Competition Laws in Conflict

Antitrust Jurisdiction in the Global Economy

Editors

Richard A. Epstein and
Michael S. Greve

The AEI Press

Publisher for the American Enterprise Institute

WASHINGTON, D.C.

Available in the United States from the AEI Press, c/o Client Distribution Services, 193 Edwards Drive, Jackson, TN 38301. To order, call toll free: 1-800-343-4499. Distributed outside the United States by arrangement with Eurospan, 3 Henrietta Street, London WC2E 8LU, England.

NRI NATIONAL RESEARCH INITIATIVE

This publication is a project of the National Research Initiative, a program of the American Enterprise Institute that is designed to support, publish, and disseminate research by university-based scholars and other independent researchers who are engaged in the exploration of important public policy issues.

Library of Congress Cataloging-in-Publication Data

    Competition laws in conflict: antitrust jurisdiction in the global economy / edited by Richard A. Epstein and Michael S. Greve
        p. cm.
    Includes bibliographical references and index.
    ISBN 0-8447-4201-5 (pbk.)
    1. Conflict of laws—Antitrust law. 2. Conflict of laws—Jurisdiction. 3. Extraterritoriality. 4. Antitrust law—United States—States. I. Epstein, Richard Allen, 1943- II. Greve, Michael S.

K3850.5.C66 2004
343'.0721—dc22

                                           2004041129

10 09 08 07 06 05   2 3 4 5

Printed in the United States of America

Competition Laws in Conflict

Contents

Foreword

"Globalization" is a loaded word these days, fraught with many negative political connotations and dire implications. In economics, however, globalization has a distinct, politically neutral meaning. It refers to the emergence of geographic markets that extend beyond the boundaries of individual nation-states, and more specifically to the emergence of worldwide markets in goods and services. Fifty years ago, most important goods and services were sold in markets that were no larger, and often smaller, than the nations in which they were produced. Today many essentials—including those from the "old economy," such as automobiles, consumer goods, and financial services, and those from the "new economy," such as computers and cellular telephones and the software that drives them—are sold in markets that are larger than those of individual political jurisdictions, even those of the United States and the European Union.

Economic globalization has important implications for antitrust policy, which polices corporate mergers and other aspects of market competition. When two firms merge, antitrust authorities want to know if the merged firm will gain market share sufficient to confer significant power to raise prices; the critical step in answering this question is "defining the market"—deciding on the geographic size of the market in which price competition takes place. In times past, a merger of two banks in a single city could raise serious antitrust concern, because most consumers of banking services (business loans, home mortgages, savings and checking accounts) were limited to banks just in their own cities. Today, when individuals and small businesses routinely secure financial services from among hundreds of sellers across the country, and when larger businesses have even greater choices including foreign banks, the merger of two local banks could not conceivably give rise to pricing power. Even goods with high transportation costs, such as consumer durables and industrial machinery, are now often sold in markets that include sellers and buyers in different nations, thousands of miles apart.

This development may seem to have made antitrust obsolete where globalized markets are concerned. It has not, because the same economic forces that have generated global market competition—falling "transaction costs" of communications, transportation, and data processing—have also facilitated the growth of individual firms. Consumers can now choose from among distant as well as local suppliers. But the suppliers are also larger and more global than in times past, so the net effect on market concentration and pricing power remains a legitimate topic for antitrust inquiry. One has only to glance at the morning's newspapers to notice that many important markets, from consumer electronics to heavy construction and engineering, are characterized by very large firms with worldwide operations. So antitrust remains an important government function in the global economy.

But globalization has produced a problem for antitrust procedure and enforcement that is systematic and, as the essays in this volume demonstrate, complex and troubling. When a merger's economic effects are limited to a single nation, all of the effects can be assessed by a single political authority whose decision may be rendered without the delays and uncertainties associated with multiple reviews. Today, many important mergers affect markets that spread across America, Europe, Asia, and elsewhere. If they are subject to an exhaustive independent review—and potential veto—in every affected nation, the potential for delay in consummating important economic transactions can be very great.

And the costs of delay are compounded by problems of uncertainty, differing legal standards, and protectionism. Americans take justifiable pride in the progress of their antitrust policies in recent decades, where an infusion of economic analysis in merger review, monopolization, and other areas of antitrust enforcement has yielded great improvements in market efficiency. If other political jurisdictions with less disciplined legal standards—which often lead to "industrial planning" and "competitor-protection" decisions in individual cases—gain an effective veto over transactions important to our own economy, much of what we have gained can be put in jeopardy. And, formal standards aside, when several nations have antitrust jurisdiction over transactions affecting domestic and foreign firms, political pressures to use antitrust for protectionist purposes—favoring one nation's firms over foreign competitors—may introduce new enforcement distortions that pervert antitrust from its proper purpose of enhancing market competition and consumer welfare.

The papers in this volume, first presented at an AEI conference in April 2003 and thereafter revised to take account of the conference discussions, are the first attempt to examine the dilemmas of global antitrust enforcement, and practical steps for addressing them, in a rigorous and systematic fashion. Many of them also address the related problems resulting from the rise in state antitrust enforcement activity—in parallel or sometimes in conflict with federal enforcement—within the United States. I am very grateful to Richard Epstein and Michael Greve for attracting such an outstanding group of scholars, jurists, and practitioners to this important project, and for their own superlative introductory and summary essays which bracket the volume.

CHRISTOPHER DEMUTH
American Enterprise Institute
for Public Policy Research

Acknowledgments

We gratefully acknowledge the generous support of the National Research Initiative, a program of the American Enterprise Institute. The National Research Initiative is designed to support, publish, and disseminate research by university-based scholars and other independent researchers who are engaged in the exploration of important public policy issues.

Kate Rick organized and supervised the two-day conference on which this book is based. Thereafter, she performed the unenviable task of keeping the editors and contributors on schedule, and she moved the manuscript along from rough drafts to final copy. Kate handled her varied duties with exceptional competence, uncommon grace, and unfailing good cheer. Competent assistance on these many dimensions is hard to find; we enjoyed it in abundance. To borrow a phrase, we owe Kate— big time.

RICHARD A. EPSTEIN
MICHAEL S. GREVE
American Enterprise Institute
for Public Policy Research

1

Introduction: The Intractable Problem of Antitrust Jurisdiction

Richard A. Epstein and Michael S. Greve

The success of a complex legal system depends first and foremost on the soundness of its substantive rules. Sound substantive rules, however, are easily undercut by choosing the wrong legal institutions and procedures to enforce them. That observation applies with full force to the topic of this volume—the jurisdictional and procedural problems arising from the enforcement of antitrust laws by multiple authorities on both the domestic and international fronts. To a greater extent than other regulatory regimes, anti-trust law is informed—at least in the United States—by a well-understood, well-developed economic theory that sets its initial presumption in favor of competition and against monopoly. The rules used to implement those policy preferences, however, operate in a context of institutional fragmentation, confusion, and conflict. Within the U.S. federal system, the law enforcement function is uneasily parceled out among the federal government, the individual states, and private parties, acting under a mix of federal and state law. Structurally similar problems are revisited in the international arena, where the central questions concern the extraterritorial enforcement of antitrust laws by individual nations, the collective articulation and enforcement of antitrust laws by supranational bodies such as the European Union, and the desirability and feasibility of a global antitrust regime.

The essays in this volume address the basic question of institutional design in both the domestic and international contexts. In a world of multiple (and proliferating) antitrust authorities, whose law should govern any given case—and under what rules of engagement? The professional consensus on these second-order questions is rather more limited than it is with respect to substantive doctrines. We hope that a rigorous examination, by authors with a wide range of perspectives, will deepen that understanding.

The inquiry delves into complex jurisdictional and procedural issues that will strike the uninitiated as forbidding, turgid, and dull. Practicing antitrust lawyers, for their part, may tend to view an extended analysis of basic institutional design questions as a futile distraction from the urgent task of identifying politically acceptable and economically workable (even if piecemeal and small-scale) solutions to a myriad of recurrent conflicts. Laymen and experts alike tend to see nothing but the trees, albeit for different reasons. But the basic choice of how to organize and enforce the law in overlapping jurisdictions starts with the grand questions of legal theory. Thus, the purpose of this introduction is to sketch the broad intellectual framework for the full range of jurisdictional issues, as they relate to both the articulation of policy and the control over individual cases. If that general analysis seems to lead far afield, so be it: We mean to guard against the more common error of treating a legal field, merely because it is defined and fortified by professional specialization and bureaucratic organization, as an intellectual autarky with rules and problems all of its own.

In attempting to develop the intellectual baseline, we will draw heavily on the American experience. We understand, or at any rate hope, that no one is seriously proposing a "United States of the World" for antitrust or other purposes. Far less do we hold out "Our Federalism" (antitrust or otherwise) as a model for the world. Our point, in drawing on the American experience, is quite the opposite: False starts, detours, and all, the American solution—more accurately, the mismanagement—of jurisdictional problems holds more than one cautionary lesson for the management of structurally similar problems in an international context.

The Intellectual Framework

All contributors to this volume start from the proposition that the object of law in general and of antitrust law in particular is to advance some systematic conception of human welfare. This global and consequentialist orientation does not come easily to most people, who tend to think of law as dealing with particular disputes whose underlying questions of right and wrong are best resolved by an appeal to the principle of corrective justice—render to each his due. That approach works well enough with individual contracts of employment and sale or with routine intersection collisions. In these cases, public and private officials are more concerned with the conduct of the parties than with the soundness of the basic institutional framework—and sensibly so: No society could survive if it had to reexamine first principles with each routine case.

In big antitrust cases, often involving multinational corporations and the collective wealth of nations, neither the stakes nor the legal and institutional questions seem in any way routine. When it is no longer possible to look at the transactions in isolation from their larger social context (as the traditional corrective justice model requires), participants and observers quickly resort to arguments of a more basic nature. But the local car collision and the multinational merger at the uncharted legal frontier are not a dichotomy but the extremes of a spectrum: Behind the most humdrum case lies some fundamental social norm. At least once, someone has to decide that it is wise for a social order to enforce contracts of sale and employment or to adopt some set of liability rules for intersection collisions. These questions of antecedent rights then lead into inquiries about the overall desirability of the rules of the game. *Ex post*, we enforce individual contracts because they are breached. *Ex ante*, we enforce contracts because we think that they generate joint gains between the parties in ways that typically have no adverse, and some positive, effects on third persons. Push hard on any individual suit after the fact and it becomes imperative to justify the soundness of its governing rules.

What should these rules provide? The traditional libertarian approach rests on a firm attachment to concepts of individual liberty, private property, and freedom of contract. In economic terms, these concepts boil down to a preference for competitive markets supported by a strong social infrastructure. Make government prevent force and fraud; otherwise, let people do what they will. That position leads quite naturally to the development of ordinary markets where private parties exchange goods and services at mutually agreeable prices. The role of the legal system is primarily to facilitate exchanges and to protect the exchange relationship from illicit interference by others. At no time can competitive harm count as compensable injury. No seller may complain when a rival offers goods or services at a lower price; no buyer can do so when a rival offers a higher price. Count us firmly in this camp.

Yet, one must question the breezy assumption that *all* contracts should be enforced in accordance with their terms. The libertarian program does not distinguish between a contract to buy or sell some commodity and a cartel arrangement between two rival sellers to restrict output and raise prices. This simple hypothetical raises a profound question both for political theory and economic policy: Should we continue to support an unqualified libertarian ideal of freedom of contract if we can envision an alternative regime under which everyone is better off and no one is worse off? Forget for the moment how one demonstrates the truth of the unstated premise. The real question is this: *If* this demonstration turns out to be true, why defend an independent view of individual rights if *no one* benefits from its implementation from the *ex ante* perspective? The question is whether this criterion shakes the traditional libertarian substantive program to its roots or only compels a qualification of its core insights. We think that the latter is true.

The key question that gave rise to both social contract theory and the libertarian prohibition against force and fraud is this: Is everyone better off in a state of nature in which all individuals may do just as they please, or do we prefer a situation in which we swap collectively (and coercively) any rights to attack another individual in exchange for protection against like attacks by others? The answer is, let's swap. The consequentialism buried in the closet of social contract theory gets us, roughly speaking, to the minimal state. The traditional language of inherent natural rights gets translated into a consequentialist program that satisfies the Pareto criterion: At least some are better and none are worse off than in a state of nature, at least to the extent that any imperfect human institutions can achieve.

The libertarian baseline must remain the basic reference point because it represents so great an improvement over the state of nature. Even so, one must allow for the possibility of at least some further collective and coercive bargains that conform to the pattern and the constraints of the original, if hypothetical, meta-transaction: At least some are left better off and no one worse. In the case at hand, the antitrust control of monopoly represents a Pareto improvement over the libertarian world that fails to distinguish between contracts of sale and contracts in restraint of trade.

In an ordinary contract of sale or employment, we cannot identify any systematic, negative external effects to a contract of sale. Rather, the transactions produce positive effects on third parties because the increased wealth of the trading partners increases the opportunities for further beneficial exchanges. Both of these elements are also present with cartels. They are overshadowed, however, by the social losses that arise when goods are priced above marginal cost, which precludes sales to anyone willing to pay the competitive but not the monopoly price.

Once the door is set ajar with contracts that create cartels, it cannot be slammed shut again. Entrepreneurs are ingenious on whatever margins they are allowed to operate. In ordinary sales, they will find terms and practices that squeeze the last element of productive gain out of the relationship, to the benefit of us all. The same merchants, though, will display equal ingenuity in maximizing their gain from cartel arrangements with their unfortunate third-party effects. Adam Smith understood the difference: He praised the energy of the entrepreneur but denounced the cartelist. The invisible hand, in modern language, translates into the proposition that competitive markets generate a perfect alignment of private and social incentives. But Smith had harsh words for combinations.[1] Many of his concerns were directed to the practice of issuing special corporate charters to entrepreneurs whose resulting limited legal liability gave them a real advantage over their unincorporated rivals. But even after nineteenth-century law gradually eliminated this source of monopoly power, Smith's challenge remains: What, if anything, should the state do to regulate monopoly power? If cartels are bad, can they be identified and eliminated at reasonable cost? If so, how? Do we just refuse to enforce contracts in restraint of trade, or do we allow injured parties to sue cartel members? Do we have direct criminal enforcement of antitrust laws? And do these policies carry over from cartels to mergers, to exclusive dealing arrangements, and to vertical combinations? On these second-order questions of remedial strategy, overconfidence is dangerous. Legislatures and courts do not automatically find the right set of social outputs for any given set of inputs. As political actors, they are vulnerable to ignorance and favoritism.

Unwise antitrust laws could block competitive practices (as by imposing strong sanctions against predatory pricing), or they could place undue obstacles in the path of proving cartel-like arrangements. Between the polar cases of pure competition and pure cartels, moreover, antitrust law has to deal with all sorts of intermediate arrangements that generate a mixed bag of positive and negative effects. (Many of these are conscious efforts to skirt the limits of the law.) Legislatures, administrators, courts, and (yes) scholars must tease out the efficiency gains from restrictive practices in an effort to maximize the former while controlling the latter. All horizontal contracting arrangements need not be unjustified, even if most of them are—certain forms of cooperation among competitors are necessary to run a banking system and any network industry. However, some vertical arrangements may support cartel arrangements or, more doubtfully, hold out some special peril of their own. The initial task of an intelligent antitrust policy is to decide which of myriad contractual arrangements with structural overtones should be approved and which should be rejected.

Undertaking this treacherous business only serves as a prelude to some of the issues raised in this volume. It is commonplace to assert (however difficult it is to demonstrate) that certain other values—a preference for small competitors, the desire to promote infant industries, special policies for agricultural produce, subsidies for export cartels— rank higher than "mere" efficiency in the grand scheme of things. Deciding how much weight to accord these considerations is a difficult issue. In our view, the only safe and sensible policy is to turn a deaf ear to all special pleas. But the persistence of special rules that protect all of these interests suggests that our position may not have the self-evident virtue that we attach to it. On a matter this difficult, we have to learn to live with a certain amount of irreducible disagreement, both within and across jurisdictions, on the proper use of cooperative arrangements among firms on the same side of the marketplace.

Territory, Federalism, and Discrimination

How do we select and organize social institutions to prevent backsliding from sound antitrust policy—assuming we know what it is? That monumental task requires the construction of governments that are strong enough, and focused enough, to achieve their desired ends, without engaging in the horrible excesses that beset not only tyrannies but also to a lesser degree democracies. We could aspire to a system of world governance that secures peace and good will across the entire planet. History, though, militates against this idealistic solution. It is a pipedream to contemplate herding billions of individuals into a single state, with no effective check on the citizens-turned-oligarchs who patrol at the top. We might as well abolish all private property in the futile hope of finding some viable system of common ownership that herds all people under a single roof. For both sovereignty and property, it is safer and saner to organize political and economic life around smaller geographical units, and to police boundaries between them. On the political frontier, this requires governments that should have, but often lack, the desire to promote trade across borders. The larger the potential market, the greater the gains from specialization in labor and product markets—provided that we can prevent political boundaries from becoming tariff walls.

Thus, questions of jurisdiction (who governs what, on what terms) and substantive norms are of central concern in any full-fledged system of trade policy—which deals with the formal restriction of the movement of goods and services across national and state boundaries—as well as antitrust law, which deals with the regulation of those firms, domestic and foreign, that do business within the nation. The power to impose trade regulations and antitrust restrictions is diffused across different sovereigns, each of which faces internal political pressures to favor its own interests and constituencies. Noncooperative behavior thus becomes a persistent danger. In a worldwide jurisdiction, the organizers and the victims of monopoly would be in the same state. But within nations, they operate in different spheres, where it is all too easy for the local monopolist to have decisive home-court advantage when the adverse consequences of its behavior are felt beyond its borders. The challenge is to secure cooperation between jurisdictions so that all will internalize the negative as well as the positive effects of their local decisions. The central question is how globally wise decisions are made in a world in which all political actors occupy limited jurisdictions.

One possible response is the development of a federalist system that distributes power between a central government and local governments (states or provinces). Federalism in this elementary sense adds complexity to the overall governance structure, because someone has to figure out how to parcel out government business among several layers of political organization and then make sure that the various government entities do not expand their influence beyond the preassigned limits. The question is whether those additional costs are worth bearing in the overall situation. This choice reflects our basic theme of the choice between monopoly and competition and thus receives, we believe, a guardedly optimistic answer.

Political power is easily abused unless some counterweight emerges. Federalism provides partial protection so long as individuals are guaranteed the right to exit a state that they do not like in favor of one that they do.[2] This competitive pressure reduces the force of the state monopoly by giving individuals a different mix of goods and services from some other government that might prove eager to obtain their patronage. Even in the absence of explicit protections of individual rights to liberty and property, a federalist system reduces the power of a local government to extract tribute from the individuals who live within its boundaries and allows individuals to select that jurisdiction whose mix of taxation and public services best meets their desires. The exit threat may not be perfect in light of the local connections that people must abandon. But it is potent and useful nonetheless.

Yet, federalism is a mixed blessing. On the negative side of the ledger, federalism can foster state monopoly power in three related senses. First, even if individuals are mobile, land and other natural resources are not. These are therefore subject to heavy taxation and regulation by local governments. Second, numerosity proves to be both a blessing and a curse: While fostering competitive industries for ordinary goods and services, it creates the risk of balkanization for network industries that operate across state lines. Multiple, inconsistent local regulations—to say nothing of schemes of petty extortion or outright blockades—could force the abandonment of an interstate project before it is even born. Third, a state may erect monopolistic schemes whose burdens fall exclusively, or at least predominantly, on consumers and producers outside its own jurisdiction, while the benefits accrue at home.

Coordination problems among competing jurisdictions, along with the attendant welfare losses, may arise even when each sovereign's political institutions operate without distortion. Conflicting local regulations need not be motivated by avarice or spite to bring a network industry to its knees. But the most common and stubborn source of anticompetitive practices is the operation of the factions or interest groups that dominate local politics. Precisely because the threat of exit—competitive federalism's operative principle—disciplines local politics in some domains, factions naturally turn to the exploitation of people who have no exit—the owners of immobile resources, network industries, and outsiders.

What then should be done to counter the downsides of federalism without returning to a unified system of economic control that deprives us of federalism's competitive advantages? The most obvious option, and the usual starting point for regimes that seek to protect and preserve the potential gains from political competition, is an outright ban on the most blatant interferences with exit and mobility—tariffs, duties, and similar exclusionary practices. Such prohibitions, though, capture only a small—albeit important—chunk of the problematic universe. In that light, it makes sense to look for additional collective rules of the road and, ideally, for an overarching principle or criterion to select and structure those rules.

The American constitutional doctrine of enumerated powers and the continental principle of "subsidiarity" serve that function. (Though perhaps somewhat mysterious to American ears, subsidiarity essentially requires that any decision be made by the smallest unit of government that covers the effects of the regulated transaction.) Both principles cede to local governments the greatest control (at the limit, exclusive control) over matters that are local in their impact. Local knowledge could well generate greater sophistication, in circumstances in which the negative consequences of all decisions, good and bad, are localized within the community that makes them. But again, beware: Local control also increases the risk that provincialism will increase our first risk that state governments will use their local monopoly power to impose unfavorable economic and political measures on the immobile resources of minorities with no place to go. To counter that risk, the central government can put into place explicit protections of property against confiscation and regulation to limit the power of local governments to exact concessions from some segment of their population. The carryover of these *federal*

guarantees from the national government to state governments is captured in the "incorporation" movement under which the specific protections of the Bill of Rights were extended through the Fourteenth
Amendment to limit the power of the states to protect local monopolies
against internal competition. The most ambitious of these decisions,
Lochner v. New York (1905), was harshly criticized even at the time, and
today remains discredited or, at least, intensely controversial. Yet, even
with the demise of substantive due process, the Takings Clause and the
Contracts Clause of the U.S. Constitution still offer some protection,
albeit weak and uneven, of individual rights against local exploitation.[3]

The more sustained legal interventions, however, deal with national
regulation of local markets. Here, we have witnessed a sea change in constitutional attitude within the American framework. Before the constitutional revolution of 1937, the American synthesis rested largely on an
interpretation of the Commerce Clause ("Congress shall have the power
to regulate commerce with foreign nations, among the several states, and
with the Indian tribes.") that was roughly consonant with competitive
principles. The national power was always freely available to regulate
what we now term network industries whose tentacles extended beyond
any single state. The railroad, telecommunications, and airline industries
all fell quickly and easily under national regulation before the 1937
watershed events. Battles arose over lower-level issues, such as whether a
freight car that traveled from Albany to New York City was in interstate
traffic because the train continued its run into Pennsylvania—to which
the answer was sometimes no. In short order, though, federal power
extended to cover local lines in competition with interstate ones and,
finally, to all elements of the transportation grid, even those that faced no
interstate competition.[4]

Outside the network setting, the Supreme Court used a variety of
(changing) doctrines to police the boundary between internal state affairs
and interstate commerce—until 1937, when the Court got out of the
business of seeking to enforce a competitive legal regime on Congress and
the states. That signal political transformation has major implications for
trade and antitrust policy: Thenceforth, Congress could choose to prop
up or strike down cartels, and it frequently did both in different arenas at
the same time. *Wickard v. Fillburn* (1942) stretched the Commerce Clause

beyond its natural contours—to allow the federal regulation of wheat grown for home consumption—for just this functional reason. The physical actions involved in growing wheat or feeding farm animals are all intensely local; their economic consequences, taken in the aggregate, extend far beyond local borders to national markets. To limit total agricultural production and to prevent the migration of farmers from a federally regulated product line (wheat) to an uncontrolled one (livestock), Congress had to be granted the authority to regulate the level of local consumption. The principle of subsidiarity, it turns out, speaks with a forked tongue.

As a constitutional matter today, it is up to Congress to decide whether it should regulate at the center or allow decisions to be made locally. Congress does not always exhaust its authority to the limit. For example, even as its constitutional powers expanded, Congress effectively ceded local control over important portions of the communications network to local governance.[5] Antitrust policy continues to exhibit the same bifurcated structure. But it is only federal policy choices, not constitutional imperatives, that shape the American collective response to monopoly.

What if Congress does not act at all? Within the American context, the constitutional bias in favor of competitive federalism in a unified common market continues to assert itself to this day. The commerce power itself reads like an affirmative grant of power to the federal government, as distinct from an independent limitation on the powers of the states. But from the initial decision in *Gibbons v. Ogden* (1824), the clause was read to have, in addition to its undeniable affirmative power, a negative or dormant power, which—when Congress was silent—restricted *of its own force* the application of state power that hampered coordination of network industries. This "dormant" commerce power poses no threat to state regulation of the terms and conditions of local labor and product markets, but any regulation that impedes the operation of national networks passes muster only if it advances a strong local interest in health or safety. If not, the regulation could be struck down, unless Congress chooses to save it.

In practice, this seemingly elegant doctrine does not define its own reach. When the state wishes to engage in *explicit* discrimination against out-of-state activity, the legislation or regulation is subject to a virtual per se condemnation. Perhaps the state has the power to impose the restrictions on local and foreign business, or on both. But it cannot discriminate in favor of its own businesses by exempting them from regulation that applies to outsiders. (Cases of local discrimination *against* local interests are, predictably, exceedingly rare.) As one moves beyond the case of explicit discrimination, though, the task of sorting out proper from improper local regulation gets more difficult. In the easiest case, the state that wishes to secure competitive advantages for its local members knows the kinds of neutral rules that will have those effects and has the motivation to put them in place. Additional curbs on such flagrant evasions of the nondiscrimination rule are tempting—but also problematic. In most cases, it is hard to wire direct consequences through rules of general application, as other firms could comport with the local strategy in order to undercut the competitive edge. At the same time, the costs of ferreting out subtle forms of disparate impact are high, with error rates to match. There is a danger that every neutral statute could be subject to challenge once it becomes evident that it has a disparate impact on some portion of the market. For this reason, even ardent academic defenders of free markets rarely propagate the dormant Commerce Clause much beyond a prohibition against facial discrimination and, perhaps, a rule against de facto discrimination that will preclude the most egregious evasive maneuvers.[6]

The current U.S. Supreme Court cares enough for its competitive edifice that it is prepared to march a long way toward knocking out discriminatory regulations and taxation for ostensible health and safety purposes, at least insofar as state regulation governs the instrumentalities of interstate commerce. (The imposition of distinctive safety devices on highways and railroads with common grades and configurations has been routinely struck down.)[7] But it is much more difficult to apply a disparate impact test to ordinary commercial actions within a state, even when the potential for abuse remains great. In one notable case, *Exxon Corp. v. Governor of Maryland* (1978), the state of Maryland imposed a restriction on the ability of refiners to own local retail outlets. The provision was neutral in form but was passed against a background knowledge that Maryland had no local refiners. The Supreme Court refused to strike the statute down, in part because it allowed competition from nonlocal retailers who did not own refineries. The decision is, we think, on balance incorrect, but it does highlight the great difficulties of designing a system of interstate competition rules that will reliably sort legitimate from destructive regulation.

The same dynamics substantially characterize the constitutional trajectory of our third federalism risk, that of extraterritorial state legislation for the benefit of insiders. Enforced under various doctrines but with considerable vigor before 1937, constitutional obstacles to such state laws have since atrophied. The modern dormant Commerce Clause still contains an injunction against state regulation of purely extraterritorial transactions, and the Supreme Court occasionally parks extraterritoriality injunctions under the capacious roof of the Due Process Clause.[8] But neither of these prohibitions captures more than a tiny sliver of problematic state practices. In fact, at a (barely) subconstitutional level, the post–New Deal Court continues to create doctrines to *protect* mutual state exploitation. Nothing better illustrates this phenomenon than the endorsement of state-created cartels under the "state action" doctrine of *Parker v. Brown* (1943), the subject of Frank Easterbrook's famous 1983 article on antitrust federalism (reprinted, on account of its perspicacity and on the occasion of its twentieth anniversary, in this volume).

In large measure, our federalism's discontents are a result of historical accident and force. Louis Brandeis, the principal architect of the Supreme Court's New Deal revolution, understood perfectly well that competitive federalism's ground rules constrain monopolization and interest group politics. The New Deal, though, believed in cartelization and interest group politics, and for precisely that reason, the New Deal Court, under Brandeis's leadership, engineered a judicial reversal at all fronts—property rights, the Commerce Clause, and extraterritoriality.[9] (Below, we shall turn to Brandeis's crowning achievement, the demolition of federal common law, which was followed shortly after his death by an expansion of the extraterritorial powers of state courts in a manner that he surely would have approved.) Both the national regulation of local affairs and extraterritorial state legislation generate regulatory interventions in excess of what any jurisdiction (left to its own devices, under competitive conditions) would choose.[10] Precisely such interventions constituted the New Deal program, and the Court obliged by creating a complementary institutional structure. Behind the political story, though, lurk larger structural problems.

The most obvious problem is one of institutional design. The protection—or, as in the case of the dormant Commerce Clause, the creation—of competitive ground rules has always and everywhere been the achievement of judicial bodies, rather than political agencies. Over time, though, those bodies display a pronounced tendency to turn from competition to monopoly.[11] The skids are greased by a genuine theoretical problem: The rules of the game operate on an extremely messy, heterogeneous universe of state laws (and on a set of actors who have every incentive to evade and eviscerate the rules). As our cursory discussion of the dormant Commerce Clause suggests, it is devilishly difficult, and quite probably impossible, to specify an optimal set of rules that will consistently, in all contexts, unleash federalism's competitive potential while curbing its destructive features.[12]

One way of dealing with the problem is to treat the competitive norms not as ironclad rules but as default principles: The interferences are presumptively void, unless and until Congress legislates some other arrangement. Here again, though, experience reveals the flaws of a seemingly attractive solution. When confronted with state infractions, Congress rarely (if ever) responds by applying and tailoring general competitive rules (nonaggression, nondiscrimination) to a particular context. Instead of prohibiting specific state interferences with interstate commerce, Congress typically preempts the states (as the Europeans say, harmonizes) through affirmative regulation of private transactions.

We will return to this shift and its consequences in the postscript. Suffice it here to observe that the federal regulation of interstate commerce has, as an empirical matter, taken the form of a series of uneasy compromises. Some issues, such as those pertaining to international trade, remain dominated by the national government. At the other end, issues such as zoning have largely remained at the state and, indeed, local level, notwithstanding the expansion of federal power. Between those extremes lies a vast regulatory realm of overlapping and competing state and federal regulation. As noted, the regulation of network industries falls into this category. So, for that matter, does antitrust. One shudders to call this arrangement, which has sputtered along for close to seventy years, an "equilibrium." The once-exclusive federal and local domains show alarming signs of erosion—at one end, through the enactment of de facto federal land use statutes such as the Endangered Species Act (1973); at the other end, through increasingly frequent state regulations of foreign firms and transactions.[13] Moreover, the contributions to this volume show that the vast realm of concurrent jurisdiction resembles not a compromise but rather a combat zone where the rules of engagement may shift frequently, radically, and without regard to considerations of social welfare.

Jurisdiction and Choice of Law

Not only does the fragmentation of power across different government entities affect the formulation and enforcement of regulatory policy, but it also has profound implications for the treatment of disputes between individuals who are subject to the tug of different jurisdictions and to the influence of multiple systems of public law. Here again, the central questions are not unique to the antitrust laws. The first question concerns the exercise of state jurisdiction over a particular transaction or dispute when some of the parties to it lie outside the sphere of the state's control. The second question has to do with the choice of law that this sovereign will apply to the dispute in question.

To start, consider a controversial but, we believe, appealing presumption: In contract disputes, personal jurisdiction and choice of law should as a first approximation be settled by private contract, just like any other contract term. The general libertarian preference for freedom of contract works as well with the selection of jurisdiction or law as with any other contract term. As in the general context, though, the contractual solution to jurisdictional and choice-of-law questions fails in cases of monopoly. Here, as there, libertarians are compelled to play in a second-best world, structured by incomplete and imperfectly operating nondiscrimination rules. The checkered history in both areas (jurisdiction and choice of law) provides ample reason to be cautious about the capacity of political institutions to fashion sensible rules for the governance of multijurisdictional conflicts.

Jurisdiction: Territoriality, Contracts, and Minimum Contacts. In its first foray into matters of jurisdiction, *Pennoyer v. Neff* (1878), the Supreme Court promptly started off on the wrong foot. The case originated in a contract for legal services entered into between Neff (the client) and Mitchell (his lawyer), both Oregon citizens, for work to be performed in Oregon. Neff moved to California before he paid for the services in question. He received (it appears, actual) notice from Mitchell to answer the claim in an Oregon court but declined to appear. A default judgment was entered against him, and the Oregon sheriff seized property that Neff had acquired *after* the onset of the lawsuit, which in turn was sold to Pennoyer. Neff then reappeared to claim this property, arguing that the sheriff's sale was of no effect because the underlying judgment against him was void for want of jurisdiction. In the crucial part of its decision, the Supreme Court held that Neff was not subject to personal jurisdiction.

As a constitutional matter, the states must extend "full faith and credit" to judgments rendered by another state.[14] The right procedure appears to be to allow Mitchell to obtain the default judgment against Neff and to have California give full faith and credit to that ruling. (Neff's only legitimate interest is one of due process, which is satisfied by his receiving notice of a suit that has been brought against him.) The fly in the ointment, however, was that the guarantee of full faith and credit only applied where the initial judgment was not void.

So why was Mitchell's initial judgment against Neff void? Justice Field insisted that personal jurisdiction is determined by effective power *at the time of suit*, which requires the state to have physical control over the defendant's person (and Neff was domiciled outside the state when the suit began). This territorial assumption is central to *Pennoyer*. It is, however, neither sufficient nor necessary to confer personal jurisdiction. The territorial assumption is not sufficient because a state's physical control over a defendant may arise solely out of happenstance. The ordinary traveler could fly over a dozen states or nations on a single trip. Yet, it hardly makes sense to allow "transitory" jurisdiction in a case worth millions because the prospective defendant has been served with process while flying over North Dakota or Bangladesh.[15] Conversely, and more importantly for present purposes, the proposition that power is *necessary* for jurisdiction hardly holds either.[16] Suppose Neff and Mitchell had contracted explicitly for the enforcement of the contract in Oregon: Why should any conception of state sovereignty frustrate the validity of an agreement that seems the soul of good sense at the time of its formation? From an *ex ante* perspective, both parties would have been better off if each could have enforced the contract in Oregon where it was both made and performed. The opposite, territorial presumption only creates a danger of *ex post* opportunism, in which the party who wishes to defeat the agreement flees unilaterally from the jurisdiction with the maximum contacts to the transaction. In *Pennoyer* and cases like it, then, the choice of jurisdiction can easily be regarded as within the sphere of contractual issues that should be set by the parties. Both are informed, and their agreement over jurisdiction poses no risks to third persons.

After much tribulation, the U.S. Supreme Court cautiously reached that position, by deciding to enforce what we now call contractual forum selection clauses.[17] In *Carnival Cruise Lines v. Shute* (1991), cruise ship passengers had signed an agreement providing that all disputes arising out of the contract of passage "shall be litigated, if at all, in and before a Court located in the State of Florida, U.S.A. to the exclusion of the Court of any other state or country." The plaintiffs were injured in a slip and fall accident on the high seas and sought to bring their tort action in the United States District Court for Western Washington. No luck: They had to traipse off to Florida.

The Supreme Court treated *Carnival Cruise Lines* as arising under *admiralty* law. Outside that context, forum selection clauses are routinely enforced in mercantile transactions (such as franchise agreements). Their status in consumer transactions is more uncertain: Forum selection clauses in consumer contracts are widely held to be unenforceable and are in many areas prohibited by state law. Even here, though, *Carnival Cruise Lines* has exerted some influence on state courts dealing with this matter. That is all to the good, because *Carnival Cruise Lines* is right in treating forum selection clauses on a par with, and inseparable from, all other contract terms. The contract itself is one strong piece of evidence in that direction, for the defendant's choice of forum is in all likelihood matched by a reduction in the cost of carriage.[18]

What if the parties do *not* explicitly agree to a particular forum—as in *Pennoyer*? Here, the contractual baseline suggests an analogous *default rule*. If the original agreement could reasonably have contained a clause that calls for Oregon as the forum of choice, then the job of a court is to ask whether the appropriate default rule allows Oregon to rule in a case that had its origins and functions entirely within its boundaries. Of course, the plaintiff Mitchell has no duty to avail himself of the Oregon courts. An *ex ante* agreement could have explicitly allowed either party to pursue the other in a state, here California, where he has taken up permanent residence. But if—in the absence of an explicit agreement—the parties can and should be taken to have *chosen*, albeit by implication, Oregon as the forum for resolving their dispute, then Oregon exercises its sovereign power with the strongest of justifications.

Over time, the Supreme Court abandoned *Pennoyer's* misguided territorial approach to personal jurisdiction. By common reckoning, the decisive case is *International Shoe Co. v. Washington* (1945), a trade case of direct relevance to the matters covered in this volume. The International Shoe Company, a Delaware corporation operating out of Missouri, employed several traveling salesmen who lived and worked exclusively within the state of Washington. Washington imposed a tax on their wages to support that state's Unemployment Compensation Fund. When the state sued the company in its own courts for unpaid taxes that arose solely out of the company's business within Washington, the company claimed that it did not do business in Washington and could only be sued in its home forum of Missouri.

Repudiating *Pennoyer*, the *International Shoe* Court found personal jurisdiction so long as the defendant in the underlying transaction had "minimum contacts" with the state that asserts jurisdiction. And why not? International Shoe ventured into Washington for its own advantage, and all the relevant contacts in the dispute took place in Washington. Looked at from the *ex ante* perspective, the rules of personal jurisdiction should minimize the joint costs of both sides to the arrangement. (The Court called this rough calculus an "estimate of the inconveniences.") If International Shoe is able to make its way into Washington to do business, then it should be able to find its way back to defend its undertakings there. In all events, it is easier for the firm to come to Washington than for the state to go to Missouri.

What is true in the individual case becomes even more so in light of the huge volume of foreign corporations that do business in the state of Washington. It will not improve legal administration to require states to travel to the four corners of the globe in order to enforce their tax laws. As a first cut, then, the local forum is the efficient low-cost solution to the jurisdictional question. Closer inspection, though, shows that the minimum contacts rule is subject to significant limitations with respect to both its scope and the potential for discrimination.

Thus far, we have treated *International Shoe* as setting the default provisions for allowing out-of-state corporations to do business within its borders. But default provisions can be varied by *explicit* agreements. So, should there be any limitations on the power of the state to impose explicit conditions on outside firms that wish to do business within its borders? The condition in *International Shoe* looks like the kind of condition that one would expect to see between two parties from different states who did business in Washington and used that state to resolve their disputes. Just as this sort of private arrangement would extend only to disputes arising over the underlying business transactions (but not, say, to an unrelated automobile collision among those same parties in another state), so the *International Shoe* Court allowed Washington to exercise its power only over the activities that the defendant carried on within its borders. (Washington could not, for example, assert jurisdiction over a dispute that International Shoe had with one of its employees in the Missouri home office.) Minimum contacts, in other words, establish "specific" but not "general" jurisdiction. That limitation makes good sense, just as the rule that requires (through the fiction of implied consent) an out-of-state individual who has an accident on the roads of Massachusetts to litigate that dispute (but not his personal divorce) within the Bay State.[19]

But suppose that the state requires that anyone who wants to do business within its borders, drive on its roads, or buy goods from its local businesses must submit to general as well as specific jurisdiction: Get into an accident in Massachusetts and, by golly, the Bay State has jurisdiction over your divorce or business practices.[20] Out-of-staters will find that their sole protection lies in their refusal to do business. But because the need for use of public highways is pressing, and the possibility of being subject to a criminal prosecution is remote, people faced with the unhappy up or down choice will sign on—in droves. "Take it or leave it" is not likely in many contexts to generate the optimal social results. Mercifully, though, the state is not the exclusive owner of its territory.

While that averment may sound jarring at a time of judicial encomiums to states that joined the Union "with their sovereignty intact,"[21] the right to exclude others is qualified even for property owners in competitive markets.

Common carriers, as monopolists, were required at common law to take all comers at reasonable rates, which creates a big-league exception to the owner's absolute right to exclude.[22] In some cases, it must accept reasonable rates; in others, the state does not set the rates in question but only holds that the party must take all comers on a *nondiscriminatory* basis. For analogous reasons, the nondiscrimination principle occupies a central role in intergovernmental arrangements in both the domestic and the international arenas when states—whose monopoly position is far more difficult to erode than that of the common carrier—seek to block the entry of a new business.

The U.S. Constitution enshrines the nondiscrimination principle in the Privileges and Immunities Clause, which commands each state to treat the citizens of sister-states (though not, by common understanding, corporations) on equal terms with its own citizens. Here, as in the case of the dormant Commerce Clause, the antidiscrimination norm itself does not fully forestall the danger of subjecting out-of-state firms to general jurisdiction: The state could always say that out-of-state companies are not subject to any greater burdens than local firms that must accept general jurisdiction. That position, however, is almost universally rejected, probably in recognition of the disparate impact of general jurisdiction on firms located outside the state. Viewed globally, parity arises only when all firms are subject to general jurisdiction at home and specific jurisdiction in places that they do business. Any insistence on imposing general jurisdiction on out-of-state firms thus operates as a real trade barrier to out-of-state firms. It is, moreover, never sufficient from a social point of view to have the excluded firm operate elsewhere if it does not like the terms and conditions of a particular state. Decisions that restrict opportunities to sell cut more deeply than those that relate to the location of a firm (and restrictions on product characteristics cut more deeply than restrictions on how it is produced). The firm that cannot locate in the state of Washington may do just fine setting up shop in Missouri, so that competitive federalism works well in that case. But if the firm cannot sell in Washington, it cannot recoup those losses by selling elsewhere, and its potential customers suffer real losses if forced to do business with other less desirable vendors. The firm that locates in one state should be able to do business in fifty.

Should we then offer even greater protection to the outsider by allowing it to do business in the state free of local regulation? The short answer is no. Local firms are not autonomous agencies that can operate free of all forms of taxes and regulations. Someone has to provide for the maintenance of public goods and services, and outsiders would gain an unwarranted advantage if they could do business in a state without bearing their pro rata cost for maintaining local public infrastructure. With the rise of the New Deal state, the functions of local and state governments have expanded to encompass programs such as the Unemployment Compensation Fund set up under Washington state law. Once a constitutional challenge to such a program has been rebuffed (as it was in *International Shoe*), it becomes intolerable to allow the outsider to freeload on the expenditures of insiders.[23]

The antidiscrimination norm thus forges the middle way between forced exclusion by the state and forced entry by the outsider. Without judging the merits of Washington's scheme, the rule requires outsiders to play by the rules of the game once the state must let them in. That arrangement has obvious appeal when there is a genuine difference of opinion as to the right legal regime. For all its manifest imperfections, it is the only principle that allows states with fundamentally different views to trade without having to resolve their differences on domestic policy.

And that, alas, is as far as contractual principles will carry. The role of freedom of contract, both for better and for worse, is the same in jurisdictional contexts as it is elsewhere: decisive in cases of competition, but uncertain in cases of monopoly—including, emphatically, antitrust. When a member of a cartel enters into a contract of sale with a citizen of a foreign state and insists that all disputes must be resolved in its home base (where the judges are likely to be sympathetic to the local scheme), it is hardly self-evident that the interests of the foreign citizens are so slender that they should be ignored in cases of this sort. At this point, the language of minimum contacts—in the international context, the so-called "effects test"—serves the sensible function of allowing personal jurisdiction wherever the cartel sells its merchandise. If the law does not allow freedom of contract on substantive terms, then it must place analogous restrictions on the choice of forum.

To announce this proposition, however, shows the clash of cultures that can arise on so simple a jurisdictional question. If the home state props up its export cartels, it is on a collision course with any foreign state in which that cartel operates. In principle, the home state should require its local export cartels to back off. But our purportedly united states rarely accede to that demand, and our "state action" doctrine offers a ready means of resistance. (Internationally, the United States has strengthened the operation of domestic export cartels, and the World Trade Organization [WTO] has remained mute.) The nondiscrimination principle does not decide whose law applies when both sides use neutral but conflicting rules within their own jurisdictions. We could hold that the foreign state may not attack a cartel that also operates within its home state, but that rule only provides an incentive to impose small social losses at home in order to reap larger gains in foreign markets. Alternatively, we could allow a target state to restrain foreign cartels if it is prepared to impose like restrictions on local producers, which it may do if these are few and far between. A target state, though, may have legitimate policy reasons (including sheer size, or lack thereof [24]) for tolerating domestic market concentration, and that is no reason for making the state suffer exploitation by outsiders. Barring a uniform approach on substantive grounds, we are faced with a set of painful choices and no clear solution.

At the same time, a minimum contacts or effects test has the distinct disadvantage of exposing companies that operate on a national or global scale to an n-front war in countless and often hostile jurisdictions. Discretionary rules of comity or forum non conveniens may occasionally provide relief; but they are a matter of good manners, not a reliable protection against unwarranted exercises of jurisdiction. The more formal doctrines that cabin minimum contacts—the distinction between general and specific jurisdiction and the injunction against discrimination—likewise often fail to serve their intended function. The harsh reality is that the local forum will often be biased in two ways. It will extend its own jurisdiction unduly, and then top it all off by using that new power unfairly.

Precisely in recognition of that difficulty, the U.S. Constitution provides litigants in "diversity" cases—that is, cases involving parties from more than one state—with access to federal rather than state courts. State courts, the Founders believed, could not be trusted to deal fairly with outsiders. Federal courts would provide an impartial forum and, within limits, offer escape from parochial exercises of state court jurisdiction. That institutional solution, though, is available at the international level only within very narrow limits, and, as the contributions to this volume illustrate, its general implementation at that level would present great difficulties. Even in the United States, moreover, the scope of federal jurisdiction has proven quite vexing and controversial. The current law cuts back on the exercise of that jurisdiction in multiple fashions. For example, the minimum jurisdictional amount is now $75,000 per individual claim, which in ordinary litigation keeps small cases that are unlikely to provoke local abuse out of the federal courts. Yet, ironically, this provision often slams the door on the federal forum when that protection is most needed—in class actions brought in state court by thousands of plaintiffs, none of whom presents claims for the jurisdictional amount.[25] Similarly, current law only allows for diversity jurisdiction when there is complete diversity between the parties, that is, when every plaintiff is a citizen of a different state than every defendant. Today, the astute plaintiff will commonly join a local distributor as a defendant in a class action that is in truth directed against a large corporation, solely to keep the case in state court. The diversity restrictions on class actions have been subject to harsh criticism. As the Supreme Court has made clear, Congress could extend diversity jurisdiction to cases of minimum diversity, that is, where a single plaintiff and single defendant are citizens of different states.[26] Legislative efforts in that direction, however, have consistently failed. The lack of resolve in protecting diversity jurisdiction even where it is most urgently needed illustrates the difficulty of protecting sensible jurisdictional rules against politically induced erosion.

Choice of Law. What (or rather whose) substantive rules should be applied in any given dispute involving parties from different jurisdictions? In our judgment, the arguments over choice of law parallel those with respect to jurisdiction, with important qualifications.

Presumptively, we see no reason why the parties to a particular contract should not be allowed to hold that all substantive disputes between them should be governed by the law of Oregon even if the dispute is litigated in California. In many cases, the transaction in question may have contacts with multiple jurisdictions, so that a choice-of-law provision will reduce the burdens on the court to decide whose substantive law governs in any individual case. If the parties can choose their own terms by explicit contracts, then the use of default terms should seek to approximate the desired terms in question. As with jurisdiction, this task is easy when the formation and performance of the contract are slated to take place within a single state. It becomes far less elegant when formation and performance are fragmented across many jurisdictions. The rule that applies the law of the place of formation will not look attractive when parties exchange drafts, e-mails, and telephone calls across multiple jurisdictions. It could also lead to positive anomalies if parties in New York and California solidify their agreements at a convention in Florida, when that state has nothing to do with the performance of the agreement. All that conceded, the hypothetical default rule solves a broad range of choice-of-law problems.

The real problem lies elsewhere: As with personal jurisdiction, the principle of freedom of contract does not work well in noncontractual settings or in contractual settings with third-party costs—such as antitrust. It hardly seems efficient to permit a monopolist to secure protection under a choice-of-law provision that allows the law of his home state to control even if sued in the courts of the consuming party. Conversely, and especially under a latitudinarian minimum contacts rule, there are genuine risks to a rule that permits plaintiff campaigns in any state where a—real or perceived—monopolist may have set foot. Two possible solutions come to mind. Neither is wholly satisfactory, and both have been rejected.

The first approach is to trump local law with a federal rule—that is, the famous or perhaps notorious rule of *Swift v. Tyson* (1842). In that case, a series of property transactions eventually turned on conflicting state law definitions of what did or did not constitute a "negotiable instrument." In a unanimous decision, the Supreme Court through Justice Story held that the question had to be settled under neither state's law but rather under federal common law that responded to, one hoped, the timeless principles of the law merchant. At some level, *Swift* is compelling: Legal arcana are the stuff that often make or break national markets (in *Swift*, credit markets that require ease of negotiability), and the monstrous risk of local bias in adjudicating matters involving parochial state interests well-nigh dictates a federal common law (as well as access to a federal forum). Those considerations explain both the Court's unanimity in *Swift* and the lasting appeal of its decision. *Swift v. Tyson*, however, was overruled in

Justice Brandeis's 1938 opinion in *Erie Railroad v. Tompkins*, which held that there is no such beast as a federal common law and instructed federal courts to follow the law of the local (state) jurisdiction.

The second approach, this one running parallel to the personal jurisdiction question, is a constitutional nondiscrimination rule: In cases in which more than one state's law could apply, state courts must give full faith and credit to laws of sister states. As a practical matter, however, virtually all state courts have long adopted choice-of-law doctrines that systematically prefer home state law to sister state law (and home state plaintiffs to out-of-state defendants). Those doctrines—commonly called "interest analysis"—are constitutionally unconstrained. The Full Faith and Credit Clause, like federal common law, has been eliminated with respect to legislative enactments, although not with quite the decisive swiftness of *Erie*: It was gradually eviscerated and finally put to rest last year.[27]

While the necessity and sagacity of this one-two punch against federal common law and neutral choice—as the only available options to ensure nondiscrimination—are the subjects of a difficult and occasionally acrimonious debate, two observations are in order. First, the intuitions behind the pre-*Erie* regime were essentially sound. Unfortunately, though, both the federal common law and the nondiscrimination rule were burdened with the same territorialist, anticontractual misunderstanding that animated the ill-fated *Pennoyer* decision. Because parties were precluded from contracting out of federal choice-of-law and common law rules, those rules had to carry more weight—including the allegation of excessive nationalism—than they could bear, or should have been made to bear. Second, the demise of federal common law (as a safeguard against state bias) should by all rights have led to a greater emphasis on the federal protection of impartial choice-of-law rules by and in state courts—and to improved access to federal courts as an escape from biased state courts. On both fronts, the opposite happened. As noted, the federal courts' diversity jurisdiction was curtailed (especially by the statutory requirement of "complete diversity"), and the Supreme Court held—as a guard against both forum shopping and perceived national overreach—that federal courts must follow the lead of state courts within their jurisdiction *even on the choice of law*.[28] Even where diversity jurisdiction remains available, state court doctrines tag after defendants into federal courts. Out-of-state defendants can occasionally obtain protection against the personal bias of state courts—but not against the doctrinal bias of state law.

This Book

When contracts fail, the world gets messy. The jurisdictional problems that have proven so difficult in the domestic context seem even more intractable in an international context. As the sheer number of jurisdictions and the range of interests and opinions among them increase, so does the difficulty of establishing mutually agreeable rules of the road. It is easier for Pennsylvania to give full faith and credit to the laws of New Jersey than to ask a Nigerian court to respect Japanese law in a comparable case. Personal jurisdiction is more easily exercised in a single (albeit federalist) nation with long-arm statutes and reciprocity agreements than in a world of far-flung and often hostile nations.

International discord, then, is one risk. Excessive, runaway "harmonization" is the other. *Swift v. Tyson* was plainly prompted by a desire to forge, not simply a common market but a nation (at least in commercial transactions, to which the decision was originally restricted). A comparable aspiration seems rather problematic in an international context. No dreamy aspirations, moreover, may be needed to produce harmonization creep. Seemingly minimalist nondiscrimination rules, as noted, do not define their own range of application, and their underlying rationale constantly pushes toward more elaborate restrictions against de facto discrimination and discriminatory enforcement. Whatever one may think of extending the dormant Commerce Clause in those directions, the creation of international rules and institutions with a capability to police nonobvious infractions against neutrality strikes us as a rather ambitious proposition. To add—to these loose comparisons between the American experiment in multijurisdictional governance and incipient international efforts in the same direction—a more pointed observation: For all their mercantilist inclinations, the architects of the American project were free traders at home. Their work reflects a profound respect for private bargains and competitive arrangements. The protection of those arrangements was in some measure the point of the Founders' attempt to create a (particular kind of) political constitution. We are not at all sure that current attempts to strengthen international institutions are driven by the same spirit—or rather by an abiding desire to suppress its manifestations.

Having tipped our hand, we shall let the authors speak for themselves. The book is divided into two parts: the first, on international antitrust problems and the desirability of harmonization; the second, on the jurisdictional malaise of American antitrust law and possible remedies. The postscript provides a review and tentative conclusions.

Notes

1. Adam Smith, *The Wealth of Nations* (New York: The Modern Library, 1937), 123.

2. This is not always the case. For a discussion, see Richard A. Epstein, "Exit Rights and Insurance Regulation: From Federalism to Takings," *George Mason Law Review* 7 (1999): 293–311.

3. See, for example, *Lucas v. South Carolina Coastal Comm'n.*, 505 U.S. 1003 (1992).

4. See the *Shreveport Rate Cases* (*Houston, East & West Texas Railway Company v. United States*), 234 U.S. 342 (1914).

5. See, for example, *AT&T v. Iowa Utilities Board*, 525 U.S. 366 (1999).

6. See, for example, Saul Levmore, "Interstate Exploitation and Judicial Intervention," *Virginia Law Review* 69 (1983): 563–631; Stephen F. Williams, "Severance Taxes and Federalism: The Role of the Supreme Court in Preserving a National Common Market for Energy Supplies," *University of Colorado Law Review* 53 (1990): 281–314; Richard A. Epstein, "The Proper Scope of the Commerce Power," *Virginia Law Review* 73 (1987): 1387–1455; and Daniel N. Shaviro, *Federalism in Taxation* (Washington, D.C.: AEI Press, 1993).

7. See, for example, *Southern Pacific v. Arizona*, 325 U.S. 761 (1945); and *Kassel v. Consolidated Freightways Corp.*, 450 U.S. 662 (1981).

8. See, respectively, *Healy v. Beer Institute*, 491 U.S. 324 (1989); and *State Farm v. Campbell*, 123 S. Ct. 1513 (2002).

9. See Stephen A. Gardbaum, "New Deal Constitutionalism and the Unshackling of the States," *University of Chicago Law Review* 64 (1997): 483–566; and Edward A. Purcell, Jr., *Brandeis and the Progressive Constitution* (New Haven: Yale University Press, 2000).

10. James M. Buchanan and Gordon Tullock, *The Calculus of Consent* (Ann Arbor: University of Michigan Press, 1962), 135–40; Andrew Guzman, "Choice of Law: New Foundations," *Georgetown Law Journal* 90 (2002): 906–7.

11. The United States Supreme Court is not an exception. The European Court of Justice has shown a similar tendency, and the World Trade Organization's judicial bodies may soon follow suit. For the Court, see *Rush Portuguesa/Office national d'immigration* (Rec.1990, p.I-1417), C113-89. For the WTO, see Daniel K. Tarullo, "The Hidden Costs of International Dispute Settlement: WTO Review of Domestic Anti-Dumping Decisions," *Law and Policy in International Business* 34 (2002): 109–81.

12. See Guzman, "Choice of Law," 900.

13. *Barclay's Bank PLC v. Franchise Tax Board*, 512 U.S. 298 (1994); *Crosby v. National Foreign Trade Council*, 530 U.S. 363 (2000); *American Insurance Association v. Garamendi*, 123 S. Ct. 2374 (2003).

14. U.S. Constitution, art. 4, sec. 1: "Full Faith and Credit shall be given in each State to the public Acts, Records, and judicial Proceedings of every other State; And

Congress may by general Laws prescribe the Manner in which such Acts, Records and Proceedings shall be proved, and the Effect thereof."

15. The Supreme Court has held that transitory jurisdiction remains viable under the American Constitution: *Burnham v. Superior Court*, 495 U.S. 604 (1990). But cases of this sort are few and far between. Most courts exercise their discretion to decline jurisdiction under the doctrine of forum non conveniens when the sole contact with the forum state is as evanescent as that just described.

16. For a fuller treatment of this proposition, see Richard A. Epstein, "Consent, Not Power, as the Basis of Jurisdiction," *University of Chicago Legal Forum 2001* (2001): 1–34.

17. For an exhaustive account of the subject, see Larry Ribstein, "From Efficiency to Politics in Contractual Choice of Law," *Georgia Law Review* 37 (2003): 363–471.

18. The Supreme Court hedged its bets and noted that it might not enforce a forum selection clause in which the litigation was directed to a jurisdiction that had no connection with either of the parties or that had special laws that favored the defendant. Such caution makes sense in cases in which local law places limitations on freedom of contract that the parties might try to escape by choosing a remote forum unconnected with either the events or the parties. But in the ordinary contract of carriage, these restrictions rarely matter.

19. *Hess v. Pawloski*, 274 U.S. 352 (1927).

20. The state could go further and insist that anyone, inside or outside the state, who wishes to use public highways must waive his constitutional protection against unreasonable searches and seizures, not only with respect to driving but with any other activities. For the rejection of these hypotheticals, see *Frost v. Railroad Commission of State of California*, 271 U.S. 583 (1926).

21. See, for example, *Alden v. Maine*, 527 U.S. 706, 713 (1999) (citing *Blatchford v. Native Village of Noatak*, 501 U.S. 775, 779 [1991]).

22. For discussion, see Richard A. Epstein, *Principles for a Free Society: Reconciling Individual Liberty with the Common Good* (New York: Perseus Books, 1998), 282–86.

23. Lest this averment be misconstrued as wholesale endorsement of the social welfare state, we hasten to observe that the Constitution itself adopts the logic just sketched. The Import/Export Clause (U.S. Constitution, art. 1, sec. 10, cl. 2) provides that "No State shall, without the Consent of the Congress, lay any Imposts of Duties on Imports or Exports, *except what may be absolutely necessary for executing its inspection Laws:* and the net Produce of all Duties and Imposts, laid by any State on Imports or Exports, shall be for the Use of the Treasury of the United States; and all such Laws shall be subject to the Revision and Control of the Congress" (emphasis added). The clause is plainly designed to allow states to make out-of-state commerce pay its fair share of a public good, without, at the same time, permitting them to discriminate against such commerce. In James Madison's words, the provision "seems well calculated at once to secure to the states a reasonable discretion in providing for the conveniency of their imports and exports, and to the United States, a

reasonable check against the abuse of this discretion." Alexander Hamilton, James Madison, and John Jay, *The Federalist Papers*, no. 44 (Norwalk, Conn.: The Eastern Press, 1979), 300.

24. See Michal S. Gal, "Size Does Matter: The Effects of Market Size on Optimal Competition Policy," *Southern California Law Review* 74 (2001): 1437–78. See also chapter 6 by Trebilcock and Iacobucci in this volume.

25. See, for example, *Zahn v. International Paper Co.*, 414 U.S. 291 (1973).

26. See, for example, *State Farm Fire & Casualty Co. v. Tashire.* 386 U.S. 523 (1967).

27. *Allstate v. Hague*, 449 U.S. 302 (1981); *Franchise Tax Board v. Hyatt*, 123 S. Ct. 1683, 1690 (2003) ("[W]e decline to embark on the constitutional course of balancing coordinate states' competing sovereign interests under the full faith and credit clause"). For sharp critiques of the Court's constitutional agnosticism on choice of law, see Douglas Laycock, "Equal Citizens of Equal and Territorial States: The Constitutional Foundations of Choice of Law," *Columbia Law Review* 92 (1992): 249–337; and William F. Baxter, "Choice of Law and the Federal System," *Stanford Law Review* 16 (1963): 1–42.

28. *Klaxon Co. v. Stentor Electric Mfg. Co.*, 313 U.S. 487 (1941).

2

Competition of Competition Laws:
Mission Impossible?

Wolfgang Kerber and Oliver Budzinski

The rapid integration of international markets has generated an intense debate about the coordination, convergence, and harmonization of competition laws, both on a global level and within the European Union (EU). Many scholars have argued for a greater convergence or harmonization of competition laws. Others, in contrast, have insisted that harmonization would impede a fruitful "competition of competition laws." Unfortunately, the academic debate leaves very unclear what exactly "competition of competition laws" might mean. In this article, we distinguish four types of regulatory antitrust competition: (1) mutual learning, or "yardstick competition"; (2) international trade; (3) locational (or interjurisdictional) competition; and (4) free choice of law. We analyze these types of competition of competition laws with respect to their meaning and practical feasibility, and we conclude that the viability of such competition depends crucially on specific institutional preconditions. A decentralized system of competition law regimes allows for experimentation and mutual learning. Beyond this type of competition, however, competitive feedback mechanisms from international trade, factor mobility, or choice of law will suffer from considerable failures unless they are part of an institutional framework that impedes defective processes of competition.

Four Types of Regulatory Competition

Competition of competition laws represents a special case of the general theory of regulatory competition, which in turn is closely linked to the discussions about interjurisdictional (and locational) competition, systems competition, and competitive federalism.[1] More narrowly, the notion of a beneficial competition of competition laws draws on the general theory of regulatory competition and, in particular, on the theory of a "race to the top" in U.S. corporate law.[2] In terms of policy applications, the discussion over the merits and problems of competition among U.S. corporate laws and about the (de)centralization and harmonization of legal rules and regulations within the EU illustrate the practical significance of the theoretical debate.[3]

Because firms in the United States have the right to incorporate in any of the federal states irrespective of the location of their business, there has been regulatory competition between the corporate laws of the states for decades, driven by the incentive of "franchise taxes." The scholarly debate has focused on the question of whether this regulatory competition generates a "race to the bottom" or is rather efficiency-enhancing (as most scholars now suggest).[4] After the *Centros* decision of the European Court of Justice (ECJ) in 1999, the U.S. debate has also become relevant in the EU. The ECJ's earlier, pathbreaking *Cassis de Dijon* judgment had introduced the principle of "mutual recognition" as a fundamental element of European law: Companies may generally (and in the absence of affirmative regulation by the European Commission) export their goods to any member-state, provided they comply with the laws of their home or "origin" country. The *Centros* decision extended that principle beyond product regulation to national corporate laws, implying the possibility that in the long run firms might use the corporate law of their home country also in other EU member-states.[5]

So far, however, no fully elaborated general theory of regulatory competition exists. Even within the narrow context of corporate chartering, scholars continue to ask whether regulatory competition will lead to an improvement of legal rules or whether legal rules will deteriorate. Certainly, both the theoretical and empirical research show that the lessons of the corporate charter debate are not easily transferable to other contexts. The working properties of regulatory competition seem to depend crucially on specific preconditions, the institutional framework for regulatory competition, and the attributes of legal rules and regulations.[6]

The debate is also plagued by a rather vague and indifferent terminology. Often, it is not clear whether "regulatory competition" refers to

TABLE 1

TYPES OF REGULATORY COMPETITION AND THE EXTENT OF MOBILITY

Type of Regulatory Competition	Mobility of			
	Information/ Theories	Goods/ Services	Factors of Production	Legal Rules
(1) Yardstick Competition	X		–	–
(2) International Trade	X	X	–	–
(3) Locational Competition	X	X	X	–
(4) Choice of Law	X	X	X	X

a direct competition of legal rules by choice of law, to a more or less indirect one through "voting by feet" (interjurisdictional competition), a principle of origin, or a metaphorical "competition" among regulatory concepts and theories.

In an effort to bring conceptual clarity to the discussion, we distinguish four basic types of regulatory competition (see table 1). The distinguishing criterion is the extent of mobility among jurisdictions or regulatory regimes. Unless noted otherwise, the emphasis is on *extent*, as opposed to *degree*. The distinctions rest on theoretical assumptions about *what* can move across borders, not on how easily or cheaply it can move as an empirical matter. Varying assumptions about mobility, in turn, imply different transmission mechanisms for competition among legal rules.[7] Our discussion will move from most to least restrictive mobility assumptions. The assumptions are cumulative: Each step along the way, we assume (realistically) that the stuff that "moved" in an earlier theoretical model will continue to move in the next, more flexible model.

Type 1: Mutual Learning (Yardstick Competition). Jurisdictions are assumed to be isolated with the exception of information flows, which allow for mutual learning about the advantages and disadvantages of different legal rules. Jurisdictions can learn from other countries and imitate superior competition rules or enforcement techniques. Such parallel experimentation and mutual learning can occur without presupposing that the competition policy of one jurisdiction affects the welfare of other jurisdictions. In other words, the analysis neither implies nor requires international markets or an international mobility of individuals, firms, and factors of production. The transmission mechanism for the imitation of successful policies from other jurisdictions is *intra*jurisdictional political competition: Voters assess the performance of their government by comparing it with the performance of governments in other countries.

Type 2: International Trade. This type reflects the assumptions of the traditional theory of international trade: mobility of goods/services and immobility of factors of production. Because the design of the institutional and legal framework influences the competitiveness of domestic firms in international markets, a kind of indirect competition exists between the legal rules of different countries. Because competition laws can also influence the international competitiveness of domestic firms, success or failure in international trade can be an important additional feedback mechanism for competition laws. Therefore, governments may have incentives to take into account the international competitiveness of domestic industries in shaping competition policy. However, those same considerations may create incentives for strategic competition policies—for example, lenient merger policies to create "national champions" that can reap rents from market power in international markets.

Type 3: Interjurisdictional Competition. If we extend Type 2 competition by allowing for factor mobility, producers (particularly capital) can choose legal rules by moving between jurisdictions. Jurisdictions can shape their competition laws to attract investment. This direct form of regulatory competition provides additional incentives either for the improvement of competition laws or for strategic competition policies.

Type 4: Free Choice of Law. Under this model, individuals and firms can choose legal rules without having to move their physical location. In contrast to Type 3 competition, firms may choose a jurisdiction's regulations without having to accept its entire bundle of public goods, taxes, and regulations. This can lead to a much more intensive regulatory competition.

The competition of corporate laws in the United States is an example of such direct choice-of-law competition.

The mobility that determines the type of competition of competition laws depends both on real mobility conditions (such as costs of transportation, communication, and moving) and on legal rules that permit or preclude the movement of goods and services, individuals, firms, and factors of production. In competition law, the most important of these rules is the "effects doctrine," which permits a jurisdiction to apply its competition law to restraints of competition that have negative effects within its territory regardless of where those restraints of competition originate. If this extraterritorial application of competition laws were perfectly enforced, firms that want to do business in a particular jurisdiction would *not* have the right to choose between different competition laws, either through direct choice of competition laws or by moving their location to another jurisdiction. However, because of the limited enforceability of domestic competition laws in foreign countries, the effects doctrine does not necessarily exclude the possibility of interjurisdictional or choice-of-law competition. We return to this issue below. Note here that the rules that define the competencies of competition law regimes profoundly affect the dynamics and working properties of different types of regulatory competition.

Another preliminary note concerns the multilevel structure of existing competition laws. Within the EU, competition laws and authorities exist both at the national level of the EU member-states and at the EU level. The United States likewise features a two-level (federal and state) structure, particularly in regard to the enforcement of antitrust laws. The establishment of (additional) international competition rules would lead to a three-level structure of competition law regimes. In other words, competition of competition laws can take place not only horizontally (as between German and French competition policy) but also vertically, for example, between competition law regimes of the EU and its member-states. For this reason, the debate over antitrust "harmonization" or competition is closely linked to the discussion about centralization or decentralization of competition law regimes, and, therefore, to the possibility of applying the concept of federalism to competition laws.[8]

Mutual Learning (Yardstick Competition)

Knowledge Problems and the Quality of Competition Laws. Many authors have emphasized that the existence of different competition laws allows jurisdictions to learn from each other how to carry out competition policy successfully.[9] Their views are often informed by the epistemological reasoning of Hayek and Popper, which stresses the fundamental limitations of our knowledge especially in regard to rules for human societies.[10] Hayek in particular voiced a profound skepticism about the ability of governments to shape market processes. If we take the Hayekian knowledge problem seriously, we must not assume that governments (or even academic scholars) already know the best legal rules. Particularly in the long run, then, a legal system should have a high endogenous capability for improving the knowledge about the quality of its legal rules through innovation and adaptation. From this perspective, a process of parallel experimentation with legal rules in different jurisdictions (and mutual learning from these experiences) is a crucial device.

Each competition law regime consists of a complex set of rules, institutions, theories, and practices that determine its overall quality. Different *substantive* competition rules can be expected to lead to different qualities of competition law. This applies both to the legal statutes (such as the Sherman Act, the German Law Against Restraints of Competition, or Articles 81 and 82 of the EC Treaty) and to official regulations and interpretive guidelines. In addition, general legal standards may vary, as the U.S. concept of "substantially lessening competition" differs from the "market dominance test" in the EU or "public interest" as a prohibition standard for mergers. Each competition regime also features *procedural* rules, such as filing requirements, deadlines for merger procedures, investigation rights, rules for dealing with confidential business information, and sanctions for noncompliance. Other aspects of the quality of enforcement include the organization of enforcement authorities and of courts, as well as rules that determine the extent and the incentives for private enforcement. Competition agencies' degree of independence from political and private influence plays a particularly important role. The application of substantive competition rules also depends on the specific theories of competition (industrial economics) that are used by competition authorities (including courts), because those theories provide the criteria for assessing particular cases.

Different theories (for example, about entry barriers or predatory pricing) can produce qualitatively differing competition laws. Beyond that, competition laws differ in more technical practices, such as methods to define relevant markets or to determine market shares or turnover thresholds.

Although theoretical and empirical studies can provide valuable information, knowledge problems exist in regard to nearly all elements of competition law regimes. Despite a broad consensus on some basic elements (such as a prohibition against hardcore cartels), our knowledge about the best set of criteria for reviewing mergers or exempting cartels or about the most appropriate procedural rules is rather limited. Experiences with already-implemented rules, established competition authorities, and applied theories and practices are an important source of valuable information.

Experimentation, Mutual Learning, and Competition. If different competition law regimes exist in different countries, and if mutual observation of these competition policies and their relative success (or failure) is possible, governments and citizens (as voters) can use the experiences of other countries to reassess their own competition law regimes. This permits error correction; the imitation of superior legal rules, enforcement mechanisms, and theories and practices; or simply the avoidance of mistakes others have made. Even if one competition law regime might seem in general superior to another, it cannot be expected to be superior in regard to all substantive and procedural rules, theories, and practices. This ensures mutual rather than one-way learning with respect to at least some traits of competition law.

What examples of mutual learning about competition policy exist? The most important illustration is the innovation of modern competition policy through the establishment of U.S. antitrust policy at the end of the nineteenth century; its spread in the second half of the twentieth century in many industrialized countries; and, since the 1990s, its increasing diffusion in developing countries. Comparable innovation-imitation processes can also be observed in regard to particular instruments of competition policy (such as merger control), specific practices (such as methods for defining relevant markets), and particular theories (such as the spreading of arguments of Chicago economics for the evaluation of vertical restraints or the theory of contestable markets). Current discussions about whether an "efficiency defense" should be introduced in European merger control or whether the concept of "substantially lessening competition" might be superior to a "market dominance test" further illustrate the possibility of mutual learning. A detailed analysis of mutual learning processes between the German and the European competition law regime would be particularly instructive: Until the 1980s, European competition policy learned much from the more developed German competition policy, whereas since the 1990s, the main direction of learning (and imitation) has run the other way.[11] This shows that in a multilevel system of competition law regimes, processes of experimentation and mutual learning are also possible between competition law regimes on different jurisdictional levels.

Parallel experimentation and mutual learning can be described as a "competition process" only in a broad, nontechnical sense. Still, both the Schumpeterian concept of competition as innovation-imitation processes and the Hayekian concept of "competition as a discovery procedure" can be interpreted as encompassing the notion of parallel experimentation and the imitation of the successful solutions. New knowledge (here, about the protection of competition) is endogenously generated and spread.[12] Information about the quality of the performance of governments or policies (and legal rules) is revealed through comparisons with the performance of others.

Note that yardstick competition implies *permanent* parallel experimentation and ex-post revelation of superior solutions. Some authors have argued that mutual learning processes facilitate the convergence or harmonization of competition laws (for example, by identifying and spreading best practices).[13] The positive knowledge-generating effects of parallel experimentation, however, presuppose a degree of diversity among the competition policies of different jurisdictions. Therefore, yardstick competition implies (1) the right of the jurisdictions to decide freely on the details of their competition policies, and (2) the acceptance of a certain diversity of the competition policies of all jurisdictions. From this perspective, endeavors to achieve a convergence (or even a harmonization or centralization) of competition law regimes (particularly on the global level) may hamper or even eliminate the positive knowledge-generating (or error-correcting) effects of experimentation and mutual learning.

From a Hayekian point of view, the concept of competition of competition laws as a device for ex-post harmonization is equally misleading. The benefits of endogenous knowledge creation are not a temporary phenomenon, leading to an optimal solution that makes further learning unnecessary. Instead, processes of mutual learning have to take place permanently in order to secure error tolerance and allow for continuing improvements in changing environments. Therefore, the advantages of experimentation and mutual learning should be maintained in an international system of competition laws, which requires a certain degree of diversity that is not only tolerated but also seen even as a fundamental precondition for the future workability and adaptive flexibility of the system—despite other problems that result from these differences.

Problems. In practice, yardstick competition is not entirely unproblematic. If the aims of competition policy (or other important conditions) differ to a considerable extent among jurisdictions, different competition law regimes might be best for different countries. In those cases, the potential for mutual learning might be limited. Similarly, transplanting particular rules or policy instruments from one competition law regime to another might be difficult because of compatibility problems with other elements of the legal system or because the same rules have different effects in a different legal environment and judicial system.[14]

Moreover, comparative assessments of other countries' experiences with legal rules, theories, and practices will not be error-free. In some cases, countries will fail to identify the relatively best solutions, or they will imitate the "wrong" competition policies. Incentives within jurisdictions, arising from politically influential rent-seeking coalitions, might lead governments to imitate on purpose welfare-reducing competition policies, for instance, the protection of special interests through cartel exemptions or selective nonenforcement. In short, experimentation and mutual learning alone cannot ensure that superior competition policies are selected and spread. If the intrajurisdictional political processes that ultimately shape competition law are systematically deficient, mutual learning can mean the learning of inferior policies and, therefore, a deterioration of competition law regimes. Those problems, however, have to be solved by addressing the cause of the deficiencies—the institutional framework of intrajurisdictional political markets.

One may doubt whether yardstick competition, which is principally driven by intrajurisdictional political competition and excludes more direct and tangible incentives (such as firm migration), provides sufficiently strong incentives for politicians. Independent agents within each country, however, can influence innovation and imitation. Economists and legal scholars influence the academic discussion on competition policy, and they may have large incentives for the innovation of new theories and arguments and/or for importing them into domestic academic discussions. Administrative officials, judges, and lawyers likewise have incentives to adopt new theories and to develop new arguments. The complex incentives and transmission mechanisms that might foster yardstick competition of competition laws merit detailed study.

International Trade and Regulatory Competition

We now extend the analysis by allowing for the mobility of goods as well as information. Factors of production are still assumed to be immobile, and no direct choice of law is permitted. Yardstick competition remains effective; however, international cross-border trade offers an additional transmission mechanism through which competition of competition laws can become effective. It works primarily through the effects of domestic competition policies on the competitiveness of domestic firms in international markets.

Improving the Protection of Competition. The enhancement of the international competitiveness of domestic firms through competition policy has long been a popular argument in competition policy discussions.[15] One position holds that a resolute fight against market power will produce highly competitive domestic markets, which in turn will render domestic firms fitter for international competition, especially with—and in comparison to—foreign firms that are used to less competitive market conditions.[16] Moreover, such policies may lead to cost reductions in markets for intermediate goods, leading to competitive advantages for domestic firms compared to foreign firms with noncompetitive and therefore less-efficient suppliers of intermediate goods.

A second incentive effect of international trade on competition-increasing policies operates in jurisdictions with only few producers and, consequently, a high stress on consumers' interests. Because such jurisdictions would have to bear the costs of monopolization in international markets without participating much in the profits, they have powerful incentives to focus predominantly on protecting consumers and, moreover, to try to extend their regime into international markets.

Intrajurisdictional political competition will probably reinforce those incentives. In the case of increased international competitiveness, both export-oriented and import-substituting firms (including their employees) will benefit. In the case of protection of domestic consumers against foreign market power, large groups of consumers will benefit. Citizens in jurisdictions with less-protective competition policies, in contrast, will experience negative feedback from international trade, because their export-oriented firms suffer from low international competitiveness and their import-substituting industries are strongly challenged by foreign competitors, or because their consumers finance foreign monopoly rents by bearing higher prices. This provides political-economic incentives for politicians to adjust their competition policy regime toward more competition. Thus, international trade may generate a competition of competition laws and lead to an improvement of competition laws. The parallel existence of yardstick competition supports this mechanism—and vice versa. Legal innovations (or imitation) of substantial or procedural competition rules, theories, or practices improve the protection of competition and imply lower enforcement costs for both competition authorities and firms. Conversely, the international trade mechanism improves the incentives for learning, adaptation, and imitation.

Strategic Competition Policy: Deliberate Toleration of Market Power and Anticompetitive Behavior. In contrast to the positive scenario just sketched, certain theories suggest that the deliberate toleration of market power and the lessening of (domestic) competition can increase the international competitiveness of domestic firms and, thereby, contribute to domestic welfare. As an analogy to well-known strategic trade policies, which use tariffs, subsidies, and other protectionist trade policy instruments to increase domestic welfare, we can speak of strategic competition policies.[17]

A jurisdiction can strategically allow its firms to obtain market power in domestic markets to facilitate the reaping of efficiency gains in international markets as a result of synergies and economies of scale and scope. (This applies predominantly to formerly national markets that are in the process of becoming international.) Because international markets usually are larger than national ones, the efficient size of firms in international markets may be larger. Thus, cooperation between domestic enterprises and a higher domestic concentration may be efficient. This can be called an "international competitiveness defense," referring to a trade-off between market power effects (allocative inefficiencies) in domestic markets and efficiency effects on international markets.

A recent example is the merger of E.ON and Ruhrgas. Because the merger threatened to create a near-monopolistic position on the German gas market, the German Federal Cartel Office (Bundeskartellamt) initially prohibited the merger. However, the German Federal Ministry of Economics overruled the Office and allowed the merger because it promised to strengthen the international competitiveness of Ruhrgas in international gas markets. Although the Ministry did not deny the emergence of market power in the domestic market, it assumed that gas markets are on their way to internationalize and found efficiency advantages for the merged company in these emerging larger international markets.[18]

The deliberate toleration of market power in domestic markets can also help domestic firms to attain market power in international markets. In this case, profits do not result from efficiency gains, but from monopoly or oligopoly rents. The benefits for the domestic firms are based on higher prices, predominantly for foreign consumers, and the deterrence of foreign competitors. Competition policy strategies in this vein include the exemption of export cartels, selective nonenforcement of competition laws, the strategic use of merger control to support the creation of "national champions" and "domestic global players," and the promotion of research-and-development cooperation in "key industries" and "future trend-setting technologies." For example, in the well-known U.S.-EU dispute over the Boeing-McDonnell Douglas merger, both sides were suspected of abusing competition law for strategic industrial goals. The U.S. approval of the merger was perceived as an attempt to create a U.S.-based world monopoly for large civil jet aircraft, whereas the European Commission's (EC's) opposition was said to protect Airbus against a more efficient competitor.[19]

Finally, domestic competition policy can allow some firms to reap profits from domestic market power and use them to cross-subsidize foreign market activities. One strategy to promote a "national global player" is to grant monopoly privileges in national or regional markets, thus allowing the privileged firm to use the monopoly rents to finance predatory strategies in international markets. An example is the Deutsche Post AG's use of its monopoly privilege for standard-letter postal services in Germany. This remnant of the former government-organized German mail market is under pressure from liberalization claims by the EC, but the German government has so far refused to withdraw the monopoly privilege. Meanwhile, Deutsche Post has aggressively expanded in the international logistic markets, including takeovers of Global Mail (1998), Danzas (1999), Air Express International (1999), and DHL (in several steps between 1998 and 2002). The postage for standard letters remains significantly higher than in other European countries, while the prices of Deutsche Post and its subsidiaries in the international logistic markets have been reduced considerably.[20]

Export promotion through dumping strategies represents an interface between trade and competition policy. On the international level, an anti-dumping policy regime, implemented within the framework of the World Trade Organization (WTO), addresses various dumping strategies that are made possible and supported by public authorities. It is not at all clear, however, whether the WTO rules apply to a dumping strategy based on lax competition policy.[21] On the whole, the role of the WTO remains rather limited in such cases.

Strategic competition policies almost always reduce global welfare. True, the creation of large international firms, even at the price of tolerating domestic market power, may produce efficiency gains in international markets, and consumers might benefit from decreasing prices—at least in the long run. But disadvantages may result for remaining domestic competitors of the new global player and for consumers of the monopolized domestic market. From a welfare perspective, this strategy might still be Kaldor-Hicks-superior, because the winners could compensate the losers. But this is true only if the efficiency gains (scale and scope effects) become in fact realized, which often is not the case. From a political-economic perspective, the losers—probably small firms and domestic consumers—would probably not possess enough lobby power to prevent this strategy. Strategic competition policies to create international market power and allow for anticompetitive cross-subsidization do not produce efficiency gains for the world economy. Instead, international competition is harmed by the national competition policies, and international allocation becomes inefficient.

Antitrust policy, like any other policy field, can be captured by interest groups. Strategic competition policies become rational from a political economy viewpoint, if the agents that benefit are better organized to lobby than the losers. Both export-oriented and import-substituting industries, which have incentives to lobby for a strategic abuse of competition policy, have relatively low organizational costs and are represented by well-organized industry associations. "National champions" and their stakeholders (such as labor unions) may be big enough to participate successfully in the lobbying game. On the other side, the losers consist of groups with high organizational costs (consumers) or who live abroad and have no voice in the domestic political competition. Thus, it can be rational from a political economy perspective to adopt strategic competition policies even if they lead to a net welfare decrease within the domestic jurisdiction.

Moreover, modern trade theory shows that under certain assumptions, the national welfare gains from strategic restrictions or distortions of international competition may be high enough to compensate the domestic losers. (There remains a net welfare loss, which is completely imposed on the foreign jurisdiction.)[22] Incentives from intrajurisdictional political competition may induce politicians to direct domestic competition policy to alleged "national" (but in fact partial) interests.[23] Internationally discriminating competition policy strategies can eventually become a profit-maximizing strategy for one country, even as these "beggar-my-neighbor" competition policy strategies reduce the level of world welfare. For each jurisdiction, it is individually rational to choose a beggar-my-neighbor strategy. A jurisdiction that chooses a procompetitive strategy while all other jurisdictions use strategic competition policies will bear the costs of others' beggar-my-neighbor strategies, and, thus, have an incentive to adapt its competition policy. This prisoner's dilemma might lead to a defection race and a deterioration of protection of competition. Yardstick competition might reinforce this process: Mutual learning can include learning about more effective beggar-my-neighbor strategies.

The Role of the Effects Doctrine. On the basis of the effects doctrine, a national competition authority claims jurisdiction over any cartel or merger, which affects domestic markets, irrespective of their location. Consequently, whenever national competition authorities would allow a foreign-market-oriented cartel or merger, the adversely affected jurisdiction would intervene to prevent the anticompetitive effects. Thus, a perfectly enforced effects doctrine would render strategic competition policy impossible and preclude competition policies with beggar-my-neighbor effects. In reality, however, the effects doctrine cannot be applied in a perfect and complete way, because of problems of investigation, information gathering, and rule enforcement abroad. At the same time, the doctrine has the potential to generate jurisdictional conflicts among the many countries where a given merger or cartel practice may have an effect. In addition, the effects doctrine increases the transaction costs of international mergers, because it compels the parties to comply with several national and supranational merger controls with different and sometimes contradictory requirements. As a practical matter, the effects doctrine can impede but not eliminate strategic competition policies, and even that advantage carries a cost.

Moreover, the effects doctrine itself can be strategically applied to handicap foreign competitors of domestic firms. There are considerable asymmetries concerning the jurisdictional power to enforce the domestic competition laws against the resistance of another jurisdiction. Whereas big jurisdictions with important markets (such as the United States and the EU) can easily protect domestic competition against restrictions from abroad, small and developing countries often have difficulties in doing so. Therefore, the power asymmetries between the jurisdictions offer the possibility for powerful jurisdictions to abuse the effects doctrine to serve protectionist interests.[24]

Summary. The relative importance of international trade and export-import relations differs considerably from jurisdiction to jurisdiction (from small, open countries with a high significance of international trade to large countries dominated by domestic markets). Often, the international competitiveness of domestic firms has only a small importance for intrajurisdictional political competition, and is dominated by other issues. If a jurisdiction's performance in international trade is important enough for its citizens to set incentives via domestic political competition, political influence on export-import relations might be more efficiently directed to the use of trade policy instruments than to competition policy instruments. However, because of the development of an international free trade framework under the governance of the WTO, trade policy competencies have been delegated (although incompletely) to an international level and the national authorities have become restricted in the application of trade policy instruments. This process probably will continue and create a "vacuum" that can be filled by replacing strategic trade policy with strategic competition policy as a second-best solution.[25]

It remains unclear, then, whether this type of regulatory competition improves competition laws or leads to a prisoner's dilemma with suboptimal competition laws as a result of the dominance of strategic competition policies. Institutional arrangements have an important influence on the outcome of regulatory competition. The effects doctrine, as noted, reduces the scope of strategic competition policies, but it also limits all regulatory competition of competition laws. The application of rules other than the effects doctrine would entail different effects. Well-designed rules might procure the advantages of trade-related competition processes, while curbing their potential defects.

Interjurisdictional Competition

In addition to the mobility of information and goods, we now consider the mobility of capital and labor. Enterprises and individuals may choose between different institutional arrangements by choosing their domicile. Direct choice of law independent from a firm's (physical) location is still excluded from the analysis. The competitive transmission mechanism is the inflow and outflow of production factors as a result of different competition laws and policies. The idea is that an inflow of production factors increases national welfare, whereas a significant exit of factors diminishes it. Politicians have incentives to adjust their regulations in order to attract mobile factors.

Most of the extant literature on competition of competition laws draws exclusively or predominantly on this type of interjurisdictional competition. The focus is on the effects of different competition laws on the locational choice of enterprises and the strategic use of competition laws to attract business. Arguably, if highly competitive domestic markets improve the competitiveness of firms located within a jurisdiction, it is a rational strategy for firms to choose that location. The deliberate choice of a jurisdiction with strict competition laws can be interpreted as a kind of self-commitment to remain competitive, which might generate positive signals to investors, shareholders, competitors, and consumers. In addition, lower prices for intermediate goods, which can be expected if strict competition laws secure intensive competition in these markets, can be an argument for choosing a procompetitive jurisdiction.

For these reasons, some authors have concluded that interjurisdictional competition will improve competition laws.[26] Because mobile factors will move to the jurisdiction that supplies the best competition laws, jurisdictions with inferior institutions will experience actual exits and threats to exit. This provides incentives for politicians to adjust their competition laws accordingly. Again, the parallel existence of yardstick competition reinforces the dynamic. Conversely, interjurisdictional competition provides additional incentives for the innovation and imitation of substantial and procedural competition rules, theories, or practices in order to improve the competition law regimes. It is also possible, however, that firms are attracted to competition laws that tolerate domestic market power and anticompetitive business behavior. If firms value the freedom to cartelize and monopolize more than they value the protection against such behavior by others, a strategy of reducing the level of protection of competition can improve the competitiveness of jurisdictions in the international market for locations (for example, by running a cartel haven, by granting monopoly privileges, or through the selective nonenforcement of domestic competition rules).

Analogous to the dynamics that drive regulatory competition via international trade, jurisdictions can attempt to attract firms by offering competition policies that allow the reaping of efficiency gains (for example, by introducing an efficiency defense in merger control), even if market power in (related) domestic markets might ensue. Because economies of scale effects can increase international competitiveness, firms might prefer this kind of competition policy, leading to an inflow of firms and capital into the jurisdiction. Similarly, a lower level of protection of competition, either through lenient competition laws or a policy of (selective) nonenforcement, can be an important argument for locational decisions if firms want to restrict competition by cartels, build up market power by mergers, or engage in anticompetitive behavior in international markets. If the negative effects of market power and anticompetitive behavior primarily affect markets in other jurisdictions, the positive welfare effects of the inflow of resources can overcompensate possible negative effects in domestic markets. The strategy to allow firms to build up market power in domestic markets in order to use these profits to cross-subsidize business activities in foreign markets (maybe to finance predatory strategies) can be attractive for firms in regard to their locational decision.

A jurisdiction can allow for market power that can be used only to reap profits from domestic markets. It may be attractive for firms to move their location into that jurisdiction, even if they produce exclusively for its domestic market. Under certain conditions, this strategy might prove attractive for certain jurisdictions, particularly if domestic suppliers would otherwise be unable to produce the goods in question (for example, because of a lack of technology or expertise).

Because such strategies may often be successful, some authors have argued that interjurisdictional competition will trigger a race to the bottom in antitrust policy.[27] (Even policies directed purely at domestic markets may produce that result.) If firms prefer jurisdictions with a low level of protection of competition, jurisdictions with a high level of protection of competition might suffer exits and a subsequent decrease in welfare. Consequently, agents in those jurisdictions have incentives to vote in favor of a policy imitating the successful jurisdictions in order to reattract mobile factors. Thus, stiff interjurisdictional competition can lead to a deterioration of competition laws: Although all jurisdictions could be better off with appropriate competition laws, there can be a suboptimal equilibrium with an insufficient level of protection of competition.

Although interjurisdictional competition represents a more direct competition of competition laws than yardstick or trade competition, obstacles remain. If firms can choose more attractive competition laws only by moving to another jurisdiction, they have to accept the entire bundle of public goods, regulations, and taxes of that jurisdiction. It is doubtful whether competition laws will dominate locational decisions in light of the importance of other jurisdictional characteristics (such as taxes and labor market regulations). In addition, mobility costs have to be overcompensated by the benefits of the locational change. The effects doctrine further limits interjurisdictional competition. Under a perfect effects doctrine regime, moving the location of a firm to another jurisdiction with a lower protection of competition does not help because the jurisdictions of the affected markets will nevertheless enforce their (stricter) competition laws against anticompetitive behavior of the firm. Again, no room would be left for a competition of competition laws.

Summary. Interjurisdictional competition of competition laws can be expected to have beneficial effects if firms prefer a more competitive market environment because of its beneficial effects on their competitiveness and on downstream markets. However, race-to-the-bottom processes can emerge if jurisdictions engage in strategic competition policies that allow for restrictive practices and the development of market power in domestic and international markets. In these cases, interjurisdictional competition of competition laws can create an international prisoner's dilemma, which cannot be solved without international coordination. Whether prisoner's dilemma problems result or competition of competition laws proves beneficial depends largely on the institutional framework of that regulatory competition, that is, on the rules that shape the behavior of jurisdictions in interjurisdictional competition. Again, the effects doctrine can play an important limiting role, but other rules—such as comity principles—could also be an important part of an institutional framework that allows for productive interjurisdictional competition and precludes race-to-the-bottom phenomena.

Choice of Law

Choice-of-law competition implies that firms have the right to choose directly between regulations of different jurisdictions without having to move their location to that jurisdiction. As noted, U.S. corporate law operates on this principle. Can this type of regulatory competition be applied to competition law?

To a limited extent, firms may already have a choice of competition law. In Europe, firms can influence, through the design of their mergers or cooperative agreements, which competition law rules apply to them. For example, because European merger control was seen as less restrictive than German merger control, firms had an incentive to design mergers that fell under the European merger control rules. (It depends on the turnover thresholds in national markets and in the European market whether the EC or the national competition authorities have jurisdiction over a merger.) Such forum shopping between national and European competition rules also existed with respect to cartel exemptions, albeit in only a limited way.[28]

Forum shopping is also seen as one of the potential problems of the decentralization approach in the EC's reform of Articles 81 and 82 of the EC Treaty. The competition authorities of the member-states obtain the right to enforce the European competition rules on behalf of the EC, so that the latter can concentrate on the most serious cases. In doing so, however, firms may have an increased opportunity to pick the enforcement agency that is most sympathetic to their arrangement.[29]

At the international level, the situation is different. Here, the effects doctrine has the opposite effect—a cumulating of competition law proceedings in one and the same case (although the practical limits of the effects doctrine might permit forum shopping in specific cases). Regardless of its precise current scope, though, forum shopping is not a consequence of institutional or policy design. It is unintended and undesired, even by the most ardent opponents of harmonization.[30]

The aim of competition law is the protection of competition, that is, the protection of markets, not particular firms. If firms may choose the competition rules under which they do business, a prisoner's dilemma emerges. Individually, each firm is interested in avoiding restrictions on its business practices, leading to the choice of less-restrictive or poorly enforced competition laws. Although firms might be interested in being protected from anticompetitive behavior of others (and in that sense, they might prefer a stricter competition law), the desire to attract firms will induce jurisdictions to dilute their competition laws. In short, the idea that choice of law can be applied to competition law seems absurd.

Another train of thought leads to the same result. Competition in a particular market is a public good, which can only be produced if all firms in this market contribute to the production of this public good by subjecting themselves to the same restrictive rules.[31] Antitrust law concerns itself with injuries to third parties that are not involved in the competition-violating arrangement (for example, consumers harmed by a cartel). In contrast to the corporate law context, no contractual link exists between anticompetitive firms and harmed consumers or competitors. Instead, significant externalities occur because of the firms' jurisdiction shopping, and no workable mechanism would force the law-choosing firms to internalize these costs.

In two cases, pure choice of law *might* improve competition law regimes. First, choice of law can help to improve competition laws if the choice depends not on the substantive strictness of competition law but on the efficiency of *procedures*. For example, merger reviews under different competition law regimes might entail different costs and require a different time exposure for the merging firms, completely irrespective of the strictness of the review. If the same level of protection of competition would be ensured by other means (for example, international arrangements), a free choice of the competition law regime in case of a merger review might lead to a productive competition between the competition authorities. Second, efforts to circumvent competition laws through choice of law can enhance national (and global) welfare if the competition laws are excessively strict or distorted by rent-seeking activities. If the existing laws stifle competition and impede efficiency, exit through choice of law might induce jurisdictions to enact more appropriate competition laws.

It is *only* in these special cases (procedural rules and overregulation), however, that choice-of-law competition might lead to an improvement in competition laws. In all other cases, the prisoner's dilemma will lead to a deterioration of the legal rules. Because competition law aims to protect markets rather than market participants, the competition of U.S. corporate laws cannot serve as a model for competition of competition laws. The widespread suspicion against forum shopping in competition law is justified.

What Follows? Toward a Decentralized International Multilevel System of Competition Laws

Our analysis strongly suggests that mutual learning (or yardstick competition) is the most promising type of competition of competition laws. Trade and interjurisdictional competition might strengthen the incentives for improving competition laws. Both, however, would require institutional arrangements to avoid deleterious effects (particularly prisoner's dilemma situations). Choice-of-law competition of competition laws leads to the most serious problems; a productive use of this mechanism does not seem practically feasible.

Competition laws cannot be separated from the markets they are supposed to protect. Because competition laws necessarily have to restrict the behavior of firms in order to exclude anticompetitive practices, choosing between competition laws implies the possibility of circumventing competition rules. Therefore, it can be expected that interjurisdictional and choice-of-law competition of competition laws will generally lead to a deterioration of the protection of competition.

Under the international trade scenario and the interjurisdictional competition scenario, jurisdictions will use strategic competition policies to enhance their welfare or at least the welfare of powerful interest groups. Both types of competition of competition laws can lead to an improvement of competition laws if theories dominate in intrajurisdictional political competition that a high level of protection of competition enhances the international competitiveness of domestic firms or the competitiveness of the jurisdictions as locations. However, jurisdictions can also engage in competition policy strategies that reduce the protection of competition in order to promote domestic firms in international markets (or protect them against foreign competitors) or to attract firms in interjurisdictional competition. Generally, strategic competition policies have negative (external) effects on other jurisdictions and lead to a global prisoner's dilemma. In most cases, therefore, competition of these strategic competition policies has to be assessed negatively because it tends to reduce the protection of competition both in domestic and international markets. Hence, trade and interjurisdictional competition can improve competition laws only if the negative effects of strategic competition policies are avoided by appropriate institutional arrangements, such as the effects doctrine or comparable, agreed-upon international rules. Such rules, in turn, would limit considerably the extent of competition of competition policies. Thus, the applicability of trade, interjurisdictional, and choice-of-law competition of competition laws is limited. Putting aside the special case of universal overregulation, competitive mechanisms have to be severely restricted if a deterioration of the protection of competition is to be avoided.

The general assessment is different in regard to yardstick competition of competition policies. If we take the knowledge problem seriously, parallel experimentation and mutual learning become very important. Mutual learning can take place between competition law regimes on the same jurisdictional levels (horizontal dimension) and on different jurisdictional levels (vertical dimension). Although it also can suffer from problems in regard to imitation and incentives, no systematic race-to-the-bottom problems emerge (in contrast to all other types of competition of competition laws). Yardstick competition offers the opportunity for a long-term process of improving the knowledge about effective competition laws.

In the extensive debate on international competition policy over the past decade, three main avenues to cope with international competition and globalizing markets have emerged:

- *No systematic international competition policy.* Despite a widespread consensus about the existence of problems in regard to the protection of competition in international markets, proponents of this view believe that the costs of an international competition policy regime might exceed its benefits. Instead, they favor the application of the effects doctrine combined with discretionary bilateral cooperation between antitrust agencies.

- *Convergence and harmonization of national competition laws toward centralized international regulation.* Proponents of this view eventually strive for a uniform international competition policy in the long run. The (realistic) way toward this first-best solution includes a step-by-step process of convergence of national competition policies in a multilateral framework. Consequently, the focus lies on the harmonization of substantial competition law.

- *Regulation of the allocation of jurisdiction within an (international) decentralized system of competition laws.* Proponents of this perspective believe that an international convergence and harmonization of substantial competition law is either not feasible or not desirable, except to a very limited extent. A workable solution is rather seen in an international consensus on procedural rules for policy problems in multijurisdictional antitrust cases.

These rules particularly address the delimitation of jurisdictional competencies, conflict resolution, and enforcement assistance.

Following our analysis, we reject the first line of thought. The problems and deficiencies of purely national competition policies in international markets—such as loopholes in the protection of competition (as a result of deficient extraterritorial enforcement), negative externalities (as a result of beggar-my-neighbor strategies), and cumulating competition law proceedings (as a result of overlapping jurisdictions with resulting jurisdictional conflicts)—will increase with the ongoing globalization of markets and firms. Competition of competition laws that is not guarded by an appropriate international arrangement cannot be reliably expected to yield welfare-enhancing results.

We are equally skeptical about the substantive convergence and harmonization of national competition policies, which would eventually imply a centralization of international competition policy. Establishing a substantial international competition policy regime would be very costly,[32] and pessimism in respect to the possibility of agreeing on harmonization of substantial competition laws is justified. However, this is not our main concern. Rather, we question whether harmonization (and centralization) of competition laws is the first-best solution at all. The different goals of competition policy and varying economic and cultural conditions across different countries raise severe doubts whether a uniform competition policy would be the best one for all countries (irrespective of their state of development, their cultural background, their size, their openness to international markets, and their institutions). Decentralized competition policies might be more appropriate to cope with the enormous divergences in the world economy.

Our principal objection, though, derives from our Hayekian perspective. Our limited knowledge about the most appropriate competition law regime, coupled with the necessity to protect flexibility and openness for improvements in light of rapid—and continuous—technological and economic change, is a powerful argument against the establishment of an inflexible centralized or harmonized solution. A decentralized system of competition laws would allow for parallel experimentation with different solutions and mutual learning from their performance.

To some extent, the International Competition Network (ICN) embraces the advantages of parallel experimentation and mutual learning. Its main features are the systematic exchange of information and the evaluation of current competition laws and policies of the member jurisdictions. Thereby, best practices concerning antitrust procedures, institutional arrangements, and substantial rules shall be identified and published. In doing so, the ICN promotes mutual learning through two channels: the creation of transparency concerning different solutions to competition policy problems, which enhances the possibilities for interjurisdictional comparisons, and the public identification of superior solutions (best practices), which facilitates their diffusion by putting "peer pressure" on the member jurisdictions to imitate the best practices. It is not clear, though, whether the ICN will develop to be a road to *ex post* harmonization: Processes of imitation are strongly emphasized, while the role of future innovations remains rather vague.[33] This is a cause for concern: Taking competition through mutual learning does *not* mean to identify best practices "once and for all" and then to harmonize competition policies according to that standard. On the contrary, the knowledge problem requires that an international system of competition laws must sustainably produce variety and generate new knowledge.

How can a decentralized approach to competition policy be made compatible with the necessity to solve the many problems that result from the current situation of multiple, independent national competition laws? In our view, the most promising perspective is the development of a consistent international multilevel system of competition laws. Within this system, substantive competition rules and enforcement agencies might exist on two or three different jurisdictional levels (for example, the international level, the European level, and the national level). Although policies on these different levels should remain (to a considerable extent) independent from each other, a coherent institutional framework should govern the whole multilevel system so as to reduce gaps in the protection of competition, to resolve conflicts between different competition policies, and to save transaction costs by limiting parallel proceedings. It is crucial that this multilevel system of competition laws work as an integrated system.

True, a minimum consensus about the basic principles of competition policies is a precondition for such an international system. The focus, however, is on the development of the institutional framework for making a decentralized system work in a satisfactory way. In this sense, our suggestion parallels the aforementioned third perspective for international competition policy—that is, the search for an international consensus on the allocation of jurisdiction in transborder antitrust cases.

So far, there is no comprehensive proposal for a multilevel system of competition laws that would allow us to derive detailed policy conclusions. However, well-developed economic theories of federalism can be applied to determine the appropriate mixture of centralization and decentralization within an international multilevel system.[34] The primary questions to be answered are, What kinds of competition problems should be dealt with on what jurisdictional level? What extent of centralization or decentralization should be chosen in regard to substantive competition rules, on the one hand, and in regard to the enforcement of competition rules (competition authorities, courts) on the other hand? The geographic scope of competition problems, economies of scale, transaction costs, the extent of local knowledge, and the homogeneity or heterogeneity of the aims of competition policies are among the criteria that will determine the optimal balance between centralization and decentralization.

Our analysis of the different types of competition of competition laws should further assist in providing an answer. Parallel experimentation and mutual learning are powerful arguments for a decentralized system—but not a complete answer. To the extent that other types of competition of competition laws are working in a positive way, they are reinforced by yardstick competition—just as, conversely, those competitive mechanisms provide additional incentives for learning. But under different conditions, yardstick competition may in fact aggravate the problems of strategic, welfare-reducing policies, as countries "learn" more effective ways of exploiting their neighbors. We should therefore ask what kinds of institutional arrangements could channel the learning processes into a positive direction. Although the application of the effects doctrine could impede negative effects (if it were fully enforceable), it also considerably limits the potential positive effects of competition of competition laws. Perhaps, though, more sophisticated rules could improve the situation.

First steps have been taken. The attempts to establish a decentralized system of enforcement of European competition law within the EU and the efforts to agree on procedural rules for national merger reviews on a global level both can be seen as treating particular aspects of the task of developing an international multilevel system of competition laws. That task, however, will require much further research. Of particular urgency is the development of rules for the horizontal and vertical delimitation of competencies of the competition policies within this international multi-level system of competition laws. The effects doctrine and its modifications by applying principles of positive and negative comity as well as other explicit rules for the horizontal and vertical delimitation of competencies can be seen as starting points for the development of a consistent set of rules.

Notes

1. See, for example, C. M. Tiebout, "A Pure Theory of Local Expenditures," *Journal of Political Economy* 64 (1956): 416–24; Horst Siebert and Michael J. Koop, "Institutional Competition: A Concept for Europe?" *Aussenwirtschaft* 45 (1990): 439–62; Daphne A. Kenyon and John Kincaid, eds., *Competition Among States and Local Governments: Efficiency and Equity in American Federalism* (Washington, D.C.: Urban Institute Press, 1991); Viktor Vanberg and Wolfgang Kerber, "Institutional Competition Among Jurisdictions: An Evolutionary Approach," *Constitutional Political Economy* 5 (1994): 364–85; Bruno S. Frey and Reiner Eichenberger, "Competition Among Jurisdictions: The Idea of FOCJ," in *Competition Among Institutions*, ed. Lüder Gerken (London: Palgrave Macmillan, 1995), 209–29; Albert Breton, *Competitive Governments: An Economic Theory of Politics and Public Finance* (Cambridge: Cambridge University Press, 1996); Hans-Werner Sinn, "The Selection Principle and Market Failure in Systems Competition," *Journal of Public Economics* 88 (1997): 247–74; Hans-Werner Sinn, *The New Systems Competition* (Oxford: Blackwell Publishers, 2003); W. W. Bratton and J. A. McCahery, "The New Economics of Jurisdictional Competition: Devolutionary Federalism in a Second-Best World," *Georgetown Law Journal* 86 (1997): 201; Wolfgang Kerber, "Zum Problem einer Wettbewerbsordnung für den Systemwettbewerb," *Jahrbuch für Neue Politische Ökonomie* 17 (1998): 199–231; W. E. Oates, "An Essay on Fiscal Federalism," *Journal of Economic Literature* 37 (1999): 1120–49; W. E. Oates, "Fiscal and Regulatory Competition: Theory and Evidence," *Perspektiven der Wirtschaftspolitik* 3, no. 4 (2002): 377–90; and Dietmar Wellisch, *Theory of Public Finance in a Federal State* (Cambridge: Cambridge University Press, 2000).

2. See Roberta Romano, "Law as a Product: Some Pieces of the Incorporation Puzzle," *Journal of Law, Economics, and Organization* 1 (1985): 225; and Frank H. Easterbrook and D. R. Fischel, *The Economic Structure of Corporate Law* (Cambridge, Mass.: Harvard University Press, 1996).

3. See Stephen Woolcock, *The Single European Market: Centralization or Competition Among National Rules?* (London: Royal Institute of International Affairs, 1994); J. M. Sun and J. J. Pelkmans, "Regulatory Competition in the Single Market," *Journal of Common Market Studies* 33 (1995): 67–89; and Wolfgang Kerber, "Interjurisdictional Competition within the European Union," *Fordham International Law Journal* 23 (2000): 217–49.

4. See, for example, L. A. Bebchuk, "Federalism and the Corporation: The Desirable Limits on State Competition in Corporate Law," *Columbia Law Review* 105 (1992): 1435; Roberta Romano, "Law as a Product," *The Genius of American Corporate Law* (Washington, D.C.: AEI Press, 1993); and Easterbrook and Fischel, *The Economic Structure of Corporate Law*.

5. See Jan Wouters, "European Company Law: Quo Vadis?" *Common Market Law Review* 37, no. 2 (2000): 257–307; and Klaus Heine and Wolfgang Kerber,

"European Corporate Laws, Regulatory Competition, and Path Dependence," *European Journal of Law and Economics* 13 (2002): 43–71.

6. See Siebert and Koop, "Institutional Competition: A Concept for Europe?" *Aussenwirtschaft* 45 (1990): 439–62; Heinz Hauser and Martin Hösli, "Harmonization of Regulatory Competition in the EC (and the EEA)?" *Aussenwirtschaft* 49 (1991): 497–512; Sun and Pelkmans, "Regulatory Competition in the Single Market"; Sinn, "The Selection Principle"; and K. Gatsios and P. Holmes, "Regulatory Competition," in *The New Palgrave Dictionary of Economics and the Law,* ed. Peter Newman (London: Palgrave Macmillan, 1998), 271–75; R. Van den Bergh, "Towards an Institutional Legal Framework for Regulatory Competition in Europe," *Kyklos* 53 (2000): 435–66; Paul B. Stephan, "Regulatory Cooperation and Competition: The Search for Virtue," in *Transatlantic Regulatory Cooperation: Legal Problems and Political Prospects,* eds. George A. Bermann, Matthias Herdegen, and Peter L. Lindseth (Oxford: Oxford University Press, 2000), 167–202; and Klaus Heine, *Regulierungswettbewerb im Gesellschaftsrecht: Zur Funktionsfähigkeit eines Wettbewerbs der Rechtsordnungen im europäischen Gesellschaftsrecht* (Berlin: Duncker & Humblot, 2003).

7. For this distinction of different types of regulatory competition, see also Wolfgang Kerber, "Rechtseinheitlichkeit und Rechtsvielfalt aus ökonomischer Sicht," in *Systembildung und Systemlücken in Kerngebieten des Europäischen Privatrechts: Gesellschafts-, Arbeits-, und Schuldvertragsrecht,* ed. Stefan Grundmann (Tübingen: Mohr Siebeck, 2000), 67–97; Heine, *Regulierungswettbewerb im Gesellschaftsrecht;* and briefly in respect to competition laws, Wolfgang Kerber, "An International Multi-Level System of Competition Laws: Federalism in Antitrust," in *The Future of Transnational Antitrust: From Comparative to Common Competition Law,* ed. Josef Drexl (Bern: Kluwer Law International, 2003), 269–300.

8. For first approaches to apply federalism to competition policy, see Frank H. Easterbrook, chapter 8 in this volume; Barry E. Hawk and Laraine L. Laudati, "Antitrust Federalism in the United States and Decentralization of Competition Law Enforcement in the European Union: A Comparison," *Fordham International Law Journal* 20 (1996): 18; Eleanor M. Fox, "Antitrust and Regulatory Federalism: Races Up, Down, and Sideways," *New York University Law Review* 75 (2000): 1781; Andrew T. Guzman, "Antitrust and International Regulatory Federalism," *New York University Law Review* 76 (2001): 1142; Kerber, "An International Multi-Level System."

9. See Karl M. Meessen, "Competition of Competition Laws," *Northwestern Journal of International Law and Business* 10 (1989): 17; Phedon Nicolaides, "Competition Among Rules," *World Competition* 16 (1992): 113–21; Phedon Nicolaides, "Towards Multilateral Rules on Competition," *World Competition* 17 (1994): 5–48; R. Van den Bergh, "Economic Criteria for Applying the Subsidiarity Principle in the European Community: The Case of Competition

Policy," *International Review of Law and Economics* 16 (1996): 363; Harry First, "Theories of Harmonization: A Cautionary Tale," in *Comparative Competition Law: Approaching an International System of Antitrust Law*, ed. Hanns Ullrich (Baden-Baden: Nomos Verlagsgesellschaft, 1998), 17–41; and A. Freytag and R. Zimmermann, "Muß die internationale Handelsordnung um eine Wettbewerbsordnung erweitert werden?" *Rabels Zeitschrift für ausländisches und internationales Privatrecht* 62 (1998): 38–58.

10. See Friedrich A. von Hayek, "The Use of Knowledge in Society," *American Economic Review* 35 (1945): 519–30; Friedrich A. von Hayek, *The Sensory Order* (Chicago: The University of Chicago Press, 1952); Friedrich A. von Hayek "The Pretence of Knowledge," *The Swedish Journal of Economics* 77 (1975): 433–42; and Karl R. Popper, *Objective Knowledge. An Evolutionary Approach* (Oxford: Clarendon Press, 1972).

11. The sixth revision of the German Law Against Restraints of Competition (GWB) in 1999 comprised several imitations of European competition rules—for example, the imitation of the EU rule on cartel exemptions (art. 81, par. 3, EC Treaty as "Sonderkartelle" [GWB, § 7]) or procedural rules for merger control.

12. For evolutionary concepts of competition, see Joseph Alois Schumpeter, *The Theory of Economic Development: An Inquiry into Profits, Capital, Credit, Interest, and the Business Cycle* (Cambridge: Harvard University Press, 1934); Friedrich A. Hayek, "Competition as a Discovery Procedure," in *New Studies in Philosophy, Politics, Economics, and the History of Ideas* (Chicago: University of Chicago Press, 1978), 179–90; Wolfgang Kerber, "Wettbewerb als Hypothesentest: eine evolutorische Konzeption wissenschaffenden Wettbewerbs," in *Dimensionen des Wettbewerbs: Seine Rolle in der Entstehung und Ausgestaltung von Wirtschaftsordnungen*, eds. Karl von Delhaes and Ulrich Fehl (Stuttgart: Lucius & Lucius, 1997), 29–78; and Israel Kirzner, "Entrepreneurial Discovery and the Competitive Market Process: An Austrian Approach," *Journal of Economic Literature* 35 (1997): 60–85. For applications of evolutionary concepts of competition to interjurisdictional and regulatory competition, see Martti Vihanto, "Competition between Local Governments as a Discovery Procedure," *Journal of Institutional and Theoretical Economics* 148 (1992): 411–36; Viktor Vanberg and Wolfgang Kerber, "Institutional Competition Among Jurisdictions: An Evolutionary Approach," *Constitutional Political Economy* 5 (1994): 193–219 ; and Manfred E. Streit and Michael Wohlgemuth, eds., *Systemwettbewerb als Herausforderung an Politik und Theorie* (Baden-Baden: Nomos, 1999). The specific concept of yardstick competition can be traced back to A. Shleifer, "A Theory of Yardstick Competition," *Rand Journal of Economics* 16 (1985): 319–27. In the theory of interjurisdictional and regulatory competition, it was introduced by Pierre Salmon, "Decentralisation as an Incentive Scheme," *Oxford Review of Economic Policy* 3 (1987): 24–43. For modeling the search for new policy solutions in decentralized federal systems with learning from others, see K. Kollman, J. H.

Miller, and S. E. Page, "Decentralization and the Search for Policy Solutions," *Journal of Law, Economics, and Organization* 16 (2000): 102.

13. See Phedon Nicolaides, "Towards Multilateral Rules on Competition," *World Competition* 16 (1994): 113–21 and A. Freytag and R. Zimmermann, "Muß die internationale Handelsordnung um eine Wettbewerbsordnung erweitert werden?" *Rabels Zeitschrift für ausländisches und internationales Privatrecht* 62 (1998): 38–58; as well as the cautious approach of Harry First in "Theories of Harmonization: A Cautionary Tale," in *Comparative Competition Law: Approaching an International System of Antitrust Law*, ed. Hanns Ullrich (Baden-Baden: Nomos Verlagsgesellschaft, 1998), 17–41, toward a "best-rule-harmonization" through regulatory competition. The best practice approach is also one important goal of the International Competition Network. See Oliver Budzinski, "The International Competition Network as an International Merger Control Institution," in *International Institutions and Multinational Enterprises—Global Players, Global Markets*, ed. John-ren Chen (Cheltenham: Edward Elgar, forthcoming); Oliver Budzinski, "Towards an International Governance of Transborder Mergers? Competition Networks and Institutions between Centralism and Decentralism," *NYU Journal of International Law and Politics* 36 (forthcoming); and Harry First, "Evolving Toward What? The Development of International Antitrust," in *The Future of Transnational Antitrust: From Comparative to Common Competition Law*, ed. Josef Drexl (Berne: Kluwer Law International, 2003), 23–51.

14. For those compatibility problems see, for example, Klaus Heine and Wolfgang Kerber, "European Corporate Laws, Regulatory Competition, and Path Dependence," *European Journal of Law and Economics* 13 (2002): 43–71, in respect to the introduction of regulatory competition of corporate laws within the EU after the *Centros* decision of the European Court of Justice.

15. See, among many others, Erhard Kantzenbach and Konstanze Kinne, "Nationale Zusammenschlußkontrolle und internationale Wettbewerbsfähigkeit von Unternehmen," in *Wettbewerbspolitik im Spannungsfeld nationaler und internationaler Kartellrechtsordnungen*, eds. Jörn Kruse, Kurt Stockmann, and Ludger Vollmer (Baden-Baden: Nomos Verlagsgesellschaft, 1997), 67–83; European Commission, *2002 European Competitiveness Report* (Brussels: Enterprise Publications, 2002), 100–119; and in special regard to innovative industries, Andreas Fuchs, *Kartellrechtliche Grenzen der Forschungskooperation: eine vergleichende Untersuchung nach US-amerikanischem, europäischem und deutschem Recht* (Baden-Baden: Nomos Verlagsgesellschaft, 1989); and Thomas M. Jorde and David J. Teece, eds., *Antitrust, Innovation, and Competitiveness* (New York: Oxford University Press, 1992).

16. This line of thought has always been emphasized in the ordoliberal tradition of competition theory and policy in Germany (and its rejection of industrial policy). See, for example, Ulrich Immenga, "Conflicts Between Competition Policy and Industrial Policy," in *Towards WTO Competition Rules: Key Issues and*

Comments on the WTO Report (1998) on Trade and Competition, ed. Roger Zäch (Berne: Kluwer Law International, 1999), 343–60. This argument is also stressed in Michael E. Porter, *The Competitive Advantage of Nations* (New York: Free Press, 1990).

17. See on strategic trade theory, for example, Elhanan Helpman and Paul Krugman, *Market Structure and Foreign Trade: Increasing Returns, Imperfect Competition, and the International Economy* (Cambridge: MIT Press, 1985); and Murray C. Kemp, *International Trade and National Welfare* (London: Routledge, 2001). See, concerning the relation to competition policies, Henning Klodt, "Rent-Shifting, Industrial Policy and Multinational Enterprises," in *Competition Policy in an Interdependent World Economy*, eds. Erhard Kantzenbach, Hans-Eckart Scharrer, and Leonard Waverman (Baden-Baden: Nomos Verlagsgesellschaft, 1993), 243–53; T. Greaney, "Strategic Trade and Competition Policies to Assist Distressed Industries," *Canadian Journal of Economics* 32 (1999): 767–84; and Rainer Markl and Werner Meissner, "Strategic Trade and International Competition Policy," in *Industrial Policies after 2000*, eds. Wolfram Esner and John Groenewegen (Boston: Kluwer Academic Publishers, 2000), 175–98.

18. The German competition policy system empowers the Federal Ministry of Economics to overrule, under exceptional circumstances, decisions of the otherwise independent Federal Cartel Office (Bundeskartellamt) for reasons of overwhelming public interest and if no solution with less anticompetitive impact can be found. Before doing so, the Ministry has to collect the advice of the German Monopolies Commission, an advisory body composed of economic and legal experts. Inter-estingly, in the case at hand, the German Monopolies Commission explicitly rejected the Ministry's line of argument and instead supported the decision of the Bundeskartellamt. On the Commission's theory, the E.ON-Ruhrgas merger does not respond to a problem of scale; rather, it looks like an official attempt to create a "national champion" for competition in international markets.

19. See Eleanor M. Fox, "Antitrust Regulation Across National Borders," *The Brookings Review* 16, no. 1 (1998): 30–32. Eventually, the merger was approved but with modifications concerning exclusive long-term contracts of Boeing and MDD with several U.S. airlines. As this example suggests, the deliberate toleration of market power can also be directed against foreign firms that intend to export their goods into the domestic markets. For example, a jurisdiction can protect import-substituting industries against their foreign competitors by enabling them to erect barriers to entry. Instruments include the permission of a defense concentration or of vertical integration that might exclude imports from domestic distribution channels. Several cases in which the United States, the EU, or Japan have acted along these lines are discussed in Eleanor M. Fox, "International Antitrust and the Doha Dome," *Virginia Journal of International Law* 43 (2003): 911; and Stephan, "Regulatory Cooperation and Competition," 167–202.

20. Complaints about cross-subsidization were raised by competitors and the European Court of First Instance, leading to several investigations by the European competition authorities (cases IP/00/562 abuse of dominant position: disturbance of international mail traffic; IP/00/919 abuse of dominant position: predatory pricing in mail-order parcel delivery service; and IP/99/530 state aid). The state aid investigation led to a fine, but Deutsche Post has filed an appeal.

21. See B. Hoekman and P. C. Mavroidis, "Competition, Competition Policy, and the GATT," *The World Economy* 17 (1994): 121–50; Edward Iacobucci, "The Interdependence of Trade and Competition Policies," *World Competition* 21 (1997): 5–33; B. Hoekman, "Competition Policy and the Global Trading System," *The World Economy* 20 (1997): 383–406; Eleanor M. Fox, "The Problem of State Action that Blesses Private Action that Harms 'the Foreigners,'" in *Towards WTO Competition Rules*, ed. Roger Zäch (Berne: Staempfli), 325–40; and Merit E. Janow, "Public, Private and Hybrid Public/Private Restraints of Trade: What Role for the WTO?" *Law and Policy in International Business* 31 (2000): 977. The standard example is the Kodak/Fuji Film case in which the United States tried in vain to stop (indirectly) government-supported anticompetitive private practices in Japan.

22. See Helpman and Krugman, *Market Structure and Foreign Trade*; P. Krugman, "Is Free Trade Passé?" *Journal of Economic Perspectives* 1 (1987): 131–44; Andrew T. Guzman, "Is International Antitrust Possible?" *New York University Law Review* 73 (1998): 1501; Kemp, *International Trade and National Welfare*; and Murray C. Kemp and Koji Shimomura, "Recent Challenges to the Classical Gains-from-Trade Proposition," *German Economic Review* 3 (2002): 485–89.

23. See Viktor Vanberg, "Economic Constitutions, Protectionism, and Competition among Jurisdictions," in *Competition and Structure: The Political Economy of Collective Decisions: Essays in Honor of Albert Breton*, eds. Gianluigi Galeotti, Pierre Salmon, and Ronald Wintrobe (Cambridge: Cambridge University Press, 2000), 364–85. Vanberg concludes that without factor mobility and without choice of law, protectionist and rent-seeking interests have a good chance to influence national policy strategies.

24. See A. Jacquemin, "Towards an Internationalisation of Competition Policy," *The World Economy* 18 (1995): 781–89; and Eleanor M. Fox, "International Antitrust: Against Minimum Rules; For Cosmopolitan Principles," *Antitrust Bulletin* 43, no. 1 (1998): 5–13; Eleanor M. Fox, "Antitrust Regulation Across National Borders: The United States of Boeing versus the European Union of Airbus," *The Brookings Review* 16, no. 1 (1998): 30–32; Fox, "Antitrust and Regulatory Federalism."

25. See Olivier Cadot, Jean-Marie Grether, and Jaime De Melo, "Trade and Competition Policy: Where Do We Stand?" *Journal of World Trade* 34 (2000): 1–20; and Oliver Budzinski, "Institutional Aspects of Complex International Competition Policy Arrangements," *Current Issues in Competition Theory and Policy,*

eds. Clemens Esser and Michael H. Stierle (Berlin: Verlag für Wissenschaft und Forschung, 2002), 109–32. For example, in the case of Kodak/Fuji Film, Japan was accused of maintaining its protection of domestic markets against foreign firms by tolerating an import cartel after the original, trade policy-based protection had to be reduced (due to WTO requirements). Thus, Japan simply "privatized protection" by selective nonenforcement of competition laws to compensate the loss of trade policy instruments. See Fox, "International Antitrust and the Doha Dome."

26. See, for example, Meessen, "Competition of Competition Laws"; Karl M. Meessen, "Das Für und Wider eines Weltkartellrechts," in *Wirtschaft und Wettbewerb* 50 (2000): 5–16; Heinz Hauser and Rainer Schöne, "Is There a Need for International Competition Rules?" *Aussenwirtschaft* 49 (1994): 205–22; Ignacio De León, "Should We Promote Antitrust in International Trade?" *World Competition* 21 (1997): 35–63; A. Freytag and R. Zimmermann, "Muß die internationale Handelsordnung um eine Wettbewerbsordnung erweitert werden?" *Rabels Zeitschrift für ausländisches und internationales Privatrecht* 62 (1998): 38–58; and First, "Theories of Harmonization," 17–41.

27. See Hans-Werner Sinn, "The Limits to Competition Between Economic Regimes," *Empirica* 17 (1990): 3–14; T. Ackermann, "Wettbewerb der Wettbewerbsordnungen im europäischen Binnenmarkt?" in *Europäisierung des Privatrechts: Zwischenbilanz und Perspektiven*, Jahrbuch junger Zivilrechtswissenschaftler, 1997 ed. (Stuttgart: Boorberg, 1998), 203–24; and, more critical, R. Van den Bergh and P. D. Camesasca, *European Competition Law and Economics: A Comparative Perspective* (Oxford: Intersentia, 2001), 133, 149–54. In *New Systems Competition* (Oxford: Blackwell 2003), Sinn derives a race-to-the-bottom (with, however, conflicting welfare effects) in a game-theoretic general equilibrium model of competition of competition policies.

28. See, for example, Van den Bergh and Camesasca, *European Competition Law and Economics*, 151–52. As a consequence, the German competition policy felt the pressure to adapt its standards to the less restrictive ones of the European competition policy.

29. See, for example, German Monopolies Commission, "Cartel Policy Change in the European Union?" (1999), http://www.monopolkommission.de/sg_28/text_e.htm; and "Problems Consequent upon the Reform of the European Cartel Procedures" (2001), http://www.monopolkommission.de/sg_32/text_s32_e.pdf; Petros C. Mavroidis and Damien J. Neven, "The Modernisation of EU Competition Policy: Making the Network Operate," in *Cahiers de Recherches Economiques du Département d'Econométrie et d'Economie Politique* (Lausanne: Université de Lausanne, 2000); and J. H. Bourgeois and C. Humpe, "The Commission's Draft 'New Resolution 17,'" *European Competition Law Review* 23 (2002): 43; however, in this case, the choice is not between laws but rather between different enforcement agencies.

30. See, for example, Stephan, "Regulatory Cooperation and Competition," 186–87, discussing the problem of "jurisdiction-shopping."

31. Ibid., 186–87, 199.

32. See Stephan (chapter 3) and McGinnis (chapter 5) in this volume.

33. For a more elaborate analysis, see Oliver Budzinski, "Institutional Aspects of Complex International Competition Policy Arrangements," *Current Issues in Competition Theory and Policy*, eds. Clemens Esser and Michael H. Stierle (Berlin: Verlag für Wissenschaft und Forschung, 2002), 109–32; Budzinski, "The International Competition Network"; and Budzinski, "Towards an International Governance of Transborder Mergers?"

34. See in more detail Kerber, "An International Multi-Level System of Competition Laws"; and for other first approaches Van den Bergh, "Economic Criteria for Applying the Subsidiarity Principle"; and Van den Bergh and Camesasca, *European Competition Law and Economics*, 125. For a general attempt to apply the criteria of federalism theory to legal rules (legal federalism), see Wolfgang Kerber and Klaus Heine, "Zur Gestaltung von Mehr-Ebenen-Rechtssystemen aus ökonomischer Sicht," in *Vereinheitlichung und Diversität des Zivilrechts in Transnationalen Wirtschaftsräumen*, eds. Claus Ott and Hans B. Schäfer (Tübingen: Mohr Siebeck, 2002), 167–94; for a first attempt to apply the concept of a multilevel system of legal rules to European contract law, see Stefan Grundmann and Wolfgang Kerber, "European System of Contract Laws: A Map for Combining the Advantages of Centralised and Decentralised Rule-Making," in *An Academic Greenpaper on European Contract Law*, eds. Stefan Grundmann and Jules Stuyck (The Hague: Kluwer Law International, 2002), 295–342.

3

Against International Cooperation

Paul B. Stephan

Antitrust coordination problems have three possible solutions. First, states might adhere to a common standard of competition law. Second, states might accept a body of rules for allocating regulatory jurisdiction that ensures that one, and only one, state imposes its competition standards on any given transaction. Third, states might decline to cooperate.

Most commentators have argued for solutions one or two. The effort to incorporate competition law into the Doha Round negotiations of the World Trade Organization (WTO) reflects, if weakly, the impulse to harmonize competition law across states. The growing network of cooperation agreements among competition regulators and the negotiations over a Hague Convention on Jurisdiction and Recognition and Enforcement of Foreign Judgments reflect the desire to allocate jurisdiction. I argue, in contrast, that states might do better by *not* trying to impose an international framework on competition law.

The argument against international cooperation has both negative and affirmative elements. On the negative side, we have good reasons to doubt whether international imposition of either substantive rules of competition law or binding assignments of regulatory jurisdiction will result in welfare-enhancing outcomes. These reasons rest on a positive explanation of why nations have different rules and why their regulatory jurisdictions overlap. The common thread is a prediction that government failure at the national level will replicate itself at the international level and an observation that international regimes are more difficult to unwind than domestic regulation is.

On the affirmative side, forces underlying international economic relations among the world's most prosperous and powerful states can punish nations that use competition policy to produce substantial losses in global welfare and reward those that use competition policy to enhance global welfare. In an information-based economy with substantial international mobility of financial and human capital and significant levels of international trade, states that protect domestic producers from welfare-enhancing competition will tend to experience lower levels of investment and innovation. Countries that use competition law to punish more efficient foreign producers will suffer losses in consumer welfare without obtaining any offsetting competitive gains, once innovation losses are taken into account. Countries that use competition law to punish foreign producers engaged in inefficient forms of industrial organization, however, should experience some economic benefits.

I do not argue that economic forces unconstrained by international cooperation will lead inevitably to an optimal distribution of competition policies among states. Countries that underinvest in competition law may free ride on those countries that make optimal investments. Moreover, shortfalls in local political accountability, whether they are due to underdeveloped democratic processes or public choice factors, will often prevent political actors from fully internalizing the costs of their suboptimal choices. But one cannot claim with confidence that the world would be worse off without international cooperation over antitrust law.

The Protean Nature of Competition Policy

What Is Competition Policy? Under the aegis of competition policy, governments regulate producer choices, including decisions to cooperate with other producers. Regulation of prices, marketing practices, and the array of products offered comes under competition policy. Notwithstanding the label, states do not necessarily invoke competition policy either to enhance competition or to maximize global welfare, much less consumer welfare. Competition policy, in practice as much as in theory, involves decisions about competition but does not imply a preference for competitive markets. Support for a national champion, suppression of large-scale and efficient producers that threaten politically influential small producers, and setting quotas on output all represent competition policies.[1]

In fact, competition cannot be an end in itself. Some kinds of collusion can be unambiguously desirable, such as (some) provision of standardized goods or long-term supply contracts. Markets and organizational hierarchies often offer themselves as alternatives, and there are no a priori reasons always to prefer one over the other.[2] One cannot have a competition policy, then, without some concept of desirable cooperation. It follows that a state concerned about the level of competition in a given market might either forbid or mandate particular forms of cooperation. Competition policy necessarily merges with industrial policy. In a world where international trade occurs, competition and trade policy also become the same subject.

Why does a conviction persist that competition policy constitutes an autonomous discipline with its own technical expertise? Competition law appeared in the United States in response to private decisions to consolidate production. Its principal manifestation was the Sherman Act, which attacked cooperative actions "in restraint of trade" and abuses of monopoly power. We should see this congruence between competition law and public restrictions on private cooperation and consolidation as a historical accident, however, and not as the core of what constitutes competition policy.

Even in the United States, moreover, competition law has never manifested an implacable hostility to all forms of industrial consolidation. It accepts, for example, cooperation among producers organized or mandated by the U.S. states as well as collusive political action to bring about such state mandates. The United States traditionally has encouraged collusion among exporters and more recently has supported similar cooperation among producers in supposedly strategic economic sectors such as semiconductor design and production.[3] When one turns to Europe or Japan, the illustrations of competition policy coexisting with coordinated producer behavior become abundant.

A broad, nonparochial understanding of competition policy underscores the difficulties of achieving an international consensus about its content. Even if states could agree that efficiency—optimization of welfare—is the only legitimate objective of competition policy, agreement as to whether a particular regime advances or detracts from efficiency would remain elusive. Specifying the optimal mix of competition and cooperation in a particular economic sector is inevitably controversial.[4] Technological change and other kinds of innovation, as well as shifting consumer preferences, limit the lessons one can learn from analyzing a sector's history. Once legitimate differences over the optimal level of competition arise, it becomes nearly impossible to determine whether a regulator is pursuing efficiency-driven competition policy or not. And once one relaxes the constraint on objectives, by allowing regulators to prefer something other than efficiency, the possibility of monitoring regimes for compliance with their professed objectives becomes even more remote.

Competition Policy and Local Interests. If governments sought to maximize general welfare, presumably competition policy would seek to identify and compel the optimal mix of competition and cooperation in any given economic sector. Two factors, however, complicate the analysis: international trade, which implies the possibility of externalizing both the costs and benefits of a particular competition policy; and public choice considerations.

International trade. As a conceptual matter, three considerations can influence a state's incentives to externalize the effects of its competition regulation. First, producers may be over- or underrepresented in a state, compared to the global distribution of producers in that sector. For example, a few national economies are dominated by oil and natural gas production, while many important economies produce virtually none. Second, consumers of the good in question similarly may be over- or underrepresented in the state. Third, the global market for the good may be more or less competitive. This last factor will affect the distribution between producers and consumers of potential gains from industrial consolidation.

Consider first a good, the production of which has increasing returns to scale up to the market clearing price. In this economic sector, the most efficient producer is a monopolist. Further assume that consumption of this good is more or less evenly distributed globally (if not per capita then per gross domestic product). Ignoring strategic issues and the possibility of coordination, a state should prefer to function as the home of this industry.[5] The state can capture some portion of the producer's monopoly rents, while its consumers will suffer no more than if any other state hosted the monopolist. Under these conditions, a rational competition policy would entail protecting the local producer and inflicting costs on the producers of all other states. Monopoly leads to no global welfare losses (netting producer and consumer surplus) and benefits the host state to the extent of producer surplus; the host state can externalize a large portion of the losses in consumer surplus to outsiders. The production of operating system software for microcomputers, semiconductors, and large-body civilian aircraft may have these characteristics.[6]

Strategic trade theory, as developed by Paul Krugman and others in the late 1970s, addresses exactly these circumstances.[7] It maintains that in many sectors, production has increasing returns to scale. Monopoly industrial organization thereby becomes common, and greater levels of international trade will lead to greater levels of industrial concentration. Strategic trade theory argues that the premises of liberal trade theory about competitive markets no longer hold; that the conventional story of comparative advantage is seriously incomplete; and that the distribution of monopolist producers, rather than the distribution of producer endowments, explains more about trade patterns.

What does strategic trade theory suggest for countries that have no hope of hosting an industry with increasing returns to scale? A country's choices depend on its share of the global market for the good in question. Those with small shares usually would not be able to prevent the foreign producer from moving toward monopoly. If such a country tried to regulate the producer, the latter could either raise prices in the local market or refuse to import. Both outcomes would hurt consumers in the regulating country with no offsetting benefits.[8]

A country with a large share would have another option. Assuming a sufficiently large market share, such a country would have the capability to force the producer to internalize the costs of its regulation. It rationally would block efficient growth by the producer in instances in which the benefits from consolidation, no matter how large, would accrue to the producer and the increase in competition would generate some benefits for local consumers, no matter how small. Put simply, under some realistic conditions, some countries will have both an incentive and the capacity to restrict producers from undertaking welfare-enhancing consolidation and cooperation. These states will choose a competition policy that, in terms of global efficiency, requires too much competition and not enough hierarchy.

Conversely, some states may host producers that have diminishing returns to scale and export most of their production. (Examples include industries that depend disproportionately on factor endowments, such as extraction or farming.) These states might benefit if their producers participated in a successful cartel: Monopoly rents would stay at home, and the lion's share of the lost consumer surplus would fall on consumers in the export markets. Under these conditions, states would embrace a competition policy that tolerates or even mandates cartelization. In other words, these states would seek to effect a competition policy that, in terms of global efficiency, requires too much hierarchy and not enough competition.

These incentives become even more salient to the extent that states can evade the national treatment obligation and discriminate against foreign producers. Enforcement authorities may oppose collusion that benefits the foreign competitors of local producers while ignoring or even coordinating collusion that benefits local producers. Selective enforcement can have the same effect as does trade protection.[9] Because selective enforcement is harder to detect and monitor than a direct trade barrier is, however, it may generate greater costs. Uncertainty about when competition law will apply may deter risk-averse transactors and require wasteful investments in precautions (such as legal services and lobbying). The ambiguous and elusive nature of protection realized through selective enforcement also may make it more difficult to mobilize coalitions to oppose it. Trade barriers, which conventionally take the form of high tariffs or quotas, are quantitatively precise, easier to detect and to oppose, and generally entail lower costs of organizing opposition.

Political economy. Governments will pursue outcomes that reflect the preferences of homogenous and compact interest groups at the expense of the general welfare. This dynamic applies with particular force to national competition policies. Producer groups tend to have lower organizational costs relative to consumer groups; thus, they generally achieve outcomes that favor them to the detriment of society as a whole. Because the ability of particular groups to minimize the costs of organization and political action varies across countries, we should not expect similar groups to come out winners in different countries, much less win to the same extent.

If political economy predicts more protection than one otherwise would expect, then one should look for states to expand the available tools of protection, including competition law. We should see not only differences among states in the content of their competition law (horizontal variation) but differences within states in the application of their competition law as a function of the subject's status as insider or outsider (vertical variation). And so we do.

Horizontal and Vertical Variation.

Horizontal variation. The United States, the European Community (EC), and Japan use different institutions to pursue competition policy, articulate different substantive objectives, and reach different outcomes.

The United States disperses enforcement power among two federal agencies (the Antitrust Division of the Justice Department and the Federal Trade Commission) and private attorneys general, who benefit from various financial (treble damages) and procedural (class actions, broad pretrial discovery, jury trials) incentives. A residual and not well-defined power of states to apply their own regulatory regimes further complicates the picture. In the EC, by contrast, the Competition Directorate of the European Commission has a virtual monopoly over enforcement powers. The fifteen member-states have some residual power to regulate competition, but all rely on a single national authority with virtually no private enforcement. Japan has a unified regulatory authority (the Fair Trade Commission), no subnational entities with regulatory powers, and high barriers to private litigation.

The substantive goals of U.S. antitrust law reflect the shifting preferences of administrations as well as changes in the courts' understanding of competition regulation. Over the past thirty years, U.S. regulators have taken a more relaxed attitude toward forms of collusion and industrial concentration that seem driven by efficiency considerations. Consumer welfare remains the touchstone of competition policy, rather than opposition to the accumulation of power and influence in the hands of private firms. The courts have also embraced efficiency as the principal criterion and permitted anticompetitive practices that plausibly may increase consumer welfare.[10] Finally, for sixty years, the courts have permitted state-level experimentation with alternative approaches to the competition/collusion trade-off.

The substantive goals of EC competition law seem in form virtually identical to those of the United States. Articles 81 and 82 of the current revision of the Treaty of Rome closely track Sections 1 and 2 of the Sherman

Act: Article 81 prohibits "concerted practices" that "may affect trade between Member States" and "have as their object or effect the prevention, restriction or distortion of competition," whereas Article 82 outlaws "any abuse" of "a dominant position." These capacious words, however, have achieved a significantly different meaning in the EC. At the risk of over-simplification, EC competition law evinces greater skepticism, relative to recent U.S. practice, about the benefits of producer consolidation and coop-eration. One aspect of this skepticism, not so much articulated as displayed, is concern about private concentrations of power threatening governmen-tal authority. In particular, EC competition law clearly opposes the substi-tution of lower-level (that is, national) supervision for EC-administered competition policy. Unlike the United States, the lower-level entities cannot authorize anticompetitive practices.

Japan's antimonopoly law in form follows closely the competition law of the United States. But its Fair Trade Commission, although not quite the lapdog that some commentators portray, has not had the opportunity to develop as rich and informative a practice as have its U.S. and EC counter-parts. While the Commission has brought criminal prosecutions against core anticompetitive behaviors (that is, price-fixing and output restric-tions), it has not attacked other practices that result in significant costs to Japanese consumers, and it has no influence on government policies in some industries that protect numerous small producers from efficient com-petition by consolidated firms.[11]

Vertical variation. No government acknowledges that it uses its competi-tion law as a means of protecting domestic producers, and the practice almost certainly violates the national treatment norm embodied in multi-lateral trade agreements administered by the WTO. In many cases, how-ever, protectionist purposes supply the most plausible explanation of competition law and policy.

In all major countries and in the EU, competition law takes the form of broad, nonspecific standards that maximize enforcement discretion, as opposed to precise rules that tie the enforcer's hands. Of course, the enforcement bureaucracy may seek to maximize its discretion for reasons unrelated to protection, and even a welfare-maximizing lawmaker might regard bonding costs as unacceptably high relative to other means of supervising the enforcement process. Nonetheless, examples from all three major jurisdictions—the United States, the EU, and Japan—illustrate that the discretion afforded the enforcers has allowed actions that seem inexplicable except as a way of advancing the interests of local producers.[12]

Similarly, all major industrial economies with competition laws exempt export cartels from their law. This practice manifests a welfare calculation that gives no weight to foreign consumers and suggests some indifference to local consumers who probably bear some costs from foreign export cartels. Looking at the exemption of export cartels as a global norm, rather than as local aberrations from good competition policy, reinforces the impression that competition law, among its many functions, serves as a source of trade protection.

Transparency. Wherever regulators have the capacity to act arbitrarily, there is a risk that they will exercise their powers to the advantage of specific groups and to the cost of outsiders. Yet, squeezing this capacity out of competition law seems unlikely.

Competition law has not yet come to grips with many fundamental problems. No consensus exists on the distinction between successful consolidation and abuse of monopoly power; on when vertical supply and purchase commitments encourage productive firm-specific investments and when they unnecessarily restrict consumer choice; or when core misconduct (such as cartelization or predatory pricing) constitutes a genuine threat to consumer welfare and when the strategy contains the seeds of its own failure, thus making regulatory intervention unnecessary. Given this indeterminacy about the content of competition policy, one should not expect unambiguous commitments to clear rules. But without clarity, supervision of both the content of the rules and their application is extremely difficult, if not impossible. The history of the General Agreement on Tariffs and Trade (GATT) and the WTO illustrates the point.

The GATT's great achievement was postwar liberalization of the international economy through tariff reduction. High tariffs are an ideal subject for international cooperation. This form of protection neither disguises itself nor hides its effects. Tariffs single out goods traded internationally for special excises stated in precise quantitative terms, and quantification of their effects presents no great challenge. Reciprocal tariff reduction agreements thus are easy to negotiate, easy to monitor for compliance, and generally do not produce sore losers.

Building on its earlier success in promoting tariff liberalization, the GATT sought to expand its responsibilities. It achieved this goal with the 1994 Uruguay Round Agreements, which converted the old secretariat administering the GATT into the WTO. Along with expanded jurisdiction, however, came an increasing frequency of embarrassments. The shift in the international trade regime's focus to nontariff trade barriers, including health and safety rules and environmental regulation, has placed the WTO at the center of great controversies. Its new agreements largely involve ambiguous commitments that raise profound interpretative problems. The efforts of the WTO organs to apply these standards to concrete cases has triggered intransigence on the part of the states accused of violation, sharp criticism of the dispute resolution process among trade experts, and passionate attacks from populist forces.[13]

International Antitrust?

Competition policy embodies imprecise normative judgments that invite controversy and defection rather than consensus and commitment. Because its scope extends to such a wide range of economic activity, it has the potential to inflict significant costs on many transactors. In particular, competition policy tempts states both to impose nominally neutral policies that favor local producers and consumers at the expense of global welfare, and to administer their policies in a discriminatory fashion to similar ends. Uncertainty about the willingness of states to pursue this strategy further burdens international transactions. In short, states engaged in significant international trade have incentives to adopt competition laws that fail to maximize global welfare. That being so, should we seek to create some mechanism that will coordinate national competition policies?

Experts have suggested various strategies for harmonizing and unifying global competition law. One would locate negotiations over the content of an international agreement to harmonize competition law in the WTO and give that organization the authority to enforce such an agreement.

Alternatively, the major economic powers might agree to allocate regulatory jurisdiction in a way than minimizes conflicts among regulators. A series of bilateral agreements to which the United States is a party represents modest steps in this direction, and scholars have suggested other architectures for jurisdictional allocation. I first describe what these proposals might look like and then discuss their drawbacks.

International Coordination of Substantive Competition Law. Many, perhaps the majority, of the specialists writing on international antitrust have supported "soft" harmonization of competition laws. For example, the Organisation for Economic Co-operation and Development has promulgated guidelines for competition policy to which its members should adhere. These recommendations establish a minimum level of regulation that each state should impose and also suggest a baseline to which each state should gravitate. Along similar lines, in 2000, the U.S. Department of Justice's International Antitrust Advisory Committee called for greater standardization of merger review, technical assistance to encourage the creation of competition policy and enforcement agencies in countries that have none, and gradual assimilation of international practice leading toward standardization of competition policy rules. This report led to the creation of the International Competition Network (ICN), an international organization of government regulators that sponsors conferences to promote harmonization.

Going further, Andrew Guzman and others have called for an agreement on competition policy modeled on the Trade-Related Aspects of Intellectual Property Rights Agreement (TRIPS).[14] They would have the WTO serve both as the forum for negotiating the substance of such an agreement and as the agency that resolves disputes over its meanings and enforces its obligations. Guzman argues that because harmonization would require some states to forgo regulatory choices that, at least in the short run, would further their national interest, negotiations must take place in an environment that maximizes the opportunity for winners to compensate losers with concessions in unrelated areas.[15] The WTO seems ideal for this purpose both because of its scale (146 countries as of the end of 2003) and scope (its regulatory subjects comprise trade in goods and services, intellectual property, agricultural health and safety, and certain forms of investment regulation, among others).

Guzman also has argued for changes in the organizational structure of the WTO to accommodate its expanded jurisdiction. He calls for the division of the organization into departments, each with responsibility for substantive areas such as trade, competition, environment, labor, and intellectual property. Depicting these policy areas as rivalrous, Guzman would have each department act as an advocate for its particular subject and rely on WTO internal dispute resolution processes to reach compromises. The bold new world that Guzman hopes to usher in would entail a single body of competition law applicable to firms operating internationally. States would enforce this law, but a department of the WTO would supervise their actions to ensure that they did not neglect their obligations or exceed the international regulatory limits. To the extent conceptions of optimal competition law conflicted with those of, say, intellectual property, labor standards, or food safety, the WTO would strike the proper balance and then require WTO members to observe it.[16] Having questioned proposals such as Guzman's in earlier writing, I summarize my objections here.[17]

Agency costs. Designing an international body to administer and enforce an agreement on substantive competition policy presents serious issues of instrumentality design and incentives. It is useful to conceptualize such a body as the agent of the various states that collectively wish to implement an agreement on competition policy, much as the managers of a business serve as the agent of the firm's investors. In both cases, the fundamental problem involves aligning the agent's interests with its principal to maximize the value of the agency relationship. The principal—here, the states seeking to implement a collective competition policy—cannot fully anticipate how it wants the agent—here, the WTO or some comparable body— to respond to future problems. The principal understands that the agent might want to maximize some good—its budget, power, glory, leisure, or compensation—that it would not want maximized. It must respond to this challenge by structuring the agency relationship so as to limit *ex ante* the agent's discretion (what the literature calls bonding), supervising what the agent does *ex post* (what the literature calls monitoring), or otherwise tolerating outcomes that do not reflect its preferences.

Just as investors cannot just hand over their money to managers and ask only that the managers maximize their return, states cannot ask an international organ simply to choose a competition policy that maximizes global welfare. The states either must accept the risk that the organ will make suboptimal choices—perhaps embracing a harebrained economic theory or using competition law as a guise to advance some redistributive project—or rein in its discretion through some mix of bonding and monitoring. But bonding forecloses some policy responses that, in hindsight, would turn out to be optimal. Monitoring consumes resources and, if coupled with a right of retaliation, also may induce unwarranted conservatism on the part of the organ's officials.

These general problems have proven manageable in many instances. But in the case of international antitrust, they loom especially large. Two features of competition policy exacerbate the agency problems accompanying a delegation to an international organization. First, the absence of any clear understanding and definition of good competition policy makes bonding more problematic. The architects of an international regime either must find the few areas where clarity and consensus exist and settle for a seriously incomplete regime, or they must trust the international organ with broad discretion. Second, because it is likely that any universal competition regime that increases global welfare will make some countries worse off, effective monitoring of the organ's performance will only clarify the scope of the injury particular states will experience.

When regulation takes the form of case-by-case application of general standards shaped by complex policy goals with significant potential for international wealth redistribution, those affected by the regulation and those who impose it cannot easily commit to a mutually beneficial agreement. As noted, the shift in the international trade regime's focus to non-tariff trade barriers, including health and safety rules and environmental regulation, has already embroiled the WTO in great controversy. To date, the WTO has had little direct involvement with competition policy, but the few times it has engaged with these problems illustrate the shortcoming of international supervision of national competition law.

In the Kodak-Fujitsu dispute, the WTO dispute settlement process rejected the claim that Japan's tolerance of inefficient retail distribution networks, which impeded the entry of foreign products, constituted an impermissible trade barrier.[18] The case had murky facts and suffered from less-than-deft advocacy by the United States, but it still suggests the difficulty of detecting disguised protection. Arguably, Japan tolerates the gross inefficiencies of small-scale retail outlets in part because they protect domestic producers from foreign competition, but the inference necessary to reach this conclusion was beyond the grasp of the WTO. A symmetrical dispute, involving a European attack on the U.S. Antidumping Act of 1916, reinforces the point. That statute, as interpreted by the U.S. courts, simply recapitulates the substantive requirements of a predatory pricing violation under the Sherman Act.[19] No criminal or civil suit under the 1916 Act has ever succeeded. But, because in form the 1916 Act regulates dumping in a manner not authorized by the WTO agreements, the WTO condemned it as violating U.S. obligations under the 1994 Agreement on Antidumping Duties.

Institutional limitations provide the key for understanding both decisions. The WTO dispute resolution process involves a review of national laws and regulations in light of the text of the Uruguay Round Agreements, rather than an empirical investigation into government practice and the effects of regulatory choices. The approach is formalistic rather than substantive. As both cases indicate, the WTO bodies are reluctant to stray from the uncontroversial meaning of the agreements that form the organization's charter, even at the cost of the substantive ends that these agreements purportedly pursue. Both also reveal an inability to evaluate governmental practice independent of published law. This incapacity to deal effectively with as-applied regulation means that the WTO dispute resolution process cannot identify and condemn de facto discrimination and in particular cannot ferret out discriminatory uses of competition policy for trade protection purposes. For the same reason, it has no difficulty condemning a purely hypothetical case of de jure discrimination.[20]

Dispute resolution. Limiting an international agency to the task of settling disputes over the meaning and application of an international agreement does not avoid the agency problems.[21] In theory, an international tribunal might follow in the footsteps of the U.S. judiciary and become the source of international competition law. In reality, this outcome is implausible.

U.S. federal judges have life tenure and a great fund of social capital. They come to the bench after achieving distinction in any of a number of legal fields, and they wind up on the Supreme Court after facing intense public scrutiny and surviving a daunting political gauntlet. They benefit from a tradition of judicial lawmaking that for the most part has gained acceptance and even admiration from the general public.

None of this applies to adjudicators in the international system. For example, the members of the WTO appellate body, the closest analog to a common law appellate court, serve for six years, with nomination and replacement at the pleasure of specific countries or blocs, rather than of the WTO membership as a whole. Given this short leash, the possibility for articulating and imposing a competition policy that any significant state opposes seems unlikely.

Executive branches as national agents. In both international bargaining and monitoring of international agencies, states act not through their parliaments but through their executives, which have a tendency to commit to harmonization and unification projects that provide officials with high-profile venues to display themselves. Even in parliamentary systems, actors within the executive branch may have interests that diverge from that of the legislature, including possibly a preference for larger budgets, projects that show off the executive to good effect, and work that increases the actors' future returns from their post-political careers.

Even projects that produce little hard law (such as the ICN) offer such temptations. They may seem harmless enough, but they have the potential to destabilize the legal environment in which firms operate. Soft harmonization may also distract individual states from desirable changes in their competition laws, induce cosmetic changes to appeal to the international audience, and send confusing signals to bureaucrats and judges responsible for interpreting and applying national law.

Inflexibility. International institutions are hard to create and even harder to reform. The principle of unanimity that applies to treaty systems means that amendments, like the initial institution, require unanimous consent. As circumstances change, it often becomes desirable to alter the mandate and tools of the regime, but holdouts are likely. For this reason, international regimes tend to administer broad standards and norms rather than precise rules, and they tend to collapse or become irrelevant rather than reform themselves.

International bureaucracies. Guzman appreciates that asking an international agency to make challenging policy judgments based on competing, and to some extent contradictory, commitments will not be easy. His response to this challenge is Weberian. He would rely on bureaucratic rationality embodied in distinct, policy-defined departments to formulate good policy and negotiate the competing interests. In effect, he would replace national governments, representing the material interests of their producers and consumers, with technocratic elites. Guzman hopes to see the WTO, which operates out of Geneva, reorganized to take on a wide array of social and economic problems, including competition policy.

As noted, however, the WTO has already taken over dispute resolution responsibility in areas such as food safety and intellectual property protection. It has increasingly found itself responding to disputes with decisions that the parties find unacceptable, and with which commentators find fault. Going still further down this path seems ill advised. Bureaucratic rationality typically masks a powerful urge for aggrandizement; in the international arena, we have few examples of agencies that have avoided the temptation. Budgets grow, capacities for effective intervention decline, and faith in international policymaking falters, only to rise up again in new areas. Geneva seems a graveyard for past idealism, not a hotbed of innovative solutions.

Coordination of Regulatory Jurisdiction. Recognizing the many obstacles to substantive harmonization of competition law, some governments and commentators have considered coordination of jurisdiction as an alternative way of addressing the problem of overlapping jurisdiction.[22] The ideal is universal acceptance of jurisdictional criteria that would submit transactions to one, and only one, regulatory authority.

Judicial allocation. Disputes over jurisdictional scope typically take place in the judicial arena. Legislators almost always fail to address the issue of extraterritorial regulation, and courts conventionally craft choice-of-law rules to fill in statutory lacunae. In a simpler, long-gone world of formalistic jurisdictional tests, overlapping regulatory authority did not pose a problem: Only the sovereign on whose territory a transaction occurred would impose its rules. But with the rise of multijurisdictional transactions, territoriality came under pressure. U.S. courts initially relaxed the traditional test by requiring that only some part of the transaction in question occur in U.S. territory. By the end of World War II, the lower courts cast aside even that constraint, instead applying U.S. antitrust law to any action that had direct and intended effects in the United States.[23] Europe and the Commonwealth countries resisted this approach, but by the end of the 1980s, the EC had incorporated the effects test into its own competition law.[24]

Almost as soon as the effects test emerged as the U.S. standard for international antitrust, some courts and commentators proposed to limit it. Their efforts dominated most discussion of international antitrust during the 1970s and 1980s. The leading treatise on international antitrust proposed that courts use a "rule of reason," based on multiple criteria, to limit U.S. jurisdiction in cases that satisfied the effects test.[25] The object of the test was to restrict the exercise of jurisdiction in some instances in which the effects test would permit regulation. It did not purport to create a world where every transaction would have one and only one regulator, but it did aspire to reduce the instances of multijurisdictional conflicts

The Ninth Circuit embraced this standard, and the Third Restatement of the Foreign Relations Law of the United States proclaimed it the general rule.[26] But the campaign to limit antitrust jurisdiction suffered a setback in 1993, when, in *Hartford Fire Insurance Co. v. California*, a narrow majority of the Supreme Court endorsed the effects test and rejected the rule-of-reason limitation.[27]

Intergovernmental agreements. Straightforward analysis demonstrates that none of the three rules used by the courts for allocating state regulatory jurisdiction—territoriality, the effects test, or the rule of reason—will produce optimal outcomes.[28] A universal commitment to territoriality would prevent a state from regulating offshore producers intending inefficiently to limit competition in the state's market. Barring all such desirable regulation can be justified only if one can demonstrate that on balance extraterritorial regulation would decrease welfare. Some instances of extraterritorial regulation probably are inefficient. States can use competition law as a form of protection for local producers or as a means of attacking changes in foreign producers' organizational structure that greatly reduces production costs at the price of some reduced consumer welfare. But some states might limit competition rules to cases that both maximize efficiency and increase consumer welfare. Moreover, in industries in which production is movable, and firms thus can induce states to compete for their activities, producers probably would exploit a territoriality regime to increase opportunities for monopoly rents.

Symmetrical arguments expose the flaws in the effects test. That approach multiplies the number of states with jurisdiction over transactions and thus increases the likelihood that private organizational decisions will confront governmental resistance. As with the territorial rule, whether governmental intervention will increase welfare is an empirical question. There is no categorical reason to believe that the benefits from desirable competition rules permitted by the effects test necessarily will be greater than the costs generated by inefficient regulation.[29]

The rule of reason seems clearly flawed. Application of its criteria increases the likelihood that only one state, presumably the place of production, will impose its competition rules. But unlike either the territoriality rule or the effects test, the rule of reason contains a high degree of instability and unpredictability. It allows courts to balance unweighted factors on an *ex post* basis, making reliable guesses about regulatory jurisdiction difficult if not impossible. It creates legal risk without necessarily eliminating the costs of either underregulation or overregulation.

In spite of its flaws, the rule of reason has become the default jurisdictional position of most developed economies through the device of intergovernmental agreements. For example, the U.S. Department of Justice has negotiated compacts with Australia, Canada, the EC, Japan, and Mexico, among others. Superficially, these agreements appear to address the problems of overlapping regulation. A review of their terms, however, reveals that they do not even create soft law. Rather, the bilateral agreements express only a desire to consult and cooperate, and do not limit the discretion of regulatory authorities in any jurisdiction. None of these instruments has terms that a U.S. court could enforce, and the U.S.-EC agreement entails judicial enforcement only in the sense that it provides the EC Commission with additional grounds for making demands of national regulators. The agreements purport to embrace the rule of reason as the basic concept for allocating regulatory jurisdiction, but all use a long list of unweighted criteria that have the effect of insulating almost all exercises of regulator review from attack. Moreover, the agreements do not seek to coordinate merger approval, the area that has caused the greatest recent tension. If anything, the bilateral agreements illustrate the conflicting interests that jurisdictions have in imposing their competition law on international transactions, and the difficulties of surrendering regulatory discretion in spite of the potential costs caused by overlapping constraints on private transactors.

The Hague Convention on International Jurisdiction and Foreign Judgments in Civil and Commercial Matters, if adopted, might limit the power of a signatory state to exercise some regulatory jurisdiction over extraterritorial transactions and would make civil judgments produced by proceedings that conform to the convention subject to execution by all parties to the Convention. But no one who follows these negotiations seriously believes that the United States will sign the Convention or that Congress would accede to it.

An evaluation of jurisdictional allocation. The use of rules that allocate regulatory jurisdiction as a substitute for unification of substantive law is most closely associated with U.S. corporate law. During the past decade, Roberta Romano has produced an influential reappraisal of this subject.[30] Her work has developed a conceptual apparatus that translates into other substantive areas and, in due course, has led to a rich and lively scholarly debate about regulatory competition generally.

The traditional critique of the U.S. choice-of-law rule for corporate law (place of incorporation) asserts that managers incorporate in jurisdictions that maximize their opportunities to enrich themselves at the expense of investors. (The race-to-the-bottom metaphor arose in this context.) Romano showed, however, that managers often will have to internalize the costs associated with rules that enabled them to exploit investors and, thus, should have a preference for rules that maximize firm value. She found in corporate law a virtuous race to the top, where her predecessors had seen only a regrettable regulatory collapse. Stephen Choi and Andrew Guzman extended her argument to the international arena, advocating a regime that would allow the issuers of securities to choose which jurisdiction would regulate their transactions.[31]

While no consensus exists regarding the validity of Romano's empirical claims about U.S. corporate law (much less Choi and Guzman's extension), most scholars agree with the analytics underlying Romano's claim. The degree to which transactors should have the freedom to choose which rules will govern their transaction depends primarily on externalities. To the extent that the ratio of externalized costs to benefits matches that of those internalized, the transactors, at least if they meet minimum standards of competence, should have the freedom to choose their regulatory environment. Under these conditions, a race to the top can occur.

Using Romano's framework, the argument that competition regulation is susceptible to a race to the bottom and, therefore, should *not* be subject to transactor choice, is straightforward. At its heart, competition law involves producer conduct, either unilateral or in concert, that may have harmful effects on consumers. Allowing producers to choose which regime will regulate the harm they impose on consumers would make sense only if consumers could boycott producers that choose consumer-unfriendly regimes. But competition law, at least in theory, focuses on exactly the kinds of producer actions that reduce consumer choice. In most instances, producer choices about competition law should have no significance.[32]

Summary. Judicially crafted formulas for allocating jurisdiction produce suboptimal outcomes. Extant governmental agreements to allocate jurisdiction suggest that we already have reached the limits of state-to-state bargains. No state seems willing to submit to serious and enforceable constraints on its regulatory jurisdiction. Two reasons for this reluctance suggest themselves. First, states will not surrender jurisdiction to regulate without some clear and reliable expectation of what substantive rules other states will apply. Second, states recognize that the jurisdiction issue simply recasts the question of preferences for substantive competition rules.

This last point suggests why a global bargain to allocate competition policy jurisdiction may be undesirable as well as unattainable. On reflection, the jurisdictional question presents exactly the same issues and problems as does substantive harmonization. There is no neutral template for allocation that transcends the interests engaged by competition law, and no reason to believe that those interests would not affect the structure of any international bargain.

Anarchy, International Antitrust, Innovation, and Investment

The faith in international cooperation is misplaced. Analogies to trade agreements do not work, because the assumptions, interests, and legal tools at stake in competition policy are far less transparent and, therefore, far less susceptible to oversight and satisfactory dispute settlement than those presented by direct trade barriers. We have every reason to believe that international supervision will be either inconsequential or pernicious.

In that light, we should reconsider what may happen if states do *not* face international constraints on their competition policies. Given certain plausible assumptions about the world economy, in particular those sectors that draw to a greater extent on skill and innovation, the anarchic international environment embodied by the status quo may contain substantial impediments to a global race to the bottom in competition law.

Under the status quo, no international regime imposes serious limitations on the competition law principles or practice of nation-states. In theory, WTO members have an obligation not to discriminate in their competition rules against foreigners, but in practice, this obligation has proven unenforceable. No binational or multilateral agreement places significant constraints on the authority of states to assert regulatory authority over transactions occurring outside their territory that have consequences within their territory. States do not necessarily exercise their full regulatory power, but these abstentions reflect each state's choice rather than international coercion. It is a system with these characteristics that I defend here.

Static models of what competition law a state will enact and enforce rest on two assumptions: (1) States seek to maximize a weighted sum of local consumer and producer interests, and (2) the choice of competition policy has no secondary effects on consumer or producer welfare. States choose among a fixed set of outcomes that proceed directly from particular competition policies. Choices in one time period do not affect the set of choices available in the next. A dynamic model, by contrast, assumes that choices made in the first time period alter the possibilities available in the next.

In this section, I sketch a dynamic model of innovation that emphasizes increasing marginal returns, and I explore the relationship of this model to competition. The model suggests that inefficient competition policy can lead to long-term losses in a globally competitive economy. In industries such as agriculture and natural resource extraction, the distribution of natural endowments may dominate welfare calculations and innovation may play a less important role. In such sectors, we would expect to find inefficient industrial structures that generate, or at least seek, monopoly rents, along with significant levels of trade protection. In other, knowledge-based sectors, by contrast, the cost of protection, either through government regulation or private collusion, may be high.

Knowledge and Industrial Structure. A considerable body of work by economists has explored the impact of knowledge-based investments on economic growth. In these models, knowledge has low reproduction costs. Returns on knowledge thus depend critically on the size of the market in which goods embodying knowledge can be sold. Increases in the scope of the market, such as the creation of the U.S. common market in the nineteenth century and of Europe's in the second half of the twentieth, expand the opportunities for exploiting knowledge and thus reward investments in knowledge more. Trade liberalization and other strategies for broadening market structure also raise incentives to invest in knowledge.[33]

Recent research tends to support this hypothesis. Studies by Jeffrey Frankel and coauthors have demonstrated a strong positive correlation between trade openness and labor productivity, a good proxy for innovation.[34] A more recent paper by Francisco Alcalá and Antonio Ciccone refines these results by looking at the relationship between productivity and openness in tradable goods, as opposed to gross measurements of an economy's openness to trade.[35] Their analysis shows an even tighter link between innovation and an economy's exposure to international competition.

Under conventional models of development, a country's economic growth depends both on its physical and human capital and on its efficiency in using these assets. Other considerations, in particular institutional quality, have a strong relationship with levels of capital stocks, and the link between economic openness and institutional quality is not well understood. What the empirical work indicates, then, is not that openness is the most influential factor in economic growth, but that it is an important factor in explaining how effectively an economy exploits its stock of physical and human capital.

This is not to say, however, that barriers to competition will not depress investment as well as innovation. Monopoly rents derive from restricting production below a level that efficient competition would dictate. Lowering production implies, although it does not require, reducing the level of investment in the industry. Barriers to entry, whether imposed by private agreement or the state, imply fewer opportunities for the deployment of capital.

To be sure, the link between investment and barriers to competition is not as well documented as that between innovation and market size. But the hypothesis that inefficient limits on competition serve as a barrier to investment is plausible. Declining industries, rather than infant ones, have the greatest demand for protection.[36] That suggests that industries that have lost their capacity to attract new investment tend to seek less competitive market structures.

These claims frame an argument as to why competition policy that does not pursue efficiency will prove costly to states. First, states that permit local producers to construct inefficient constraints on competition are functionally equivalent to states that undertake such protection directly. Tolerance of inefficient collusion in an industry is likely to lead to lower rates of investment and innovation than otherwise would be obtained. Except in the case of industries that depend heavily on local factor endowments (petroleum in the Middle East, diamonds in South Africa and Russia), these losses should lead to low growth or shrinkage in the affected sector. Gradual immiserization eventually should either impair an industry's ability to resist regulation or lead to its economic irrelevance.

Second, states that use their competition law to impose inefficient organizational structures on foreign producers, with the object of protecting local producers, encourage lower rates of investment and innovation in the protected sector. If bad competition law is the functional equivalent of trade protectionism, then equivalent consequences should follow.

The significant counterexample would be state intervention in a rivalry between oligopolists in an industry characterized by positive returns to scale. In theory, punishing foreign producers with competition law would facilitate the local producer's ascendancy as an efficient global monopolist.[37] If states generally can choose when to invest in industries that will become globally dominant, then they should include competition law among the tools that they can use to implement such decisions. However, states rarely do a good job of picking winners. A decade ago, many U.S.

scholars saw Japan as a model of successful strategic trade policy. Revisionist studies of Japanese policy reveal that the government generally supported industries that did not have much success in international competition and did little for those sectors—automobiles and consumer electronics—where Japanese producers did enjoy some success.

This argument for virtuous pressures to produce efficient competition law is subject to two important qualifications. First, states that serve as a base of operations for firms that largely export their products may seek to free ride on the regulatory efforts of importing states. If no single importing state were to consume a substantial share of the global output of such producers, those states might not invest sufficient resources in imposing competition rules. Under these circumstances, consumers over the short run would suffer losses due to excess prices and low supply, while the producing country might witness the eventual decline of the industry it hosts. Here, collective action by the affected states to impose an appropriate competition policy might produce a better outcome.

Second, the argument assumes that states eventually will respond to the decline of local producers by withdrawing the protection that contributes to their decline. There is some point at which this assumption must be correct: An industry that collapses completely obviously lacks the ability to procure desired outcomes from government. But economic and political decline need not be symmetrical. A sense of beleaguerment might lead an industry to overcome internal divisions and to concentrate more directly on influencing governmental outcomes. The U.S. steel industry provides a case in point: Although some firms have increased their international competitiveness through increased investment and higher labor productivity, others have used adversity as a ground for procuring repeated episodes of protection from import competition and have made no significant improvements in their production methods. There is plenty of evidence that failing industries can obtain costly protection until collapse becomes imminent.

These qualifications, however, do not seriously undermine the claim that virtuous forces make international cooperation less imperative. First, the free-ride scenario seems somewhat hypothetical. States generally have some incentive to protect their consumers from anticompetitive practices, whether or not the local injury is a large portion of the global injury. Most importantly, they do not have to limit their remedies to recovery of the cost of local injury. Criminal sanctions, punitive damages, and injunctions give local authorities the capacity to address a local harm proportionately to its global ramifications. Second, the disconnect between economic and political power is a general problem and not limited to local law production and enforcement. Any state that will protect a failing industry by prosecuting its foreign rivals will use international relations to pursue similar goals. In particular, such a state will block any international accord that takes away its discretion to impose such protection.

I do not mean to suggest that the appeal of a competition law that both frustrates inefficient collusion and does not impede beneficial industrial cooperation is always manifest, or that the consequences of bad competition law are immediately painful. Rather, I make two claims. First, in industries that compete for capital internationally and that can realize significant returns from increases in labor productivity, good competition law matters. Second, the political mechanism that mediates between an industry's economic status and a state's policy preferences should not change when the state pursues those preferences through international cooperation rather than by domestic lawmaking and enforcement. These claims in turn suggest that, with respect to economic sectors to which the argument applies, states have some incentive to eschew competition policies that otherwise might generate short-term gains at the expense of global welfare.

Regulatory Competition and International Antitrust Revisited. Models of regulatory competition (such as Romano's) invoke a stylized market in which states (putative sellers) offer packages of law to firms (putative buyers) that have the capacity to select among them. States gain some benefit by having firms choose their law and thus wish to attract these buyers; firms choose laws that maximize benefits to the firms' decision makers. As noted, allowing states to market their competition law to producers seems undesirable. Instead of choosing laws that maximize general welfare, firms would seek opportunities for monopoly rents. For this reason, we do not find it disturbing that, in the contemporary world, firms have little influence over the choice of competition regulation that will apply to their activities. For the most part, firms can avoid a state's competition law only by abandoning that jurisdiction entirely, that is, neither producing, selling, basing personnel, or holding attachable assets in the territory of that state.

The dynamic model of competition law's effects on innovation and investment, however, introduces an indirect form of regulatory competition. If states compete for capital and opportunities to generate returns from knowledge, they should have some incentive to choose competition law that increases its opportunities for both. Under this model, states would not compete for producers as such, but rather for capital and innovation. To the extent good competition law increases a state's attraction for either, a virtuous cycle may proceed without the need for international coordination of state choices.

This vision of virtuous competition for innovation and investment is not as far-fetched as one might think. Explanations of the rise of Europe stress the pressure placed on states by their neighbors.[38] Rent seeking becomes more expensive in the face of a neighbor's technological progress, and competition among neighbors offers a powerful explanation for a state's willingness to sacrifice vested interests in the service of adaptation. Europe, a geographically fragmented entity, experienced more of this competition; the vast, hermetic empires of China and Russia did not. And in today's world, with lower costs in transportation and communication, geographical contiguity plays less of a role in economic competition among states than in the past.

My hypothesis also requires important qualifications. First, it applies largely to high value-added goods, including services, and not to industries that depend mostly on factor endowments. Second, the mechanism driving the virtuous cycle is considerably less transparent than the competition for corporate charters (and even that contest remains subject to debate). The incentive for virtuous policy involves a long-term effect rather than short-term payoffs. One might argue that political cycles do not run this long and that no one can realistically expect political actors to respond reliably to such forces. The example of Japan, which has resisted structural reform in spite of more than a decade of serious economic problems, bolsters this argument.

The force of these objections depends largely on guesses about the future—foremost, the nature and extent of the "new economy" at the international level. For virtuous competition in competition policy to have much purchase, two current trends in international economic relations will have to become more pronounced. First, the portion of international transfers involving high value-added goods will have to grow even more. Second, the pace of technological innovation, and the response of mobile capital to this pace, will have to quicken. These developments would increase the importance of competition policy and shorten the time between policy choice and economic consequences.

Looking only at the past two years, one might argue that the new economy never was much more than a pipe dream and that any expectation of its near-term recovery rests on delusion more than evidence. If one were to expand the horizon to the past decade, however, the story becomes more complicated and less crazy. Japan, a country that exports capital rather than investing it at home and that displays considerable structural rigidity and resistance to domestic competition, has experienced zero or negative growth during the period. The EC, with a competition policy that has more bite than Japan's but still seems more slanted toward protecting local producers than does U.S. policy, has not enjoyed nearly the same growth in labor productivity or inflows of capital that the United States has seen. To be sure, neither jurisdiction has yet seen its way clear to reforming its competition policy. My claim, however, is that the pressure to reform exists and over time may become irresistible, regardless of the absence of any international regime to harmonize or constrain competition law and practice.

Serious risks of government failure attend proposals for international governance in competition policy. Under certain assumptions, the market failures in this area may not be as great as they appear at first glance. In that light, international anarchy can start to look good. The chance that trends now at work in the world economy may reduce the need for hard law at the international level should temper our enthusiasm for lawmaking projects that may exacerbate, rather than remedy, the problems of international antitrust.

Notes

1. See Daniel J. Gifford and Robert T. Kudrle, "Alternative National Merger Standards and the Prospects for International Cooperation," in *The Political Economy of International Trade Law—Essays in Honor of Robert E. Hudec*, eds. Daniel L. M. Kennedy and James D. Southwick (Cambridge: Cambridge University Press, 2002), 208; Michael Trebilcock and Robert Howse, "Trade Liberalization and Regulatory Diversity: Reconciling Competitive Markets with Competition Politics," *European Journal of Law and Economics* 6 (1998): 5. National champions proliferate, among others, in the airlines and telecommunications industries.

2. See Oliver E. Williamson, *Markets and Hierarchies: Analysis and Antitrust Implications: A Study in the Economics of Internal Organization* (New York: Free Press, 1975).

3. *National Cooperative Research Act of 1984*, P. L. No. 98–462, 98 Stat. 1815 (1984), 15 U.S.C. §§ 4301–06; *Webb-Pomerene Act of 1918*, 15 U.S.C. §§ 61–65 (1994); *Export Trading Company Act of 1982*, 15 U.S.C. §§ 4001–21 (1994); *Foreign Trade Antitrust Improvements Act of 1982*, 15 U.S.C. § 6a (1994).

4. See Frank H. Easterbrook, "Does Antitrust Have a Comparative Advantage?" *Harvard Journal of Law and Public Policy* 23 (1999): 5, 7. ("And here's the big point: *by and large, we can't know when competition has 'failed.'*")

5. A state that has no hope of hosting a global monopolist would derive no gains from attacking the monopolist. The monopolist producer presumably would regard the attack as a cost of doing business and transfer those costs to that state's consumers, either directly by raising prices or indirectly by withdrawing from the market from which the attack would emanate.

6. Laura D'Andrea Tyson, *Who's Bashing Whom? Trade Conflict in High Technology Industries* (Washington, D.C.: Institute for International Economics, 1991).

7. See Paul R. Krugman, ed., *Strategic Trade Policy and the New International Economics* (Cambridge: MIT Press, 1986); Elhanan Helpman and Paul R. Krugman, *Market Structure and Foreign Trade—Increasing Returns, Imperfect Competition, and the International Economy* (Cambridge: MIT Press, 1985); Avinash K. Dixit and Victor Norman, *Theory of International Trade* (Cambridge: Cambridge University Press, 1980); Kelvin Lancaster, "Intra-industry Trade Under Perfect Monopolistic Competition," *Journal of International Economics* 10 (1980): 151; and Paul R. Krugman, "Increasing Returns, Monopolistic Competition, and International Trade," *Journal of International Economics* 9 (1979): 469.

8. Compare Alan O. Sykes, "Countervailing Duty Law: An Economic Perspective," *Columbia Law Review* 89 (1989): 199.

9. The possibility of strategic deployment of competition law is manifest where governments have a monopoly over enforcement, the situation that exists almost everywhere except for the United States. Even in the United States,

governmental enforcement decisions have a powerful effect on private suits, as evidenced by the preference of private plaintiffs to follow in the wake of Justice Department litigation. See also Mark R. Joelson, *An International Antitrust Primer: A Guide to the Operation of United States, European Union and Other Key Competition Laws in the Global Economy* (The Hague: Kluwer Law International, 2001), 168–76 (arguing that administrative control over the content of U.S. antitrust control has grown significantly in the past quarter century).

10. Gifford and Kudrle, "Alternative National Merger Standards," 220–23.

11. See John O. Haley, *Antitrust in Germany and Japan—The First Fifty Years, 1947–1998* (Seattle: University of Washington Press, 2001), 154–57, 162–68.

12. Perhaps the clearest U.S. example is the epic battle between U.S. television set manufacturers and the Japanese consumer electronic industry. The trial court, the Third Circuit, and four justices of the Supreme Court embraced the theory that producer collusion in the home market of the Japanese producers, coupled with successful price competition in the U.S. market, sufficed to make out a violation of the Sherman Act. *Matsushita Electrical Industrial Co. v. Zenith Radio Corp.*, 475 U.S. 574 (1986). This theory merges antitrust law with antidumping law. In fact, a few years after a narrow majority of the Supreme Court rejected the suit, the U.S. government successfully collected antidumping duties based on the evidence that the U.S. industry had presented in its antitrust claim. *Zenith Electronics Corp. v. United States*, 755 F. Supp. 397 (C.I.T. 1990). Later, U.S. legislation closed the gap even further by requiring distribution of antidumping (as well as countervailing) duties to protected domestic producers. *Continued Dumping and Subsidy Offset Act of 2000*, P.L. 106–387, § 1(a), 114 Stat. 1549, codified at 19 U.S.C. § 1675c. The permissibility of this law under the Uruguay Round Agreements is currently the subject of a WTO dispute proceeding.

In the EC, the European Commission's refusals to approve mergers of U.S. firms that compete with important European producers are legendary. In the notorious Boeing/McDonnell Douglas transaction, for example, the suspicion that the Commission sought to give a leg up to Airbus, Boeing's European rival, has been impossible to suppress. See Daniel J. Gifford and E. Thomas Sullivan, "Can International Antitrust Be Saved for the Post-Boeing Merger World? A Proposal to Minimize International Conflict and to Rescue Antitrust from Misuse," *Antitrust Bulletin* 45 (2000): 55. Other examples of EC protectionism involve prosecutions for "abuse of dominant position," which disproportionately seems to take in successful competition by non-EC firms. A classic case is its prosecution of United Brands, the American banana producer. *United Brands Co. v. Commission* (Case 27/76), 1978 E.C.R. 207 (1978). The Commission embraced an improbable theory of abuse against a background of Community trade regulation that systematically protected bananas produced in former European colonies from competition by United Brands. Consumer welfare, in particular that of banana-loving Germans, mattered not at all here.

In Japan, one does not find prosecutions of foreign firms so much as tolerance of private collusion to keep out foreign competition. Whether the government activity encourages and guides these policies or only accepts them is a matter of debate. Yoshiro Miwa and J. Mark Ramseyer, "Capitalist Politicians, Socialist Bureaucrats? Legends of Government Planning from Japan," *Antitrust Bulletin* 48 (2003): 595–627.

13. Robert L. Howse and Elisabeth Tuerk, "The WTO Impact on Internal Regulations—A Case Study of the Canada-EC Asbestos Dispute," in *The EU and the WTO: Legal and Constitutional Issues*, eds. Gráinne de Búrca and Joanne Scott, (Oxford: Hart Publishing, 2001), 283; Alan O. Sykes, "Domestic Regulation, Sovereignty, and Scientific Evidence Requirements: A Pessimistic View," *Chicago Journal of International Law* 3 (2002): 353 (technical barriers to trade and WTO dispute resolution process); Daniel K. Tarullo, "Norms and Institutions in Global Competition Policy," *American Journal of International Law* 94 (2000): 494, n. 57 (citing disputes over Cuba sanctions, meat hormones, preferences for former colonies, and dolphin protection).

14. Andrew T. Guzman, "International Antitrust and the WTO: The Lesson from Intellectual Property," *Virginia Journal of International Law* 43 (2003): 933–57; and Guzman, chapter 4 in this volume. See also Eleanor Fox, "International Antitrust—A Multi-tiered Challenge: The Doha Dome," *Virginia Journal of International Law* 43 (2003): 911–32; Einer Elhauge, "Preference-Eliciting Statutory Default Rules," *Columbia Law Review* 102 (2002): 2243–45; Joel P. Trachtman, "Economic Analysis of Prescriptive Jurisdiction," *Virginia Journal of International Law* 42 (2001): 72–74; Hannah L. Buxbaum, "Conflict of Economic Laws: From Sovereignty to Substance," *Virginia Journal of International Law* 42 (2002): 962–66.

15. Guzman, "International Antitrust and the WTO."

16. Andrew T. Guzman, "Global Governance and the WTO," *University of California Berkeley Public Law Research Paper*, no. 89 (2002).

17. See Paul B. Stephan, "Accountability and International Lawmaking: Rules, Rents and Legitimacy," *Northwestern Journal of International Law and Business* 17 (1996–97): 681; Paul B. Stephan, "The New International Law—Legitimacy, Accountability, Authority, and Freedom in the New Global Order," *University of Colorado Law Review* 70 (1999): 1555; Paul B. Stephan, "Sheriff or Prisoner? The United States and the World Trade Organization," *Chicago Journal of International Law* 1 (2000): 49; Paul B. Stephan, "International Governance and American Democracy," *Chicago Journal of International Law* 1 (2000): 237; Paul B. Stephan, "Institutions and Élites: Property, Contract, the State, and Rights in Information in the Global Economy," *Cardozo Journal of International and Comparative Law* 10 (2002): 801; Paul B. Stephan, "Courts, Tribunals and Legal Unification—The Agency Problem," *Chicago Journal of International Law* 3 (2002): 333.

18. See World Trade Organization, "Japan—Measures Affecting Consumer Photographic Film and Paper," *Report of the Panel*, WT/DS44/R §§10.378-10.382

(March 31, 1998). For discussion, see Stephan, "Courts, Tribunals," 348–49; Stephan, "Sheriff or Prisoner?" 56–61; Tarullo, "Norms and Institutions," 484.

19. See *In re Japanese Elec. Prods. Antitrust Litig.*, 807 F. 2nd 44 (3rd Cir., 1986).

20. World Trade Organization, "United States—Antidumping Act of 1916," *Report of the Appellate Body*, WT/DS316/AB/R, WT/DS162/AB/R (Aug. 28, 2000). For discussion, see Stephan, "Courts, Tribunals," 349.

21. But see John O. McGinnis and Mark L. Movsesian, "The World Trade Constitution," *Harvard Law Review* 114 (2000): 572–89 (arguing for welfare benefits of WTO dispute resolution). I consider the McGinnis-Movsesian argument strongest where the WTO addresses disputes over clear and therefore transparent principles. As the clarity of the principle dissipates, so does the likelihood of efficacious dispute resolution.

22. For a thorough review of the literature, see Joel P. Trachtman, "Prescriptive Jurisdiction."

23. *United States v. Aluminum Co. of America*, 148 F.2nd 416 (2nd Cir. 1945).

24. *In re Wood Pulp Cartel* (Case 89/85), 1988 E.C.R. 5193 (1988).

25. James R. Atwood and Kingman Brewster, *Antitrust and American Business Abroad* (Colorado Springs, Colo.: Shepard's/McGraw-Hill, 1981), 166.

26. *Timberlane Lumber Co. v. Bank of America*, 549 F.2nd 597 (9th Cir. 1976); Restatement (Third) of the Foreign Relations Law of the United States § 403 (1987).

27. *Hartford Fire Insurance Co. v. California*, 509 U.S. 764 (1993). Poor argumentation in that majority's opinion has enabled litigants to keep alive the prospect of the rule of reason's reemergence. See *United States v. Nippon Paper Industries Co.*, 109 F.3rd 1, 26–27 (1997), cert. denied, 522 U.S. 1044 (1998).

28. See Andrew T. Guzman, "Choice of Law: New Foundations," *Georgetown Law Journal* 90 (2002): 904–13.

29. William Dodge argues that courts should express a bias in favor of over-regulation on the grounds that special interests find it easier to block regulation they disfavor than to have enacted legislation that they favor. William S. Dodge, "An Economic Defense of Concurrent Antitrust Jurisdiction," *Texas International Law Journal* 38 (2003): 33–36. The argument confuses prudential concerns with welfare claims. Courts might defer to legislative choices about jurisdiction on the grounds that they do not have the capacity to second-guess legislative choices. But it does not follow that because special interests have a comparative advantage in blocking adverse legislation, only public-regarding regulation will pass through this filter. It is just as plausible that we see less legislation than we might because of the comparative advantage of compact groups but that the legislation we do see still reflects private rather than public interests.

30. Roberta Romano, *The Genius of American Corporate Law* (Washington, D.C.: AEI Press, 1993); Roberta Romano, "Empowering Investors: A Market Approach to Securities Regulation," *Yale Law Journal* 107 (1998): 2359; Roberta Romano,

The Advantages of Competitive Federalism for Securities Regulation (Washington, D.C.: AEI Press, 2002).

31. Stephen J. Choi and Andrew T. Guzman, "Portable Reciprocity: Rethinking the International Reach of Securities Regulation," *Southern California Law Review* 71 (1998): 903; Andrew T. Guzman, "Capital Market Regulation in Developing Countries: A Proposal," *Virginia Journal of International Law* 39 (1999): 607. See also Roberta Romano, "The Need for Competition in International Securities Regulation," *Theoretical Inquiries Law* 2 (2001): 387; Paul B. Stephan, "Regulatory Cooperation and Competition—The Search for Virtue," in *Transatlantic Regulatory Cooperation: Legal Problems and Political Prospects*, eds. George A. Bermann et al. (Oxford: Oxford University Press, 2000), 193–96; Frederick Tung, "Passports, Private Choice, and Private Interests: Regulatory Competition and Cooperation in Corporate, Securities and Bankruptcy Law," *Chicago Journal of International Law* 3 (2002): 369.

32. Some subjects, such as contracts implementing vertical cooperation, may present sufficiently debatable competition issues to justify deference to the transactors. See *Mitsubishi Motors Corp. v. Soler Chrysler-Plymouth, Inc.*, 473 U.S. 614 (1985). These contracts typically involve merchants who have some competitive choices before their entry into the agreement and involve project-specific investments that on balance may increase welfare. See generally Charles J. Goetz and Robert E. Scott, "Principles of Relational Contracts," *Virginia Law Review* 67 (1981): 1089. Under these circumstances, the parties are more likely to internalize the costs of whatever competition regime they choose, and without the freedom to choose, they may pass up valuable transactions.

33. For empirical evidence, see Richard R. Nelson and Gavin Wright, "The Rise and Fall of American Technological Leadership: The Postwar Era in Historical Perspective," *Journal of Economic Literature* 30 (1992): 1931.

34. Jeffrey A. Frankel and David Romer, "Does Trade Cause Growth?" *American Economic Review* 89 (1999): 379; Jeffrey Frankel and Andrew Rose, "An Estimate of the Effect of Common Currencies on Trade and Income," *Quarterly Journal of Economics* 117 (2002): 437.

35. Francisco Alcalá and Antonio Ciccone, "Trade and Productivity," *Economics Working Papers, Universitat Pompeu Fabra*, Barcelona, Spain (June 2002).

36. For a review of the evidence and a theoretical justification, see Oona A. Hathaway, "Positive Feedback: The Impact of Trade Liberalization on Industry Demands for Protection," *International Organization* 52 (1998): 575.

37. Bruce Scott and George C. Lodge, eds., *U.S. Competitiveness in the World Economy* (Boston: Harvard Business School Press, 1987); James A. Brander and Barbara J. Spencer, "Export Subsidies and International Market Share Rivalry," *Journal of International Economics* 16 (1985): 83. For claims about the feasibility of government selection of winning technologies by persons whose later record in government to some extent undermines their thesis, see Ira Magaziner and Robert Reich, *Minding America's Business* (New York: Vintage Books, 1982).

38. Douglass C. North, *Structure and Change in Economic History* (New York: W. W. Norton, 1981), 29; E. I. Jones, *The European Miracle: Environments, Economies, and Geopolitics in the History of Europe and Asia* (Cambridge: Cambridge University Press, 1987); Azam Chaudhry and Phillip Garner, "Political Competition Between Countries and Economic Growth" (Draft, August 29, 2002).

4

The Case for International Antitrust

Andrew T. Guzman

We already live in a world of international competition policy. Although no international institution or agreement governs the subject, firms doing business internationally face a de facto regime generated by the overlap of domestic regimes. The question, then, is not whether there should be an international competition policy, but rather whether the existing system is better than what might otherwise exist. Examination of how globalization and trade interact with domestic competition policies and how they influence the incentives of domestic policymakers suggests that there is significant value to increased cooperation. Furthermore, this cooperation must extend beyond the current set of information-sharing agreements or bilateral negotiations and include substantive antitrust issues.

The Costs of Noncooperation

The regulation of international activity by national regulators generates costs and benefits that are not fully internalized by domestic decision makers. This failure to take all effects into account is inevitable in a world with neither a single governmental body charged with establishing objectives and policies nor a forum in which domestic authorities can negotiate effectively over their domestic policies and the international implications thereof. Among the costs generated by the current noncooperative system are the effects of multiple regulators reviewing a single transaction (including redundant filing and reporting obligations), the risk of biased prosecutions based on the nationalities of the parties, and the impact of international activity on the substantive rules chosen by states.

Transaction Costs. The most obvious problem is the duplication of costs. Firms must satisfy regulatory agencies in many countries, meaning they must hire legal representation in each state and meet the reporting and disclosure requirements of each jurisdiction. At a minimum, this generates duplicative costs and wastes time. It may also impose conflicting requirements on firms. Additional costs are borne by the regulatory agencies that must review a firm's documents. Because each country's regulators act independently, each country must review and evaluate the firm's filing *de novo*, generating redundancy and waste in the review process.

Bias. When transactions cross borders, regulatory authorities review the activities of both foreign and domestic firms. Agencies will be tempted to be lenient toward locals and tough on foreigners in this review process, even if no such double standard is called for in the relevant legislation. Furthermore, even if the process is unbiased, foreign firms subject to review—as well as their governments—may believe that an unfavorable ruling represents an attempt to penalize foreign firms. This perception is itself costly because it may chill firm behavior or generate hostility among states.

Ample evidence suggests that states are, indeed, biased in their application of competition policy. Export cartel exemptions are the most obvious example.[1] Perhaps less obvious are the industry exemptions that American law provides to several privileged industries, including international aviation, international energy, international ocean shipping, and international communications. To the extent local firms benefit from these exemptions, they enjoy an advantage over their foreign rivals.

Although it is more difficult to demonstrate bias at the administrative level than at the statutory level, favoritism toward locals is likely in the selection of cases to pursue. One would expect more aggressive prosecution of foreign firms than domestic firms, either because the regulators themselves view local firms more favorably or because political leaders bring pressure to bear on regulators and encourage them to pursue foreign firms rather than national champions.

The increased transaction costs of noncooperation and the impact of bias are both familiar in the international antitrust literature, so this chapter does not discuss them further. It focuses instead on the question of how and why international trade distorts substantive antitrust policies and makes sound policymaking virtually impossible without cooperation.

The analysis that follows requires only the modest assumption that each state pursues its own interests without regard for the interests of other states. If this is so, international trade will distort decisions on antitrust relative to the regime each state would choose if it were a closed economy. These systematic and predictable deviations represent attempts to externalize the costs and internalize the benefits of the exercise of market power across borders. The analysis holds for any reasonable assumption about government behavior, whether based on public choice assumptions or the alternative hypothesis that governments seek to maximize the well-being of citizens.[2] To keep the presentation simple, I assume that states do not consider foreign costs and benefits at all, but even this assumption of complete disregard for foreigners could be relaxed. The only necessary assumption is that local interests are favored over foreign interests.

International Trade and Domestic Policy

To see how international trade can distort policy decisions in antitrust, suppose that a country exports virtually all of its production in imperfectly competitive industries.[3] (Only imperfectly competitive industries are of concern here because firms in competitive industries are not problematic from an antitrust perspective.) When domestic firms engage in activities that might be considered anticompetitive, the great majority of the harm is felt by foreigners, whereas the benefits are felt by local firms. Policymakers, looking only to local costs and benefits, will take into account all of the resulting benefits enjoyed by firms, but will consider only that fraction of the harm that is felt by local consumers.

A government designing an antitrust policy in this context would, therefore, favor the interests of producers over those of consumers. Note that this effect operates in addition to any preference for one group or the other generated by domestic political concerns. One way to think about this is to imagine that the policymaker adjusts the payoffs to local consumers and producers to reflect the relative weights or priorities that he or she assigns to each. In contrast to local interests, foreign interests are not considered at all—they receive a weight of zero. Thus, trade causes the country to favor producers over consumers more than would be the case in the absence of international trade.

To illustrate, imagine that a state favors firm interests over consumer interests. If the country is a closed economy, it will adopt policies that favor firms but, in evaluating policy options, will give consumer interests at least some weight. Now consider a country that has the same political economy but that exports most of the production of its imperfectly competitive industries. Because the political economy favors firms, the interests of domestic producers are still weighted more heavily than those of domestic consumers. In addition to this effect, the impact of the antitrust regime on consumers is underestimated because foreign consumers receive zero weight in the government's calculus. This generates policies that are still more favorable to firms, at the expense of consumers, than was the case in the absence of trade.

Several strategies are available to governments that wish to favor firms over consumers. The easiest of these, the already-discussed export cartel exemption, is a relatively crude instrument because it applies only if all of a firm's production is exported. A more nuanced strategy is to change the state's substantive laws. This benefits all firms, including those that sell some of their goods domestically. Returning to the example of a country that exports most but not all of its production in imperfectly competitive industries, the government could react to the pattern of trade by weakening its competition laws. This strategy opens the door to more anticompetitive activity by local firms than would be the case in the absence of trade, yet it retains some limits on conduct to protect local consumers.

Imports generate an analogous distortion. If a country is able to regulate extraterritorially, it has an incentive to tighten its policy (relative to what a closed economy would do) in response to the importation of goods in imperfectly competitive markets. In the case of imports, the full amount of harm suffered by local residents is included in the policy calculus, whereas only the benefits to local firms are considered. As with imports, this generates a predictable distortion regardless of how policy-makers weigh the interests of firms and consumers.

The combination of trade, consumption, and production patterns in imperfectly competitive markets sheds light on the competition policies a rational state will adopt. Because states are only concerned with consumption and production that occurs within their own borders, rational states will regulate with the relationship between trade and these variables. Once we know a state's pattern of trade with respect to imperfectly competitive goods, then, we can make predictions about how its policies will deviate from what it would do if it were a closed economy. For simplicity it is assumed that if a country's firms are responsible for x percent of global production of imperfectly competitive goods, those same firms enjoy x percent of the monopoly rents generated by the sale of those goods.[4] The government of that country, then, will take into account x percent of the producer surplus generated by a change in its policies. Thus, for example, if a country relaxes its competition policies, this might lead to an increase in producer surplus. But the government ignores the portion of that surplus that falls outside the country. If the same country's consumers account for y percent of global consumption of goods sold in imperfectly competitive markers, then the government will take into account y percent of the global effect of its policies on consumers.

The net effect of trade, then, depends on the ratio of a country's global share of production to its global share of consumption of imperfectly competitive goods. Notice that a closed economy would be one in which these are equal (x = 100 = y). If a country is a net exporter (meaning that its share of global production exceeds its share of consumption, x > y), then the country will take into account a larger portion of its policy's impact on producers than on consumers. Relative to what it would do if it were a closed economy, then, the country will favor the interests of producers, yielding a more permissive competition policy regime. If a country is a net importer of these goods (x < y), the opposite is true—the preferred policy is stricter than would be the case in a closed economy.

International activity, then, causes a state's domestic antitrust laws to deviate in systematic and predictable ways from what that state would choose if it were a closed economy. These deviations represent attempts to externalize the costs and internalize the benefits of the exercise of market power across borders.

Choice of Law

In part because of the divergent interests just discussed, the current level of cooperation in international competition policy is quite modest. This lack of cooperation, however, has generated an "accidental" competition policy regime created by the interaction of national regimes and their choice-of-law rules. Because of these rules, a single activity may be over-regulated or underregulated, depending on how it intersects with jurisdictional policies. Independent from, and in addition to, the distorting effects of international trade, the choice-of-law rules chosen by domestic systems interact to create a complex regulatory system that is not controlled by any single authority and that impacts international activity.

Overregulation. The activities of firms doing business in the United States, the European Union (EU), and other states that apply their laws extraterritorially are often within the jurisdiction of two or more domestic regimes. The net effect is a more restrictive and burdensome set of substantive rules than exists under the legal regime of any single state. Consider a proposed merger of two or more large firms doing business in both the United States and the EU and subject to merger review in both jurisdictions: Those firms face more regulation than they would under either of the domestic regimes. First, even if the substantive criteria for review were identical in the United States and Europe, the proposed merger could go forward only if both regulatory authorities permit it. This duplicative review would not matter if regulatory review were a precise science, but of course it is not. Any review by regulators is affected by the idiosyncratic views of the individual reviewers, the culture of the reviewing agency, the political climate in the country, and other factors. Requiring the approval of two independent regulatory bodies, therefore, increases the likelihood that an activity will be deemed a violation and increases the regulatory burden.

Second, firms doing business in states that apply their laws extraterritorially face a heightened burden because the substantive provisions of those laws are not identical across jurisdictions. Where legal rules vary across jurisdictions and all such rules must be followed, the relevant international legal regime consists of a medley of the strictest elements of each national regime. Suppose, for example, the activities of a firm are subject to the competition laws of countries A and B. Assume that country A has, relative to country B, a restrictive policy with respect to horizontal restraints of trade and a permissive policy with respect to vertical restraints. For its own reasons, country A believes this combination represents the optimal competition policy. Country B, however, believes that its regime, which is relatively permissive with respect to horizontal restraints but restrictive with respect to vertical restraints, is optimal. Firms subject to the jurisdiction of both states face a de facto regime that includes the strict horizontal restraint regulations of country A and the strict vertical restraint regulations of country B. This is a stricter policy than either country A or country B believes should exist.

In short, firms doing business in both the United States and the EU face an international competition policy regime that is more burdensome than the regime of either the EU or the United States and very likely more restrictive than what either jurisdiction would choose if it were a closed economy. The only way to prevent such overregulation is to end the extraterritorial assertion of jurisdiction—which would impose its own costs, as discussed below—or enter into some form of cooperative policymaking.

Underregulation. Although some jurisdictions, including the United States, apply their laws extraterritorially, many countries (including most developing states) either do not have effective competition laws or do not apply their competition laws to conduct beyond their borders.[5] Business activity that takes place within these states also faces an accidental international competition policy, but its contours are more complex than is the case for businesses operating in the United States and the EU.

Consider, first, the impact of international trade on the domestic competition policy of a country that does not apply its laws extraterritorially. With respect to imported goods, the country is unable to prevent anticompetitive activity by the foreign producers of those goods. Recognizing this, when policymakers shape the state's substantive competition policy, they only consider the impact of the law on domestic production. Put another way, because the domestic law cannot affect the behavior of foreign firms, the optimal policy for the state is the same as it would be if there were no imports. As long as domestic firms sell at least some of their products abroad, then, the state has an incentive to adopt competition laws that are more permissive than would be the case in a closed economy. (If local producers in imperfectly competitive markets only sell domestically, the local competition policy will be the same as it would be in a closed economy.) This is so because a tightening of the antitrust laws affects both producers and consumers. Producers are hurt by more restrictive laws, while consumers benefit from more competitive pricing.[6] Policymakers will tighten the laws until the marginal benefit to consumers equals the marginal cost to producers.[7] In a closed economy, all gains enjoyed by consumers are taken into account because all consumers are local. In a trading economy, however, this is not so. At least some consumers are located abroad, and the policymaker ignores all benefits conferred on these consumers by domestic laws. Because some of the benefits of tougher laws are ignored, the optimal policy for the state is less restrictive in the presence of trade.

One of the predictions of this analysis is that small, open economies—whose firms export a high percentage of their goods and whose consumers import a high percentage of their consumption—will have weak or nonexistent antitrust laws. This prediction is consistent with the empirical observation that small states rarely have significant antitrust laws. It is also consistent with the experience of the EU. When competition policy was made at the national level, the EU's competition policies were relatively permissive. When policy moved to the regional level (and as extraterritoriality came to be the practice), the EU adopted a much stricter antitrust regime.[8]

If no states applied their laws extraterritorially, the above analysis would lead to the conclusion that substantive competition laws are systematically more lenient than would be the case if all costs and benefits were taken into account. In fact, however, the conduct of states that apply their laws extraterritorially affects the legal regime facing many firms, including some that do business in states that do not apply their laws to foreign conduct.

Because the United States and the EU apply their laws to foreign conduct that has a local effect, firms active in those markets are at least potentially subject to the laws of both jurisdictions. This is relevant to all states, including those that do not apply their laws extraterritorially, because the EU and U.S. regimes affect the global operations of producers. Imagine, for example, that two or more producers of passenger aircraft wish to merge. If they do so, they will enjoy greater market power, earn more profits for the newly merged firm, and increase the price of aircraft. A state that does not apply its laws extraterritorially can only reach the proposed merger if one of the firms happens to be located within its borders, and even then it can—at most—prevent its local firm from participating. The same proposed merger, however, will trigger jurisdiction in both the EU and the United States and can be blocked by either of those states. If the merger is blocked, this affects all states, including those that do not apply their laws extraterritorially. Economic activity within these states, then, is influenced by the competition policies of foreign states. This can yield benefits for a state that does not apply its laws extraterritorially, because it is able to free ride on the regulatory supervision of those countries that do apply their laws in this way.

A strategy of free riding is especially effective in the presence of an open trading regime because a firm can retain local market power only if it also has global market power. A firm that operates monopolistically locally but not internationally will earn excess profits from its local operations, attract competitors from abroad, and see its market power erode. If, however, a firm has market power internationally, it is likely to sell its products into the United States and/or the EU.

Although free riding can operate as a substitute for domestic competition policy, it falls short of a satisfactory legal regime for states that do not apply their laws extraterritorially. In addition to the distortions already discussed, there are at least two further reasons why free riding is likely to yield suboptimal policy. First, if the impact of a particular activity is small in developed states but large in developing states, the EU and the United States may not bother to pursue a case. There is no reason to think that the costs and benefits of an activity are the same in all countries, especially when comparing developing countries to developed ones. As a result, a decision on whether to bring a case in the United States or the EU may be quite different from what is in the interests of a developing country.[9] Similarly, there are at least some goods that are sold only regionally (for example, regional periodicals) and that will not trigger jurisdiction in the United States or the EU.

Second, even when goods trade globally, the existence of a strong and effective competition policy, complete with extraterritorial application, in the United States and the EU may not prevent firms from engaging in anticompetitive conduct in other countries. Consider how a profit-maximizing firm with market power and global sales will react if it faces effective competition laws in some but not all of the states in which it does business. In states with an effective policy, the firm would restrain its anticompetitive activities so as to remain within the law. But the firm need not sell at the same price everywhere. As long as arbitrage between markets is costly, the firm can charge higher prices in markets without effective competition laws or without laws that apply extraterritorially. Although the United States and the EU have jurisdiction over the firm, they have no reason to pursue a case if the firm's conduct in the United States and the EU mimics that of a firm in a competitive industry. Countries whose laws cannot reach the firm, then, may not be able to free ride on the competition laws of the EU and the United States. The empirical evidence suggests exactly this sort of market segmentation and price discrimination has taken place.[10]

Overall, the de facto competition policy regime that exists in countries that do not apply their laws extraterritorially is almost certainly a mix of overregulation in some markets (where EU and U.S. laws apply) and underregulation in other markets (where those laws do not apply or are not effective). Cooperation has the potential to reduce the level of regulation in the former markets and increase it in the latter.

The Promise of Cooperation

If we assume that governments pursue some measure of national welfare, government decisions in a closed economy represent optimal decisions in the sense that they take into account all relevant costs and benefits. Deviations from this closed economy policy represent attempts by states to externalize cost while internalizing benefits. The resulting policies are, by assumption, domestically optimal but are suboptimal from a global perspective because some costs and benefits are ignored. If we instead assume a public choice model of government, the analysis is more complex. Under this model, trade causes policies to move away from the closed economy policy, which may represent a move toward or away from the optimal policy, depending on the way in which public choice issues affect decision making.

To isolate the impact of trade on policy, assume for the moment that there is an international consensus on the objectives of antitrust policy and the appropriate way to achieve those objectives. Even under these assumptions, noncooperative states will not all adopt the same policies: Net importers will adopt relatively strict antitrust laws (assuming they can apply their laws extraterritorially), and net exporters will adopt relatively permissive laws. Nevertheless, because states have a shared view of the optimal antitrust law for a closed economy, they will be able, absent transaction costs, to reach an agreement that implements that policy on a global scale. That is, states will agree on the most efficient global antitrust regime. This result is an application of basic theories of federalism, which suggest that decision-making responsibility should be assigned to the lowest level of government that is capable of internalizing economic externalities.[11] In the case of antitrust policy, the externalities provide a strong argument for international regulation or cooperation.

Assuming a consensus of opinion and zero transaction costs is, of course, wholly unrealistic. The proper role of competition policy is a subject of considerable disagreement, and international negotiations are plagued by transaction costs. In recognition of these realities, we now relax these assumptions.

For the moment, continue to assume that transaction costs are zero, but allow that the objectives of competition policy differ from state to state. There are any number of reasons why states might have divergent goals. For example, some countries may understand what competition policy can and cannot do, and others may simply be mistaken. In this situation, agreement may be possible through dialogue and debate. Over time, one view may come to be accepted while the other is discredited, and international agreement on a common policy will be possible.

Another possibility is that disagreements are not the result of differences in information but, rather, differences in preferences. Diversity of preferences may exist for many reasons, ranging from differing priorities to differing conditions in domestic markets to different interest group constellations. If the preferences differ, the sharing of information cannot by itself generate consensus. This will not preclude an optimal agreement, however, so long as states can compensate one another for accepting a policy that differs from their preferred policy. Just as parties to a contract will bargain to maximize the joint value of the agreement, states will bargain to maximize the joint value of competition policy. Imagine, for example, that one state prefers a relatively restrictive policy toward mergers—perhaps because it values the existence of small and medium-sized businesses—while another prefers a more permissive merger policy based solely on efficiency grounds. This difference in preferences can be overcome through the use of transfer payments. An agreement will be struck in which the party with the stronger preferences gets its preferred policy and in exchange makes a compensatory payment to the other state.

The same result holds if the divergent preferences stem from the trade-induced distortions discussed earlier. Specifically, the parties would enter into an agreement that puts in place the globally optimal competition policy and provides for a transfer from states that benefit from this policy to states that suffer losses relative to their noncooperative payoffs. Because cooperative policy is globally optimal, it must be the case that there are sufficient gains for a Pareto improving agreement to be reached.

Thus, putting aside political economy issues (discussed below), the real impediment to achieving an optimal policy is transaction costs. Because the interests of net importers and exporters diverge, cooperation can only be achieved through transfers from prospective winners to prospective losers. It follows that ad hoc attempts at cooperation, limited to competition policy alone, stand little chance of success: States that stand to gain from a particular agreement have no way to compensate those that stand to lose. Negotiation over competition policy must occur in a sufficiently broad institutional context to allow for compensation in other areas such as trade, or the environment.[12] The negotiation of transfer payments through concessions in other areas of negotiation is, of course, difficult. This difficulty, however, is unavoidable because without it, cooperation at a substantive level is likely impossible. Before considering the possible forms of cooperation, I now turn to discuss the main arguments advanced in opposition to cooperation.

The Problematic Case Against Cooperation

The problems of noncooperative policymaking, combined with the realities of international business activity, make it impossible to defend the status quo as an optimal competition policy regime. If there were a well-functioning international governmental system, the case for making antitrust policy decisions at that level would be irrefutable. Because the case against international regulation fails as a matter of theory, sophisticated opponents of international cooperation argue, as they must, that cooperation is too difficult or too costly as a matter of practice. The most common and powerful argument is that policymaking at the international level is too inefficient, undemocratic, and corrupt to be trusted with competition policy.[13] Even skeptics of international cooperation must admit, though, that it has proven effective in some instances. Few, if any, observers would argue that the General Agreement on Tariffs and Trade, the Trade-Related Aspects of Intellectual Property Rights Agreement, the Basle Accord, the North American Free Trade Agreement, and the EU have all generated net social costs. That said, there is no doubt that international agreements come with costs. The question in any given case is whether the costs outweigh the benefits.

The greatest risk posed by international cooperation in antitrust is that the international process itself will generate undesirable outcomes—foremost, because negotiators might favor the interests of certain groups over those of others. For example, business interests may enjoy greater influence than consumer interests, generating a bias toward lenient rules. But while public choice problems will certainly occur at the international level, there is no way to know how large these effects will be or if they will be larger or smaller than the corresponding domestic problems.

As a first cut, international public choice problems are likely to reflect domestic public choice problems. That is, interest groups will be able to influence negotiators because they can influence the politicians who control the negotiators. This influence is not created by internationalization but, rather, by the political structure of domestic government. If policy is made domestically, the same interest group biases will be present. Furthermore, international negotiations may help to offset the power of interest groups. Interest groups in one country may have significant control over policy, but when governments must negotiate with one another, powerful interest groups in one state may be offset by opposing groups in another. For example, trade agreements counter protectionist pressure by giving policymakers the ability to open foreign markets and thereby please exporters. The net result is less influence on policy for import competing industries and freer trade. Given the clear evidence that domestic policies are frustrated by a noncooperative regime, it seems appropriate to demand that skeptics advance a more precise model of the political economy of domestic and international policymaking to support their account of international public choice problems.

In this volume, John McGinnis presents the most comprehensive extant attempt to show that public choice problems on the international level are likely to generate higher costs than domestic regulation (see chapter 5). Although his arguments have some theoretical merit, their validity in any particular context turns on empirical questions that cannot be resolved here. More importantly, the modest level of proposed cooperation in international antitrust fails to trigger most of the costs McGinnis identifies. McGinnis's principal concern is that international negotiators and function-aries have an interest in generating complex rules or other devices to maximize their own influence. But this legitimate concern is not a reason to resist cooperation altogether. The same problem exists—and, in the competition policy context, is much more acute domestically. International bureaucrats have considerably less rule-making authority than their domestic law counterparts, so they have a more limited ability to pursue their own interest in this way. Outside the EU and a very small number of quasijudicial bodies, there are very few, if any, instances in which international bureaucrats have any policymaking authority that is independent of national governments. In the area of international antitrust, no serious proposal exists for an international antitrust agency authorized to develop its own rules and policies.[14] In other words, international cooperation in antitrust can and should proceed without significant bureaucracy.

Ultimately, the issue here concerns the form of cooperation rather than its merits. If cooperation is desirable, concerns about bureaucracy should not frustrate it. To the extent bureaucratic capture is a concern, there should be less delegation to those bureaucrats.[15]

Along similar lines, McGinnis expresses concern about the enforcement of a cooperative regime. He argues that centralized enforcement entails significant costs while *decentralized* enforcement leads to the problem of divergent standards. Though a regime of harmonization might well present that dilemma, a more modest level of cooperation (described below) avoids it. An adjudicatory body—such as the WTO's Appellate Body—could adjudicate disputes that arise with respect to a small number of general rules while leaving other issues to the states themselves. That arrangement would also leave room for innovation and experimentation and, in that fashion, allay McGinnis's fears over the rigidity and inflexibility of international institutions.

Two additional arguments against international antitrust cooperation warrant a brief discussion. First, in antitrust, as in many other areas, the internationalization of business activity can and has been viewed as a welcome challenge and discipline for regulators. Until the *Alcoa* case (1945) in the United States and the *Wood Pulp* decision (1988) in Europe, for example, activities that took place offshore but that had an effect in the jurisdiction were (at least arguably) beyond the reach of local authorities.[16] Even today, many countries make no attempt to exercise jurisdiction over foreign conduct. Where national law is applied on a strictly territorial basis, it may fail to reach conduct that is alleged to impose harm on local interests. If one believes that existing domestic antitrust laws are excessively tough (or, indeed, entirely unnecessary), internationalization that removes conduct from the local jurisdiction may be seen as desirable. On this view, the internationalization of business corrects a failure of the domestic political system and reduces the authority of local regulators in a desirable way. As McGinnis puts it, "[F]oreign bias may counteract public choice biases against wealth maximizing laws and thus move competition law toward a more optimal state."

The readiest—and sufficient—reply is that this argument ignores the current state of international antitrust. Both the United States and the EU, among others, now apply their laws to conduct that takes place abroad but has local effects. Rather than undermining the authority of local regulators, a failure to cooperate will generate overlapping jurisdictional claims and, at least among developed states, more rather than less regulatory review.

Second, and finally, one could argue that a global market reduces the potential for monopolization or other anticompetitive conduct to the point of rendering antitrust law unnecessary. Trade can certainly substitute for competition policy in some instances. The clearest example is a small, closed economy whose consumers are harmed by local monopolies. Opening the country to foreign trade would undermine the market power of local firms and force them to compete. Trade here works as a substitute for competition policy, with the added advantage of promoting competition without government intervention.

Still, trade is not a full substitute for competition policy. Trade can only undermine monopolies that rely on trade barriers for their existence. When firms have *international* market power, one would expect them to behave as monopolists just like domestic firms with market power. Although it may be more difficult to establish and maintain market power internationally, there is no reason to believe that it is impossible or, for that matter, rare. Industries such as pharmaceuticals, passenger aircraft, and software illustrate the phenomenon.

The Form of Cooperation

Although international cooperation on competition policy is necessary, its critics are right that cooperation carries costs. As decisions are moved further from individual citizens, democratic control is weakened. For this and other reasons, special efforts may be necessary to rein in international bureaucracies. Cooperation can be frustrated by weak and unreliable international enforcement mechanisms. And of course, international agreements involve transaction costs. They are slow to negotiate, distract officials from other tasks, and can cause animosity among states. Even when negotiations are successful, the ensuing cooperation can be costly, especially if new institutions are needed. Once completed, these same costs, typically coupled with a unanimity requirement, make international agreements difficult to change. Attempts to reduce the cost of change by delegating authority to international bureaucrats generate their own costs in the form of entrenchment and lack of democratic control.

To reduce these inevitable costs, the preferred form of cooperation is the lowest level that avoids the distortions of noncooperative policymaking.[17] Cooperative strategies on international competition policy come in essentially three forms, from lowest to highest levels of cooperation: voluntary information sharing and consultation (the system that currently exists); procedural cooperation on choice-of-law rules, with an eye toward restricting the number of legal systems claiming jurisdiction; and substantive cooperation, which imposes on states more or less demanding requirements in terms of their domestic substantive rules. A review of these options shows that effective regulation of antitrust requires at least some cooperation with respect to substantive laws. Although such a strategy has drawbacks, including the fact that it may be difficult to reach any agreement, it represents the only way for states to address the externalities associated with international competition policy.

Information Sharing

Faced with continuing growth in international business activity, domestic antitrust authorities have been forced to adopt new strategies. Without at least some sharing of information among national regulators, it would often be difficult to build a case against international firms. If prosecutors were helpless beyond their own borders, a firm could violate the law with little risk by keeping key documents offshore, holding offshore meetings among participants in the violative activity, and residing in a foreign jurisdiction. To prevent erosion of their authority and enforcement powers, antitrust authorities have cooperated with one another.

With few exceptions, cooperation has been limited to voluntary information-sharing agreements.[18] A typical agreement calls for the sharing of information between enforcement authorities when the actions of regulators in one country affect the interests of the other state.[19] In addition, the agreements provide for consultation to resolve concerns between the states, indicate that the parties should cooperate in enforcement when this is possible, and call for each state to take into account the effects of anticompetitive conduct on the other state when considering an enforcement action. This last element, taking the effect of domestic conduct on other states into account, would go a long way toward addressing the problems with the existing international competition policy regime. Unfortunately, though, existing agreements do not lay out any details about how this consideration is to be given, do not include any sort of sanction for a failure to take the interests of the other party into account, and say nothing about how the interests of other states should affect domestic policy decisions.

Although these information-sharing agreements play an important role in international antitrust enforcement, they are not and cannot be a solution to the problem of international cooperation. There is, for example, no coordination of substantive laws, no compromise of domestic control,[20] and no minimum standards. Furthermore, compliance is voluntary. Each state is free to refuse cooperation when it wishes and remains guided by its own interests in deciding when to do so.

Information sharing, or "soft" cooperation, has also been pursued at the Organisation for Economic Co-operation and Development, which has generated several aspirational texts.[21] None of these impose obligations on states, and they are not intended to do so. Their goals are modestly limited to improving communication on competition issues. This dialogue—and, more recently, multilateral cooperation through the International Competition Network—is important and may have contributed to greater harmonization of substantive laws than would otherwise exist. Still, it barely exceeds the level one would expect from self-interested states and administrative agencies seeking to preserve their own influence.[22] By sharing information, enforcement agencies cooperate in such a way as to allow both themselves and their sister agencies to continue their work, but they do not surrender any of their authority over domestic matters. This form of soft cooperation furthers the enforcement goals of regulators but does virtually nothing to address the over- and underregulation of antitrust at the international level.

Choice of Law

Stepping one rung higher on the cooperative ladder, states could set the terms of their interaction through choice-of-law rules that assign jurisdiction (based on some criteria) to one or more states. The criteria for such a selection are familiar and include factors such as the location of the disputed activity and the principal place of business of the firm. But choice-of-law rules cannot, without more, address the problems of over- and underregulation. A choice-of-law system that allows for overlapping jurisdiction leaves the problem of overregulation unresolved. A system that assigns jurisdiction to a single state can reduce the problem of overregulation but may exacerbate the problem of underregulation. Nor can a choice-of-law strategy prevent local favoritism and trade-induced distortions of national substantive policies.

Theoretically, the problem of underregulation in states that cannot extend their laws extraterritorially could be addressed through a choice-of-law rule that grants standing to plaintiffs if the relevant firm activity took place within the jurisdiction, even if the injuries occurred abroad. (An even more aggressive rule would grant standing to any plaintiff regardless of where the conduct took place.) This rule would give injured plaintiffs a remedy against the actions of foreign firms that target states whose laws do not apply extraterritorially, as long as the conduct was within a state with effective antitrust rules. Such a rule would at a minimum ensure that Western firms faced some regulation when selling into countries without extraterritorial reach. The justification for this rule is essentially the same as the justification for eliminating export cartels exemptions: It requires states to pursue some anticompetitive behavior even when it benefits local firms and harms foreign consumers. This arrangement would obviously be a dramatic change from the status quo, and implementation would face numerous difficulties. If one concludes (as is almost surely correct) that the adoption and operation of such a rule in the current context are unrealistic, the lesson is that deeper cooperation is needed.

Deep Cooperation

Once it is accepted that cooperation with respect to substantive laws is required, the question becomes how to achieve it. Experience and theory show that a substantive agreement will be difficult to reach. This is so because the transaction costs of negotiation in this context are significant. The challenge, then, is to reduce transaction costs as much as possible.

I have argued elsewhere that the WTO represents the best forum for negotiations on the subject.[23] Regardless of the chosen forum, however, the distortion of domestic incentives cannot be corrected short of cooperation on substantive competition policy. This need not take the form of harmonization because states may conclude that policy differences across regimes are desirable, but it does require negotiation over substantive policy in a forum where transfers are available. For the reasons noted, it seems prudent to start with a relatively modest agenda—without foreclosing greater cooperation in the future.

The most plausible agenda item is a nondiscrimination principle.[24] This would ideally include both national treatment and most favored nation components, although national treatment is the more important element. Chapters in this volume by McGinnis (chapter 5) and by Trebilcock and Iacobucci (chapter 6), as well as past writing of my own, support the notion of a national treatment requirement.[25] A national treatment obligation appeals to our sense of fairness, is consistent with the spirit of existing WTO obligations, and would address export cartel exemptions.

Although a national treatment obligation could eliminate explicit discrimination, it would be less successful at addressing the problem of discrimination in application and enforcement. In attempting to deal with discriminatory enforcement, Trebilcock and Iacobucci observe that international trade law addresses the problem of de facto discrimination in other contexts. The antitrust context, however, differs from other areas where discrimination is prohibited. In the trade context, for example, discrimination against an imported product is relatively easy to identify by comparing the treatment of one product with the treatment of another "like product." One can carry out a meaningful inquiry, for example, into the question of whether a country treats imported watches differently from locally produced watches. This sort of comparison is much more difficult in the antitrust context because each prosecution turns on a unique set of facts. It will not typically be the case, for instance, that the prosecution of an alleged international price-fixing scheme can be reviewed by looking at a domestic scheme carried out in the same fashion and in the same industry. A lack of a closely analogous set of facts will often obviate comparisons. True, some benchmarks (such as the Hirfindahl-Herschman Index, or HHI) may permit comparisons, but even in those cases, the prosecution of antitrust violations involves much more discretion and case-specific facts than a conventional trade case.

Moreover, other areas subject to nondiscrimination requirements are not always policed effectively, and the national treatment obligation is often more of a de jure than a de facto standard. This is especially true in areas where fact-specific inquiries are involved, as would be the case in antitrust. Under the WTO's Agreement on the Application of Sanitary and Phytosanitary Measures, for example, WTO members may adopt measures necessary "for the protection of human, animal or plant life or health." As applied, this requirement is extraordinarily modest, requiring only that there be a "rational relationship" between the disputed measure and the required risk assessment.[26] Similar nondiscrimination requirements exist in other parts of the WTO agreements, and where the obligations go to nontrade issues, the result is virtually always the same: De facto discrimination is largely ignored because the WTO is hesitant to second-guess domestic decisions with respect to such policies.

A national treatment obligation for antitrust, then, is useful primarily to prevent the use of export cartel exemptions and perhaps to constrain egregious forms of de facto discrimination. It cannot prevent regulators from favoring locals in the day-to-day administration of the law or, for that matter, resolve the problems associated with the domestic adoption and enforcement of rules to govern international activity, for example, the strategic choice of domestic law by states engaged in trade.

The slightly more ambitious WTO agenda for reform is a good first step toward more meaningful cooperation. This approach would focus on "core principles, including transparency, non-discrimination and procedural fairness, and provisions on hardcore cartels; [and] modalities for voluntary cooperation."[27] Seeking cooperation on the most agreed upon violations such as hard-core cartels is sensible, as are efforts to increase transparency and voluntary cooperation. Eventually, it would be helpful to see other forms of cooperation emerge, including mandatory information-sharing arrangements (subject to appropriate confidentiality provisions),[28] streamlining cooperation in international merger review,[29] and jurisdictional agreements that at a minimum commit states to decline jurisdiction if the impact of a measure on their own citizens is sufficiently small. Cooperation of the sort described here is difficult to achieve, but it is the only way to achieve a sensible competition in our globalizing world.

Notes

1. American antitrust laws have long provided an explicit exception for export cartels. The Webb-Pomerene Act, 15 U.S.C. §§ 61–66 (1994), adopted in 1918, creates an exemption from the Sherman Act and from Section 7 of the Clayton Act for export associations formed for the sole purpose of engaging in export trade and actually engaged solely in such export trade. Export associations must register with the FTC. The Act does not protect activity that has an anticompetitive effect within the United States, and there are other restrictions on its applicability. See A. Paul Victor, "Export Cartels: An Idea Whose Time Has Passed," *Antitrust Law Journal* 60 (1991): 572. By the early 1980s, it was widely agreed that the Webb-Pomerene Act was, for various reasons, not being used by exporters and was, in that sense, no longer effective. See id. at 573–74. Congress responded by enacting the Export Trading Company Act of 1982, 15 U.S.C. §§ 4001–16 (2000), and the Foreign Trade Antitrust Improvements Act, 15 U.S.C. § 6a (2000). The Export Trading Act allows a firm to apply for and receive a Certificate of Review from the Secretary of Commerce by demonstrating that its activities will not have harmful effects on the United States. The certificate does not grant complete immunity to the firm, but it does provide immunity from treble damages and criminal liability. It also establishes a presumption of legality for any activity that is covered by the certificate. The Foreign Trade Act offers a more direct exemption for export activity. It exempts from Sherman Act prosecution activity that does not have a "direct, substantial, and reasonably foreseeable" effect on American commerce, 15 U.S.C. § 6a (2000). Other countries have similar exemptions.

2. For example, if government officials behave as public choice models predict— pursuing campaign contributions, political support, and a good public image— the discussion that follows applies just as it does if governments pursue some measure of national welfare, as long as the goals of those officials are influenced primarily by domestic interests. In other words, as long as campaign contributions are dominated by domestic contributors, important political supporters are locals, and the public image that matters is domestic, the discussion that follows is consistent with public choice assumptions.

3. See Andrew T. Guzman, "Is International Antitrust Possible?" *New York University Law Review* 73 (1998): 1501–48 for a more detailed discussion of the impact of trade on competition policies.

4. This assumption could be relaxed without changing the analysis, but at a cost of considerably more complexity.

5. A country might choose to limit the jurisdiction of its laws to territorial conduct, or it may simply lack the ability as a practical matter to apply its laws abroad. Historically, every nation limited its laws to conduct within its territory. See, for example, *American Banana Co. v. United Fruit Co.*, 213 U.S. 347 (1909).

Even as extraterritoriality has become accepted, states have retained limits on the reach of their laws. In the United States, for example, the reach of the securities laws is limited by a variety of rules. Many developing countries have little choice but to opt for a territorial jurisdiction because they lack both the capacity and the political power to enforce their laws more broadly.

6. Consumers need not always benefit from stricter antitrust laws, of course. In particular, they can be harmed if the tougher laws prevent firms from achieving efficiency gains. Even in that event, however, domestic policies will be weaker for a trading country without extraterritoriality than for a closed economy.

7. To account for the realities of the political economy, it may be more accurate to say that policymakers will tighten the laws until the net marginal gain to those policymakers is zero. As long as the policymakers' gains from tougher laws stem from the benefits to consumers and the costs stem from the burden on producers, the analysis presented above applies. That policymakers may weigh producer interests more heavily than consumer interests (or vice versa) does not affect the results.

8. See Guzman, "Is International Antitrust Possible?" 1537–38.

9. In the market for pharmaceuticals designed to treat tropical diseases, for example, firms with market power may act in a way that would violate the substantive laws of the United States and the EU without attracting the attention of regulators in either jurisdiction.

10. See Margaret Levenstein and Valerie Suslow, "Private International Cartels and the Effect on Developing Countries," Background paper for the *World Development Report* 2001 (Washington, D.C.: World Bank, 2001); John M. O'Connor, *Global Price Fixing: Our Customers Are the Enemy* (Boston: Kluwer Academic Publishing, 2001); Lawrence J. White, "Lysine and Price Fixing: How Long? How Severe?" *Review of Industrial Organization* 18 (2001): 23–31; Julian L. Clarke and Simon J. Evenett, "The Deterrent Effects of National Anti-Cartel Laws: Evidence from the International Vitamins Cartel," *AEI-Brookings Joint Center for Regulatory Studies, Working Paper* 02-13, December 2002.

11. See, for example, Robert P. Inman and Daniel L. Rubinfeld, "Rethinking Federalism," *Journal of Economic Perspectives* 11, no. 4 (1997): 45. This desire to internalize externalities explains why competition policy is carried out by the federal government in the United States and by the regional government in the EU.

12. See Andrew T. Guzman, "International Antitrust and the WTO: The Lesson from Intellectual Property," *Virginia Journal of International Law* 43 (2003): 933–57 (arguing that the TRIPS agreement was possible because negotiations took place in the WTO, where transfer payments are possible).

13. For a generalized argument opposing international cooperation on these grounds, see Paul B. Stephan, "Regulatory Competition and Competition: The Search for Virtue," in *Transatlantic Regulatory Cooperation—Legal Problems and*

Political Prospects, eds. George A. Bermann, Mathias Herdegen, and Peter L. Lindseth (Oxford: Oxford University Press, 2000), 167; Paul B. Stephan, "Accountability and International Lawmaking: Rules, Rents, and Legitimacy," *Northwestern Journal of International Law & Business* 17 (1996–97): 681–735; Paul B. Stephan, "The Futility of Unification and Harmonization in International Commercial Law," *Virginia Journal of International Law* 39 (1999): 743–97; Paul B. Stephan, "The Political Economy of Choice of Law," *Georgetown Law Journal* 90 (2002): 957–70.

14. A proposed "International Antitrust Code" includes the establishment of an "International Antitrust Authority," that arguably would possess some of the bureaucratic characteristics that concern McGinnis. See Draft International Antitrust Code as a GATT-MTO-Plurilateral Trade Agreement (International Antitrust Code Working Group Proposed Draft 1993), published and released July 10, 1993, *Antitrust and Trade Regulation Report* (BNA) 64, no. 1628 (Aug. 19, 1993) (Special Supp.). For a discussion of the Draft Code, see Daniel J. Gifford, "The Draft International Antitrust Code Proposed At Munich: Good Intentions Gone Awry," *Minnesota Journal of Global Trade* 6 (Winter 1997): 1–66. This proposal, however, was advanced in 1993 and does not seem to have generated any significant support. Were it made as a serious proposal today, I would share many of McGinnis's objections.

15. Ultimately, the dispute here turns on empirical questions. I have previously outlined my views on how to proceed with international cooperation in the face of the inevitable uncertainty regarding public choice issues. See Andrew T. Guzman, "Public Choice and International Regulatory Competition," *Georgetown Law Journal* 90 (2002): 977–80.

16. *U.S. v. Aluminum Company of America* (Alcoa) 148 F.2d 416 (2d Cir. 1945); *In re Wood Pulp Cartel* (Case 89/85) (1988), E.C.R. 5193.

17. I have previously written on the question of how to manage cooperation in a wider set of regulatory areas. See Andrew T. Guzman, "Choice of Law: New Foundations," *Georgetown Law Journal* 90 (2002): 883–940.

18. See Eleanor M. Fox, "Antitrust and Regulatory Federalism: Races Up, Down, and Sideways," *New York University Law Review* 75 (2000): 1785–88.

19. See, for example, Agreement Between the Government of the United States of America and the Government of Canada Regarding the Application of Their Competition and Deceptive Marketing Practices Laws, Aug. 3, 1995, U.S.-Can., reprinted in Trade Regulation Reporter (CCH) 4, par. 13,503; Agreement Between the Government of the United States of America and the Government of the Federal Republic of Germany Relating to Mutual Cooperation Regarding Restrictive Business Practices, June 23, 1976, reprinted in *Trade Regulation Reporter* (CCH) 4, par. 13,501. The United States has entered into similar agreements with Australia, the European Communities, Israel, Japan, Brazil, and Mexico. For a detailed discussion, see John J. Parisi, "Enforcement Cooperation

among Antitrust Authorities," *International Quarterly* 12 (2000): 691–720; see also Spencer Weber Waller, "The Internationalization of Antitrust Enforcement," *Boston University Law Review* 77 (1997): 343–404.

20. There are two significant exceptions. Canada and the United States have entered into The Treaty on Mutual Legal Assistance in Criminal Matters, Mar. 18, 1985, Can.–U.S., 24 I.L.M. 1092 (1985), which provides for the use of compulsory powers to gather evidence in criminal antitrust cases and allows the exchange of compulsory information. The United States has also entered into an agreement with Australia under the International Antitrust Enforcement Assistance Act of 1994, P. L. No. 103-438, codified at 15 U.S.C. §§ 6201–12. The text of the agreement is available at http://www.ftc.gov/os/1997/9704/lastaus.htm.

21. See *OECD Guidelines for Multinational Enterprises: Ministerial Booklet* (Paris. OECD, 2000), available at http://www.oecd.org/document/28/0%2C2340%2Cen_2649_34889_2397532_1_1_1_1%2C00.html; 1978 Council Recommendations Concerning Actions Against Restrictive Business Practices Affecting International Trade Including Those Involving Multinational Enterprises, OECD Doc. C(78)133 (Final) (August 9, 1978); 1978 Council Recommendation Concerning Cooperation Between Member Countries on Restrictive Business Practices Affecting International Trade, OECD Doc. C(79)154 (Final) (October 1979); 1998 Recommendation of the Council Concerning Effective Action Against Hard Core Cartels, OECD Doc. C(98)35 (Final) (May 13, 1998), available at http://www.oecd.org/dataoecd/39/4/2350130.pdf.

22. See Parisi, "Enforcement Cooperation among Antitrust Authorities," 691. ("As business concerns have increasingly pursued foreign trade and investment opportunities, antitrust compliance issues have arisen which transcend national borders and, thus, have led antitrust authorities in the affected jurisdictions to communicate, cooperate, and coordinate their efforts.")

23. See Andrew Guzman, "Antitrust and International Regulatory Federalism," *New York University Law Review* 76 (2001): 1156–58; Andrew Guzman, "Global Governance and the WTO," forthcoming, *Harvard International Law Journal* (2004). At least two of the chapters in this volume argue against the inclusion of competition policy in WTO negotiations. See Michael Trebilcock and Edward Iacobbucci (chapter 6 in this volume), 169–72; Paul B. Stephan, (chapter 3 in this volume), 75–81.

24. One could argue persuasively that the WTO's national treatment obligation in art. III:4 of the GATT applies to antitrust rules. I take no position on the applicability of this provision and simply note that the Doha Declaration's charge to the WTO Working Group in Trade and Competition Policy to consider nondiscrimination suggests that there is at least serious doubt about the applicability of the most-favored-nation (MFN) and national treatment clauses. See Ministerial Declaration, Doha WTO Ministerial 2001, par. 25.

25. See Guzman, "Antitrust and International Regulatory Federalism," 1162. Trebilcock, Iacobbucci, and McGinnis resist labeling a nondiscrimination provision substantive harmonization, although it is hard to know what else to call an obligation that forbids states from adopting substantive rules or practices that favor locals over foreigners.

26. See, for example, Michael J. Trebilcock and Robert Howse, *The Regulation of International Trade*, 2nd ed. (London/New York: Routledge, 1999), 147. ("[I]f countries generally feel committed to adopting more stringent health, safety, consumer protection, environmental or conservation standards . . . they remain largely free to do so, subject to demonstrating that there is some rational scientific basis for their actions . . . and that such measures do not gratuitously encumber international trade.")

27. Ministerial Declaration, Doha WTO Ministerial 2001, par. 25.

28. See John McGinnis (chapter 5 in this volume), 144 (supporting the notion that nations should be required to "permit the extraterritorial application of another nation's laws, at least on the same antitrust theories deployed by the nation whose producers are the target of antitrust enforcement").

29. For example, a firm proposing to merge might be required to seek approval for the merger from only one or two states (perhaps its home states or the state with the most affected consumers), and the same forms could then be submitted (with translations if necessary) to authorities in other states who would have the option of requesting further submissions.

5

The Political Economy of International Antitrust Harmonization

John O. McGinnis

Many academics have called for harmonization of the substantive content of antitrust laws, and the World Trade Organization (WTO), through the Doha Round, is taking tentative steps in that direction. In my view, substantive harmonization—even if limited to core competition standards—would be a major mistake. While multiple regimes undoubtedly impose some of the costs that commentators have decried (such as high transaction costs and a substantial risk of parochial bias), substantive harmonization is hardly cost free. An international lawmaking regime is less subject to democratic control and discourages beneficial change. The lock-in costs of an international regime are particularly high in a fast-changing world. Advocates of substantive antitrust harmonization have so far failed to show why substantive harmonization will cure the defects of a decentralized regime, without introducing new and potentially more serious ones.

A more persuasive form of harmonization would look to international antidiscrimination standards rather than international substantive standards. As it happens, the WTO already applies antidiscrimination rules that focus on preventing foreign bias in regulations that affect importers, as opposed to engaging in substantive harmonization of national rules. Thus, if domestic competition regimes harbor foreign bias, we should add an antidiscrimination antitrust code to make the WTO's general prohibition against discriminatory regulations more effective in the antitrust context, just as previous rounds of the General Agreement on Tariffs and Trade (GATT) have produced separate agreements that make national treatment principles more comprehensive and concrete in such contexts as the regulation of food and in technical regulation of products.[1] Such an anti-discrimination code would advance values integral to the WTO as well as to competition law. Foreign bias in competition laws is likely to become a greater problem as the WTO clears away other trade restrictions, because interest groups will substitute discriminatory competition laws as other protectionist barriers decline. The need to protect the efficacy of the WTO's elimination of overt trade restrictions is a neglected rationale for policing domestic antitrust law—and is the reason why, unlike Paul Stephan, I do not favor complete autarky in international antitrust law.

Compared to substantive harmonization of antitrust laws, an international antidiscrimination regime will have several advantages. First, it will preserve substantive diversity and experimentation. Second, it will avoid many public choice problems that likely render substantive harmonization suboptimal. Third, an antidiscrimination model comports with the rest of WTO jurisprudence and, if located there, will benefit from its already established institutional structure, including a sophisticated jurisprudence for ferreting out discriminatory laws. Unlike substantive rules, an antidiscrimination model will not require substantial transformation of WTO institutions—changes that would be counterproductive to the rest of the WTO regime. As I describe below, such antidiscrimination rules should nevertheless be limited in scope, incremental in application, and sensitive to issues of institutional design.

Traditional Arguments for Substantive Antitrust Harmonization

The case for international harmonization of substantive competition law has traditionally rested on two arguments. First, in a world of multinational corporations, multiple antitrust regimes raise transaction costs. Second, in a world with extraterritorial application of antitrust laws, the most restrictive antitrust laws will govern business behavior. Neither of these arguments, however, attempts to compare the costs of diverse antitrust laws to the costs of harmonization. Even if uncoordinated national regimes are inefficient, it does not follow that an international regime will be more efficient.[2] The debate over substantive harmonization thus should center on whether the decisions under a harmonized law system are likely to prove better than the sum of the legal applications of diverse systems. While my analysis assumes that economic efficiency should be the exclusive goal of antitrust law, other objectives would be subject to a similar public choice inquiry to determine whether centralization is more likely to retard than advance these objectives.

The Political Economy of Domestic Antitrust. In developed nations, several factors tend to make competition law depart from a consumer welfare ideal. Foremost, government antitrust officials have an interest in an excessively interventionist antitrust policy.[3] A more interventionist policy allows them to gain more rents. In return for enforcing the antitrust law against a particular company, officials can gain rents from its competitors.[4] Bureaucrats also have an interest in the larger budgets and staff attendant to more interventionist policies. Larger budgets and staff both bring more prestige and postbureaucratic employment opportunities, as interventionist policies require more consultants and lawyers to handle the effects of such policies on behalf of corporations. The rationally ignorant public confronts large agency costs in monitoring public officials. The technical nature of competition law tends to exacerbate that general difficulty.

Broadly speaking, campaign contributions and other benefits of excessive intervention will tend to affect elected officials, while the desire for prestige and employment opportunities will tend to affect the permanent bureaucracy. Legislators can extract rents by setting up a system that permits excessive intervention because they can use legislative hearings and the budget process to influence regulatory and enforcement proceedings.[5] Moreover, even if *legislators* were motivated entirely by the public interest, antitrust statutes cannot be written like a code, because no code can capture all anticompetitive business practices.[6] Thus, *regulators* inevitably enjoy substantial discretion to shape the interpretation of antitrust statutes to pursue their own interests.

The judiciary's ability to restrain regulators can also be limited. First, regulators often render judicial review ineffective. For instance, particularly in Europe, regulators can block a merger. By the time effective judicial review can reverse that decision, business considerations may well have forced a termination of the merger.[7] Second, the judiciary often defers to regulators, because judges incur costs in standing up aggressively to the democratically elected branches—particularly when the law, like antitrust law, does not provide bright-line rules. The tendency toward self-aggrandizement that drives bureaucrats is also not unknown in the judiciary. For instance, the prospect of transforming and supervising an entire industry—as Judge Harold Greene did with the phone industry—cannot be discounted as a possible distorting motive.[8]

Besides rent seeking, the mismatch between the short-time horizons of politics and the longtime horizons of markets may lead to excessive antitrust intervention. The central question in antitrust is whether government intervention will correct anticompetitive practices better than the market itself.[9] In the long run, the market erodes wealth-decreasing cartels and monopolies. But humans have a heuristic bias that causes them to discount long-run facts.[10] Political actors will thus tend to underestimate the likelihood that markets will destabilize cartels and monopolies.

The Political Economy of International Antitrust. The factors that distort national antitrust laws shed light on the question of whether internationally harmonized antitrust will prove better. In my view, an international regime would likely generate higher agency costs, while depriving us of distinctive benefits of a diversified regime.

In a political context, international harmonization can become the song of the oligarchs. Because agency costs are likely to be higher at an international level, bureaucrats will have more ability to fashion more interventionary rules. First, average citizens will find the international process even more opaque than the domestic process; their monitoring costs are much higher.[11] Second, more rents are available on a global scale. If business groups can manipulate international intervention in their favor, they can disable a whole world's worth of competitors.[12] Third, international antitrust regulators become a distinct class with a distinctive interest—that of growing the international antitrust apparatus—that is not likely to mirror the interests of national governments, let alone citizens. As a result, rules and standards fashioned at an international level may be more excessively interventionist than those of any major nation.

The costs of an international harmonized regime also depend on whether an international agency enforces international competition law directly or whether nations themselves enforce the international standards. The enforcement of international standards by individual countries would allow nations, over time, to diverge dramatically in their application of the standards. Even within a single nation, the judiciary has interpreted essentially the same antitrust law with spectacularly different results in different eras. The results would surely be as disparate in different nations, as the interpretation of international standards will be influenced by the preexisting substratum law of competition.[13]

In contrast, direct enforcement of international norms by international bureaucrats would be without precedent. Any new regime has start-up costs; the lack of appropriate traditions, rules, and institutions will produce errors. Furthermore, an international corps of decision makers will depend ultimately on the support of national governments. International bureaucrats will need to take the national identity of actors into account in making decisions, thus distorting agreed-upon competition principles. They may lack the political legitimacy to make decisions stick when a powerful nation vehemently disagrees.

Most distressingly, direct enforcement would necessitate changes in the constitutional structures of nation-states. For instance, the U.S. Constitution represents a serious obstacle to giving international institutions the authority to render decisions that would directly affect U.S. citizens.[14] Changing the applicable constitutional provisions would require a constitutional amendment process and, moreover, might well destabilize constitutional norms that serve to ameliorate public choice problems (for example, by ensuring an accountable executive and an independent judiciary). Even if these constraints are worth relaxing for the cause of antitrust harmonization, that step may create costs in other areas where the price is not worth paying.

The Costs and Benefits of (De)Centralization. It might be argued that antitrust law can hardly get worse: In a globalized but decentralized world, the most restrictive system already governs. For reasons just noted, though, agency problems may make international standards more excessively interventionist than those of any major nation. Even in a globalized world, moreover, some nations will lack jurisdiction to apply their antitrust law. For instance, a merger with implications for the United States and Asia may not affect Europe. In that case, the most restrictive antitrust regime (assuming it is Europe's) will *not* govern, because only the United States and Asian nations have jurisdiction. We would have to compare the sum of the antitrust applications in a decentralized system to that of the harmonized system.

More importantly, a diversified regime creates opportunities for legal innovation and change. In a rapidly changing world, we should preserve some process by which excessively restrictive regimes may undergo transformation.

Commentators have rightly noted that jurisdictional competition will not smoothly and routinely optimize domestic antitrust laws. Because of its extraterritorial reach, a nation can apply its competition law to firms that do not choose to locate there, and firms thus cannot exit to put pressure on the antitrust law to become more optimal. Conversely, if firms could choose their antitrust law without regard to their domicile, some might choose the least restrictive regime—which may well prove suboptimal.[15] Still, one should not dismiss the possibility that jurisdictional competition will do some good. Antitrust law, like business and tax law, affects business conditions, and nations will prosper insofar as they have good antitrust rules, at least as applied to purely domestic transactions. While they may then choose to discriminate and apply worse law to antitrust practices in order to help domestic producers at the expense of foreign producers or consumers, such a strategy can be policed by an antidiscrimination rather than a substantive antitrust regime.

Moreover, even in the absence of the formal conditions for efficient jurisdictional competition, a decentralized regime will foster innovation and the debate that it engenders. The harsh criticism of the European Union's (EU's) merger laws in the wake of the blocked GE/Honeywell merger, for example, appears to have prompted changes in the EU regime.[16] Of course, academics can critique antitrust law at any point, but the question is whether anyone will listen. Open conflicts can focus the attention of the press and other elites outside government circles on the wisdom of government antitrust intervention. Such focal points of criticism would be lost with harmonization.

Such focused criticism is very valuable, because revolutions in social thought and changing political institutions sometimes can upset the tendency in industrial democracies toward excessively interventionist policies. The U.S. antitrust revolution of the 1980s is a clear case in point. Some might suggest that centralized institutions today could take advantage of the growing knowledge of the benefits of Chicago School antitrust learning, disseminated by graduate students the world over. But public choice analysis suggests that knowledge is not a sufficient condition for good antitrust decision making.[17] The decision makers need to have the right motivation. Conflicts will give academic views salience among the press and other elites, constraining decision makers whose utility will not otherwise be maximized by correct decisions.

The need for continually innovative perspectives on antitrust law is especially important because the comparative advantage of government intervention depends on how swiftly the market will correct for super-competitive prices in the absence of intervention.[18] The effectiveness of the market process depends on transportation, information costs, and trade restrictions, and the appropriate set of rules authorizing government antitrust intervention will vary correspondingly. Thus, the optimal shape of antitrust rules, like market prices themselves, is always changing. An international regime faces a higher degree of stasis because the transaction costs of getting agreement from almost all nations in the world to change the rules are higher than those of getting change from a single nation.[19] If, however, one were to delegate substantial discretion to international bureaucrats, their power would exacerbate the problem of agency costs.

The Failure of Domestic Antitrust to Take Foreign Interests into Account

Andrew Guzman, a leading proponent of substantive antitrust coordination, argues that nations will systematically fail to take account of the interests of foreign producers and foreign consumers. Application of antitrust law under national systems will be suboptimal, because nations will neglect the interests of foreign companies and, hence, not even attempt to maximize consumer and producer welfare. A country with only exporters of a product and no consumers of that product will turn a blind eye to anti-competitive practices that detract from consumer welfare. Conversely, nations with only consumers and no producers will ignore foreign producers' profits in reviewing corporate transactions.

Guzman's arguments represent the most comprehensive attempt to show that a structure of international competition law, or least substantive international principles, will represent an improvement over the present decentralized regime. First, the objective sought—that antitrust laws should be applied without respect to nationality—is a modest one that may well command consensus. Second, the claim that domestic antitrust laws neglect foreign interests has a ring of truth. Third, as global trade increases, and as corporate actions affect more and more foreign producers and foreign consumers, it is at least superficially plausible that national indifference to external effects has large costs. If the world were to move toward a single antitrust law enforced by an international organization, parochial bias might be substantially reduced, just as the federal enforcement of antitrust laws in the United States has reduced concern about state bias.

The tendency to neglect foreign interests can produce two kinds of divergences from the competition law that a nation would have chosen in the absence of trade. First, it may result in either de jure or de facto exceptions to the antitrust laws. Export cartels are a conspicuous example of such "exception divergences." Second, a nation might change its general antitrust principles from what it would optimally deploy in a closed economy.[20] If a nation consumed less than it produced and did not distinguish antitrust laws by sectors, it would tend to have weaker antitrust laws than it would in a closed economy, because antitrust laws protect consumers while depriving producers of monopoly profits. This tendency would be particularly pronounced if the nation exported imperfectly competitive products (such as pharmaceuticals), because monopoly profits from exports would redound to the nation's benefit. Conversely, if a nation consumed more than it produced, it might tend to have stronger laws than it would in a closed economy. This tendency would be particularly pronounced if the nation exported perfectly competitive products, because antitrust laws would not affect those anyway. I will call this kind of divergence "distortion divergence."

Guzman suggests that cooperation on substantive international antitrust provides a potential solution to both kinds of divergence because international rules and enforcement would have no reason to discriminate on a parochial basis. In my view, however, in some circumstances, bias may be less of a problem than Guzman's formal model suggests. Moreover, in other circumstances, bias might even compensate for other public choice problems of antitrust, paradoxically leading to more optimal competition laws. And, even assuming that local enforcement is suboptimal, harmonizing substantive international antitrust rules may sacrifice so much in experimentation and potential for beneficial transformation that the costs may outweigh the benefits.

Exception Divergences. Guzman is certainly correct that antitrust will sometimes be deployed systematically to consider only local interests and will be biased against foreign interests in some circumstances. Exception divergences will result from laws that discriminate on their face. Congress, for instance, has exempted export cartels from the reach of antitrust laws and may be influenced by the predominance of exporter interests in exempting certain sectors from antitrust altogether.[21] There is no reason to believe that the executive and the judiciary will not vigorously enforce laws that call for such discrimination

But many antitrust laws are neutral on their face, particularly in that they do not discriminate among foreign and domestic producers.[22] When the laws themselves are neutral, it is not so clear that foreign interests will be slighted, because the legal institutions charged with enforcing the rules may not be as subject to parochial bias as legislators.

Assume that the United States has only consumers of a product. Will our antitrust system fail to take account of producer surplus of foreign companies in deciding whether to challenge a merger? Not necessarily. First, classifying the nationality of multinational corporations is often difficult. Such firms have shareholders and employees around the world; thus government decision makers would often take some substantial account of their interests. Second, advanced industrial democracies such as the United States have developed formal rules and a legal culture that require decision makers to consider only those criteria that the law makes relevant. Thus, the judiciary, and to some extent the bureaucracy, will be constrained to take foreign interests into account so long as the law does not formally eliminate them from consideration.

In fact, the Antitrust Enforcement Guidelines for International Operations issued by the U.S. Department of Justice make clear that unless the law otherwise requires, "the agencies do not discriminate in enforcement of the antitrust laws on the basis of the nationality of the parties."[23] Of course, decision makers may still slight foreign interests, but it is not entirely clear what mechanism will guide them. Bureaucrats have craft interests that militate against blatant favoritism, and judicial review often offers some protection. In the United States, at least, institutional screens reduce the risk of bias in cases involving the anticompetitive conduct of foreign companies.

Now assume that the United States has only producers of a product and no consumers: Will antitrust fail to intervene to protect foreign consumer interests? Here, there is more reason for concern. Federal law suggests that the interest of foreign consumers need not be taken into account in most circumstances, and the Antitrust Enforcement Guidelines for International Operations confirm this stance.[24] Even in the absence of such a direction, in initiating a prosecution, bureaucrats must take account of budgetary constraints. In the context of case selection, bias may be more likely to creep in because it is less obvious. Moreover, because there is no judicial review of a failure to take action, the judiciary will not be a bulwark against bias.

Still, bias against foreign interests will not necessarily make antitrust laws depart from an economically optimal regime.[25] Indeed, such foreign bias may counteract public choice biases against wealth-maximizing laws and, thus, improve competition law. Suppose that prosecutors in the United States give greater weight to producer interests (when they are primarily domestic) and less weight to consumer interests (when they are foreign) than is justified by the letter of the law (or official policy). In that event, parochial bias may push toward optimal antitrust enforcement by making prosecutors less likely to go after monopolies and other commercial practices in the marginal case, where public choice factors may otherwise lead to overenforcement.

One might suggest that the bias against foreign interests would have the opposite effects when the United States has almost all the consumers and few of the producers of a product. For instance, in deciding whether to allow a merger initiated by a foreign corporation, administrators' tendency to disallow the merger because of bias toward overenforcement may be exacerbated by a bias against foreign producer interests. But there are relatively few examples of laws that are biased on their face against producers, and foreign bias can be constrained when neutral laws are enforced by an impartial judiciary. Without a careful investigation of public choice and institutional factors, one cannot really measure the extent to which exception divergence moves us away from the optimal enforcement of neutral antitrust laws. Only when we make our models institutionally rich can we assess the degree of damage that a diverse antitrust regime will inflict through the tendency toward bias against foreign interests.

Distortion Divergences. Distortion divergence is supported by less empirical evidence than exception divergence. In fact, there are some reasons to doubt that it is more than a theoretical possibility. First, a nation's balance between production and consumption changes as does the mixture of goods it exports. Nations are unlikely to change antitrust law to follow changing patterns of consumption and production: The transaction costs are too high. Second, antitrust law does not appear to track the predictions of Guzman's model. Developed nations that export imperfectly competitive goods tend to have more interventionist laws than developing nations. The theory suggests the reverse.

Even if distortion divergences exist, it is not clear whether they will make antitrust law better or worse. If, as I have suggested, developed nations tend to deploy excessively interventionist competition laws and developing nations tend to have excessively lenient competition laws, trade is likely to make the laws better than they would be under a closed economy. For instance, because of their export of imperfectly competitive goods, developed nations will adopt laws that are less suboptimally stringent than they otherwise would be.

In the end, Guzman's sophisticated model is subject to the objections that apply to traditional arguments for substantive coordination: It is not at all clear that the costs of parochialism are as high as might be initially assumed. These costs, moreover, must be weighed against the cost of substantive harmonization—which, as noted, may be quite high.

Antidiscrimination Antitrust

Beyond the confines of antitrust law, the world trade regime already contains a rationale and a structure for opposing discrimination in antitrust law. As WTO agreements progressively reduce tariff barriers, nations are likely to use discriminatory competition laws as a nontariff barrier. This likely substitution by special interests, although never discussed in the debates over antitrust harmonization, is in my view the best reason for an antidiscrimination antitrust regime.

I stress that my support for an antidiscrimination antitrust regime based on a trade rationale is nevertheless limited in scope, incremental in application, and sensitive to issues of institutional design. WTO enforcement of such rules should, at least at first, be limited to discrimination that creates a nontarriff barrier substitute for tariff barriers such as antitrust rules that discriminate in market access. Second, until evidence develops that antitrust laws are applied in a discriminatory manner, the antidiscrimination rules should apply only to expressly discriminatory laws. Third, if the WTO expands its antidiscrimination regime to include discriminatory application of antitrust laws, it should consider ways of assuring nondiscrimination through domestic institutions rather than increasing the power of WTO tribunals. For instance, the antidiscrimination regime might provide a safe harbor for nations that have administrative directives not to discriminate on the basis of nationality and an independent judiciary. This differential institutional scrutiny would decrease the need for international oversight while giving nations incentives to build institutions that protect against foreign bias.

An antidiscrimination antitrust regime, put into the existing WTO system, has several advantages over substantive harmonization. First, it would preserve diversity of antitrust approaches. Conflicts on the substance of antitrust law could still occur, generating publicity and cutting through agency costs. Better norms could thus still evolve from the debate that diversity may engender. Second, neither the formulation nor the enforcement of antidiscrimination rules would be subject to the peculiarly high agency costs and other public choice problems involved in choosing substantive rules. Third, insofar as discrimination is a problem in international antitrust, it justifies a nondiscrimination regime, not a substantive regime. Thus, invigorating the WTO antidiscrimination model to combat discriminatory antitrust law provides an international framework that is just sufficient, and no more intrusive than necessary, to address the problem of discrimination.

The Shape and Logic of a WTO Antidiscrimination Regime. Generally, the WTO requires its members not to discriminate against other members in their regulatory regimes, but refrains from imposing substantive restrictions on the content of regulation. For an antidiscrimination regime, the WTO thus affords a better institutional match than other possible institutions, such as the United Nations Conference on Trade and Development or the Organisation for Economic Co-operation and Development. Moreover, an antidiscrimination antitrust regime will not set an unfortunate precedent for substantive regulatory rule making by the WTO.[26]

The WTO creates a structure for liberating world trade by creating a reciprocal relation between tariff reductions domestically and those in other countries. In that fashion, the WTO changes the constellation of political interests at play in debates over tariff reductions.[27] Because exporter groups gain from low tariffs, they will enter the political struggle against the protectionist interest groups at home, thus virtually representing the public's interest in wealth-enhancing free trade.[28] Thus, the WTO blunts the ability of protectionist interest groups to obstruct lower tariffs that would benefit the majority of citizens in their countries.[29] Under this view, the WTO is a regime that facilitates democratic choice within individual states even as it increases wealth by decreasing tariff barriers.

Interest groups, however, tend to substitute more subtle nontariff barriers for the reduced tariffs. Discriminatory health and safety regulation is a well-known example, and much of the current WTO dispute settlement regime is aimed at preventing such discriminatory regulation.[30] By that same logic, the WTO should prohibit discriminatory antitrust laws that interfere with market access. Otherwise, protectionist interest groups will frustrate the effect of tariff reductions. Exporter groups will lack *ex ante* incentives to fight for lower tariffs in their home country if they recognize that their reciprocal gains abroad can be reduced by foreign competition laws that discriminate against their market access. An example of discriminatory antitrust regulations that impede market access includes discriminatory restrictions that prevent importing companies from integrating vertically with domestic companies, if such mergers would facilitate competition against domestic companies. Other discriminatory practices include refusing to apply rules against boycotts for the benefit of foreign companies, as well as a domestic requirement of providing competitors "an essential facility," even while giving domestic companies the advantages of such rules.

While Article III of the GATT—containing the national treatment requirement—already provides protection in some instances, it fails to reach all discriminatory antitrust legislation that could interfere with market access.[31] In particular, Article III requires only that a member nation refrain from providing less favorable treatment to foreign "like products." Under that rule, a nation could apply its competition law differently depending on the product at issue, so long as it applied the competition law equally to industries making the same product. For instance, if the new low-cost provider of a product were a foreign import, a nation might well permit boycotts and other anticompetitive measures to frustrate all new entrants, both domestic and foreign, of this product, because the actual incidence of the anticompetitive practice would fall mostly on the foreign imports. This may well be permissible even if the nation were not to permit such practices in other industries making different products, because it would not be discriminating against foreign and domestic producers of "like product." A WTO panel actually gave this limited but defensible reading to Article III when it held that Japan had not discriminated against U.S. photographic film producers, because its competition law treated Japanese film producers in the same way.[32] The panel failed to explore, however, whether Japan was applying its competition law in the photographic film industry as it does in other industries. The problem of divergent application of antitrust law driven by foreign bias is likely to become a bigger problem as the General Agreement in Trade in Services reduces other kinds of barriers in an increasing number of service sectors.

If evidence develops of widespread instances of such discrimination in application, a new antitrust code within the WTO can require that antitrust laws be applied consistently, at least within the same industrial and service sectors. There is precedent for a consistency requirement within the WTO. For instance, the Sanitary and Phytosanitary Standards Agreement (SPS, the GATT agreement that governs food regulation) requires members to avoid "arbitrary or unjustifiable distinctions in the level [of protection it considers] to be appropriate in different situations, if such distinctions result in discrimination or a disguised restriction on international trade." A WTO competition agreement could deploy a similar consistency requirement, requiring nations not to arbitrarily vary their competition law depending on the products and services at issue. (As discussed below, such a requirement should be even easier to apply than the SPS consistency requirement.)[33] To avoid requiring the WTO dispute-resolution process to engage in unnecessary scrutiny, an agreement could create a strong presumption that a law is not discriminatory when nations have enforcement guidelines that do not distinguish among nationalities of corporations and when they have an independent judiciary to scrutinize the application of antitrust laws.

A thoroughgoing antidiscrimination antitrust model would admittedly conflict with the WTO regime's toleration of antidumping laws under certain conditions.[34] Antidumping laws generally permit tariffs to be raised on foreign imports if they are sold at a price lower than the price in their home country or lower than the cost of production. In contrast, domestic antitrust law often (as in the United States, for instance) permits suits against domestic companies only if their cost is lower than their cost of production and even then only under very specific circumstances. Because antidumping laws define predatory practices much less sensibly than antitrust law and are intended to protect competitors rather than competition, they are potentially subject to attack under a serious antidiscrimination antitrust regime that seeks to guarantee market access. For political reasons, it may be impossible to subject antidumping laws to the discipline of an antidiscrimination antitrust model. Nevertheless, it would be all to the good if an antidiscrimination antitrust regime eventually undermined GATT's tolerance of antidumping laws.

Finally, the WTO regime is best interpreted to permit nations to apply their antitrust laws to activities in other jurisdictions so long as those activities affect that jurisdiction. Permitting nations to regulate activities that affect their citizens (wherever those activities occur) is consistent with long-established legal norms and promotes regulations that will be more responsive to the interests of citizens than those generated by a distant international bureaucracy. In contrast, domestic authorities are not well positioned to assess the needs or views of foreign citizens, nor are they easily accountable for the effects of their decisions on foreigners. Thus, the WTO rationale and practice would suggest that nations have the authority to apply their competition laws extraterritorially so long as their regulation meets an effects test.

Minimizing Agency Costs. Antidiscrimination rules curtail the policy discretion of international decision makers. For that reason, antidiscrimination rules pose far fewer public choice problems than substantive rules.[35] In other contexts (such as health and safety regulation), the WTO enforces antidiscrimination principles through a variety of procedure-oriented rules. The WTO's antidiscrimination jurisprudence considers whether a nation's rules are transparent, consistently applied with respect to foreign and domestic producers, and avoid regulatory processes that are unnecessary to advance the regulations' objective.[36]

The transparency requirement does not require substantive judgments, yet it helps ensure that both foreign and domestic producers face similar compliance costs for antitrust regulations. Foreign firms may have greater difficulty complying with generally applicable regulations because domestic producers may better understand the opaque requirements of their own bureaucracy. Transparency helps level the regulatory playing field by ensuring that regulations are publicized and the steps for compliance are clear.[37]

Even transparent regulations can be unequally applied. Thus, the antidiscrimination regime should ensure that regulations are applied consistently. For example, if a nation enforced its law against cartels only among foreign producers, that practice would violate a nondiscrimination rule. Evaluating consistency within an industrial sector would not require a review of the substance of a nation's competition regulations—just a comparison of its treatment of foreign producers or consumers and its treatment of domestic producers or consumers.

This comparison should in fact be easier than similar comparisons undertaken by the WTO in evaluating health and safety regulations. In the latter context, a consistency evaluation requires identifying the true objectives of a vast array of regulations. For instance, in deciding whether an Australian regulation prohibiting the importation of salmon was discriminatory, the WTO compared the regulation with weaker regulations relating to domestic herring (which, the WTO concluded, posed higher risks.)[38] In the competition context, in contrast, nations tend to have somewhat more unified rules and objectives. Instead of conducting difficult and contestable comparisons among disparate regulations, international decision makers would only inquire whether a particular nation applies its competition law consistently across the range of product markets within an industrial sector. As already noted, a WTO Competition Code should adopt a stance of substantial deference to enforcement decisions if those decisions were made under neutral laws and reviewed domestically by an independent judiciary.

Nations might also adopt procedural requirements that do not serve their objectives but disproportionately burden foreign producers. Once again, the antidiscrimination regime could rely on WTO precedent and require a least-restrictive alternative to eliminate provisions extraneous to competition objectives. The review would not be deeply substantive (and thus would not be subject to public choice pathologies). It would not need to evaluate the merits of the competition objectives that the law served, only to make sure that the regulations actually served those objectives and not the cause of discrimination.[39]

Enforcement of WTO Antidiscrimination Competition Law Decisions. Because WTO tribunals are already familiar with applying a nondiscrimination jurisprudence, an extension of that regime would not require construction of a new and untested institution. Like the rest of the WTO regime, a Competition Code would also allow, except for discrimination issues, final responsibility for antitrust decisions to rest with officials of the country concerned, thus ameliorating fears that international decisions create a democratic deficit.

The WTO's dispute resolution system also minimizes enforcement problems. It requires international review of domestic decisions, avoiding the parochial interpretation of its principles that will over time lead to divergence. Yet, WTO rulings are binding only as a matter of international law. They have no direct effect, leaving the final decision to implement the ruling to member-states. Thus, the WTO permits domestic systems of constitutional accountability to work and avoids the substantial costs of direct implementation of international rulings.

The WTO nevertheless deploys a fairly effective method of gaining compliance with its rulings. If a nation fails to comply with a WTO ruling, the offended nation can generally seek to withdraw concessions from the offending nation in value equal to the harm caused by the violation of WTO rules. For instance, if a nation were found to have violated the (hypothetical) Competition Code by failing to afford a foreign market entrant the protection that it gave to domestic market entrants, the offended foreign nation would be authorized to raise its tariffs on a product of the offending nation in the amount of the value of the violation. Such sanctions will energize the exporters adversely affected by the sanctions to lobby their governments to comply with the WTO ruling.[40]

Limitations

Having described the operation and advantages of an international antidiscrimination regime for antitrust policy, I conclude by defining its scope. Two limitations merit discussion. First, in contrast to Trebilcock and Iacobucci's otherwise very similar proposal in this volume (see chapter 6), I conclude that dispute resolution under the WTO (or at least withdrawal of concessions authorized by dispute resolution) should be available only for violations of WTO Competition Code provisions that impair market access. For instance, Trebilcock and Iacobucci would subject domestic decisions to immunize export cartels to international antitrust enforcement; I, however, would not subject them to WTO dispute resolution. Second, international organizations should firmly resist calls for a "minimum harmonization" of substantive antitrust norms.

Market Access. Not all discriminatory laws relate to market access. For instance, a country could ignore foreign consumer welfare and permit export cartels while still prohibiting cartels that impose costs on its domestic consumers. With respect to such unfortunate and discriminatory (although nonexclusionary) practices, the WTO should create hortatory or educational practices and mechanisms for reform. The WTO has already created informal structures such as the Trade Review Mechanism, which encourages nations to improve their laws from a trade perspective. Along the same lines, a WTO competition committee could issue periodic reports and exercise peer review, thus creating pressure for nations to change their practices. Because of the WTO's experience in applying antidiscrimination rules, it may be a better forum for such reports than other organizations. However, discriminatory but nonexclusionary practices should *not* be subject to formal dispute resolution.

As noted, the WTO structure relies on exporters to lobby for lower tariffs in their own countries in return for concessions abroad. The prospect of future sanctions will reduce *ex ante* the value of these concessions and cause exporters to lobby less for the lowering of tariffs in their own countries. This cost is worth paying if, as I have argued, enforcing a prohibition on discriminatory regulation is necessary to prevent nations from substituting discriminatory regulations, including discriminatory antitrust regulations that affect market access, for tariff barriers. But if the discriminatory antitrust regulations do not affect market access (as when a nation permits export cartels at the expense of foreign consumers), the use of WTO sanctions to enforce a prohibition against such regulations will impose costs on a class of companies that can never receive benefits from the enforcement of such provisions. As a result, expanding the withdrawal of concessions beyond market access issues would tend to reduce the expected value of the WTO regime to exporters, thus diminishing their activism in support of reciprocal tariff reductions.[41]

No "Minimum Harmonization." The WTO's Doha Round could usefully provide a separate agreement devoted to antitrust law to make national treatment principles more comprehensive and concrete in the area of competition law. Unfortunately, though, the Doha agenda contemplates that all WTO members also be held to certain "core competition principles." In support of that project, it has been argued that nondiscrimination principles are not sufficient to force nations to treat foreign interests equally. Some countries, for instance, may choose to have no antitrust law because they want to help their producers at the expense of foreign consumers. Moreover, it may not be rational for a small country to have an antitrust law, because it will lack the clout to apply its competition law extraterritorially to protect its own consumers.[42]

An international agreement could address the latter objection by requiring nations to permit the extraterritorial application of another nation's laws, at least on the same antitrust theories deployed by the nation whose producers are the target of the antitrust enforcement. That principle would remove obstacles to the enforcement of domestic antitrust laws that derive from weaker nations' inability to enforce their rules extraterritorially. But nations should not be required to choose some particular form of antitrust law. Small or undeveloped nations may rationally choose a low level of antitrust enforcement for reasons wholly related to their domestic situation rather than to any foreign bias. Small nations may reasonably conclude that monopoly prices of both domestic and foreign products can be best constrained by foreign competition rather than by domestic antitrust intervention. (The smaller the size of a nation's market, the easier it is for a foreign company to redirect part of its supply to discipline any supercompetitive prices in that nation.)[43] Underdeveloped nations may rationally take account of their relatively weak institutional competence in assessing the likelihood that government intervention will lead to better results than market processes. Finally, in a variety of situations, *no* antitrust enforcement may be superior.[44] While it is easy to say that cartels are always bad, distinguishing a horizontal agreement that constitutes an anticompetitive cartel from one that may have market benefits is a matter of debate even under U.S. antitrust law. It is an advantage of a diversified system that some countries can test this or that regime, while others may study its fruits. The antidiscrimination model of antitrust harmonization, then, should exclude substantive harmonization even in the form of agreement on "core principles."

It is true that one WTO agreement, the Trade-Related Aspects of Intellectual Property Rights Agreement (TRIPS), does require WTO members to enforce core intellectual property principles. For instance, WTO members now have to offer basic copyright and patent protections. But the theoretical and practical reasons that support WTO-enforced intellectual property principles do not apply in the antitrust context. Some nations— for instance, a small developing nation with few, if any, inventors—have no incentives to provide any intellectual property laws at all. (Such countries might rationally decide to free ride on the inventions of others.)[45] All nations, however, have consumers—and, therefore, incentives to have antitrust laws. The incentives may not be perfect and may be affected by the mix of imported and exported goods, but that is true of all regulations. With the single exception of TRIPS, the WTO does not require nations to have a floor of substantive regulations but requires only that regulations be nondiscriminatory. In light of the public choice defects that afflict substantive international regulatory regimes, the usual WTO antidiscrimination model remains the proper framework for its antitrust regime.

The intensely pragmatic reasons for the inclusion of TRIPS are also inapplicable to antitrust standards. The developing world most wanted tariff reductions in textiles and agriculture where it often holds a comparative advantage. But it could only succeed in obtaining these reductions with the help of the most powerful exporters in the developed world, such as film producers and pharmaceutical companies. These exporters would not have been enthusiastic, however, about the prospect of increasing their exports to the developing world through reciprocal tariff reductions, if the developing world continued to expropriate what was in their view their intellectual property. Accordingly, the grand bargain at the heart of the Uruguay Round required nations, particularly developing nations, to adopt minimum standards for intellectual property in return for the agreement of developed nations to lower tariffs on textiles and agriculture.[46] Key export sectors are not demanding substantive harmonization as a price for making fundamental tariff reductions in the coming rounds of WTO talks.

Conclusion

Substantive antitrust harmonization is inadvisable because it has high agency costs and will reduce experimentation and innovation in antitrust that over the long run is likely to be beneficial. In contrast, an antidiscrimination antitrust model has fewer agency costs, particularly if it is conducted in the WTO, because the antidiscrimination precedent of the WTO will provide a stable guide to the development of antidiscrimination rules. The antidiscrimination regime will also allow continued beneficial experimentation and innovation in competition law. Insofar as this antidiscrimination regime helps police nations' denial of market access to importers, it will advance the goals of the WTO by inhibiting nations from substituting discriminatory competition regulations to negate the value of tariff reductions and other concessions that liberate trade.

Notes

1. World Trade Organization, Agreement on the Application of Sanitary and Phytosanitary Measures (Uruguay, 1994) vol. 27, http://www.wto.org/english/docs_e/legal_e/15-sps.pdf (hereinafter SPS agreement); World Trade Organization, Agreement on Technical Barriers to Trade (Uruguay, 1994) vol. 27, http://www.wto.org/english/docs_e/legal_e/17-tbt.pdf (hereinafter TBT agreement).

2. Moreover, some of the transaction costs of compliance with multiple laws can be reduced by nonsubstantive harmonization, such as enhanced cooperation among antitrust authorities. Steps for such procedural harmonization are already being taken bilaterally and multilaterally. See Spencer Weber Waller, "The Internationalization of Antitrust Enforcement," *Boston University Law Review* 77 (1997): 400.

3. Private enforcement is unlikely to correct for public choice bias in favor of excessive antitrust intervention. First, executive regulators tend to shape the law with their decisions on antitrust both because judges are more likely to defer to their judgments and because much private litigation simply piggybacks on their decisions. Second, private litigation has its own structural difficulties. Because private litigation can be filed by competitors as well as by consumers, much private litigation will attempt to advance theories that protect competitors rather than competition and so be excessively interventionist.

4. It is true that in refusing to exercise official discretion to enforce laws against a company, officials can obtain rents from that company, but to make that threat of enforcement credible, they have to intervene at times. See Fred S. McChesney, "Economics Versus Politics in Antitrust," *Harvard Journal of Law and Public Policy* 23 (1999): 134 (giving examples of political influence on antitrust enforcement).

5. See Michael P. Kenny and William H. Jordan, "United States v. Microsoft: Into the Antitrust Regulatory Vacuum Missteps the Department of Justice," *Emory Law Journal* 47 (1998): 1376 (detailing how Orrin Hatch, who was the home-state senator of many of Microsoft's competitors, tried to influence the Department of Justice to bring the Microsoft case).

6. For this reason, U.S. antitrust law uses a common law rather than code approach. See Christoper M. Barbuto, "Toward a Convergence of Antitrust and Trade Law: An International Trade Analogue to Robinson-Patman," *Fordham Law Review* 62 (1994): 2055. See also Alan J. Meese, "Price Theory, Competition, and the Rule of Reason," *Illinois Law Review* 1 (2003): 89–92 (explaining that *Standard Oil* in particular and Rule of Reason in general contemplate application of evolving economic theory in a manner that could produce changing treatment of various business practices).

7. See Eric S. Hochstadt, "The Brown Shoe of European Competition Law," *Cardozo Law Review* 24 (2002): 302 (suggesting that European regulators have substantial discretion because of lengthy time for judicial review of their decisions).

8. Harold Greene was called the czar of telecommunications during the pendency of his antitrust oversight. See Leslie Cauley, "Telecom Czar Frets Over New Industry Rules," *Wall Street Journal*, 12 February 1996, sec. B6.

9. See Frank H. Easterbrook, "The Limits of Antitrust," *Texas Law Review* 63 (1984): 2.

10. The representativeness heuristic tends to make people overconfidently extrapolate about predicted characteristics of a class from a small sample size of which they happen to be aware. See Amos Tversky and Daniel Kahneman, "Belief in the Law of Small Numbers," in *Judgement Uncertainty: Heuristic and Biases*, eds. Daniel Kahneman, Paul Slovi, and Amost Tversky (Cambridge: Cambridge University Press, 1982), 23. If the sample consists of events rather than objects, the heuristic should tend to make people extrapolate in a similarly irrational manner from events of which they are aware to uncertain future events. Thus, individuals will tend to think that future events will resemble past events more than probability warrants. See Kenneth Arrow, "Risk Perception in Psychology and Economics," *Economic Inquiry* 20 (1982): 5. For an important present-day application, see Robert Schiller, *Irrational Exuberance* (Princeton, N.J.: Princeton University Press, 2000) (using work on representativeness heuristic to suggest that people will think stock market patterns today will be those of tomorrow).

11. See Paul B. Stephan, "Accountability and International Lawmaking: Rules, Rents and Legitimacy," *Northwestern Journal of International Business* 17 (1996–97): 699–702.

12. Compare Frank Easterbrook, "The State of Madison's Vision of the State: A Public Choice Perspective," *Harvard Law Review* 107 (1994): 1337–38.

13. See Spencer Waller Weber, "Neo-Realism and International Harmonization of the Law: Lessons from Antitrust," *University of Kansas Law Review* 42 (1994): 559 .

14. See Jim Chen, "Appointments with Disaster: The Unconstitutionality of Binational Arbitral Review Under the United States-Canada Free Trade Agreement," *Washington and Lee Law Review* 49 (1992): 1456–67 (discussing the reasons that direct enforcement of the United States-Canada free trade agreement by international arbitrators violates Article II's Appointment Clause because international arbitrators are not appointed by the president).

15. See Andrew T. Guzman, "Antitrust and International Regulatory Federalism," *New York University Law Review* 76 (2001): 1148–49.

16. See, for example, remarks of Mario Monti, Commissioner for Competition Policy, "Feedback to the Green Paper: An Overview," at the Conference on Reform of European Merger Control, British Chamber of Commerce, Brussels, Belgium, (June 4, 2002) (acknowledging criticisms of European merger review process in setting forth reform proposals) (available at the European Commission website, http://europa.eu.int/comm).

17. See Alan J. Meese, "Farewell to the Quick Look: Reconstructing the Scope and Content of the Rule of Reason," *Antitrust Law Journal* 68 (2000): 486

(explaining that government simply ignored defendants' explanation of the virtues of the restraints involved in *TOPCO* and their reliance on sound economic theory already articulate in law review scholarship).

18. See Easterbrook, "The Limits of Antitrust," 2 (suggesting that the scope of antitrust should be limited to instances in which it has a comparative advantage over market-correcting forces).

19. See William J. Alceves, "Institutionalist Theory and International Legal Scholarship," *American International Law and Politics* 12 (1997): 244.

20. See Andrew T. Guzman, "International Antitrust and the WTO: The Lesson from Intellectual Property," *Virginia Journal of International Law* 43 (2003): 936.

21. See, for example, Webb-Pomerene Act, P. L. No. 65–126, 40 Stat. 516 (1918) (codified at 15 U.S.C. §§ 61–66 [1994]).

22. It is interesting to speculate why Congress does not overtly discriminate between foreign and domestic companies in merger laws. A possible answer is that blatant discrimination would invite retaliation against U.S. companies. U.S. companies might thus lobby against such discrimination. In contrast, American consumers are a diffuse group and are not in a position to prevent discrimination against foreign consumers, even if such discriminatory U.S. law were to encourage foreign nations to discriminate against foreign consumers in their own competition laws. See note 21 and accompanying text.

23. See Antitrust Enforcement Guidelines for International Operations, U.S. Department of Justice and the Federal Trade Commission (April 1995) at p. 3, www.usdoj.gov/atr/public/guidelines/internat.htm.

24. See Foreign Trade Antitrust Improvements Act, 15 U.S.C. 6(a) 1994; Antitrust Enforcement Guidelines for International Operations, 9–15 (requiring an effect on U.S. commerce or U.S. producers to assert U.S. antitrust jurisdiction).

25. As Guzman acknowledges. See Andrew T. Guzman, "Is International Antitrust Possible?" *New York University Law Review* 73 (1998): 1531.

26. Others have argued that another advantage of placing antitrust law in the WTO would be the possibility of bargains. Nations that would be made worse off by antitrust harmonization can trade it for other items (that is, lower tariffs, stricter enforcement of an antidumping regime) that they would prefer but that other countries would not. See, for example, Guzman, "Antitrust and International Regulatory Federalism," 1157.

27. See John H. Jackson, *The World Trading System: Law and Policy of International Economic Relations* (Cambridge: MIT Press, 2002), 157–74 (discussing the reciprocal nature of the most favored nation obligation of the WTO).

28. See John O. McGinnis and Mark L. Movsesian, "The World Trade Constitution," *Harvard Law Review* 114 (2000): 545 (noting that producers who enjoy a comparative advantage gain new markets when foreign countries reduce tariffs, which creates incentive for such producers to lobby for lower tariffs in their own countries).

29. Ibid., 546.

30. Ibid., 566–72 (explaining the antidiscrimination model of the WTO).

31. Article III does not interfere at all with discriminatory laws that do not affect market access, because it is only concerned with discrimination related to the sale of foreign products. Thus, a decision to exempt industries that exempt exports from foreign consumers from the antitrust laws would not violate Article III.

32. See World Trade Organization, "Japan—Measures Affecting Consumer Photographic Film and Paper," *Report of the Panel*, WT/DS44/R §§10.378–10.382 (March 31, 1998).

33. Even this more muscular requirement will not ensure market access if a nation refuses to punish anticompetitive behavior even when directed against some of its own producers. But in that case, these domestic producers would be a lobbying force against the denial of market access and likely improve the substantive content of domestic competition law.

34. See Wesley A. Cann, Jr., "Internationalizing Views Toward Recoupment and Market Power: Attacking the Antidumping Dichotomy through WTO-consistent Global Welfare Theory," *University of Pennsylvania Journal of Internal Economic Law* 17 (1996): 231 (describing tension between antitrust and antidumping law).

35. See McGinnis and Movsesian, "World Trade Constitution," 566–67.

36. For fuller discussion of this jurisprudence, see McGinnis and Movsesian, "World Trade Constitution," 572–81.

37. See Edward A. Laing, "Equal Access/Non-Discrimination in International Economic Law," *Wisconsin International Law Journal* 14 (1996): 296.

38. World Trade Organization, "Australia—Measure Affecting Importation of Salmon," *Appellate Body Report*, WT/DS18/AB/R §§ 154–58, http://www.wto/org/english/tratop_e/dispu_ds/18abr.doc.

39. See Alan O. Sykes, "Regulatory Protectionism and the Law of International Trade," *University of Chicago Law Review* 66 (1999): 25 (noting that the least-restrictive means test allows governments to pursue their chosen objectives).

40. See Mark L. Movsesian, "Enforcement of WTO Ruling: An Interest Group Analysis" (paper on file with author). Admittedly, there is risk that nations will nevertheless refuse to comply with the WTO ruling and, in that event, innocent exporters will have been penalized with no result. So far, however, withdrawal of concessions and the threat of such withdrawal have been fairly successful.

41. It is true that some exporters might in any event expect that they will fail to benefit from the dispute resolution process, because they know from their position that they will be likely targets of sanctions. Still, the fact that some exporters operate under a less-than-perfect veil of ignorance is no reason to extend the dispute resolution regime to provisions that exporters know are of no help to them. It is also true that some provisions of the GATT that were necessary concessions to obtain tariff reductions, especially the permission for

antidumping laws, do not help exporters at all. Even in this context, however, the dispute resolution system serves the interests of exporters, because it enforces the GATT's limits on the scope of permissible antidumping laws.

42. See Guzman, "Antitrust and International Regulatory Federalism," 1153.

43. See A. E. Rodriguez and Mark D. Williams, "The Effectiveness of Proposed Antitrust Programs for Developing Countries," *North Carolina Journal of International Law and Commercial Regulation* 19 (1994): 218 (Competition from imports "is a countervailing force against whatever power domestic firms may have to raise prices above the competitive and socially efficient level.").

44. See Lino A. Graglia, "Is Antitrust Obsolete?" *Harvard Journal of Law and Public Policy* 23 (1999): 21 (arguing that in many instances antitrust law does more harm than good).

45. See John Duffy, "Harmony and Diversity in Global Patent Law," *Berkeley Technical Law Journal* 17 (2002): 698–99 (explaining the international externalities of intellectual property systems that justify TRIPS).

46. See, for example, Jayashree Watal, *Intellectual Property Rights in the WTO and Developing Countries* (The Hague: Kluwer Law International, 2001), 9–47 (discussing this bargain).

6

National Treatment and Extraterritoriality: Defining the Domains of Trade and Antitrust Policy

Michael J. Trebilcock and Edward M. Iacobucci

In an increasingly integrated global economy, a multiplicity of national competition policies is costly. First, there are enforcement costs. These include the additional costs that antitrust authorities incur when investigating conduct in other jurisdictions, as well as the additional costs from attempting to enforce their orders extraterritorially. Enforcement costs also include the higher transaction costs that accrue to parties from complying with the laws of several jurisdictions. Prenotification of mergers, for example, can become a substantial burden when many different laws require different information or entail different decision time lines.

Additional costs arise from the effect on substantive laws from the interaction of trade and competition policies. Countries may strategically distort antitrust policies in order to capture a larger share of the surplus in a supranational market even at the expense of reducing the overall surplus. An obvious example is the exemption for export cartels in several countries, including Canada and the United States. (Export cartels earn supracompetitive profits at the expense of foreign consumers, increasing domestic but harming global welfare.) Thus—proponents of international harmonization of competition laws argue—divergent domestic competition laws impose major economic costs on firms that are active in international markets. In addition, domestic laws likely entail distortions that reduce global economic welfare.

All true. Yet, it is hardly self-evident that domestic competition laws (relative to other domestic laws) create distortions that require *special* efforts at international harmonization. Firms trading into or investing in a foreign market must comply with foreign laws and policies relating to taxation, health and safety, environmental protection, employment, labeling, and civil rights. All those rules will diverge from the laws and policies that prevail in a corporation's home jurisdictions and in many other jurisdictions in which the company may choose to trade or invest. Why, then, is competition law special? Why should a foreign firm trading into or investing in the United States have any greater right to complain that U.S. antitrust law on horizontal or vertical arrangements is more stringent than in their home jurisdiction or in other jurisdictions in which they do business, relative to a variety of other distinctive domestic laws that they will have to comply with in the United States? Similarly, why should U.S. firms seeking to trade or to invest in, for example, Japan have any greater right to complain of laxer Japanese competition laws on horizontal arrangements or vertical restraints than apply to U.S. firms at home, relative to a variety of other Japanese laws that impose distinctive requirements on firms doing business in Japan (for example, large-store laws, store opening hours, labeling laws)?

On the assumption that nation-states have chosen laws or policies that are in their own public interest, requiring them to abandon or modify these laws and to adopt internationally harmonized policies is likely to reduce national welfare and to have an ambiguous impact on global welfare. Where public choice factors explain the adoption of domestic laws or policies that reduce both global and domestic welfare, international trade regimes may facilitate their mitigation through reciprocal tariff and related concessions that enlist export interests as a political counterweight to domestic import-sensitive interests and through the reciprocal adoption of a principle of nondiscrimination or "national treatment." Short of abandoning any notion of national sovereignty, though, and short of assigning a very large role to supranational institutions—as in the European Union (EU)—in negotiating and mandating harmonization of a vast array of policy domains, costs from divergent policies are simply a fact of life in a world of nation-states. While multiple compliance costs do represent a kind of "tax" on the international movement of goods, services, capital, and people, requiring states to forgo policy autonomy—beyond constraints on discriminatory application of domestic laws to foreigners—may entail significant domestic welfare losses.[1]

Here, we review the benefits of having localized antitrust policies and focus on the role of national treatment and extraterritoriality in addressing the costs from self-interested competition policies. We further suggest that the extraterritorial application of domestic antitrust law can be desirable from a domestic and global perspective, but that it requires some organizing principles.[2] First, domestic laws should adhere to the national treatment principle enshrined in Article III of the General Agreement on Tariffs and Trade (GATT). Consistency with national treatment avoids many of the blatant beggar-thy-neighbor applications of domestic competition policy, but not all. Second, when there is a genuine conflict between laws (as opposed to a conflict resulting from a violation of national treatment), resolution of this conflict should build on the principles that animate competition and trade policies. The former requires an examination of where consumers are alleged to suffer harm; the latter looks to harm to producers.

National Treatment

The attraction of national treatment as a principle to govern domestic competition policies is best understood in light of the costs and benefits of maintaining distinctive local competition policies. That is, why do policies diverge in the first place? The best place to start the analysis is to ask what competition policies countries would adopt in an autarkic (closed economy) world, and then ask how a liberal international trade and investment regime may influence countries to change competition policies that they deemed optimal in autarky.[3]

In autarky, it seems reasonable to assume that public-interested governments would adopt competition policies that are designed to maximize domestic social welfare. (Social welfare here obviously means the welfare of local residents, because the costs and benefits of domestic policies are fully internalized.) For various reasons, one should expect significant policy differences across countries. First, countries may differ as to the objectives of competition policy, ranging from an efficiency (total welfare) objective to a consumer welfare objective, to a populist (decentralization of power) objective, to preserving small businesses, to integrating regional markets, or even to promoting the "public interest" broadly defined. Moreover, as is evident in the history of various countries' domestic competition laws, these objectives may vary over time. Second, material conditions may vary from one country to another, requiring a different mix of policy instruments.[4] For example, very small economies with thin markets may have to live with much higher concentration levels than would be acceptable to countries with much larger markets. High concentration levels may be necessary to obtain scale economies, which helps explain why Canada has an explicit efficiencies defense to mergers and the United States does not. For similar reasons, small economies may assign a larger role to economic regulation or even state ownership.[5] Third, countries may have different understandings of relevant and contested bodies of economic theory that inform their policy choices (for example, on the efficiency properties of various kinds of vertical restraints) or have cultural traditions that are more hospitable to certain practices or arrangements than other traditions (for example, vertical and horizontal *keiretsu* in Japan).

If one drops the assumption of public-interested governments, differences in competition policies are likely to emerge because different configurations of political interests in different countries will shape competition policies in different ways. In some countries, concentrated producer interests may dominate diffuse consumer interests in the political process and succeed in obtaining lax competition laws that permit an abuse of market power. In other countries, a politically engaged citizenry may be more effective in resisting this distortion. In countries with authoritarian or despotic governments, it is difficult to predict what policy objectives are likely to motivate the government in formulating competition laws.

Now assume a world with substantial trade and investment flows between and among countries: Are the differences in competition policies that one might observe in an autarkic world likely to diminish or to increase, and in what ways and for what reasons? There are some reasons why countries might choose to assimilate their competition laws to those of other countries. For example, in order to attract foreign investment or imports, there may be incentives to avoid imposing burdens on foreigners that they do not face in their home countries. Alternatively, countries may wish to facilitate the investigation or review of international cartels or mergers.

On the other hand, an open international trade and investment environment may provide incentives to adopt protectionist or beggar-thy-neighbor competition policies. These interjurisdictional externalities may increase domestic welfare but reduce foreign and perhaps global welfare.[6] In addition, some countries may adopt lax competition laws or sectoral exemptions to promote "national champions" or to provide local businesses with an opportunity to grow to minimum efficient scale before exposing them to foreign competition (a version of the "infant industry" argument). Finally, various theoretical models suggest that a country with a strong competition policy may reap gains from international trade; therefore, countries may face incentives to pursue stricter competition policies than their trading partners, resulting in divergence of competition policies.[7]

Self-interest is most manifest in laws that explicitly discriminate against foreign interests. (We return below to the question of dealing with nondiscriminatory laws whose substantive content is nevertheless distorted by international trade.) The widespread exemption for export cartels in general or in particular sectors provides an excellent example: Domestic producers benefit at the expense of foreign consumers. Another example is Section 96 of the Canadian Competition Act, which provides an efficiency defense to mergers. In applying the defense, authorities are to consider whether efficiency gains will result in "(a) a significant increase in the real value of exports; or (b) a significant substitution of domestic products for imported products." Obviously, self-interested competition policies also include the discriminatory application of domestic laws.

In addressing the costs of self-interested, divergent competition policies, several scholars have proposed some kind of harmonization of competition policies. International efforts in this direction have encountered serious political and practical obstacles, as our brief discussion below will show. Regardless of their feasibility, however, we find comprehensive-harmonization proposals unattractive.[8] There are significant benefits to maintaining independent policies, including accommodation of divergent objectives across countries and divergent means of achieving those objectives.[9]

We would instead rely in part on the national treatment principle. As elucidated in trade law, this principle requires countries not to discriminate between domestic and foreign producers of like or directly competitive products by treating the latter less favorably than the former, either through legislation or through discriminatory enforcement. Adherence to this principle in the competition law context could play a valuable role in permitting a diversity of competition policies and its attendant benefits to flourish, while limiting harmful forms of local self-interest. Prohibiting the discriminatory application of laws would be the most difficult aspect of the national treatment principle to enforce, but this is also true with respect to the interactions of many aspects of domestic law or regulation and international trade law, in which very difficult questions of adverse effects or de facto discrimination are raised in the national treatment context.[10] Problems of enforceability, while real, are not insuperable.

The national treatment principle would prohibit countries from framing or enforcing domestic competition laws, such as laws on abuse of dominance, predatory pricing, or vertical restraints, so as to favor domestic producers over foreign producers of like or competitive products. However, probably reflecting its mercantilist history, international trade law emphasizes market access rather than consumer welfare. As Daniel Tarullo notes, "Trade policy is usually concerned with promoting the interests of specific competitors, whereas competition policy is usually concerned with promoting competitive markets . . . trade negotiators tend to stress the result of 'effective' access (that is, sales), rather than the relative competitiveness of the market in an economic or antitrust sense."[11] Thus, the national treatment principle, as traditionally understood in trade law, fails to prohibit discrimination between domestic and foreign consumers of like or competitive products. To address this problem, we favor a limited form of extraterritoriality (an "effects" doctrine) that would permit countries to sanction conduct originating abroad that adversely impacts either consumer or total welfare in the importing country, provided that such action satisfies the national treatment principle. We develop this principle in the next section.

The Jurisdictional Scope of Trade and Competition Laws

The national treatment principle, as traditionally formulated, compels state actors not to discriminate between domestic and foreign producers of like or directly competitive products. This eliminates some of the most egregious forms of self-interested, globally harmful policies. But it leaves open some potentially difficult questions of conflict resolution, particularly over the scope for extraterritorial application of local laws. The advantages of a relatively weak supranational principle in preserving local choice over antitrust policy also present disadvantages in leaving open the possibility of conflict. This section reviews principles of conflict resolution that allocate authority over particular problems to trade or competition laws. We begin with two case examples, based loosely on actual antitrust experience.

> *Example 1: Export Cartels.* Suppose that Japan has no competition laws dealing with cartels and that members of a Japanese cartel export their output to the United States at inflated prices that reduce the welfare of U.S. consumers. Suppose further that domestic U.S. antitrust law would prohibit such cartels if they involved domestic parties. (This scenario is similar to *Hartford Fire Insurance Co. v. California*[12] decided in 1993 by the U.S. Supreme Court.) Applying Japanese laws to the conduct in question would entail a form of extraterritorial application of these laws to the market most impacted by the conduct, that is, the U.S. market. Applying U.S. laws to the conduct of the Japanese firms would entail the extraterritorial application of U.S. laws to parties and conduct located elsewhere. Given our assumption—no Japanese anticartel laws, a U.S. ban on cartelization—neither a Japanese decision not to prosecute the cartel nor an American decision to prosecute would violate national treatment. The divergent approaches to the same fact pattern produce a conflict in need of resolution.

> *Example 2: Vertical Restraints.* Assume that Japanese competition law permits exclusive dealing arrangements (or at any rate, that Japanese law is much more permissive than U.S. law

in this respect). Assume further that U.S. firms seeking to export into the Japanese market face difficulties in securing distribution outlets because of exclusivity arrangements between local distributors and suppliers. (This broadly parallels the claim of the United States before the WTO in *Japan— Measures Affecting Consumer Photographic Film and Paper*.)[13] If U.S. law prohibits those exclusive arrangements, the extraterritorial application of U.S. exclusivity laws would enhance U.S. exporters' access to the Japanese market. Again, the divergent approaches of U.S. and Japanese law do not violate the national treatment principle. (We assume for purposes at hand that each jurisdiction applies its own laws without discriminating between foreign and domestic producers.)

These two examples are structurally very similar. Neither the export cartel nor the vertical restraints example involves a violation of national treatment with respect to competition policy. In both cases, moreover, local Japanese laws and conduct harm U.S. interests. We conclude, however, that the extraterritorial application of U.S. antitrust law is legitimate in the first case (inbound commerce) but not in the second case (outbound commerce). There is a crucial asymmetry in the distribution of the effects. Because the vertical restraints case results in harm to foreign producers in export markets (outbound commerce), it is appropriately left to trade law. The cartel case, in contrast, results in harm to foreign consumers in import markets (inbound commerce). It is therefore an appropriate context for the extraterritorial application of U.S. antitrust law.

To elaborate on these conclusions about the scope of trade and competition law, it is clear that competition policies around the world universally take maximizing consumer welfare in any particular market as a central objective. To be sure, "central" does not mean "exclusive." The EU, for example, seems sometimes to consider harms to rival producers when two firms propose to merge. Still, competition policies in Europe, and throughout the developed world, rest on the premise that antitrust law is at base not about protecting competitors but rather about protecting competition.[14] Nowhere will a bare complaint that low prices are driving a firm out of business get far; rather, the complainant would need to show that the prices are unreasonably low and predatory, which in turn requires a careful examination of the facts, including price-cost comparisons.

Trade law, however, recognizes that domestic governments may pursue objectives other than domestic consumer or total welfare. Free trade maximizes domestic welfare on net, but this does not prevent those harmed by it from lobbying against it. Public choice theory predicts that concentrated interest groups may distort domestic law to impede trade. As a consequence, countries enter into agreements with other countries entailing reciprocal commitments to allow foreign producers access to their markets.[15] These involve commitments to abolish tariffs and quotas, as well as commitments not to adopt laws that discriminate, explicitly or in their operation, against foreign producers. Trade law, in short, focuses on producers who are excluded from foreign markets. That focus will generate incidental (and often substantial) benefits for domestic consumers, but the law in its operation seeks to constrain domestic governments, on a basis of reciprocity, from adopting laws that deny foreign producers access to a market. To substantiate a complaint, the producer must show harm and discriminatory conduct; the effect on domestic consumers from trade-reducing laws is mostly beside the point.

The different principles that animate trade and competition law lead in many different contexts to a coherent method of determining the appropriate scope for the extraterritorial application of competition law (on the assumption that no country has violated the national treatment principle). In particular, extraterritorial application of competition law remedies the harm that domestic antitrust laws seek to address: harm to domestic consumer or total welfare. This implies that extraterritorial application is appropriate in the first example, where a Japanese export cartel aims to raise prices and harm U.S. consumers. Because the conduct would be illegal under U.S. law (that is, the U.S. authorities do not violate national treatment by applying their law to such a cartel) *and* because the alleged conduct would harm U.S. consumers, U.S. antitrust law should apply extraterritorially. Recent evidence suggests that international cartels impose severe costs on importing countries, including many developing countries.[16] Our limited principle of extraterritoriality permits importing countries to act unilaterally in all such cases. It does not, however, suggest a need for international competition laws beyond voluntary cooperation between states in investigating and prosecuting such practices.

In our vertical restraints example, the only harm to the United States affects producers. Barring a violation of national treatment by either country, first principles rule out an extraterritorial application of U.S. vertical restraints law. U.S. antitrust law is explicitly not about protecting producers, but rather about protecting competition. Applying U.S. antitrust law to protect U.S. producers in foreign markets would therefore be inappropriate.

Our position conflicts with the practice and legal position of the United States. Especially since the amendments in 1992 and 1995 to the U.S. Antitrust Enforcement Guidelines for International Operations (repealing note 159), the United States has asserted jurisdiction over conduct that harms U.S. exporters in outbound commerce even if U.S. consumers are *not* harmed.[17] And a recent decision of the D.C. Circuit Court held that the Foreign Trade Antitrust Improvements Act permits foreign plaintiffs to sue in the United States for antitrust damages arising outside the United States.[18] The U.S. position, however, fails to leave other jurisdictions with the discretion not to penalize local behavior, which approach is unwarranted and inefficient. If applied by a large number of countries, it would entail a global race to the most stringent competition laws, which are unlikely to maximize global welfare. It is better to leave room for local competition policies.

Harm to producers as the result of exclusionary practices *is*, however, the domain of trade law, as is the broader issue of market access by foreign producers. If Japanese permissiveness toward vertical restraints is a form of protectionism, U.S. producers may have a complaint under trade law (as they claimed, unsuccessfully, in the photographic film and paper case mentioned previously), at least if the law is being applied in a discriminatory fashion. Where this is not the case, but Japanese policy on exclusionary policies reduces consumer welfare in Japan, that cost is internalized to Japan. It is that country's prerogative to decide whether to amend or apply its competition laws to address this harm.

> *Example 3: Monopoly.* Assume that a monopoly in the EU exports all of its output to the United States, along with monopoly overcharges.[19] Under U.S. antitrust law, monopolization

does not include supracompetitive pricing per se, but requires proof of some exclusionary, disciplinary, or market foreclosure practice. Under European Community law, in contrast, monopoly pricing per se may constitute an abuse of dominant position. U.S. consumers are harmed—but not in a way that would attract liability for a U.S. producer under U.S. domestic antitrust law. EU consumers are not harmed, but the conduct at issue would potentially violate EU laws if it took place within the EU.

First principles again resolve the potential conflict. The U.S. would not challenge high prices *simpliciter* charged by a local monopolist; therefore, it would be a violation of the national treatment principle to challenge the European monopolist on this basis. However, it would *not* be a violation of national treatment for the EU to address the monopolist's conduct, because it would do the same in the case of a local monopolist selling in the EU market. EU enforcement would create a conflict with U.S. law in this context, which should be resolved by reference to our extraterritoriality principles that assign jurisdiction in cases of conflict to the jurisdiction where consumer welfare is prejudiced (the United States in our example). (Also, as a matter of European law, the European Commission or courts may lack jurisdiction if EU citizens are not harmed. If the monopolist sells some of its output in both U.S. and EU markets, the EU would obviously have jurisdiction over the monopoly overcharges.)

> *Example 4: Dumping.* Japanese steel producers sell steel into the United States. U.S. steel producers object that the steel is being sold at low prices that cause them material injury. What law should resolve the dispute?

Current trade law would permit U.S. producers to seek trade remedies under antidumping provisions in the GATT (Article VI), depending on the prices charged by Japanese producers in the United States relative to their home market. Our approach suggests that this is inappropriate. Trade law (as opposed to trade theory) is about harm to producers excluded from foreign markets; competition law is about harm to local consumers. In the steel example, U.S. producers are obviously not being excluded from Japanese markets, and it is inappropriate to rely on trade law as a remedy. If, however, Japanese producers are preying on U.S. steel firms, there may be a claim that U.S. consumers will be harmed in the long run. This would be an appropriate case for the extraterritorial application of U.S. predation laws.

Standards for predation, which serve consumer rather than producer interests, are much more difficult to meet than antidumping standards. (That is why local firms typically pursue trade remedies, not competition remedies.) However, but for the special dispensation for antidumping laws in the GATT, such laws would clearly violate the national treatment principle, because they subject foreign producers to pricing constraints that do not apply to domestic producers of like or competitive products. There is a strong case for abolishing this flagrant exception to the national treatment principle and relying instead on nondiscriminatory domestic antitrust predation or abuse of dominance laws, albeit applied extraterritorially.[20]

The key advantage of the national treatment principle and the jurisdictional limitations on extraterritoriality (applicable to inbound but not outbound commerce) is to preserve the benefits of localized competition policy. The principles allow local governments to devise competition laws to suit local conditions and to engage in policy experimentation. Absent a national treatment principle, countries could adopt globally undesirable self-interested laws. Conversely, an overly permissive approach to extraterritoriality would interfere with local governments' ability to adopt distinctive competition laws (for example, extraterritoriality in the vertical restraints example would hinder Japan's ability to adopt its own distinctive vertical restraints regime). Looking to the country whose consumers are affected by conduct helps resolve the jurisdictional division between trade and competition policies.

Another instrumental advantage of our proposed conflicts regime is one of institutional competence. Antitrust authorities determine the effect of conduct on consumer or total welfare, while trade authorities typically only seek to determine whether foreign producers have been excluded from a market by discriminatory restraints on trade.[21] Allocating matters engaging consumer or total welfare to antitrust authorities and matters engaging producer welfare to trade authorities exploits the comparative advantage of the different agencies.

Hard Cases

The principles just described solve many problems that arise through the interaction of trade and competition policies but not all such problems. Again, a case example provides a useful context for tackling the hard cases.

> *Example 5: A Supranational Merger.* Consider a merger between two firms selling their output into supranational or global markets (for example, large commercial aircraft manufacturers). Suppose one country—perhaps where the two merging parties are located—approves the merger on the grounds of efficiencies (cost savings) likely to be generated by the merger, while another country disapproves the merger on account of a likely increase in the price of the product in question as a result of the reduction in competition. The latter country does not realize in any direct way the efficiencies associated with the merger.

This example broadly reflects the De Havilland case, in which the European Commission prohibited the acquisition of De Havilland, a Canadian-based commuter aircraft producer (owned by the American firm Boeing) by a European joint venture, ATR (owned by French and Italian interests), on the grounds that the merger would give the merged entity excessive market power in the European market. The Canadian authorities, meanwhile, approved the merger. The example is also similar in some respects to the interjurisdictional conflicts between the United States and the EU in the McDonnell Douglas/Boeing merger and the GE/Honeywell merger. The example is conceptually similar to Example 1 (export cartels) and does not differ in important analytical respects from major international cartels (such as the vitamin cartel)[22] that affect many domestic markets. Several issues arise. We consider them in order, from most to least troubling.

Multiplicity of Jurisdictions/Race to the Strictest. Because the merging parties in our example sell in a supranational market, multiple jurisdictions can both comply with the national treatment principle and legitimately (under our analysis) apply their laws extraterritorially. This creates the potential problem of inconsistent decisions about the same merger. The nature of relief in merger cases is typically injunctive, either permitting the merger to proceed in its entirety, permitting a modified merger to proceed after divestitures, or forbidding any form of the merger. If several jurisdictions review a merger and each relies on injunctive remedies, the strictest regime will prevail. This undermines the autonomy of antitrust regimes, just as U.S. extraterritorial application of vertical restraints law in Example 2 would undermine Japanese efforts to adopt a permissive approach to vertical restraints. Furthermore, as countries impose their laws to transactions that cause them harm, they will block not only globally inefficient anticompetitive activities, but also many efficient activities (that is, activities that cause a net loss to a particular country while yielding global benefits that outweigh that loss). In this scenario, domestic law may be more stringent than the optimal global policy.[23]

The problem, however, should not be exaggerated. First, while allowing firms to merge in all jurisdictions but one is often not feasible in cases involving global or supranational markets, many other antitrust contexts permit idiosyncratic local remedies. Consider again Example 3, involving a European monopolist charging high prices in the EU and United States. There is no reason that the EU could not penalize the monopolist for high prices in the EU while U.S. authorities decline to intervene with respect to sales in the United States. Likewise, exclusivity provisions may be unenforceable in some local markets but permissible in other jurisdictions. Even mergers that involve many local markets can sometimes appropriately be addressed by local divestitures.

A second, more radical response is to rethink the injunctive nature of antitrust remedies. A damages remedy could accommodate jurisdictional multiplicity without requiring any jurisdiction to cede sovereignty over the substantive content of its antitrust regime. In the merger context, for example, antitrust authorities considering a merger involving several jurisdictions could calculate the expected local damages to consumers and require the merging parties to pay this amount (perhaps by way of a reduction in prices in that jurisdiction or a fine). If gains elsewhere offset local damages, the merger will proceed. If not, it will not.

This approach has benefits analogous to the efficient breach benefits of awarding damages rather than specific performance for breach of contract. True, individual jurisdictions will be tempted to make spurious findings in order to extract extortionate damages from foreign merging firms. But this is equally true of price-fixing damages or fines, yet these are set locally even in the case of an international cartel. Under the national treatment principle, the strictest regime would set the highest price for the merger (at least relative to the size of local sales), but this is entirely appropriate given local views of the harms from the merger. The strictest regime would *not* have a veto over the merger—a holdout right that would violate at least the spirit of the national treatment principle (because it would ignore the impact on foreign producer and consumer welfare).

A third response to the problem of jurisdictional multiplicity is a lead jurisdiction approach. Just as nations with legal jurisdiction over a matter may cede authority to other nations under principles of comity, local jurisdictions may cede authority to a lead jurisdiction in antitrust matters.[24] The least intrusive lead jurisdiction model is a coordinating agency model, in which the lead jurisdiction would coordinate a review of the merger for all affected countries, reach a dispositive decision with respect to its own jurisdiction, and make findings and recommendations for other affected countries after taking account of submissions from these countries' competition authorities. While this model would not prevent divergent outcomes, it would reduce transaction costs with regard to activities affecting supranational geographic markets.[25] A more intrusive model would entrust the lead jurisdiction with dispositive powers not only with respect to its own jurisdiction, but to other affected jurisdictions. A third model would entail some kind of supranational appeal mechanism, not on the merits of the merger but on the conflict-of-laws issue and in particular on the designation of the appropriate lead agency. In each model, the choice of lead jurisdiction should reflect the concern for consumers that animates competition policy. The country that represents the largest share of consumption should presumably be the lead jurisdiction.[26] The presence of producers in a jurisdiction should have no impact on the choice.

Conflicts of Principle. While competition laws generally serve to promote consumer welfare, in some cases, they explicitly account also for producer welfare. For example, as previously mentioned, Canada recognizes an explicit efficiencies defense in merger review that balances anticompetitive effects with efficiency gains. In some cases, Canada may approve a merger in part out of a regard for producer welfare. If a multijurisdictional conflict arises over a particular merger, resolving the conflict by reference to the location of consumers is at least complicated by the Canadian emphasis on producer welfare (as an element in a total welfare test). The De Havilland case is one example: While production of commuter airlines was in part located in Canada, customers were for the most part located in Europe. Resolving the conflict by deferring to Europe because of customer location ignores the producer (or total welfare) emphasis of the efficiencies defense in Canada.

Two of the already-rehearsed responses to the problem of jurisdictional multiplicity apply to this context. First, the problem only arises where idiosyncratic local remedies are infeasible—which, as an empirical matter, is not true in the vast majority of antitrust cases. Second, an international agreement to impose damages (or fines) rather than injunctions can better accommodate conflicting decisions. Moreover, while some nations' antitrust laws recognize qualifications to a one-dimensional consumer welfare standard, the principal purpose, always and everywhere, is to protect consumers from anticompetitive distortions. Canadian antitrust law generally protects consumers, so it is not unreasonable to ask it to cede jurisdiction to Europe on the basis of consumer welfare.

Distortions from Trade. In this volume (see chapter 4) and in his earlier writings, Andrew Guzman has argued that countries' *general* antitrust policies will be distorted by trade flows. Even if all countries adhere to national treatment, trade patterns may distort local competition laws. Net exporters in imperfectly competitive markets may often favor a lax policy; net importers in such markets may often favor a strict policy.[27] In addition, Guzman suggests that because in a world with unlimited extraterritoriality the strictest approach across jurisdictions will prevail in any given case, trade will lead to overly strict antitrust rules (from a global welfare perspective) imposed by net importers in imperfectly competitive markets.

Putting aside our earlier responses to the race-to-the-strictest concern (including consideration of local remedies), we do not view the general distortions from trade as a significant problem. First, the trade surplus in any given country in the long run must be balanced. Guzman argues that while trade overall may be in balance over time, trade in *imperfectly* competitive markets may not balance over time.[28] Imperfectly competitive markets, however, depend at least in part on local competition and trade policies. Oil, for example, would almost certainly sell in a competitive market if not for the Organization of the Petroleum Exporting Countries (OPEC). The endogeneity of the competitiveness of markets casts doubt on the predictive value of Guzman's analysis. Predicting which countries are net exporters or importers in imperfectly competitive markets—in order to predict the strictness of their policies—depends on the policies themselves. A local welfare-maximizing government cannot easily disentangle market and legal effects in order to decide whether, over time, it will be a net importer or exporter in imperfectly competitive markets and to distort its policies accordingly.

Second, although Guzman argues that the combination of trade-distorted competition policies and the veto power of the strictest policy would lead to excessively strict global policies, it is not clear that net importers in imperfectly competitive markets will always adopt overly strict rules. Suppose that two U.S. firms and two European firms each serve the European market. The market is imperfectly competitive, and Europe is a net importer. The two EU firms propose to merge. Guzman would argue that the EU should object. A welfare-maximizing EU, however, may come to the opposite conclusion. Although the merger will decrease competition and harm local consumers, it will benefit local producers. If all effects are internal to the EU, the net effect may be negative and the EU should object to the merger. But not all effects *are* internal. Rather, the merger could result in a larger or smaller share of overall profits for EU producers, depending on the model of oligopoly that prevails. This complicates the calculus for the EU: The merger may augment total producer rents and allow the EU to realize a larger share of those rents. The gains in profit for the merged EU firm could offset losses to EU consumers. Rent shifting, then, could cause net importing countries to impose an excessively *lax* policy.[29]

Finally, as an empirical matter, the net trade surplus in imperfectly competitive markets is unlikely to have significant distortionary effects on policies. The value of exports less imports was only 4.3 percent of gross domestic product in Canada in 2002[30]—a small, open economy with a relatively large trade surplus. Unless imperfectly competitive markets are disproportionately important in export as opposed to import markets, the effect of trade is even smaller if one considers only the surplus that arises in imperfectly competitive markets. If countries can discriminate in the application of their policies between foreigners and locals, their standards may indeed vary depending on the position of local firms and customers in any given case. But so long as countries adhere to a policy of nondiscrimination, we doubt that the trade surplus or deficit in imperfectly competitive markets will have a significant effect on the general choice of competition policy.

Solutions in Search of a Problem

In 1993, an International Antitrust Working Group (composed largely of German competition scholars) produced a Draft International Antitrust Code.[31] This so-called Munich Code proposed a mandatory World Competition Code of minimum standards to be incorporated into the GATT and to be enforced in domestic jurisdictions by an International Antitrust Authority operating under the auspices of the WTO. More recent events in international antitrust, however, demonstrate both the likely futility and undesirability of a substantive harmonization agenda. Even modest proposals for harmonization have engendered strong disagreements, indicating that harmonization is impractical. The reasons for disagreement may sometimes relate to self-interest, but often seem motivated by good faith differences in opinion over optimal law.

Proposals for sweeping international harmonization competition laws (such as those espoused in the Munich Code) no longer reflect mainstream preoccupations with the costs, in terms of global welfare, of divergent national competition policies. The Doha Ministerial Declaration of November 2001 identified an apparently much more modest trade and competition policy agenda, focused on the clarification of core principles, including transparency, nondiscrimination and procedural fairness, and provisions on hard-core cartels; modalities for voluntary cooperation; and support for progressive reinforcement of competition institutions in developing countries through capacity building. Full account shall be taken of the needs of developing and least developed country participants and appropriate flexibility provided to address them.

A report released by the WTO Working Group on the Interaction between Trade and Competition Policy to the WTO General Council[32] details a striking diversity of views among member-states on even this seemingly modest agenda. In principle, the report states, transparency should permeate all aspects of a country's competition regime, including legislation, policies, institutional structures, decision-making processes, enforcement priorities, policy and procedural guidelines, case selection criteria, exemption criteria, appeal processes, and details of all relevant outcomes and decisions made. However, recognizing that fifty or more members of the WTO have no competition laws at all and that many other countries' competition laws exist on paper only,[33] such a set of requirements is likely to be extremely burdensome, especially if it includes all case-specific decisions made by enforcement authorities, such as advisory opinions and settlements. Moreover, the question of the protection of confidential information, including commercial and business secrets, is likely to be viewed very differently in different legal cultures.

Similarly, countries differ on whether the principle of nondiscrimination should apply only to de jure discrimination or also to instances of de facto discrimination, and on the difficulty of distinguishing the latter from reasonable exercises of prosecutorial discretion. Moreover, several countries have general exemptions for export cartels, and most countries have various sectoral exemptions from competition laws. Developing countries argue more generally for special and differential status so that they would not be obliged to apply competition laws to expose domestic industries to foreign competition or acquisitions, and to be permitted to maintain export cartels in commodity markets, on an infant industry rationale. Thus, many developing countries argue for the addition of special and differential status to the core principles, while some developed countries argued conversely for the addition of the principle of comprehensiveness to the list of "core" principles.

With respect to hard-core cartels, the report notes that there is a lack of any consensus on the definition of a hard-core cartel as opposed to other kinds of horizontal arrangements,[34] and, even if they could be defined, whether they should be subject to per se illegality or rule of reason review. In addition, the report states that even if these two issues could be resolved, there is disagreement whether there should be some common position on penalties or sanctions for participation in such cartels. Finally, even if *all* these issues could be resolved, differences exist as to whether certain exemptions should be permitted from the prohibition against hard-core cartels. As to modalities for voluntary cooperation in the administration and enforcement of competition laws, the report again notes a wide diversity of views as to the various forms that cooperation might take and how mandatory "voluntary" cooperation should be in various contexts.

As this cursory review demonstrates, and as reflected in the EU's proposal at Cancun in September 2003 to withdraw competition policy from the WTO's negotiating agenda in the face of intense opposition from developing countries, significant harmonization on substantive areas of law seems very unlikely. Moreover, the reasons for disagreement, such as different conceptions of hard-core cartels, often seem rooted in fundamental differences in approach, not parochial self-interest. In that light, we oppose proposals (such as Guzman's) to vest in the WTO a mandate to negotiate a single, comprehensive harmonized international antitrust regime by using cross-issue trade-offs or side payments to induce countries to adopt domestic antitrust regimes.[35] Threats of trade sanctions, for example, may be effective in achieving harmonization—but only at the price of compelling countries to opt for laws that they (nonstrategically) do not consider optimal in terms of their own domestic welfare.

In the end, efforts at harmonizing international law are largely a solution in search of a problem. To the extent that diversity of national competition laws poses problems in a context of dramatically increased international trade, the two core principles that we have identified—the national treatment principle and limited (inbound) extraterritoriality—adequately address the most serious problems. With respect to the principle of national treatment, and only in that respect, the WTO has a legitimate mandate in the trade and competition policy area. That mandate already exists, and although it is difficult to discharge in the case of complaints of de facto discrimination, it is no more intractable in antitrust than in many other areas of domestic law and regulation.[36] Voluntary cooperation between national competition authorities in the investigation and enforcement of competition laws can be promoted by bilateral treaties or agreements of the kind that already exist between several national enforcement authorities. Pointless incompatibilities between international competition laws (for example, with respect to information requirements and decision time lines in merger reviews) are best addressed through forums such as the International Competition Network, which represents most significant national antitrust enforcement authorities. Similar spontaneous regulatory convergence on best practices in various other areas of antitrust law enforcement can also effectively be promoted through such a forum.[37]

It would be the ultimate incongruity that the desire to harmonize all or some aspects of national competition laws may come at the price of eliminating competitive politics and policymaking. Competition in competition policy is important for social welfare, just as is competition in the economic domain.[38]

Notes

1. See David Leebron, "Lying Down with Procrustes: An Analysis of Harmonization," in *Fair Trade and Harmonization: Prerequisites for Free Trade?* vol. 1, eds. Jagdish Bhagwati and Robert Hudec (Cambridge: MIT Press, 1996), chap. 2; Alan Sykes, "Regulatory Protectionism and the Law of International Trade," *University of Chicago Law Review* 66 (1999): 1–46; Michael Trebilcock and Robert Howse, "Trade Liberalization and Regulatory Diversity: Reconciling Competitive Markets with Competitive Politics," *European Journal of Law and Economics* 6 (1998): 5–37.

2. The United States has applied its antitrust laws extraterritorially since *United States v. Aluminum Co. of America* (Alcoa), 148 F.2d 416(2d Cir. 1945).

3. See Edward Iacobucci, "The Interdependence of Trade and Competition Policies," *World Competition* 21 (1997): 16–17.

4. William Kovacic expresses concern with the transition economies' attempts to apply regulatory frameworks based on Western models in environments that lack the institutional preconditions that are essential to the effectiveness of such frameworks in the West. William E. Kovacic, "Merger Enforcement in Transition: Antitrust Controls on Acquisitions in Emerging Economies," *University of Cincinnati Law Review* 66 (1998): 1075–1112.

5. Michal S. Gal, "Size Does Matter: The Effects of Market Size on Optimal Competition Policy," *Southern California Law Review* 74 (2001): 1437–78; Michal S. Gal, *Competition Policy for Small Market Economies* (Cambridge: Harvard University Press, 2003) (discussing the distinct needs of small economies with respect to antitrust policy).

6. Iacobucci, "Interdependence of Trade," 20–21.

7. Under certain circumstances (in particular, where competition involves strategic substitutes, such as in the case of Cournot [quantity] oligopoly competition, countries will maximize their welfare by having several local firms, rather than one, participate in international markets. Having more than one domestic firm compete reduces the total amount of profit in an international market but, in the case of strategic substitutes, increases the domestic country's share of those rents, thus potentially increasing total domestic producer welfare. In addition, competition will be beneficial to domestic consumers. The combination of these factors could result in countries racing to the top with their competition policies in an attempt to shift rents to the home country. Unlike beggar-thy-neighbor reasons for the divergence of competition policy, the race to the top may be globally welfare-enhancing. See ibid.

8. Both authors have written at greater length on this question elsewhere. See Iacobucci, "Interdependence of Trade," 5–33; Michael Trebilcock et al., *The Law and Economics of Canadian Competition Policy* (Toronto: University of Toronto Press, 2002), chap. 10; Neil Campbell and Michael J. Trebilcock, "International Merger

Review: Problems of Multi-Jurisdictional Conflict," in *Competition Policy in an Interdependent World Economy* (Baden-Baden: Nomos Verlagsgesellschaft, 1993), 129–64. Also against harmonization: See Eleanor M. Fox, "Antitrust and Regulatory Federalism: Races Up, Down, and Sideways," *New York University Law Review* 75 (2000): 1801; Karl M. Meessen, "Competition of Competition Laws," *Northwestern Journal of International Law and Business* 10 (1989): 21; Douglas H. Ginsburg and Scott H. Angstreich, "Multinational Merger Review: Lessons from Our Federalism," *Antitrust Law Journal* 68 (2000): 219–37. For a detailed review of the history of international efforts at cooperation, coordination, and harmonization with respect to domestic competition policy, see Kevin Kennedy, *Competition Law and the World Trade Organization: The Limits of Multilateralism* (London: Sweet and Maxwell, 2001), chaps. 2–4.

9. We set aside another potentially significant drawback of international harmonization: the potential lack of accountability of international bodies and thus the vulnerability of rulemaking to pernicious political influences. See Paul B. Stephan, "Accountability and International Lawmaking: Rules, Rents, and Legitimacy," *Northwestern Journal of International Law and Business* 17 (1996): 706.

10. See Michael Trebilcock and Shiva Giri, "The National Treatment Principle in International Trade Law," paper presented at the Law and Economics Workshop, University of Toronto (February 26, 2003).

11. Daniel Tarullo, "Norms and Institutions in Global Competition Policy," *American Journal of International Law* 94 (2000): 483.

12. *Hartford Fire Insurance Co. v. California*, 509 U.S. 764 (1993). For discussions of this case, see Kenneth Dam, "Extraterritoriality in an Age of Globalization: The Hartford Case," *Supreme Court Review* (1993), 289–328; Alan Swan, "The Hartford Insurance Company Case: Antitrust in the Global Economy—Welfare Effects and Sovereignty," in *Economic Dimensions in International Law: Comparative and Empirical Perspectives*, eds. Jagdeep S. Bhandari and Alan O. Sykes, (Cambridge: Cambridge University Press, 1997), 530–91.

13. WTO, *Japan—Measures Affecting Consumer Photographic Film and Paper—Report of the Panel*, WTO Doc. WT/DS44/R (1998).

14. The EU Commissioner of Competition has recently stated that EU competition laws are principally concerned with protecting consumer welfare. Mario Monti, "Europe's Merger Monitor," *The Economist,* November 9, 2002, 71.

15. See Tarullo, "Norms and Institutions," 478–504.

16. See Robert Anderson and Peter Holmes, "Competition Policy and the Future of the Unilateral Trading System," *Journal of International Economic Law* 5 (2002): 541–44; WTO, *Report of the WTO Working Group on the Interaction Between Trade and Competition Policy to the General Council*, WTO Doc. WT/WGTCP/6 (2002), 17, 18.

17. See Paul Crampton, "The 1995 U.S. Antitrust Enforcement Guidelines for International Operations: A Foreign Perspective," *International Business Law*

Journal 1 (1996): 99–109; for similar reasons, we oppose the assertion of jurisdiction by the United States in *United States v. Pilkington*, 59 FR 30604 (1994), alleging that Pilkington established a web of restrictive distribution arrangements impeding effective market access by U.S. competitors to the U.K. and other glassware markets around the world.

18. *Empagran S.A. v. F. Hoffman LaRoche Ltd.*, 315 F.3d 338, 357 (D.C. Cir. 2003).

19. See Frank H. Easterbrook, chapter 8 in this volume, for a similar example.

20. See Michael Trebilcock and Robert Howse, *The Regulation of International Trade*, 2nd ed. (London: Routledge, 1999), chap. 7.

21. See Tarullo, "Norms and Institutions."

22. See *In re Vitamins Antitrust Litig.*, 2000–1 Trade Cas. (CCH) P 72,914 (D.D.C. 2000).

23. See Andrew Guzman, "Is International Antitrust Possible?" *New York University Law Review* 73 (1998): 1524; Andrew Guzman, "Antitrust and International Regulatory Federalism," *New York University Law Review* 76 (2001): 1142–63.

24. Campbell and Trebilcock have argued for a lead jurisdiction model that comes in different variants. Campbell and Trebilcock, "International Merger Review," 149–55.

25. Ibid., 150.

26. Trebilcock et al., *The Law and Economics of Canadian Competition Policy*, 684; Campbell and Trebilcock, "International Merger Review," 153.

27. Guzman, "Antitrust and International Regulatory Federalism"; see also Iacobucci, "Interdependence of Trade," 21.

28. Guzman, "Antitrust and International Regulatory Federalism," 1155.

29. Iacobucci, "Interdependence of Trade," 24–26. The strategic trade literature shows that countries may intervene in imperfectly competitive markets in an attempt to shift rents from foreign firms to domestic firms. Applying similar analysis to international antitrust can provide valuable insights.

30. Derived by dividing gross receipts in international trade of goods and services less gross payments in 2002 (which difference was C$49.5 billion in 2001: see "Canada's Balance of International Payments," available online at Statistics Canada, http://www.statcan.ca/english/Pgdb/econ01a.htm [accessed February 24, 2004]) by Canadian GDP in 2002 (which was C$1.15 trillion: see "Gross Domestic Product: Expenditure-based," available online at Statistics Canada, http://www.statcan.ca/english/Pgdb/econ04.htm [accessed February 24, 2004]).

31. See GATT, International Antitrust Code Working Group, Draft International Antitrust Code as a GATT-MTO Plurilateral Trade Agreement, Special Supplement, *Antitrust and Trade Regulation Report* (BNA) 64 No. 1628 (August 19, 1993). For a review of the code, see W. F. Kentscher, "Competition Rules for

Private Agents in the GATT/WTO System," *Aussenwirtschaft* 49 (1994): 281 (code annexed).

32. WTO, *Report of the WTO Working Group on the Interaction Between Trade and Competition Policy to the General Council*, WTO Doc. WT/WGTCP/6 (2002).

33. See William Kovacic, "Creating New Competition Policy Institutions in Transition Economies," *Brooklyn Journal of International Law* 23 (1997): 403–54.

34. On the difficulties of drawing this distinction, see Presley Warner and Michael Trebilcock, "Rethinking Price-Fixing Law," *McGill Law Journal* 38 (1993): 679–723.

35. Guzman, "Antitrust and International Regulatory Federalism," 1142–43, 1155–58.

36. See Trebilcock and Giri, "The National Treatment Principle."

37. See Konrad Von Finckenstein, "Speech given at the 29th Annual Conference on International Antitrust Law and Policy to the Fordham Corporate Law Institute, New York," http://www.internationalcompetitionnetwork.org/news/oct312002.html, October 31, 2002; see also Tarullo, "Norms and Institutions," 495, 496.

38. Michael Trebilcock and Robert Howse, "Trade Liberalization and Regulatory Diversity."

7

Cooperation and Convergence in International Antitrust: Why the Light Is Still Yellow

Diane P. Wood

We know what antitrust "paradox" Robert Bork was talking about in his now-classic 1978 book, *The Antitrust Paradox*: It had to do with internal contradictions in antitrust doctrine. But many observers perceive a different kind of paradox in the position of the United States on the question whether we should have international antitrust rules of some kind.

From the time before I was at the Department of Justice up to the present,[1] the attitude of the United States has not been one of wild enthusiasm for international antitrust rules. It has instead been far more cautious. There was a movement just after the World Trade Organization (WTO) entered into effect in 1994 to add three new issues to the WTO's agenda: environmental regulation, workers' rights, and antitrust or competition policy. That was then; this is now. We have seen a lot of regrouping on the part of the WTO with respect to how far it could push various new agendas. Nevertheless, many working groups and other organizations have begun to look seriously at the international antitrust question.

How did antitrust laws become so popular? The short answer is that everyone loves a winner. The United States has a very successful economic system, and we have had antitrust laws for a long time. We have certainly been vocal about the benefits of having those laws. But we did not set out to originate a great movement. Canada actually passed its first antitrust law in 1889, a year before the United States came along with the Sherman Act in 1890. And that was almost the entire picture for quite a while. U.S.

antitrust law was not something that the rest of the world regarded as a model. Outside the United States and Canada, almost nobody else had antitrust or competition laws, and many countries frankly doubted whether antitrust law was such a great idea. Look at Nazi Germany's various cartels or at the *zaibatsu* in Japan before World War II. All around the world, cartels were not demonized; they were tolerated or even applauded. In fact, during the Great Depression, there were those in the United States who thought that cartels might be a fine idea. There were some modest efforts at competition regulation on the international level, even under the League of Nations. But those efforts went nowhere. After World War II, the Havana Charter was proposed for what would have been an international trade organization. The Charter had a chapter on restrictive business practices, which is what antitrust was then called. The United States actually withdrew its support for the charter, in no small part because of its concern about the competition provisions.

Between 1945 and now, national antitrust laws have snowballed. The trend began in 1952 or 1958, with the decision of the drafters of the key European treaties, the Coal and Steel Treaty in 1952 and the Treaty of Rome in 1958,[2] to include competition law as a fundamental, quasi-constitutional principle. Those provisions were contained in Articles 85 and 86 of the original Treaty of Rome, now renumbered as Articles 81 and 82. The member-states of the European Union (EU), as part of their project to create an internally harmonious system, enacted their own competition laws. The developing world started moving from a fairly *dirigiste* approach toward a more open model of economic regulation. Later, the fall of the Berlin Wall and the defeat of communism led the former socialist countries to enact competition laws.

Ten years ago, there were forty or fifty competition laws around the world that were recognizable as such. Today, officials at the U.S. Department of Justice and the Federal Trade Commission (FTC) will tell you that there are more than one hundred such laws. Having succeeded in selling antitrust law to the world, we have to ask, "What have we wrought? And what should we do now? What kinds of new problems exist because of the enormous proliferation of antitrust laws?"

Several proposals are on the table that suggest answers to these questions. Some people, Andrew Guzman (see chapter 4) among them, have argued for a regime of multilateral rules under the umbrella of the WTO, modeled on something like the Trade-Related Aspects of Intellectual Property Rights Agreement (TRIPS), which is backed up by quite a few other international conventions on intellectual property rights. Others have argued for a stand-alone international competition regime, along the lines of the convention on narcotic drugs or the postal convention. Still others have rejected all those proposals as premature. That is the group in which I find myself. In my judgment, we need to exercise caution before we take the leap into a formal international antitrust regime.

First, we need to look at the nature and purpose of competition laws, or antitrust laws. They are not all replicas of the best we have been able to develop in the United States, after more than one hundred years of experience. There are superficial similarities. Sometimes there are even real similarities. But below the surface are quite a few fault lines.

Let's begin with the goals of the competition laws. Do we have one goal, consumer welfare? If so, what do we mean by consumer welfare? Or do we have multiple goals? Obviously, we have debated that theme among ourselves in the United States. I take as a given that we have settled on "consumer welfare" (meaning, in economic terms, allocative efficiency) as the single goal of competition laws. But with respect to other countries, it is hard to generalize.

Among my responsibilities at the Department of Justice was to represent the United States on the Organisation for Economic Co-operation and Development (OECD) Committee on Competition Law and Policy. That platform provided an opportunity to talk to competition enforcement officials from the other major economic actors in the world. At the time, there were about twenty-five member-countries; now there are about thirty. I found very little argument about the proposition that consumer welfare is one purpose of competition laws, but I found great divergence over the proposition that it is the *only* purpose. The EU, for example, originally put competition principles into its treaties because the member-states viewed that policy as a complement to the dismantling of trade barriers among member-states. If a region cannot have tariffs among member-states, why should it have distribution systems that permit companies to carve up the EU into the French market, the German market, and the Italian market?

One can debate whether that perspective makes any sense, but it certainly appears in the literature as one of the reasons why this particular set of rules was seen as necessary. At the Department of Justice, I had debates with people from the U.S. Trade Representative's Office and the Commerce Department about whether that same rationale should support competition rules under the WTO's umbrella. People would say, "Look at the glass industry in Japan. Look at the film industry in Japan. They use exclusive distributors. Because they use exclusive distributors, we ("we" meaning U.S. companies) cannot break into the market. It must be illegal." And I would ask them, "What do you want to do? Do you want to change the rule about exclusive distribution in the United States, and reinvigorate the antitrust prohibition against that rule? Or do you want to have a discriminatory rule? Is it only when *other* countries have exclusive distribution systems that they violate the law? Moreover, maybe the Japanese distribution system (and I do not mean to pick on Japan) is not the reason why "our" companies cannot enter the market. And even if it is, antitrust law may be the wrong policy tool."

There was a real lack of understanding in the trade community at that time about exactly what the antitrust laws do and do not prohibit. Officials would also cite the Robinson-Patman Act as an antitrust analog to international trade rules. "Price discrimination," they would say, "is forbidden by the antitrust laws; therefore, everything we are doing under our antidumping laws is okay." The analogy, however, is not a good one. While a discussion of the wisdom of the antidumping laws and the differences between the laws and the Robinson-Patman Act would go well beyond the scope of this paper, it is important to note that few antitrust scholars want to see the Robinson-Patman Act expanded.

To return to my theme: Trade liberalization has been one of the driving forces behind competition and antitrust laws in other countries. The laws also reflect development objectives such as the elimination of the vestiges of apartheid, the opening of industries to members of aboriginal groups, and so on. Perhaps most importantly, one sees a very strong dose of unfair practices regulation. I once listened to a presentation by a gentleman from a developing country who told us about his country's new competition law. For the most part, he listed things that companies may not do. They may not have trade promotions. They may not advertise in certain ways. They may not do this, that, or the other thing. Those forbidden business practices were the kinds of things that, if we regulated them at all, would fall under the jurisdiction of either the Unfair Trade Practices branch of the FTC or a state attorney general. We do not cover them under antitrust law. On an international scale, though, there is a vagueness about what, exactly, is or should be covered under antitrust laws. We have our definitions, and other countries have theirs, to which they are equally entitled. But if definitions differ, then I worry about convergence. It is a bit obnoxious to tell other countries, "We will converge with you as long as you do all the changing." We can take that position, but the response would not be overwhelmingly positive.

Beyond that basic point of disagreement, the attitude toward regulation itself varies considerably among countries. In general, Americans distrust regulation. Our sense of individualism informs both our business regulation and our perspective on personal rights. But many other countries have long traditions of trusting bureaucrats. (Think of the continental Europeans. Think of the Japanese.) If you trust your bureaucrats, maybe you do not mind the idea of a regulatory decree that specifies, business practice by business practice, what a firm with a 30 percent or 40 percent market share may do. Those countries are just as baffled by our skepticism as we are by their trust in government.

There is yet another difference: Because it is seen as a government function, antitrust or competition regulation is very comfortably situated in the broader context of industrial policy in most foreign countries. That is why those countries put all or most of the responsibility to enforce antitrust law in the hands of government officials. Here in the United States, we have provided for private actions and, for better or worse, for an extensive role for the courts. Within that structure, antitrust policy cannot really be industrial policy, because it is not exclusively under the control of government policymakers. But that is not so in most other countries.

Finally, the size of the economy and the openness of the market may make a difference in antitrust policy. Certainly, many smaller countries believe that these factors make a difference. I have had many discussions with people from both small countries with extremely open economies (such as New Zealand) and small countries that are not so far along the way (such as some African countries). Their representatives will say, "An antitrust law that is purely consumer welfare–oriented, with no national origin discrimination, makes perfect sense for you Americans, because you have an enormous integrated market. But we are just little Country A. We can't afford your approach. Our law has to be different." They argue that antitrust is not a one-size-fits-all proposition. Previous efforts to develop global rules have always run up against this problem. A particularly striking example is the set of equitable rules and principles on restrictive business practices that the United Nations passed in 1980. Some of those rules contain propositions that are uncontroversial among antitrust experts: Cartels are bad. Monopolistic abuses are bad. But each statement is followed by huge sets of exceptions. Almost every sentence of that document included the phrase "except for developing countries." This is a general risk of global rules. Even if we assume that we are all on the same page, economic theories can differ. I think that difference largely explains the problems with the GE/Honeywell merger.

We have to ask, then, whether those differences signal a problem that needs a solution. We know that there are many differences in the laws of the fifty states of the United States, yet Congress has not chosen to federalize every area of law. It has not passed fully preemptive legislation in the insurance area, in the tort area, or in franchise protection areas. One can argue that there should be federal laws in these areas. But the truth is that we live with a certain amount of diversity. By that same token, we should ask whether some level of disagreement is acceptable within international competition law. Real problems exist as long as these differences persist, particularly as the system has ballooned. The sheer number of autonomous procedural systems has imposed ever-increasing transaction costs on international companies. Firms that want to enter into joint ventures may have to register them in some places. They may have to notify authorities and obtain substantive clearance in other places. They might not need to do anything but get decent antitrust advice in still other places.

The situation in the merger area is most worrisome. Ten years ago, I wrote a monograph with Professor Richard Whish of Kings College in London.[3] The OECD had asked us to look at eight transactions in which more than one national authority had reviewed a corporate merger or acquisition. In one case, we discovered that the parties had considered notifying twenty-one different countries. (In the end, they whittled the number down to nine.) It was quite common for companies to have notified at least four or five countries, and for those countries to have different timetables, different forms, and different substantive tests. At some point, corporate officials said, "Give us a timetable—any timetable. Give us a form—any form: We will fill the thing out, however onerous it may be." But the situation has not improved; in fact, it has deteriorated. More than sixty countries now require premerger notification. Suppose you are Gillette and Wilkinson: You both manufacture razor blades. You do business in nearly every country of the world. A razor blade is a razor blade is a razor blade. It does not become a different product when you sell it in Australia or the United States. But the laws that govern a merger of these two companies may be very different, and that is a serious problem. The same thing is true for the regulation of monopolistic practices.

The problem with regulating cartels is more substantive than procedural. I once attended an international conference on the question of hard-core cartels. Are hard-core cartels a bad thing? The answer was a universal "Yes, but. . . ." "Yes, but not if the arrangement is a price undertaking entered into by the full industry to resolve an antidumping case." "Yes, but not if the arrangement is an attempt to restructure a national industry" (such as the steel industry in the United States). "Yes, but with respect to an industry like agriculture, we do not believe that we are dealing with a hard-core cartel." "Yes, but we do not really care about export cartels, because somebody else's consumers are paying the price." The number of exceptions was staggering. Start out with a clean proposition ("Cartels are bad."), and everyone adds his favorite exception. By the time the process is finished, you do not have much of a principle left.

Remedial options also differ quite considerably among countries. The most important decision, in my view, is to criminalize or not to criminalize anticompetitive conduct. The United States has criminal sanctions. Japan does. Canada does. A few other countries criminalize certain types of behavior—but not many. Most countries resort to a combination of injunctive relief and administrative fines, and those countries do not agree on the level of fines, on the level of deterrence, or on the targets (that is, individual executives or entire companies). Maybe the trickiest problem with respect to remedies is how to preserve the right of countries to implement a nonregulatory approach if they so choose. Back in the 1950s and the 1960s, the rest of the world had that problem with the United States. The United States was constantly bringing international prosecutions of various kinds (I use the word loosely to include civil cases) on something like the following theory: "We believe that your—mostly offshore—watchmaking industry, or shipping industry, or insurance industry is violating the antitrust laws of the United States, and because you do business in the United States, your conduct is our business too." The Swiss actually took us to the World Court on the question, in a case involving the organization of the Swiss watchmaking industry. The Swiss government argued: "We do not want an antitrust law. We want to leave the industry alone. Our industry organization is none of your business." The U.S. government eventually agreed that it would not put anyone in jail for contempt of court for doing something that was required by Swiss law. That, though, was as far as we were willing to bend.

The shoe is on the other foot now, because the U.S. regime, particularly with respect to vertical restraints and monopolistic firms, is on the whole more permissive than many of the other regimes around the world. Now, it is our turn to ask why a U.S. firm should be punished for having a particular kind of distribution system or why another firm should be punished for refusing to do business with a particular customer. How then do we preserve our regime in a world where companies, and antitrust laws, have global reach? That question lies at the heart of the discussion of antitrust "harmonization."

So why not go all the way? Why not create a sensible global antitrust regime? In the course of my government service, it became painfully clear to me that the differences between governments were too great at present; that nobody would actually agree on antitrust rules that an American would support; and that a slower approach, a different approach, was the better way toward our ultimate goal.

It bears mention that the business community is no fan of cooperation among antitrust agencies. The International Antitrust Enforcement Assistance Act (IAEAA) allowed U.S. agencies to enter into bilateral agreements with counterpart authorities in other countries. If a vitamin cartel has an effect on the United States and on Canada or Europe or

Australia, U.S. officials may not sit down with their counterparts in other countries and conduct a joint prosecution without specific legal authority to do so, under a treaty or an IAEAA agreement. Even then, cooperation among governments is completely voluntary; no country is ever dragged into it against its will. But it can be allowed, and where it occurs, it simplifies, streamlines, and improves the situation for all concerned. Of course, though, sometimes businesses would rather face a fragmented prosecution than a unified one.

But even with potential benefits in sight, I believe that harmonization is, at this time, premature. First, as I have already implied, I am concerned that we will arrive at the wrong rules. Maybe the rules will acknowledge multiple "antitrust" goals. Maybe they will be excessively interventionist. Maybe they will legitimize too many exceptions—exceptions that we have been working hard to reduce. If we sign on to the wrong rules just for the sake of international harmonization, we shall be worse off than we are now, when at least we have the right rules for our own country. That counts for something. And in truth, we are muddling along fairly well at the international front. The world has not ground to a halt because of antitrust frictions.

Second, with respect to the notion of establishing an international antitrust regime within the WTO, I am concerned about institutional and political overload. For all their errors, the demonstrators at recent international trade meetings were making one important point: There is in fact a democratic gap between the WTO's rules and its insulated bureaucrats and the democratic institutions in the member-countries. With respect to the United States, that is particularly true under the president's fast-track negotiating authority. That authority is a very effective way for an administration to negotiate credibly with its foreign counterparts, but it does raise questions about democratic accountability when international bodies assume significant new responsibilities.

I also am concerned about giving the WTO dispute resolution authority in antitrust cases. I will stipulate that WTO panels have the technical expertise to adjudicate such cases. Still, as a judge who occasionally hears antitrust cases, I would not feel comfortable reviewing somebody's conduct without a full record. I would be surprised if any ultimate dispute settlement agreement in this area would give WTO panels the authority to obtain the full record—all of the confidential documents, all of the discovery products. I could be wrong, but I am skeptical.

Third, I fear that global rules would be achieved at the price of so much dilution that they would be bromides. They would provide that "cartels are bad, unless they are accepted through legislation that is published in a document of general circulation." That kind of rule solves nothing. In the 1980s, when everybody thought that Japan would become the dominant economy for the next millennium, we used to say, "So what if we pass some rule that says Japan has to have an antitrust law? The Japanese already have that law." It is a perfectly good law, and it is enforced by a very large agency, the Japan Fair Trade Commission. What we need is something other than standards that everyone already meets.

On national treatment, I agree that a commitment to national treatment might be helpful—but it seems to me that it already exists under many bilateral agreements. The United States has a vast network of friendship, commerce, and navigation treaties; bilateral investment treaties; and other kinds of treaties that commit us to national treatment. Maybe Article III of the General Agreement on Tariffs and Trade, as modified by Article XX, does not apply in this context; maybe it does. But in general, I would be surprised if national treatment were the biggest antitrust problem out there.

Let me end on a positive note. I do think there's a better way forward, which involves education, consensus building in a voluntary environment, and targeted cooperation with like-minded countries. It rests on fidelity to our own evolving vision of antitrust law. And it involves, finally, serious international efforts to eliminate the barriers to competition that are still embedded in some international rules.

The International Competition Network (ICN) is serving some of these functions. For example, it is working on well-defined problems, such as the merger review process. If the ICN could make even minor progress in that area, everyone would be better off. My own idea is that there should be a rule that permits companies to file for merger review on whatever form their home country uses. They would submit a copy of that form to an international clearinghouse, which would then send it along to other jurisdictions when necessary. Those other jurisdictions could follow up or not, as they wish. If they need additional information, they could request and obtain it. That procedure would be straightforward, and maybe it would work.

Some of our bilateral agreements are stronger than others. With Canada and Australia, we have a strong version of bilateral cooperation, where we actually share information. With Europe, Japan, Israel, and several other countries, we have the softer form. We may inform those countries when we are about to file a case, but we do not and cannot give them our case files. The idea of positive comity, which emerged in the 1992 version of the Cooperation Agreement between the United States and the European Commission, is extremely helpful. It essentially states that if there is a practice going on in a foreign country that violates that country's law and that is hurting our consumers, we can call on the other party to take steps. If the foreign country proceeds, so much the better. If it does not, we reserve the right to act. Still, the information problem remains even in that setting. It is very nice to say that you can file a lawsuit, but without information to back up an allegation of an anticompetitive practice, that lawsuit will fail. Again, information is an obstacle that we will have to surmount.

Finally, let me list a few areas where I think competition problems are still embedded in the international structure. Agricultural policy is one such area; government procurement is another. Likewise, many sectoral agreements would benefit from a good competition audit. Above all, I absolutely agree with Michael Trebilcock that antidumping and countervailing duty rules are perverse, not helpful.[4] The United States refuses to include antidumping rules in the debate about developing an overall competition policy. That is a shame, because the United States could do a lot of good if it abandoned its position. Thus far, however, the political will to do so has been lacking.

To those who are eager to put competition policy on the world stage, I say, let us start here. Let us start in areas where we can do something right away that will make a big difference. In the meantime, we can move cautiously forward with a broader international agenda, taking care not to wreck everything that we have accomplished here at home.

Notes

1. Judge Wood served as Deputy Assistant Attorney General in the Antitrust Division of the U.S. Department of Justice from 1993 to 1995.

2. Treaty Establishing the European Economic Community, March 25, 1957, 298 UNTS 11, as amended by the Treaty of Amsterdam, October 2, 1997, OJ (C340) 1 (1997).

3. Richard Whish and Diane Wood, *Merger Cases in the Real World—A Study of Merger Control Procedures* (Paris: Organisation for Economic Co-operation and Development, 1994).

4. See Trebilcock and Iacobucci in this volume (chapter 6).

8

Antitrust and the Economics
of Federalism

Frank H. Easterbrook
University of Chicago

I. Introduction: The Conflict between Antitrust and Regulation

A. Antitrust versus Regulation. There is an uneasy coexistence between federal antitrust laws and state regulatory regimes. Regulation displaces competition. Displacement is the purpose, indeed the definition, of regulation. Limitations on the number of taxicabs, licensing of barbers and dentists, health and safety codes, zoning laws, and price supports for milk depend on a belief that competitive markets should be replaced with something else.

Sometimes legislation may be justified as necessary to correct "imperfections" in markets, but in most cases legislation is designed to defeat the market altogether. Although state and local legislatures may say that their schemes are better than the markets they replace, many scholars believe,

Reprinted from the *Journal of Law & Economics*, vol. XXVI (April 1983). By agreement with the author, the article is reprinted here exactly as it first appeared, save for two minor corrections. Copyright by The University of Chicago. All rights reserved.

Several of the ideas developed in this essay were sketched in Richard A. Posner & Frank H. Easterbrook, Antitrust 1008–10, 1026–27 (2d ed. 1981), and I thank my coauthor for the customary flood of stimulating ideas he offered in the course of that enterprise. I also thank Douglas G. Baird, William F. Baxter, Robert C. Ellickson, Richard A. Epstein, Bruce E. Fein, Daniel R. Fischel, Edmund W. Kitch, William M. Landes, Richard A. Posner, and Cass R. Sunstein for helpful comments on earlier drafts. The Law and Economics Program of the University of Chicago provided support for the research and writing of this paper.

and much evidence shows, that regulatory laws owe more to interest group politics than to legislators' concern for the welfare of society at large.[1] The state and local laws reduce allocative efficiency and enhance something else—perhaps the welfare of powerful groups, perhaps "the public interest" more broadly defined.

The antitrust laws, in contrast, are designed to preserve the functioning of competitive markets that, at least presumptively, produce allocative efficiency. The Supreme Court has described the antitrust laws as a "consumer welfare prescription," a convenient shorthand for allocative efficiency.[2] And it has said that "public interest" justifications, however compelling, do not justify private restraints on the operation of markets. The purpose of antitrust analysis "is to form a judgment about the competitive significance of the restraint; it is not to decide whether a policy favoring competition is in the public interest."[3] The Court therefore rejected a "public safety" justification for a reduction of competition among engineers. Any other position, the Court thought, would require case-by-case reexamination of the wisdom of the antitrust laws.

A collision between the federal rule in favor of competition and state rules supplanting competition is inevitable. The antitrust laws apply to all "combinations" in restraint of trade, without limitation to combinations organized outside the auspices of regulation. The antitrust laws "apply" to combinations formed with the permission (even under the compulsion) of state law just as the piracy laws apply to privateers operating with the permission of states.

Under the Supremacy Clause of the Constitution, state-federal collisions are resolved in favor of federal law. Yet such a resolution would doom all state regulation. Because general "public good" justifications (other than those based on consumers' welfare) do not count in antitrust analysis, application of the antitrust laws would crimp the legislative authority of states far more effectively than the old substantive due process cases.[4] And if the Court attempted to avoid this pitfall by accepting "public good" arguments for regulation, it would be undertaking review of social welfare laws indistinguishable from those substantive due process cases.

Although a uniform resolution of the conflict in favor of antitrust is therefore unthinkable—and surely was not part of the structure forged by

Congress in 1890—it is difficult to find in the statutes any form of "inverse supremacy" principle under which state and local rules always prevail. Congress did not deliberate on the matter in 1890 and has not done so since. I therefore assume in the rest of this paper, although perhaps it is no more than an assumption, that the antitrust laws do not displace all state choices. Moreover, I again assume, subject to the same caveat, that the development of principles of accommodation lies in the hands of the courts. Here, as throughout antitrust law, the common law approach prevails; courts must make do as best they can within the confines of litigation.[5]

The problem of accommodation is not one of preemption, for preemption analysis, as usually carried out, would require courts to determine substantive antitrust policy and oust all inconsistent state laws. It is, rather, one of crafting a rule under which *despite* ordinary Supremacy Clause principles the substantive, procompetitive scheme of the antitrust laws is not to be honored. This is the task the Court set for itself in *Parker*, but which, perhaps because neither *Parker* nor any later case resolves the question why there should be such a curious inverse preemption, the Court has been unable to discharge. I sketch in this essay a function a rule of inverse preemption could serve, a function consistent with the competitive objectives of antitrust policy yet consistent with the independent roles of state and local governments.

B. The Judicial Accommodation. The accommodation between antitrust and state law has been developed since 1975. Although there were a few early cases,[6] including *Parker v. Brown*, which gave its name to the subject, these cases have not had an enduring significance. When *Goldfarb v. Virginia State Bar*[7] reached the Court in 1975 the subject had been quiescent for more than twenty years, and almost everyone had forgotten what the fuss had been about in *Parker*. Now, though, there is ample fuss to go around. *Goldfarb*, although unanimous, was opaque. Seven times since *Goldfarb* the Supreme Court has attempted to refine the *Parker* doctrine.[8] In one of these cases the Court treated *Parker* like a statute, expounding on its "judicial history."[9] The result of these exercises has been more confusion than cohesion, as new twists arise in a formerly uncluttered doctrine.[10]

I do not attempt to trace these twists and turns, both because they are not pertinent to my thesis and because they have been thoroughly treated elsewhere. It is enough here to say that the Court's current position is that when the state, acting through its legislature or an agency of statewide authority, makes a conscious decision to replace competition with regulation, that decision will not be subjected to antitrust scrutiny, provided that some state agency actively supervises the implementation of the state's policy. There are a few bells and whistles: sometimes the "supervision" requirement is not satisfied unless the state "compels" particular private acts; sometimes the state's decision to "authorize" regulation by political subunits, rather than its actual decision to regulate, may be respected; a decision to replace competition with monopoly (rather than regulation) may or may not be honored; and all bets are off when the state's regulators acquiesce in a plan proposed by a regulated entity. Predictably, such developments at Court provoke an outpouring of academic commentary variously urging radical expansions, radical contractions, and subtle reformulations.[11] State and local governments have sponsored amendments to the antitrust laws that would alter the doctrines, and the Court's decision in *Boulder* gave powerful impetus to these proposals.

C. Two Fundamental Assumptions. I do not try to manipulate or refine the principles expressed in the recent cases. That would be confusion worse confounded. I instead examine one of the two fundamental assumptions the Court has been using in its common law meanderings.

The Court's two assumptions are these. First, state regulatory laws are anticompetitive dispensations to politically powerful groups, are deleterious to consumers, and therefore ought to be strictly controlled to preserve at least some of the benefits of competition. Second, the control may best be achieved by supplying, as part of federal antitrust law, a set of rules about what kinds of regulatory mechanisms a state may employ to dispense its special interest favors.

The first of these assumptions is what distinguishes the Court's approach in modern cases from its approach in *Parker*. When considering California's raisin prorate program in 1943, the Court saw the state-enforced cartel as a remedy for the evils of excessive competition, as a palliative for demoralizing conditions; it saw the monopoly price as a fair return for industrious farmers. The Court's analysis was dominated by the belief, common during and shortly after the Great Depression, that a dose of monopoly would be just the thing to boost sagging industries.

By 1975, however, it was as clear to the Justices as it was to most economists (and many academic lawyers) that regulation often is procured by and designed for the benefit of those the regulation purports to control. The "ethical" requirement that lawyers charge minimum fees, at issue in *Goldfarb*, was seen as a simple cartel; the argument in *Cantor* that a regulatory agency had approved a joint sale of electricity and lightbulbs to foster the "public interest, convenience, and necessity" appeared to be nothing more than a brazen excuse by the regulated utility for extending its monopoly by stealth from one product to another; the ban on attorneys' advertising in *Bates* appeared as a way to jack up prices by denying clients information about the identity of low-priced attorneys. Justices convinced that state regulation was in the interest of firms at the expense of consumers were reluctant to give antitrust blessings to the results.[12]

Although the first assumption about the interest group politics nature of the regulatory process surely does not describe *all* state and local laws, it probably comes closer to the truth than the opposite presumption. I therefore do not take issue here with the Court's assumption.

The second assumption—that the best way to control the costs of regulation is for the Court to prescribe certain forms and forbid others—is nonetheless open to serious question. For example, this second assumption, combined with a belief about how regulation works, is the basis of the Court's holding that the state must "actively supervise" the regulated firms if its system is to avoid antitrust problems. The Court believes that it must tell the states *how* best to regulate in order to limit the gains of interest groups. The point I seek to develop in this essay is that any limits imposed by the Court on the methods and manners of state regulation are unlikely to be beneficial.

D. A Different Perspective. I use a developing branch of economics, one less celebrated but no less important than the economics of regulation, that the Court has embraced so enthusiastically in the last seven years. The economics of federalism deals with the allocation of functions between different governments (whether different layers of government in a hierarchical system or different sovereigns at the same level). The economics of federalism develops the implications of the fact that, just as there is competition in the market among sellers of bread, there also may be competition among "sellers" of laws. People may vote with their feet as well as with the ballot; indeed, because the feet respond to self-interest more reliably than the ballot does, competition among political bodies may be more important than elections in driving the political system.

Competition among states is not a new idea. Millions of people left their native lands and came to the United States in search of better government and living conditions. For a long time many people thought that some states, first New Jersey and then Delaware, led a "race for the bottom" in corporate law to attract corporations and their taxes.[13] Many people think that Nevada has won the "race for the bottom" in sin, attracting visitors by selling vice, although New Jersey is closing in. One of the common justifications for federal air pollution legislation is that, because no one state's residents can collect all of the benefits of cleaner air (which, after all, drifts east, while dirty air comes in with the breeze), the states lack the proper incentives to legislate. If one state adopts optimally "tough" laws, businesses will migrate elsewhere. Although the idea of interstate competition thus is familiar, it has not yet been applied to antitrust law. I now turn to that application, postponing to the end of Section II the question whether the economics of federalism is a defensible tool for the inquiry. The answer to *that* question depends, in part, on whether the economics of federalism is a useful tool.

II. The Economics of Federalism

A. Laws Have Different Effects on Welfare. I start with a commonplace: Different methods of regulation will have different effects on the welfare of the local population. This is one of the bases for the Supreme Court's requirement that states adopt certain methods of regulation if they want their plans to escape antitrust scrutiny. What may be less obvious is that carefully supervised regulation is not necessarily the style most favorable to allocative efficiency, the value protected by the antitrust laws.

A firm in search of monopoly profits would have a legislative wish list. First on the list would be a monopoly protected by the state but not regulated in any other way. The firm could charge a monopoly price, and it would not need to dissipate income protecting its position or fighting for a greater share of the business, as members of a cartel may do.[14] If the legislative grant were perpetual, perhaps backed up by a promise to pay the firm the full value of its expected future profits in the event of new legislation, the firm's only concern would be competition from new products.

Second on the list would be a cartel enforced by a state agency. The firm would not get all of the monopoly profit, but at least state regulation would put an end to the more obvious forms of cheating by other members of the cartel. The firms would also dissipate some of the monopoly profits in fighting for a greater market share. One method of fighting to engross more of the profit is to improve quality, as airlines once offered better food, movies, and wider seats to obtain more passengers while the CAB controlled prices and entry. Thus the firm would want the regulation to be as complete as possible: the more possible ways of cheating on price and product quality terms the regulator foreclosed, the better off the firm would be. Even so, however, with extensive regulation firms might dissipate profits by competing for the favor of the regulator. In the limit they would spend as much as the monopoly profit itself to influence the regulator's decisions; society would be stuck with a cartel that imposed not only the usual deadweight allocative loss of monopoly but also an additional loss of a substantial fraction of the monopoly profit.

The firm's third wish would be a law lifting the antitrust laws. It is easier to form cartels in such a regime, but cartel agreements are not judicially enforceable in the absence of antitrust laws. Before the Sherman Act cartels formed, broke down, reformed, and collapsed over and over as members cheated, seeking to make greater shares of the sales. The simple no-antitrust solution is least desirable to the firm not only because of the prospect of cheating but also because members of private cartels have an incentive to maintain excess capacity. Each firm fears that some other will cheat, and it wants to be in a position to follow suit quickly. Yet when every firm holds excess capacity, cheating becomes more likely because each firm is in a position to expand its own sales quickly. Private cartels thus often sow the seeds of their own destruction.

Under the current version of the *Parker* doctrine, the state may grant a firm its second wish but not its third, and perhaps not its first either. This is odd from the standpoint of federalism, by which I mean respect for the states' choices, a subject to which I turn in a few pages. It is equally odd from the standpoint of antitrust policy. As the brief discussion above indicates, heavily supervised state regulation has some undesirable welfare attributes that the other two options lack. It is most conducive to competition among the cartelists for rents, competition that may turn large chunks of the monopoly profits into social costs. The more extensive the regulation, the more forms of cheating on the cartel (i.e., the more forms of competition) it chokes off. Heavy supervision is conducive to graft and other offenses against the governmental process. It reduces the flow of information generated by the market and so increases the chance of error. (Incentives as well as information are changed under regulation. Has anyone heard of a regulator losing his job because of a gaffe in projecting market demand?) For one reason or another, the style of regulation often is ill adapted to the tasks given to the agency. And because employees of a regulatory apparatus have goals of their own, they may turn the agency to pursuits unanticipated by the legislature (and the regulated firms).

The inefficiencies of extensive command-and-control regulation fall on consumers and producers alike. And there is some reason to think that whenever politically powerful groups are denied their preferred methods of regulation, the result will be worse for all groups. If firms have political power, they maximize the redistribution of income in their favor by holding as low as they can the deadweight allocative efficiency loss of their chosen methods: the greater the allocative loss, the smaller the pie the "powerful" firms can slice in their favor. There is thus at least a weak presumption that politically powerful groups initially choose methods of redistribution that have relatively low deadweight losses. If these preferred methods are foreclosed, perhaps by federal antitrust doctrine, politically powerful groups will shift to other methods of redistribution that benefit them less but, perhaps, also leave less for the rest of us.[15] They may shift, for example, from demanding free cartelization to demanding state-enforced cartelization, which inhibits cheating. The antitrust laws cannot abridge political clout. They can only shift the form in which it finds expression, and in the shift we may all lose.[16]

Certainly the extensive experience with command-and-control regulation contains little promise of low-cost solutions to the problems of monopoly.[17]

Much federal regulation of this sort has been repealed or greatly modified—airline, trucking, oil, and natural gas regulation are examples—and other systems, such as regulation of telecommunications, are under review. It seems that the Supreme Court has embraced, under the *Parker* doctrine, a style of regulation in ill odor among economists and politicians as well.

At the same time, there is good reason to think that many forms of regulation may be superior to command-and-control supervision. There is a plausible if not convincing case that the best regulation of natural monopoly is no regulation, perhaps because regulation is ineffective and perhaps because the cure is worse than the disease.[18] In other cases the best form of regulation may be competition for the right to be a monopolist. For example, firms seeking to install a cable TV network might bid for the privilege; if all works well, the low, winning bid would be the competitive price. People would obtain the benefits of competition, with no continuing regulation, even though only one firm provided the service.[19] Similarly, broadcast frequencies could be auctioned off to high bidders or given away, just as oil-drilling rights in public lands are auctioned and other mineral rights in public lands are given away.[20] A bald exemption from the antitrust laws may be much better for consumers than price-setting regulation, because cartels break down while regulators punish cheating. The list of alternatives to heavily supervised regulation of the sort envisaged by the Supreme Court in its *Parker* cases could be extended almost indefinitely.[21]

It is not my purpose, though, to debate the merits and demerits of particular methods of regulation. It is enough to make two points. First, some methods of regulation may be worse, for *both* consumers and regulated firms, than other methods; second, it is usually hard to tell which method of regulation is best. These two facts set the stage for competition among governmental bodies to implement preferable systems.

The contrary line of argument would go like this. True, command-and-control regulation has greater costs than those of alternatives. But it is precisely these costs that lie at the heart of the Supreme Court's methods. The *Parker* decisions put states to an unpalatable all-or-nothing choice: they must either put the full regulatory apparatus into play or withdraw in favor of competition. The interest groups that have the political power to obtain mildly favorable legislation may lack the polit-ical power necessary to obtain monopoly-bestowing regulation, precisely because of the greater costs such regulation imposes on the rest of us. The all-or-nothing nature of the choice thus enables states to fend off the interest groups altogether.

This is a hard argument to evaluate. To do so, we would need to know the elasticities of supply and demand for special interest legislation. I cannot imagine how we could obtain such information. It is hard enough to evaluate the consequences of particular programs in particular states at particular times. Obtaining the elasticities for regulation as a whole is almost beyond contemplation.

The unavailability of data puts us to making estimates based on experience with existing systems of regulation. Mine is that the all-or-nothing choice would lead to more costly regulation rather than less, but I cannot pretend that this is a scientific estimate. How one treats estimates of this sort should depend in large measure on whether competition among jurisdictions is a powerful influence on the content of laws. If it is, then total costs, including the costs of error, are minimized under a regimen without a national all-or-nothing rule, because interest groups will be reined in by competition regardless of the national rule. As I try to show below, it is appropriate to act as if interjurisdictional competition is significant.

B. Competition among the States May Lead to Better Regulation.
People have two principles responses to dissatisfaction with the state of things: exit and voice.[22] We usually associate exit with the sale of goods and services: as the price rises or quality declines, people exit by purchasing less. And we usually associate voice with politics: as people become dissatisfied with laws they speak out and organize political campaigns.

But there is no necessary congruence between exit and economic markets, or between voice and politics. As I remarked above, people and firms leave political jurisdictions too. Firms can "move" in a sense just by changing the place of their incorporation. They may export their products to other states or nations; they may move the location of their plants and offices. Other firms may import. People also move, most of them several times in their lives. In extreme cases they emigrate to other nations.

All of these movements place pressure on governments. Whether it is city councils worried that taxes will cause a flight to the suburbs or states designing incentives to attract new industrial plants, governments establish policies that influence the rate (and direction) of the movement of people and firms. New York State, anxious to attract corporate head-quarters, decided not to levy any income tax on intercorporate dividends. New York City decided not to tax or otherwise regulate the stock exchanges lest they move to New Jersey. Many other policies are shaped explicitly by concern for exit. And for every case in which exit was the dominant consideration, there must be hundreds in which the fear of exit was a marginal, but important, influence, affecting the details of legislation even if not its elemental structure. For every recorded case of legislation influenced by exit, there are still others where the possibility of exit simply forestalled discussion. Concern about exit has been influential indeed in determining the level of government at which regulation takes place: if states collectively fear that particular programs would cause exit, they will support federal legislation.[23]

It is possible to demonstrate, albeit with some simplifying assumptions, that the goad of competition to avoid exit leads jurisdictions to enact that set of laws most beneficial to the population.[24] It is hard to place too much weight on this demonstration; the assumptions are so unrealistic that they could not be satisfied, and its predictions are not perfectly confirmed in practice. Laws surely are not optimal. But allowing for all of the difficulties with interjurisdictional competition, one still can show that exit causes a powerful *tendency* toward optimal legislation to the extent four conditions are satisfied: (1) people and resources are more mobile; (2) the number of jurisdictions increases; (3) jurisdictions can select any set of laws they desire; and (4) all of the consequences of one jurisdiction's laws are felt within that jurisdiction. The closer one comes to fulfilling these conditions, the more likely is competition among juris-dictions to be effective.[25] If people are perfectly mobile, or if there are very many jurisdictions, then the competition leads to optimal legislation; to the extent people are less mobile and jurisdictions fewer, or the other conditions less well satisfied, competition is less effective.

Competition among the states concerning corporate charters is a good example of the phenomenon. Condition 1 is well satisfied; firms are mobile, because they may change their place of incorporation even if they do not relocate their plants. Investors are even more mobile; they may elect to invest in firms from any or all states. There are fifty domestic jurisdictions and many more foreign ones from which to choose, and the jurisdictions are not significantly limited in the choices they may offer. Finally, the effects of chartering are largely confined to the investors, who choose their particular investment vehicles. In this sense, at least, there are few spillovers.

Although there has been a hubbub about the consequences of competition among the states for corporate charters, the data indicate that the competition has been beneficial to investors. Firms that announce plans to move their incorporation to Delaware realize significant gains.[26] Because of the mobility of investment capital, it could hardly be otherwise. Delaware has no monopoly of investment opportunities, and if its corporate code did not offer features valuable to investors, they would place their money with firms incorporated elsewhere.[27]

Although it is hard to name other things as mobile as corporate charters and investment capital, it is also hard to find resources—save for land—that are immobile in the long run. Over the course of a generation a very large fraction of the American population moves at least once.[28] Even the largest industrial complexes will eventually wear out, and firms must decide whether to rebuild them in the original locations or to move. The question is not whether the availability of exit puts pressure on jurisdictions but whether it puts enough pressure. I return to that question below.

C. Antitrust and Political Competition. Federal antitrust policy cannot directly affect the mobility of people and resources, but it can affect the other three things that determine the consequences of competition among jurisdictions. The Supreme Court's decisions under the *Parker* doctrine have influenced all three, each time reducing the extent and effectiveness of competition.

Take, for example, condition 2: The more jurisdictions there are, the more likely a person seeking to exit can find at least one jurisdiction with laws suited to his needs and wants, and the more pressing is the competition among them to provide such laws. There are fifty states, which is ample for competition in a sense (California, with the largest "market share," has less than 10 percent of the population) but far too few to provide a complete menu of the possible combinations of laws.[29] There are, however, tens of thousands of cities, towns, counties, and other local governmental units. These governments may supply some of the range of choices that a mere fifty states cannot.

Yet the Supreme Court has concluded that the legislative choices of these governments do not count, even if states want them to count. In *Community Communications Co. v. City of Boulder*[30] the Court held that some "home rule" legislation of the City of Boulder was to be subjected to antitrust scrutiny. Its reasoning was mechanical: only the state and federal governments (and perhaps the Indians) are "sovereign." As a result, it said, only the state's choices are to be respected. Unless the state adopts a policy in favor of (certain kinds of?) regulation of cable television—the subject of Boulder's legislation—all local acts must be scrutinized for compliance with the Sherman Act.

There is no very good reason why the constitutional location of "sovereignty" should be dispositive in common law adjudication under the Sherman Act. Neither the statute nor its legislative history draws such a distinction or suggests that Congress is unwilling to defer to whatever internal disposition a state may make of its legislative powers, and conceptions of federalism are so amorphous that they could be invoked on either side.[31] Why doesn't federalism require the Court to accept—subject to the Republican Form of Government Clause—the state's decision to allocate its powers to local governments rather than agencies of statewide jurisdiction?[32] Justice Rehnquist, speaking for three dissenting justices in *Boulder*, made a federalism argument at least as powerful as the Court's. As he pointed out, to require states to make all important choices is to limit to fifty the maximum number of mixtures of policy, and thus to reduce one of the sources of pressure on governments to provide the set of laws people value most highly.[33] And the Court achieved nothing in exchange for this sacrifice: states always have had the option to adopt statewide policies for cable television or any other subject. The decision in *Boulder* reduced the number of options open to the states in the course of reducing the number of potentially competing jurisdictions.

Or take consideration 3, the extent to which governments may tailor their laws to the desires of the people and thus offer attractive havens for the entry of those dissatisfied with (exiting from) other jurisdictions. The more options a government has, the more it can alter its laws to attract entry, the more choices people have, and thus the more pressure competition places on other jurisdictions seeking to avoid exit.

The most recent developments in the *Parker* doctrine, however, substantially limit the regulatory choices open to a state. Unless the state chooses a system of regulation with "active supervision," the antitrust laws apply.[34] Systems of regulation that simply superintend private arrangements—even if the arrangements are compulsory under state law—or that lift the application of the antitrust laws, are out of bounds even if they are more beneficial to both consumers and firms. One could easily argue that supervision is sufficient if the state's legislature supervises the results of its handiwork, ready to act if the results are unsatisfactory. This would give states full discretion to regulate as they chose. In light of *Midcal, Cantor,* and *Goldfarb,* however, states do not have the option of selecting this form of supervision. They must appoint regulators to supervise firms day to day.

Finally, there is condition 4: Competition is more effective when the consequences of each jurisdiction's rules are felt within that jurisdiction's borders. This is why states do not have the right incentives to control air pollution. All costs would be borne in state, while some of the benefits would escape to other states. This creates a prisoner's dilemma: the legislative program most desirable to each state acting independently is to let other states bear the costs of pollution control, but such a response by every state is destructive to them all. The nature of the problem justifies a national solution.[35] Similarly, states do not have the right incentive to levy taxes if some of the taxes will be paid by residents of other jurisdictions. These nonresidents cannot vote, so they lack the power of voice. To make things worse, to the extent nonresidents pay the state's taxes, the burden on residents is eased (so there is less reason to exit) *and* the gains to exit are reduced because it is necessary to pay (some of) the tax even after leaving.

A monopoly overcharge is a form of taxation. When one state has a large market share of a particular resource, it may "tax" the residents of other states by establishing a cartel. Other states' residents pay most of the overcharge. Although the first state's residents pay the overcharge too, they can be made better off by placing a significant tax on the cartel's profits.

This appears to have occurred in *Parker* itself. The Court's opinion recites that half of the world's raisins, and 95 percent of the raisins grown in the United States, came from California. California's growers thus had market power, and the record showed a substantial price increase when the prorate program went into effect.[36] More than 90 percent of California's raisin crop was shipped in interstate or foreign commerce. More than 90 percent of the monopoly overcharge produced by the prorate program (a mechanism for reducing the supply of raisins) thus fell on nonresidents of California. Even a small tax on raisin growers would have recouped for California's residents the amount they paid in overcharges for raisins consumed at home.

Competition among jurisdictions would be facilitated by prohibition on the export of monopoly overcharges. Yet in *Parker* the Court expressed no antitrust concern that the overcharge fell outside California.[37] Since *Parker* the Court has not even hinted that antitrust scrutiny of a state's program might depend on whether the effects of that program are broadcast outside the state's borders. It has left all scrutiny of interstate effects to the jurisprudence of the Commerce Clause.

In sum, at every turn the *Parker* doctrine frustrates competition among the states. Far from assisting federalism, the *Parker* doctrine undermines the effectiveness of exit in producing legal rules that maximize the welfare of each state's residents.

All of this suggests that some changes could be beneficial. In Section II, I offer a new version of the *Parker* doctrine that would promote rather than undermine competition among jurisdictions. Before doing that, however, I pause to inquire whether the economics of federalism is an appropriate way to examine antitrust policy.

D. Is the Economic Inquiry Fruitful? A reader skeptical of the argument to this point would be entitled to ask, Why the economic inquiry? Is economics an appropriate approach to limning the boundary between state and federal rules? Economics might be inappropriate for either of two reasons. First, Congress may have chosen a different approach. Second, competition among jurisdictions might be so inefficacious that its theoretical elegance is no reason to do anything. I discuss these in turn.

1. What Was the Goal of Congress? I do not argue that Congress intended courts to use economics in establishing the appropriate relation between state and federal law. I have avoided this not only because it is impossible to determine the "intent" of any collective body but also because few if any members of Congress had a personal intent on the subject in 1890. When Congress acted, the courts had such a narrow view of congressional power under the Commerce Clause[38] that few if any members reasonably could have thought that the statute applied to any actions wholly within the borders of a single state. Nothing in the legislative history addresses the matter. To the extent they had conceptions of how the statute would have applied to state legislation, members would have assumed that states could enact laws as they pleased, without interference from the new statute.

The need for accommodation between state and federal law arises only because the Sherman Act has grown with the growth of the commerce power.[39] The problem postdates the statute, and a claim that the statute (or the intent of the members) resolves the problem thus would be fatuous. The courts must use the common law method to create an accommodation; they cannot legitimately claim to *find* either the accommodation or the method of generating it in the statutory language, history, or structure.

They could, perhaps, legitimately hold that the definition of "commerce" for antitrust purposes would be limited to what Congress might have contemplated in 1890. That would obviate most of the need for accommodation and, incidentally, produce the sort of interjurisdictional competition I discuss in this essay. But that is the subject of another paper, and I assume for now that the scope of the Act's commerce jurisdiction is as broad as the constitutional commerce power. Thus the problem of accommodation is unavoidable.

Neither considerations of federalism nor considerations of allocative efficiency nor the legislative history of the antitrust laws requires respecting a state's preferences only when they are implemented in a specific form ("active supervision") or at a given level of government. The Sherman Act arose from concern that the Great Trusts were beyond the control of any one state and had to be regulated by Congress.[40] The Court was unquestionably right in concluding in *Parker* that the statute had nothing to do with a state's regulation of internal affairs.[41]

Parker itself establishes that the state action doctrine is not a limitation on the coverage of the antitrust laws. It is a substantive interpretation of them, an exercise of the Court's essentially common law power to determine which things so threaten the allocative efficiency of the economy that they should be proscribed. There is no reason rooted in the limitations on the power of courts in interpreting statutes why the Supreme Court could not adopt an interpretation of the antitrust laws that maximized the degree of competition among jurisdictions.

The question remains: Why economics? Why not history, for example, or the principle of federalism that unless Congress clearly states its purpose it is deemed not to have interfered with the power of states to pass such laws as they desire,[42] or just federalism more broadly defined? I find economics useful here not so much because it accurately reflects the statutory structure—as I have shown, no one approach would do that—as because economics alone holds out some prospect of rational accommodation.

It is clear enough, I take it, that the substantive function of antitrust is to improve the allocative efficiency of the economy by preserving competition. Whether that function is tempered by political values is of no moment here, for these values do not lead to any particular treatment of the state-federal relation. The economics of federalism offers a way to approach the state-federal relation with an eye to maximizing efficiency and thus to achieving the substantive goal of antitrust.

A historical approach, by contrast, probably would permit states to adopt any form of regulation they chose, even forms that imposed monopoly overcharges on neighbors. By 1890 states were engaged in all of the modern forms of regulation (albeit less intrusively), and they frequently granted monopolies. Because there is no evidence that Congress wanted to upset these regulatory devices or monopoly grants, a historical inquiry would require acquiescence in every state statute.

The "clear statement" form of federalism would lead to exactly the same result. Because Congress did not consider in 1890 whether to displace any state laws, it made no statement at all, clear or otherwise. I doubt, however, that it is appropriate to invoke this principle of accommodation here. The Court has used it only when Congress purports to instruct the states themselves how to behave. The "clear statement" rule is based, in substantial measure, on the Court's unwillingness to assume that Congress is skating on thin ice—as it is whenever it regulates states as states. It is an adjunct of constitutional adjudication. When, however, legislation is addressed to private parties, Congress need not pay attention to the fact that states also may regulate the conduct.[43] Its laws apply to the private parties in the ordinary course, with no serious constitutional doubts. The clear statement principle of federalism thus proves either too much or too little.

What is left is "federalism" more broadly defined. This is what the Court invokes, over and again, in its *Parker* cases. But "federalism" is an empty vessel, into which Justices may (and do) pour whatever they please.[44] "Federalism" is a catchphrase with no independent meaning. Its nebulous character is the source of the doctrinal chaos in *Parker* cases.

Now there may be some reasons *why* an argument invoking federalism leads to one or another result in cases requiring state-federal accommodation. This just leads us back to the economics of federalism, though, because the kinds of arguments I have made are the functional reasons for thinking that some decisions are best left to state and local governments. Whether these reasons are offered in the language of economics is not especially important; the point is that there are no other considerations (save, perhaps, personal political preferences of a kind alien to proper adjudication) for reaching one accommodation rather than another. In sum, economics is an appropriate tool here not only because it serves the substantive goals of antitrust policy but also because it is hard to think of anything else.

2. Does Competition among the States Work? Thinking about the *Parker* problem in terms of competition among jurisdictions is a beneficial exercise whether or not that competition is powerful. After all, to the extent federal law decrees the permissible methods of state regulation, there is even less competition in lawmaking. At the margin, a little competition is better than none, even if the effects are small.

This may seem a rather defensive way to put the proposition. Why not claim that competition among jurisdictions really produces the benefits available in theory?

I would be inclined to make that claim on grounds of casual empiricism. As I pointed out above, politicians constantly worry about exit in designing laws. We see people and firms move frequently, and we observe governments try to staunch the outflow. Governments offer inducements for firms to move in; Illinois offers inducements to stop migration to the Sunbelt; central cities constantly bemoan the exodus of residents. The movement known as white flight, in response to policies of government, is significant. Anyone may observe that suburbs acquire identifiable income, professional, and ethnic characteristics as a result of movement.

It is a commonplace of politics that the party and philosophy of local (even state) officials count for little. The median-voter hypothesis might explain this, but so might competition among jurisdictions, which leaves little leeway for discretion.

Movement is a fact of life, and it is hard to avoid the impression that enough of the movement is influenced—at the margin, of course—by laws and regulations that the movement itself strongly influences governments. It may take only a few searchers and movers to cause powerful responses by competing governments.[45]

It will seem intuitively clear to most people that state and local taxes and welfare benefits, not to mention the quality of local schools, influence migration; if this is so, then it follows that other governmental programs also have such an influence. The regulated sector of the economy exceeds state and local governments in size. Consider that state and local governments regulate utilities, insurance, and the legal and medical professions, just for starters. And it does not necessarily matter here that it is costly to move. Because many people and firms move for reasons unrelated to competition among jurisdictions, the pertinent costs are the incremental costs of diverting one's destination from one jurisdiction to another; these costs may be low indeed.

Federal banking regulation also offers some casual evidence. Because three independent agencies regulate three different sets of banks, each must strive for optimal rules lest the banks regulated by the other two dominate in the marketplace. Those who have observed this process think that it generally has led to regulation in the interest of customers rather than banks.

Nonetheless, the size of the effect of competition among jurisdictions is an empirical question, one of which we have few data. Answers based on casual empiricism may be wrong. I doubt that here: A few pieces of (solid) evidence suggest that people sort themselves out by moving to particular jurisdictions—much more so within states, where there are thousands of competing jurisdictions, than among states.[46] Other evidence suggests that many people move in response to even small changes in the level of local taxes and benefits.[47]

Perhaps contrary evidence will be developed; one can never be sure. But it is wise to act on the evidence and theories available to us, and they suggest the power of competition among the jurisdictions. In the next section of this essay I put the economics of federalism to use as a basis for substantial revisions of the *Parker* doctrine.

III. A Suggestion for a New Antitrust State Action Doctrine

A. A Sketch of a New Approach. Competition among the states to create attractive systems of economic regulation is greatest if states may adopt *any* regulations they choose, at any level of government they choose, so long as the residents of the state that adopts the regulation also bear the whole monopoly overcharge. Under such an approach states could have any rules they want, so long as he who calls the tune also pays the piper.

This approach to the accommodation of state regulation and federal antitrust is attractive because it maximizes *both* the degree of competition to produce laws (and, derivatively, the welfare of each state's residents) *and* the autonomy of the states in maintaining their traditional regulatory roles. Preservation of the states' autonomy was the foremost rationale of the Court's decision in *Parker*, as the Court concluded that Congress had not intended, in passing the Sherman Act, to impinge on the usual operation of state government. It is a happy coincidence that respect for the independence of states as regulators and concern for the competitive conditions animating the Sherman Act lead to the same result.[48]

One potential objection to this proposed state action standard is that it simply apes the negative Commerce Clause. The Court has held that, even in the absence of legislation by Congress under the Commerce power, states may not enact laws that burden commerce "too much." This doctrine has been challenged as textually and historically unwarranted and economically unnecessary.[49] An antitrust doctrine modeled on it might be subjected to the same criticisms and to the additional challenge—also frequently leveled against negative Commerce Clause decisions—that the resulting test would be too nebulous to be useful. An ambulatory doctrine proscribing state regulation that had "excessive" interstate effects might breed confusion without corresponding benefit.[50]

The textual and historical objection to the negative Commerce Clause cases does not apply to antitrust. The Sherman Act is an exercise of Congress's powers under the Commerce Clause; the Court would not be abridging states' regulatory powers in the absence of authority from Congress.

Moreover, an antitrust state action doctrine focusing on the extraterritorial incidence of a monopoly overcharge would not produce the uncertainty frequently associated with negative Commerce Clause litigation. Almost every activity affects interstate commerce to some extent, and a test that forbids "too much" effect, except for some "good reason," invites factious disputes about how much is too much and what reasons count as good ones. An antitrust state action doctrine that turned on the incidence of the overcharge would avoid these questions.

For example, even if a state's regulatory program elevated the domestic prices of liquor a great deal—and thus affected a great deal of interstate commerce by reducing imports[51]—it would be unnecessary for a court to attempt to measure the size of that effect, weigh the gains and losses of the state's program, or determine the adequacy of a proffered justification. Unless the liquor business is a natural monopoly, the industry's costs will be constant or rising, in competition, as its sales increase. When a monopoly in state C causes C to import less liquor, then, the price of spirits in other states will remain constant or fall. State C's residents will bear the whole overcharge; because state C cannot export its costs, the exit and voice mechanisms will be effective in constraining C's decisions; and there is no antitrust justification for further judicial review. So long as C's residents pay the price and obtain the benefits of C's law, justification for federal supervision vanishes, and there is every reason to think that the process of competition among jurisdictions will work to the benefit of C's residents to at least as great an extent as application of the antitrust laws would assist those people.

B. Some Illustrations. My approach to the *Parker* problem may seem complex, but it is not. It handles with ease cases that the Court has found difficult.

Parker is the prime case in point. The raisin prorate program greatly reduced the supply of raisins available for export to other states. This caused the price to rise, to the glee of California's growers but the dismay of residents elsewhere. Under an approach forbidding the export of a monopoly overcharge, the raisin prorate program would have been pre-empted by the Sherman Act. Such a holding would have abolished a cartel in the spirit of the great Sugar Trust, against which the Sherman Act was directed.

Although the preemption of California's prorate law would have reduced the legislative options of the state, it would have left California with several ways to bolster the income (and morale) of its raisin growers, if that were its desire. California could, for example, have granted subsidies to raisin farmers. The raisin growers also could have gone to Congress. (They already had a general antitrust exemption under the Capper-Volstead Act, but the exemption apparently was not enough to prevent outbreaks of competition.) It would have been much harder for them to obtain a prorate program from Congress than from California's legislature, however; California obtained net gains from the monopoly overcharge of the raisin growers, while the United States as a whole was made poorer. Congress therefore would have resisted establishing a prorate program, unless perhaps the raisin growers could have joined with other interest groups in a logrolling process. Logrolling would have been costly in two ways, though. The growers would have needed to form a coalition of many interest groups, and such coalitions are hard to keep together; and the growers would have needed to grant some favors to the partners. Both of these costs make federal legislation less attractive, even if it could be obtained.[52]

In *Schwegmann* the state adopted a system of resale price maintenance for liquor; once one wholesaler agreed to a resale price for a particular brand, every wholesaler was bound. The Court held this preempted by the Sherman Act. An approach emphasizing limits on the export of overcharges would have sustained the law; the state's residents paid any overcharge and obtained any benefits, for the fixed resale price did not extend beyond the state's borders.[53] The same is true of the California resale price maintenance for liquor, which the Court held in *Midcal* to be invalid but which my approach would leave within the states' discretion.

The Court came to contrasting conclusions in its two cases of "ethical" restrictions by bar associations. In *Goldfarb* the Court held minimum price schedules unlawful under the Sherman Act because the Supreme Court of Virginia had simply acquiesced in schedules proposed by the bar rather than promulgating or overseeing them. In *Bates* the Court held that the Sherman Act did not apply to restrictions on attorneys' advertising promulgated by the Supreme Court of Arizona: there, it observed, although the state court initially acquiesced in an ethical proposal drafted by the American Bar Association, it supervised the ethical rule carefully when applying it in disciplinary proceedings. Thus the rule had the force of state policy. The Supreme Court hinted that the same might have been true had the Virginia court been given the chance to apply the minimum fee schedules in some disciplinary case, although as things turned out it never had the chance because someone brought a suit before the court had the opportunity to consider a fee violation as a basis of discipline.

The distinction between the cases seems entirely artificial, perhaps fortuitous. An inquiry based on the incidence of any overcharge would have treated the two alike. If minimum fee schedules are a method of cartelization, the overcharge is paid by residents of Virginia. This is so even for the kinds of transactions presented to the Supreme Court— housing purchases by persons seeking to move into Virginia from out of state. The cost of attorneys' services is simply one component of the price of buying a new house. Real estate and attorneys' time are complementary inputs into housing. If the minimum fee schedules caused the price of attorneys' time to rise, they also caused the price of real estate to fall. The overcharge ultimately was paid by the Virginia residents who attempted to sell real estate. And in *Bates*, if the ban on advertising elevated the price of attorneys' services, as the Court thought,[54] Arizona's residents paid that price. Other states could obtain the benefits of competition free from any restraint imposed in Arizona. (The price in other states might have been affected if Arizona's lawyers had been allowed to practice in other states but forbidden to advertise there. But because states other than Arizona fenced out Arizona's lawyers, this problem did not arise.)

The rest of the Court's antitrust state action cases could be analyzed in the same way. In *Exxon, Orrin Fox, City of Lafayette*, and *Boulder*, the state's residents bore the whole overcharge—if, indeed, there was an overcharge. In several of the cases there is good reason to think that the state's laws improved allocative efficiency, so that there would have been no overcharge at all.[55] Two of these four cases involved regulation by local governments. If competition among jurisdictions *ever* works, it does so in such cases because of the ease of movement and the number of competing polities.

City of Lafayette nonetheless presents an interesting wrinkle. Plaintiffs there alleged that two municipally owned and operated electric utilities had committed exclusionary practices that had consequences outside the cities' borders. Plaintiffs maintained, for example, that one city had established a tie between water and electricity, so that consumers outside the City of Plaquemine, and dependent on it for water, were required to buy the city's electricity as well.

This is at least a conceivable case of an export of a monopoly overcharge. It is not, however, a plausible one, because the city's residents all were paying the same overcharge, yet the purpose of the scheme supposedly would have been to reduce rates in the city at the expense of those who lacked a voice in the city's government. At all events the export could have been corrected by the state; if a state chooses to allow its municipalities to export overcharges elsewhere within the state, it is hard to see why that should be any concern of the antitrust laws.[56] Once more, use of antitrust law to impose a rule against such intrastate activity simply decreases the options open to states and thus impairs the power of jurisdictional competition to produce beneficial laws.

IV. Conclusion

I do not deny that a rule against exporting overcharges would present some hard cases. California might adopt a health regulation, for example, requiring half of the raisin crop to be incinerated; that would create the same overcharge that existed in *Parker*. I would be inclined to leave such statutes to standard Commerce Clause doctrine, but the handling of borderline cases is not of great moment. They will be few in number, because few states control enough of any resource to have market power. Claims of exported overcharges would be handled the same way as claims of exported state taxes: most such claims fail at the threshold because the states do not have market power in the monopolized or taxed resource.[57] The overwhelming majority of antitrust state action cases that the Court finds puzzling would be handled quickly and easily.

I also do not deny that interest groups will obtain anticompetitive state legislation. There are many opportunities for such legislation when the beneficiaries are concentrated relative to the losers, and these losses may be less than the costs of moving. But the same is true of federal legislation, and competition among jurisdictions becomes less effective as the size of the legislating jurisdiction increases.

Revision of the antitrust state action doctrine along the lines I have sketched would fulfill the promise of balanced federalism contained in *Parker* without jeopardizing allocative efficiency. One need not think of states as laboratories, as Justice Brandeis did,[58] to know that the pressures of exit and voice cause governments to search for laws that strike an adequate balance between favors to interest groups and benefits to other residents. The greatest threat to consumers' welfare is not states, and their competition, but a uniform national regimen that stifles the power of exit—that is, a monopoly of lawmaking. The Court's decisions drive states to adopt more and more intrusive forms of regulation, with greater potentials for monopoly overcharges and allocative efficiency loss. If any branch of federal law is to recognize the power of competition to improve the lot of the people, it is hard to think of a more fitting place to start than antitrust.

Notes

1. The seminal article is George J. Stigler, The Theory of Economic Regulation, 2 Bell J. Econ. 3 (1971), reprinted with addendum in George J. Stigler, The Citizen and the State 114 (1975). See also Gary S. Becker, Competition Among Pressure Groups for Political Influence, Q. J. Econ. (1983) in press; Sam Peltzman, Toward a More General Theory of Regulation, 19 J. Law & Econ. 211 (1976); Richard A. Posner, Theories of Economics Regulation, 5 Bell J. Econ. 335 (1974). For evidence one could peruse, for example, Edmund W. Kitch, Marc Isaacson, & Daniel Kasper, The Regulation of Taxicabs in Chicago, 14 J. Law & Econ. 285 (1971); Alex R. Maurizi, Ruth L. Moore, & Lawrence Shepard, Competing For Professional Control: Professional Mix in the Eyeglass Industry, 24 J. Law & Econ. 351 (1981); or almost any issue of this *Journal* or the *Bell Journal of Economics*. (For a survey of "public interest" justifications for regulation, see Stephen Breyer, Regulation and Its Reform (1982).)

2. Reiter v. Sonotone Corp., 442 U.S. 330, 343 (1979), quoting from Robert H. Bork, The Antitrust Paradox 66 (1978). See also, for example, Broadcast Music, Inc. v. Columbia Broadcasting System, Inc. 441 U.S. 1, 9–10, 19–20 (1979) ; Continental T.V., Inc. v. GTE Sylvania Inc., 433 U.S. 36, 52 n. 21 (1977). For justifications of this approach, see Bork, *supra*, and Frank H. Easterbrook, Is There a Ratchet in Antitrust Law?, 60 Tex. L. Rev. 705, 713–17 (1982).

3. National Society of Professional Engineers v. United States, 435 U.S. 679, 692 (1978).

4. See Exxon Corp. v. Governor of Maryland, 437 U.S. 117, 133 (1978): "[I]f an adverse effect on competition were, in and of itself, enough to render a state statute invalid [under the antitrust laws], the States' power to engage in economic regulation would be effectively destroyed." See also Paul R. Verkuil, State Action, Due Process and Antitrust: Reflections on Parker v. Brown, 75 Colum. L. Rev. 328 (1975), for a thoughtful discussion of the relation between substantive due process and antitrust scrutiny of state laws.

5. Compare National Society of Professional Engineers, 435 U.S. 679, 688 (1978) (Congress "expected the courts to give shape to the statute's broad mandate by drawing on the common-law tradition"), and Continental T.V., Inc. v. GTE Sylvania Inc., 433 U.S. 36 (1997) (overruling an earlier case in common law fashion), with Texas Industries, Inc. v. Radcliff Materials, Inc., 451 U.S. 630, 643 (1981) ("The intent to allow courts to develop governing principles of law, so unmistakably clear with regard to substantive violations, does not appear in debates on the treble-damages action"). See Easterbrook, *supra* note 2.

6. Schwegmann Bros. v. Calvert Distillers Corp., 341 U.S. 384 (1951); Parker v. Brown, 317 U.S. 341, 350–52 (1943); Olsen v. Smith, 195 U.S. 332, 344–45 (1904).

7. 421 U.S. 773 (1975).

8. Community Communications Co. v. City of Boulder, 455 U.S. 40 (1982); California Retail Liquor Dealers' Ass'n v. Midcal Aluminum, Inc., 445 U.S. 97 (1980); New Motor Vehicle Board v. Orrin W. Fox Co., 439 U.S. 96, 109–11 (1978); Exxon Corp. v. Governor of Maryland, 437 U.S. 117, 132–133 (1978); City of Lafayette v. Louisiana Power & Light Co., 435 U.S. 389 (1978); Bates v. State Bar of Arizona, 433 U.S. 350, 359–63 (1977); Cantor v. Detroit Edison Co., 428 U.S. 578 (1976). See also Rice v. Norman Williams Co., 102 S. Ct. 3294 (1982) (using preemption analysis to evaluate a claim of conflict between state law and federal antitrust law).

9. Cantor v. Detroit Edison Corp., 428 U.S. 579, 585–92 (1976) (plurality opinion). See also *id.* at 617–22 (Stewart, J., dissenting) (challenging the propriety of the exercise but also examining the judicial history of *Parker* and reaching a conclusion opposite to that of the plurality).

10. This should not be unexpected. Frank H. Easterbrook, Ways of Criticizing the Court, 95 Harv. L. Rev. 802 (1982).

11. The more enlightening include 1 Phillip Areeda & Donald F. Turner, Antitrust Law ¶¶ 209–17, 212.1–212.7 (1978; Areeda Supp. 1982); Lawrence A. Sullivan, Antitrust 731–40 (1977); William H. Page, Antitrust, Federalism, and the Regulatory Process: A Reconstruction and Critique of the State Action Exemption after Midcal Aluminum, 61 B. U. L. Rev. 1099 (1981); and Verkuil, *supra* note 4.

12. The Court has also used the first amendment, in *Bates* and other cases, to override states' interest group regulation. See Virginia Board of Pharmacy v. Virginia Citizens Consumer Council, Inc., 425 U.S. 748, 763–66 (1976), analyzed in Thomas H. Jackson & John Calvin Jeffries, Jr., Commercial Speech: Economic Due Process and the First Amendment, 65 Va. L. Rev. 1, 25–40 (1979).

13. The impression that the race—surely real—was for the "bottom" was uninformed. Compare, for example, Ralph Nader, Mark Green, and Joel Seligman, Taming the Giant Corporation (1976); and William L. Cary, Federalism and Corporate Law: Reflections upon Delaware, 83 Yale L. J. 663 (1974); with Ralph K. Winter, Jr., Government and the Corporation (1978); Daniel R. Fischel, The "Race to the Bottom" Revisited: Reflections on Recent Developments in Delaware Corporation Law, 76 Nw. U. L. Rev. 913 (1982); and Walter Werner, Corporation Law in Search of Its Future, 81 Colum. L. Rev. 1611 (1981). See also Section II, D 2, *infra.*

14. For discussions of how the expenditure of resources in competition to engross ever larger shares of a given monopoly profit could increase the social costs of monopoly, see, for example, Keith Cowling & Dennis C. Mueller, The Social Costs of Monopoly Power, 88 Econ. J. 727 (1978); S. C. Littlechild, Misleading Calculations of the Social Costs of Monopoly Power, 91 Econ. J. 348 (1981); Richard A. Posner, The Social Costs of Monopoly and Regulation, 83 J.

Pol. Econ. 807 (1975); Gordon Tullock, The Welfare Costs of Tariffs, Monopolies, and Theft, 5 Wes. Econ. J. 224 (1967). Compare Edward M. Rice and Thomas S. Ulen, Rent Seeking and Welfare Loss, in 3 Research in Law & Econ. 53–65 (Richard O. Zerbe ed. 1981) (arguing that competition for monopoly rents may lead to efficiencies when the state does not guarantee the monopoly); William P. Rogerson, The Social Costs of Monopoly and Regulation: A Game-theoretic Analysis, 13 Bell J. Econ. 391 (1982) (complete conversion of rents into costs unlikely).

15. For the formal argument, see Becker, *supra* note 1. For an application to antitrust see Frank H. Easterbrook, Predatory Strategies and Counterstrategies, 48 U. Chi. L. Rev. 263. 311–12 (1981).

16. The Court has recognized this—partly on prudential and partly on First Amendment grounds—in holding that people may lobby for and obtain legislation that gives them anticompetitive preferences over their rivals. For example, Eastern Railroad Presidents Conference v. Noerr Motor Freight, Inc., 365 U.S. 127 (1965). Cf. NAACP v. Claiborne Hardware Co., 102 S. Ct. 3409, 3426 (1982) (applying the *Noerr* analysis to sustain concerned economic action as well as lobbying to obtain economic benefits). See also Daniel R. Fischel, Antitrust Liability for Attempts to Influence Government Action: The Basis and Limits of the Noerr-Pennington Doctrine, 45 U. Chi. L. Rev. 80 (1977).

17. For surveys of the experience, see Breyer, *supra* note 1; Paul W. MacAvoy, The Regulated Industries and the Economy (1979); Susan Phillips & J. Richard Zecher, The SEC and the Public Interest (1981); Stigler, *supra* note 1.

18. For example, Richard A. Posner, Natural Monopoly and Its Regulation, 21 Stan. L. Rev. 548 (1969); George J. Stigler & Claire Friedland, What Can Regulators Regulate? The Case of Electricity, 5 J. Law & Econ. 1 (1962), reprinted in Stigler, *supra* note 1, at 61–77. See also Richard Schmalensee, The Control of Natural Monopolies (1979) (survey of the economics of natural monopoly suggesting that much of the current regulation is ineffectual or counterproductive but that improvements often are possible).

19. For example, Harold Demsetz, Why Regulate Utilities? 11 J. Law & Econ. 55 (1968); Richard A. Posner, The Appropriate Scope of Regulation in the Cable Television Industry, 3 Bell J. Econ. 98 (1972). But compare Oliver E. Williamson, Franchise Bidding for Natural Monopolies—in General and with Respect to CATV, 7 Bell J. Econ. 73 (1976) (pointing out the difficulties in specifying the terms of exclusive contracts and enforcing the promises); Schmalensee, *supra* note 18, at 68–73 (same).

20. For example, R. H. Coase, The Federal Communications Commission, 2 J. Law & Econ. 1 (1959); Leo Herzel, "Public Interest" and the Market in Color Television Regulation, 18 U. Chi. L. Rev. 802 (1951); Leo Herzel, Rejoinder, 20 U. Chi. L. Rev. 106 (1952). Compare Watt v. Energy Action Educational Foundation, 454 U.S. 151 (1981) (oil bidding).

21. For example, Breyer, *supra* note 1; Lester Lave, The Strategy of Social Regulation (1981); Robert W. Poole, Jr., ed., Instead of Regulation: Alternatives to Federal Regulatory Agencies (1982).

22. Albert O. Hirschman, Exit, Voice, and Loyalty (1970); see also Brian Barry, Sociologists, Economists and Democracy (1970). Arguments about the utility of movement are not confined to economists and political scientists. Consider the many-utopias vision of Robert Nozick, Anarchy, State, and Utopia 297–334 (1974).

23. For a formal analysis see Susan Rose-Ackerman, Does Federalism Matter? Political Choice in a Federal Republic, 89 J. Pol. Econ. 152 (1981) (discussing effects of both positive and negative spillovers).

24. Charles M. Tiebout, A Pure Theory of Local Expenditures, 64 J. Pol. Econ. 416 (1956).

25. For good discussions, see Dennis C. Mueller, Public Choice 125–45 (1979), 125–45; Dennis Epple & Allan Zelenitz, The Implications of Competition among Jurisdictions: Does Tiebout Need Politics? 89 J. Pol. Econ. 1197 (1981); Martin McGuire, Group Segregation and Optimal Jurisdictions, 82 J. Pol. Econ. 112 (1974). But see John Yinger, Capitalization and the Theory of Local Public Finance, 90 J. Pol. Econ. 917 (1982) (competition not completely effective if the benefits of local services are capitalized into local property values and then taxed).

26. Peter Dodd & Richard Leftwich, The Market for Corporate Charters: "Unhealthy Competition" v. Federal Regulation, 53 J. Bus. 259 (1980).

27. See Winter, *supra* note 13.

28. Between 1975 and 1980 some 48 percent of the population changed residence. Although most changes are within the same metropolitan area, some 44 percent of the population is now living in a state other than the one of birth. 1981 Statistical Abstract of the United States, 13, 15 (Tables 13, 18).

29. If each jurisdiction legislates on only ten subjects, and there are only four possible laws about each subject, then the number of jurisdictions necessary to offer a full menu of the combinations is 4^{10}, or 1,048,576 jurisdictions. The maximum number required to provide the full range of desired options is limited only because there is no need to have more than one jurisdiction per person.

30. 455 U.S. 40 (1982).

31. The U.S. Reports teem with cases, many invoking the spirit of federalism, that exalt the privileges of local governments, sometimes to the point of giving them rights to legislate that states would lack because of their uneven effects on the state's residents. For example, Fair Assessment in Real Estate Ass'n, Inc. v. McNary, 454 U.S. 100 (1981) (principles of federalism prevent damages action under 42 U.S.C. § 1983 on account of county taxation, despite plain language of statute); Ball v. James, 451 U.S. 355 (1981) (local electricity district may exclude all but landowners from voting); Holt Civic Club v. City of Tuscaloosa, 439 U.S. 60 (1978) (municipality may legislate with respect to nonresidents, and nonresidents have

no constitutional right to vote; the decision contains a paean to local experimentation); County Board of Arlington County v. Richards, 434 U.S. 5 (1977) (sustaining a county ordinance giving residents of certain neighborhoods exclusive parking privileges; holding that communities may discriminate against nonresidents); National League of Cities v. Usery, 426 U.S. 833, 855 n. 20 (1976) (holding part of the Fair Labor Standards Act unconstitutional because it interfered with the autonomy of cities and with the ability of states to carry out policies through subordinate arms); McCarthy v. Philadelphia Civil Service Commission, 424 U.S. 645 (1976) (local government may deny employment to residents of the state who live outside the city); Milliken v. Bradley, 418 U.S. 717 (1974) (declining to hold state as a unit responsible for racial discrimination practiced by a municipal school district; holding, on local autonomy grounds, that remedy for discrimination ought not to involve multiple units of government); Village of Belle Terre v. Boraas, 416 U.S. 1, 8 (1974) (praise for diversity offered by local governments); San Antonio School District v. Rodriguez, 411 U.S. 1 (1973) (local governments may fund school systems in a way that produces substantial inequality of education opportunities for residents of the state); Boyle v. Landry, 401 U.S. 77 (1971) (principles of federalism bar injunction against prosecution for violation of local ordinances). The results in many of these cases could be defended with arguments, based on the economics of federalism, that any attempt to attain equal treatment within a state would be defeated by exit. See Robert P. Inman & Daniel L. Rubinfeld, The Judicial Pursuit of Local Fiscal Equity, 92 Harv. L. Rev. 1662, 1721–47 (1979). For almost every case in this list one could invoke some apparently contrary case. See, for example, Mt. Healthy City School District Board of Education v. Doyle, 429 U.S. 274, 279–81 (1977) (school districts, like cities and counties, lack the states' Eleventh Amendment immunity from suit); Hills v. Gautreaux, 425 U.S. 284 (1976) (federal courts possess equitable discretion to order suburban housing authorities to establish public housing as part of remedy for city's violation); United States v. Scotland Neck City Board of Education, 407 U.S. 484 (1972) (the creation of a local governmental unit that would hinder school desegregation may be enjoined); Waller v. Florida, 397 U.S. 387 (1970) (because city and state are not separate sovereigns, they may not bring successive criminal prosecutions); Gomillion v. Lightfoot, 364 U.S. 339 (1960) (redrawing local boundaries may violate voting rights). But these and other cases just show that the process of establishing the appropriate domain of state versus local government in a federal system is exceptionally complex business. They hardly establish, as the Court seemed to think in *Boulder*, that there is only one right way to think about the subject.

32. See Hughes v. Superior Court, 339 U.S. 460, 467 (1950). Compare Bates v. State Bar of Arizona, 433 U.S. 350 (1977) (legislative power exercised by a court of statewide jurisdiction).

33. See 455 U.S. at 60–71 (joined by Burger, C. J., and O'Connor, J.). I think that Justice Rehnquist's dissent captures the original point of *Parker* better than

anything else the Court has offered since 1943. As I discuss later on, there are problems in *Parker* itself. But if the *Parker* doctrine is to be returned to its original form, one could hardly do better than follow Justice Rehnquist's analysis.

34. For example, California Retail Liquor Dealer's Ass'n v. Midcal Aluminum, Inc., 445 U.S. 97 (1980).

35. Of course, not all forms of pollution produce out-of-state effects. When the benefits of pollution control are realized in state, there is no similar problem. Thus California, whose geography prevents much of its pollution from leaving the state, has unusually stringent laws. In discussing pollution, I do not mean to imply that the federal cure is necessarily better than the disease. Federal statutes are inviting devices for imposing handicaps on political and economic rivals, and there is some evidence that the costs of such handicapping exceed the benefits from reduction in externalities. For example, Bruce A. Ackerman and W. T. Hassler, Clean Coal/Dirty Air, or How the Clean-Air Act Became a Multibillion-Dollar Bail-Out for High Sulfur Coal Producers and What Should Be Done About It (1981); Peter H. Aranson, Pollution Control: The Case for Competition, in Instead of Regulation, *supra* note 21, at 339, 348–81 (arguing that federal legislation enables states to cartelize pollution control, while the creation of property rights in the air would handle externalities more efficiently).

36. Without market power there could be no overcharge, and there would be no need to worry about its exportation. See William M. Landes & Richard A. Posner, Market Power in Antitrust Cases, 94 Harv. L. Rev. 937 (1981). It is probably rare that producers in one state have such market power that they could export overcharges. Usually producers in a single state will have only a very small portion of the productive capacity for a particular product.

37. The Court did not discuss this problem under an antitrust heading at all but considered, instead, whether the prorate program violated the Commerce Clause by affecting the amount of interstate commerce. 317 U.S. at 359–68. The Court concluded that it did not, in large measure because, it thought, such state agricultural programs had at least implicit support from Congress. Compare Western & Southern Life Ins. Co. v. State Board of Equalization, 451 U.S. 658 (1981) (Congress may authorize what would otherwise be a violation of the "negative Commerce Clause"), with Hunt v. Washington State Apple Advertising Comm'n, 432 U.S. 333 (1977) (state statute violates the negative Commerce Clause when in practical effect it secures a monopoly, within its borders, for apples produced in state at the expense of apples produced in other states).

38. For example, United States v. E. C. Knight Co., 156 U.S. 1 (1895); Paul v. Virginia, 75 U.S. (8 Wall.) 168 (1868).

39. For example, McLain v. Real Estate Board of New Orleans, Inc., 444 U.S. 232 (1980); Hospital Building Co. v. Trustees of Rex Hospital, 425 U.S. 738, 743 n. 2 (1976); United States v. South-Eastern Underwriters Ass'n, 322 U.S. 533 (1944).

40. See William Letwin, Law and Economic Policy in America (1965); Robert H. Bork, Legislative Intent and the Policy of the Sherman Act, 9 J. Law & Econ. 7 (1966). A substantial part of the problem came from the judicial interpretation of the Commerce Clause in that era. The Court repeatedly held that states could not regulate goods that moved in interstate commerce. For example, Wabash, St. Louis & Pacific Ry. v. Illinois, 118 U.S. 557 (1886). The time in which state and federal powers of regulation were mutually exclusive is long since over.

41. Consider also the history of the McCarran-Ferguson Act. When the Court held that the Sherman Act applied to the insurance business, Congress quickly enacted an exemption. See the discussion in Group Life & Health Ins. Co. v. Royal Drug Co., 440 U.S. 205 (1979). The principal characteristic of state regulation of insurance is that, if the regulation produces an overcharge, that overcharge falls wholly on the state's residents.

42. For example, Pennhurst State School and Hospital v. Halderman, 451 U.S. 1 (1981).

43. For example, Hodel v. Virginia Surface Mining & Reclamation Ass'n, 452 U.S. 264 (1981).

44. See text and notes 31–33, supra.

45. This is essentially a problem in the economics of searching. See Alan Schwartz & Louis L. Wilde, Intervening in Markets on the Basis of Imperfect Information, 127 U. Pa. L. Rev. 630 (1979); Alan Schwartz & Louis L. Wilde, Competitive Equilibria in Markets for Heterogeneous Goods under Imperfect Information: A Theoretical Analysis with Policy Implications, 13 Bell J. Econ. 181 (1982).

46. See Edward M. Gramlich & Daniel L. Rubinfield, Micro Estimates of Public Spending Demand Functions and Tests of the Tiebout and Median-Voter Hypothesis, 90 J. Pol. Econ. 536, 551–55 (1982) (there is a substantial tendency for people with similar demands for public services to group together in local jurisdictions); Raymond M. Reinhard, Estimating Property Tax Capitalization: A Further Comment, 89 J. Pol. Econ. 1251 (1981) (collecting earlier work) (rents and property taxes tend to behave in the way they would if Tiebout hypothesis were correct); G. Miller, Cities By Contract: The Politics of Municipal Incorporation (1981) (a more casual treatment of movement among cities in Los Angeles County).

47. See David F. Bradford & Harry H. Kelejian, An Econometric Model of the Flight to the Suburbs, 81 J. Pol. Econ. 566 (1973) (a 10 percent decline in net benefits for any income class causes 5 percent of that class to leave the central city).

48. The Solicitor General's brief in Parker urged a principle similar to the one I adopt, focusing on the out-of-state effects of the regulation. Br. for the United States as amicus curiae, No. 46, October Term, 1942, at 62–66. The Court did not discuss the suggestion.

49. Edmund W. Kitch, Regulation and the American Common Market, in Regulation, Federalism, and Interstate Commerce 7–55 (A. Dan Tarlock ed. 1981), is an especially effective argument along these lines.

50. Page, *supra* note 11, at 1107, maintains that an antitrust state action doctrine focusing on out-of-state effects would be incapable of principled application. I disagree with Professor Page for the reasons stated in the following text.

51. See Burke v. Ford, 389 U.S. 320 (1967).

52. As a first approximation, it would be easier for interest groups to obtain protective legislation from states, because the coalitions needed to support the laws would be smaller. But because the detriments of the legislation would fall on a more concentrated group, and because it is easier to move away from local governments than from the United States, it is difficult to know whether interest groups in fact exercise more power at the local level than in Congress.

53. The same analysis would apply if the state had told its liquor dealers they were free to create a cartel—if they could. If they lacked market power, there would be no antitrust objection because they would be unable to increase the price. And if they possessed market power, the cartel would produce extraterritorial effects and be condemned on that ground. The approach I suggest in this paper would treat state regulation and state authorization of private cartels identically.

54. 433 U.S. 377. See also Lee Benham, The Effect of Advertising on the Price of Eyeglasses, 15 J. L. & Econ. 337 (1972), cited by the Court at 377 n. 34.

55. *Schwegmann* and *Midcal* involved restricted distribution systems. Because the manufacturers using the restricted distribution lacked market power, it is most likely that the systems improved consumers' welfare. See Continental T.V., Inc. v. GTE Sylvania Inc., 433 U.S. 36 (1977); Valley Liquors, Inc. v. Renfield Importers, Ltd., 678 F.2d 742 (7th Cir. 1982); Richard A. Posner, The Next Step in the Antitrust Treatment of Restricted Distribution: Per Se Legality, 48 U. Chi. L. Rev. 6 (1981). *Boulder* involved a system of franchise competition under which firms bid for the right to be exclusive distributors. See text at note 19, supra, for a brief analysis of such systems.

56. Cf. Holt Civic Club v. City of Tuscaloosa, 439 U.S. 60 (1978) (the exercise of governmental authority by a municipality outside its borders does not violate the constitutional voting rights of those who feel the extraterritorial effects).

57. See Charles E. McLure, Jr., Incidence Analysis and the Courts: An Examination of Four 1981 Cases, 1 Sup. Ct. Econ. Rev. —— (1982). One benefit of the approach I suggest is that it equalizes the judicial treatment of exported taxes and exported overcharges. But compare William A. Fischel, Zoning and the Exercise of Monopoly Power: A Reevaluation, 8 J. Urban Econ. 283 (1980) (suggesting that some cities have market power because of their unique attributes).

58. New State Ice Co. v. Lieberman, 285 U.S. 262, 311 (1932) (dissenting opinion). Brandeis argued that states should be given the utmost freedom to conduct

their experiments. The Justice assumed that states calmly experiment, gather information, and write "better" statutes, as if legislators were public-sprited professors. The economics of federalism arrives at the Brandeis conclusion—people benefit if state and local governments have freedom to enact different laws— without his Panglossian assumptions.

9

A Geographic Market Power Test for Sherman Act Jurisdiction

D. Bruce Johnsen and Moin A. Yahya

The greatest threat to consumers' welfare is not states, and their competition, but a uniform national regimen that stifles the power of exit—that is, a monopoly of lawmaking.
—Frank H. Easterbrook[1]

The Sherman Act (1890) prohibits restraints of trade or commerce "among the several states." Yet, during the past thirty years, the U.S. Supreme Court has routinely upheld applications of the Sherman Act to restraints that are purely intrastate by any economically sensible standard. Most recently, in *Summit Health, Ltd. v. Pinhas* (1991), a narrow majority of the Court reaffirmed a jurisdictional test—the so-called "infected activities" test—that extends the Sherman Act's reach to even the most local restraints. This position ignores Congress's original intent in passing the Act, fails to promote consumer welfare, and undermines the important role of the states as laboratories for political competition in our federal system.

Justice Scalia's forceful dissent in *Summit*, joined by three other justices, argued that the infected activities test is needlessly vague and expansive and, moreover, fails to resolve the threshold economic issues of market definition and market power that should be necessary to establish statutory jurisdiction. The question, as Scalia put it, "is not whether Congress *could* reach the activity before us here if it wanted to, but whether it *has done* so via the Sherman Act. That enactment does not prohibit all conspiracies . . . that have sufficient constitutional 'nexus' to interstate commerce to be regulated. It prohibits only those conspiracies that are 'in restraint of trade or commerce among the several States'."[2]

   This paper draws on practical antitrust economics to develop a clear and substantively reasoned test for Sherman Act jurisdiction that correctly considers the statutory issues of market definition and market power, while adhering to the consumer welfare standard first proposed by Robert Bork and subsequently adopted by the U.S. Supreme Court.[3] Our "geographic market power" test uses established antitrust practice under the federal government's 1992 Horizontal Merger Guidelines. According to our test, to establish Sherman Act jurisdiction, any party bringing an action under the Act, whether it be a private party or a federal agency, must plead with particularity that, if successful, the defendants' conduct is reasonably likely to raise prices in more states than one. This test requires the plaintiff to identify the defendants' product and geographic antitrust markets. It also requires the plaintiff to allege that the defendants' share of the geographic antitrust market is sufficiently large that their restraint would be reasonably likely to achieve an effective exercise of market power that would substantially raise prices in multiple states. In the spirit of Justice Scalia's *Summit* dissent, local trade restraints that cannot plausibly be alleged to raise prices outside the home state lie beyond the reach of the Sherman Act.

   Product and geographic antitrust market definitions, market shares, and interstate price effects are seldom capable of exact evidentiary proof. Yet, in many cases currently entertained under *Summit*, the likelihood of interstate price effects is so small that they can be presumed as a matter of law to be purely intrastate. The geographic market power test imposes an economically justified tradeoff on plaintiffs when pleading the facts necessary to establish Sherman Act jurisdiction. The wider the product and geographic antitrust markets alleged, the more likely an effective exercise of market power in that market would result in substantial interstate price effects. The wider the market, however, the smaller the defendants' market share and the less likely their alleged restraint would achieve an effective exercise of market power. Equally important, our test requires the plaintiff to make specific allegations regarding market definition and market shares that the defendant can attempt to rebut at the jurisdictional stage. Foreseeing dismissal on the pleadings, plaintiffs who are victims of purely local restraints will be forced to seek redress under state law.

Our geographic market power test resolves two current problems in the antitrust case law. First, *Summit* places virtually no limit on Sherman Act jurisdiction in spite of the Act's clear language that it applies only to restraints of trade "among the several states." This state of affairs engenders an unduly large number of suits aimed at purely local activities.[4] In many of these cases, plaintiffs succeed at the jurisdictional stage only to fail on the merits as a result of their inability to prove a substantive restraint of trade "among the several states." Under the geographic market power test, these cases would be dismissed at the outset on jurisdictional grounds.

Second, within the framework of competitive federalism, *Summit* undermines political competition among the states to resolve purely internal market failures. If price effects resulting from market power are strictly local and confined to a single state, that state's regulators have adequate incentives to address the problem, and there is no justification for federal regulation. The economic circumstances facing the citizens of the several states vary tremendously and can surely benefit from regulatory policies tailored specifically to those circumstances. The geographic market power test for Sherman Act jurisdiction thus identifies a substantively reasoned balance between state and federal antitrust enforcement. In our view, the Court should overturn *Summit* at the next available opportunity and establish the geographic market power test as the basis for Sherman Act jurisdiction.

The Scope of the Sherman Act

The Supreme Court's view of the scope of Sherman Act jurisdiction has reflected its interpretation of the constitutional limits of the Commerce Clause. The Court first addressed the question in *United States v. E.C. Knight Co.* (1895), where the U.S. attorney challenged a proposed horizontal combination between five sugar manufacturers that would have allowed it to "control" roughly 98 percent of domestic sugar refining capacity. Chief Justice Fuller reasoned that "the power to control the manufacture of a given thing involves in a certain sense the control of its disposition . . . and although the exercise of that power may result in bringing the operation of commerce into play, it . . . affects it only incidentally and indirectly." "[I]t does not follow," he concluded, "that an attempt to monopolize . . . manufacture [is] an attempt . . . to monopolize commerce, even though, in order to dispose of the product, the instrumentality of commerce [is] necessarily invoked."[5] Ten years later, in *Swift & Co. v. United States* (1905), the Court summarily dismissed *E.C. Knight's* formalistic view of federal commerce power in favor of a more functional approach, concluding that "commerce among the States is not a technical legal conception, but a practical one, drawn from the course of business."[6] The Court laid to rest any doubt about the status of *E.C. Knight* in its landmark decision in *Standard Oil Co. of New Jersey v. U.S.* (1911), where it expressly rejected as "unsound" the formalistic distinction between commerce and manufacture. Thereafter, the Court's case law on Sherman Act jurisdiction followed the expansive path of its case law on general Commerce Clause jurisdiction, which culminated in 1942 with *Wickard v. Filburn's* holding that even purely local activities are subject to federal regulation if, aggregated horizontally, they have a "substantial effect" on interstate commerce. By 1945, the Court had repeatedly affirmed that "Congress, in passing the Sherman Act, left no area of its constitutional power unoccupied."[7]

In 1948, the Court decided *Mandeville Island Farms v. American Crystal Sugar Co.*, specifically relying on *Wickard's* aggregation principle to establish Sherman Act jurisdiction over an agreement among local sugar beet refiners. The complaint alleged that the defendant, one of three refiners located in northern California, conspired with the other two to revise the standard form contract they used to buy beets from nearby growers. Before the revision, growers' receipts were based on a formula combining a percentage of the refiner's net returns from sugar sales and the measured sugar content of the grower's beets for the period covered by the contract. The revised contracts specified, instead, that the grower's receipts were based on the average net return of all three refiners combined.

The plaintiffs, a group of growers that had agreed to the revised contract, later brought an action under the Sherman Act alleging that defendant's actions illegally fixed the price of sugar beets and thereby restrained interstate commerce in sugar. The District Court judge, however, inferred just the opposite from the face of the contracts contained in the complaint, according to which the price of sugar in interstate commerce determined the price of beets. To expedite an appeal on the question of federal jurisdiction, he allowed the plaintiffs to amend their complaint to eliminate the allegation that the defendant's restraint "affected the price of sugar in interstate commerce," in essence replacing it with the charge that the restraint of trade in beets, by itself, affected interstate commerce.

Writing for the Supreme Court, Justice Rutledge found that the three refiners were the only practical market for the petitioners' beets, owing to high transport costs and barriers to entry by competing refiners. As a result, the conspirators controlled the quantity of sugar manufactured and sold in interstate commerce from northern California. In response to the defendant's claim that the three refiners were powerless to affect the national price of sugar, Rutledge found "[t]he idea that stabilization of prices paid for the only raw material consumed in an industry has no influence toward reducing competition in the distribution of the finished product, in an integrated industry such as this, is impossible to accept."[8] Drawing on *Wickard's* horizontal aggregation principle, Rutledge concluded that "Congress's power to keep the interstate market free of goods produced under conditions inimical to the general welfare . . . may be exercised in individual cases without showing any specific effect upon interstate commerce . . . . [I]t is enough that the individual activity *when multiplied into a general practice* . . . contains a threat to the interstate economy that requires preventive regulation."[9]

By 1975, a vertical aggregation principle began to creep into the Court's decisions on Sherman Act jurisdiction. In *Goldfarb v. Virginia* (1975), the Court considered a challenge to the Fairfax County Bar Association's minimum fee schedule. When the plaintiffs were unable to find an attorney willing to perform an examination for their residential real estate closing for a reduced fee, they filed a class action suit claiming that the association's minimum fee schedule violated the Sherman Act. Writing for a unanimous Court, Chief Justice Burger reasoned that as a practical matter title examinations are indispensable to the financing of real estate transactions because lenders require them as a condition for making a loan. Because a substantial volume of real estate loans originated outside the state, and "given the substantial volume of commerce involved and the inseparability of [title examinations] from the interstate aspects of real estate transactions," he concluded that "interstate commerce has been sufficiently affected,"[10] regardless of whether the fee schedule could be shown to reduce the number of title examinations or to increase fees. Thus, the Court first "aggregated" the title examinations, then looked to their vertical input in the broader stream of commerce (real estate financing), and found a substantial economic effect sufficient to support federal jurisdiction.

In spite of the Court's back-door acceptance of horizontal aggregation in *Mandeville* and vertical aggregation in *Goldfarb*, most circuits continued to require Sherman Act plaintiffs to establish jurisdiction in either of two ways. The plaintiff could claim that the allegedly unlawful conduct itself took place "in commerce" or that the allegedly unlawful conduct had a "substantial effect" on interstate commerce even though it took place intrastate. In *McLain v. Real Estate Bd. of New Orleans* (1980), however, the Court found Sherman Act jurisdiction where the defendants' broader business activities, aggregated vertically, were "in commerce" even though the allegedly unlawful conduct was not.[11]

The plaintiff class of real estate buyers in *McLain* claimed that real estate brokers in the Greater New Orleans area had engaged in a massive conspiracy to fix commission rates, split fees, and suppress useful market information. The only connection between the conspiracy and interstate commerce shown by the plaintiffs was that brokers routinely, though gratuitously, advised buyers on how to obtain title insurance and financing, often from sources outside Louisiana. The District Court found that the defendants' brokerage activity occurred entirely in Louisiana and that the plaintiffs failed to allege, as required by *Goldfarb*, that the provision of insurance and financing constituted a large volume of interstate commerce inseparable from brokerage services. Accordingly, it dismissed the complaint for lack of federal jurisdiction, and the Court of Appeals affirmed.

Chief Justice Burger reversed the lower courts, finding they had misinterpreted *Goldfarb*. That case, he asserted, addressed the "in commerce" test rather than the "substantial effects" test. To establish that the defendants' activities were in the stream of commerce, it was necessary to show that they were an "integral part of an interstate transaction." Such a showing is unnecessary where, as in the case at hand, the alleged basis for federal jurisdiction is the substantial effects test, which is "in no way restricted to those challenged activities that have an integral relationship to an activity in interstate commerce."[12]

Given the uncontroverted testimony from local lenders that an appreciable amount of their residential real estate loans occurred in interstate commerce, Burger concluded that "there remains only the requirement that respondents' activities which allegedly have been infected by a price-fixing conspiracy be shown 'as a matter of practical economics' to have a not insubstantial effect on the interstate commerce involved."[13] The infected activities version of the substantial effects test apparently requires the plaintiff to allege only that the defendants' unlawful conduct stands to have a "not insubstantial effect" on interstate commerce because, being interstate, the defendants' broader vertically related business activities— such as title insurance and real estate financing—can be presumed to have a substantial economic effect on interstate commerce when aggregated horizontally across all defendants. That is, but for the defendants' allegedly unlawful conduct, the economic effect on the quantum or character of interstate commerce would be substantial, and this, according to Burger, was enough to carry the plaintiffs' jurisdictional burden.

Finally, in *Summit*, the Court established its most expansive version of the substantial effects test, finding that a Sherman Act defendant's entire line of business can be infected by an economically trivial local restraint. The plaintiff in that case was a licensed and highly skilled eye surgeon, Dr. Pinhas, who refused to hire the services of a physician's assistant as required by the defendants' hospital policy. In response, the defendants— including the hospital at which the plaintiff held staff privileges, its parent corporation, and several of the plaintiff's fellow doctors who served on the hospital's peer review board—initiated peer review proceedings resulting in severe restrictions on the plaintiff's practice and an impending group boycott of his services by the defendants and other hospitals throughout the Los Angeles area. The plaintiff filed a complaint in federal court alleging, among other things, that the defendants had conspired to drive him out of the Los Angeles market by boycotting his services in an effort to increase their market share. To establish federal jurisdiction under the Sherman Act, the plaintiff alleged that the defendant corporate parent's hospitals served nonresident patients, received reimbursements from out-of-state insurers and the federal government, purchased supplies from the stream of commerce, and distributed peer review reports across state lines. In response to the defendants' contention that the plaintiff's complaint failed to describe an adequate nexus between the alleged group boycott and interstate commerce, the District Court dismissed the complaint. The Court of Appeals reversed.

Writing for a narrow majority, Justice Stevens found that the petitioner was unquestionably engaged in interstate commerce even though its primary activity involved the provision of general health care services in a local market. Echoing the Court of Appeals, Stevens reasoned that, "[a]s 'a matter of practical economics,' the effect of such a conspiracy on the hospital's 'purchases of out-of-state medicines and supplies as well as its revenues from out-of-state insurance companies,' would establish the necessary interstate nexus."[14] In response to the petitioners' claim that a boycott of a single surgeon was insufficient to establish jurisdiction, Stevens argued, first, that the mere existence of an illegal agreement violates the Act regardless of its actual effects, and, second, that if successful, the conspiracy would surely have reduced the supply of eye surgery in the Los Angeles market. Quoting *McLain*, he found that the respondent "need not make the more particularized showing of an effect on interstate commerce caused by the alleged conspiracy to fix commission rates, or by those other aspects of respondents' activity that are alleged to be unlawful."[15] What is more, according to Stevens, "[t]he competitive significance of respondent's exclusion from the market must be measured, not just by a particularized evaluation of his own practice, but rather, by a general evaluation of the impact of the restraint on other participants and potential participants in the market from which he has been excluded."[16]

In dissenting, Justice Scalia argued that the Act's language ("in restraint of trade or commerce among the several states") does indeed require the Court to examine the nature and likely effect of the restraint in each particular case. In Scalia's view, *McLain's* "infected activity" test was the result of the Court's confusion over the law; the Court could easily have found jurisdiction in *McLain* given the massive conspiracy being alleged, but instead, it resorted to the infected activities test under the mistaken belief that "focusing upon the effects of the restraint itself would require plaintiffs to prove their case at the jurisdictional stage. That belief was in error because the prior approach had simply assumed, rather than required proof of, the success of the conspiracy."[17] As a result, Scalia lamented, the Court missed an opportunity to clear up the confusion in the circuits following *McLain* and had in fact made things worse. Scalia went on to observe that to establish Sherman Act jurisdiction in *Summit*, the Court looked

> *neither* to the effect on commerce of the restraint *nor* to the effect on commerce of the defendants' infected activity, but rather, it seems, to the effect on commerce of the activity from which the plaintiff has been excluded. As I understand the Court's opinion, the test of Sherman Act jurisdiction is whether the entire line of commerce from which Dr. Pinhas has been excluded affects interstate commerce. Because excluding him from eye surgery at Midway Hospital effectively excluded him from the entire Los Angeles market for eye surgery, the jurisdictional question is simply whether that market affects interstate commerce, which of course it does. This analysis tells us nothing about the substantiality of the impact on interstate commerce generated by the particular conduct at issue here.
>
> Determining the "market" for a product or service, meaning the scope of other products or services against which it must compete, is of course necessary for many purposes of antitrust analysis. But today's opinion does not identify a relevant "market" in *that* sense. It declares Los Angeles to be the pertinent "market" only because that is the entire scope of Dr. Pinhas's exclusion from practice. If the scope of his exclusion had been national, it would have declared the entire United States to be the "market," although it is quite unlikely that all eye surgeons in the United States are in competition. I cannot understand why "market" in the Court's peculiar sense has any bearing on this restraint's impact on interstate commerce and, hence, on Sherman Act jurisdiction. The Court does not even attempt to provide an explanation.[18]

The *Summit* Court took vertical and horizontal aggregation to the extreme: But for the entire Los Angeles market for eye surgery, the effect on the quantum or character of interstate commerce would be substantial, and the plaintiff's complaint was therefore sufficient to establish federal jurisdiction. Scalia emphasized the absurdity of the Court's but-for approach in pointedly observing that if "the alleged conspirators in the present case had decided to effectuate the ultimate exclusion of Dr. Pinhas, *that is*, to have him killed, it would be absurd to think that the *world market* in eye surgery would thereby be affected."[19]

The Geographic Market Power Test for Sherman Act Jurisdiction

Market Definition and Market Power. As Justice Scalia noted in his *Summit* dissent, antitrust analysis requires the definition of an appropriate market. Any market definition has two dimensions: the relevant product and the relevant geographic scope. Because our ultimate concern is the proper limit of Sherman Act jurisdiction—an inherently spatial concern—our primary focus is on the geographic scope of the market.

The geographic scope of an *economic* market has been defined as "that set of demanders and suppliers whose trading establishes the price of a good" and "within which the price of a good tends to uniformity, allowance being made for transportation costs."[20] A workable empirical test for this definition is "the similarity of price movements within the market."[21] But neither this definition nor its empirical counterpart is especially useful in an antitrust setting, because each definition assumes the events that cause prices to change are beyond the discretion of market participants. In antitrust, however, the focus is on the ability of a firm or group of coordinating firms to restrict output and raise prices through the exercise of market power.

What has been characterized as the "geographic *antitrust* market" may be either broader or narrower than the economic market.[22] The accepted method of identifying the geographic antitrust market is the "hypothetical monopolist test," which is formalized in the Horizontal Merger Guidelines and used by federal antitrust agencies to assess the probable effect of horizontal mergers on market power.[23] According to this test, for any pair of firms proposing to merge, the antitrust market is defined as the *narrowest* geographic area containing the merging firms in which all firms in the area, by coordinating their operating decisions, can profitably sustain a small but significant increase in the price of the relevant product above what would prevail absent the restraint.

FIGURE 1
HYPOTHETICAL MONOPOLIST TEST ISLAND ECONOMY

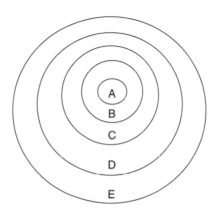

To show how this test works, consider an isolated island economy. For simplicity, assume the island is perfectly round and that consumers and producers are evenly distributed within its borders, depicted by circle E in figure 1. We assume transportation costs for all firms on the island increase at a constant rate with distance. We then take a subgroup of firms that include the firms proposing to merge, say those within circle A, and ask whether, by acting in concert, they can profitably sustain a small but significant increase in the price of widgets. If not, then circle A does not represent a geographic market for antitrust purposes because no single firm or subgroup of firms within circle A could hope to sustain a price increase if all the firms in circle A acting together are unable to do so. The geographic antitrust market is broader than circle A because outside firms must be added to the subgroup before it can hope to exercise market power.

Suppose we expand the subgroup to include all firms in circle B and again find that these firms acting together are unable profitably to sustain a price increase. By proceeding in this fashion, we can identify the narrowest geographic market in which the associated firms are capable of exercising market power. Suppose this coincides with circle C.

The geographic antitrust market, depicted in circle C, may be narrower than the entire island economy. For this to be true, the firms outside circle C must have sufficiently limited productive capacity that they are unable to expand output enough to completely undermine the hypothetical cartel. With the higher price set by the firms inside circle C, outside firms will attempt to arbitrage the price difference by expanding their production and selling into the colluders' market. As they do so, they will succeed in taking a portion of sales away from the colluders, but their marginal production costs eventually increase so much that they are no longer willing to expand. The resulting hypothetical equilibrium is one in which prices throughout the island economy are higher than they would be absent the colluders' exercise of market power, with any price differences reflecting transportation costs. This condition confirms that the entire island is an *economic* market even though the *antitrust* market is narrower.

Nothing in this analysis requires us to start the hypothetical monopolist test with circle A. In the context of a real merger proposal, antitrust agencies actually begin with the narrowest geographic area that includes the merging firms, and of course they recognize that consumers are not uniformly distributed across space and that transportation costs can vary for many reasons. If, using the hypothetical monopolist test, the agencies find that these firms would be unable profitably to sustain a small price increase, they search for the narrowest geographic area that includes the next-best substitute for production at the merging firms' location and ask whether *all* firms in this area acting together could do so. Once having identified the geographic antitrust market in this way, the antitrust agencies attempt to determine whether a proposed merger is likely to generate market power absent the cooperation of the nonmerging firms. In practice, the agencies rely on the Hirfindahl-Herschman Index (HHI) to identify changes in market concentration that raise a presumption that the merger will create market power sufficient to justify an injunction or other relief.

The antitrust agencies face a tradeoff in identifying the geographic antitrust market. The wider the product and geographic market to which they apply the hypothetical monopolist test, the more likely a hypothetical monopolist will be able to exercise market power in that market. Increasing the scope of the market in this way, though, necessarily reduces the combined market share of the firms actually proposing to merge Presumably, the agencies' recognition of this tradeoff partly explains why they identify the geographic antitrust market as the *narrowest* market in which a hypothetical monopolist could profitably sustain an increase in price.[24] While federal courts are not bound by the Horizontal Merger Guidelines, many follow their approach to product and geographic market definition. This is because the guidelines represent mainstream economic thinking and are functionally equivalent to other tests that the courts have developed over the years.

Applying the Geographic Market Power Test. Rather than focusing on the geographic scope of the price increase resulting from a given horizontal merger, the Horizontal Merger Guidelines focus solely on whether the merger is likely to generate market power. In the context of a jurisdictional challenge, it is therefore necessary to adapt the logic of the guidelines to assess the geographic scope of price effects. For example, the geographic antitrust market as defined according to the hypothetical monopolist test is likely to overlap one or more economic markets, within which the price of a good tends to uniformity, allowance being made for transportation costs. It is reasonable to expect an exercise of market power to cause a flow of goods into the geographic antitrust market as outside firms expand production in an attempt to arbitrage price differences within these overlapping economic markets. To some extent, prices will therefore rise outside the geographic antitrust market, possibly spilling into neighboring states. As the defendants' combined share of the geographic antitrust market falls below 100 percent, however, any such spillovers become less likely. In defining the relevant market for antitrust jurisdiction, a proper test should formally recognize the tradeoff between the likelihood of interstate price spillovers and the likelihood that the defendants can effectively exercise market power.

Plaintiffs seeking redress in federal court must allege and bear the burden of proving the facts necessary to support subject matter jurisdiction. The defendant, in turn, has the right to rebut the plaintiff's allegations. If the plaintiff is unable to provide substantial competent evidence to overcome the defendant's rebuttal, the defendant can move to dismiss the case, and federal subject matter jurisdiction will be defeated. To establish Sherman Act jurisdiction under the geographic market power test, then, the plaintiff must allege and prove that the defendants engaged in a restraint of trade that generated (or if successful, would be reasonably likely to generate) market power that caused prices to rise in more states than one. More particularly, the plaintiff must identify a relevant product and a geographic antitrust market in which a hypothetical monopoly of all firms, including the defendants, would be reasonably likely to sustain a profitable price increase that substantially spilled across state lines. In addition, the plaintiff must allege and prove that overall market concentration and the defendants' combined market share are sufficiently large that their restraint would be reasonably likely to generate market power.

The geographic market power test imposes an economically appropriate tradeoff on the plaintiff when alleging jurisdiction under the Act. The narrower the market identified by the plaintiff, the more likely a restraint by the defendants will generate market power. The narrower the market, however, the less likely the defendants' restraint will increase prices outside the state. Plaintiffs will naturally want to allege the narrowest market consistent with a plausible allegation of interstate price spillovers, because this strategy maximizes both the defendants' measured share of the market and the resulting change in market concentration. The defendants can respond by offering to prove they have too small a share of the market to permit an effective exercise of market power. Alternatively, they can offer to show that the market alleged by the plaintiff is so narrow that even a hypothetical monopoly of all firms would be unlikely to sustain a profitable price increase that substantially spilled across state lines. On either showing, the defendants' conduct would be presumptively intrastate. Unless rebutted by the plaintiff, either showing would support dismissal for lack of Sherman Act jurisdiction.

With respect to *vertical* aggregation, the geographic market power test provides the plaintiff with the flexibility to define the market according to the facts at its disposal and the circumstances of the particular restraint at issue. Defining the product category broadly to include vertically related goods or services, though, raises the plaintiff's evidentiary burden regarding the defendants' market share and the effects of the restraint on market concentration. As in *McLain*, for example, the plaintiffs would be free to allege a relatively broad product category that includes vertically related complements to real estate brokerage such as financing and title insurance. Although unlikely, it is economically possible that fixed minimum brokerage fees in the Greater New Orleans area would cause such a dramatic decline in the number of real estate transactions that the price of financing and title insurance outside the state would substantially decline. Including financing and title insurance in the product definition increases the likelihood that a hypothetical monopoly of the broad product category in the Greater New Orleans area would have substantial interstate price effects. At the same time, however, by reducing the defendants' combined market share, it raises the plaintiff's burden of demonstrating that their restraint could plausibly have such an effect.[25] Either way, under the geographic market power test, the interstate scope of price effects is a question to be resolved at the jurisdictional stage.

The tradeoff imposed by the geographic market power test has similar implications for *horizontal* aggregation. The plaintiff is free to allege a geographic antitrust market sufficiently broad that a hypothetical monopolist would be likely to sustain a profitable increase in prices outside the state in question, but defining the market broadly raises the plaintiff's jurisdictional burden elsewhere. As in *Mandeville*, for example, the court might hypothesize that the effect on interstate commerce would be substantial if all sugar refiners in the country adopted the same grower contracts as the defendant. In essence, the court would be applying the hypothetical monopolist test to the national market and would no doubt conclude that interstate sugar prices would suffer a substantial effect. The *Mandeville* court neglected to recognize, however, that the defendant refiners' share of such a broadly defined geographic antitrust market was trivial and beyond any plausible suggestion of market power.

Finally, the geographic market power test need not be applied identically to all restraints. No jurisdictional test can be expected to perform without error, but the geographic market power test establishes a substantively reasoned basis for Sherman Act jurisdiction that allows the legal system to iterate toward an articulate set of presumptions that minimize the weighted sum of Type I and Type II errors.[26] In the context of antitrust, judicial measurement error is small enough that practical market share and concentration thresholds can be established for various categories of restraints. Below these thresholds, the exercise of market power is economically implausible and presumptively beyond federal jurisdiction. Different restraints would very likely be subject to different presumptions regarding the thresholds necessary for the plaintiff to make out a prima facie case for federal jurisdiction. In all cases, determination of the appropriate threshold would properly be tempered by courts' recognition that the category of alleged restraints may, in fact, generate productive efficiencies that more than offset any associated allocative inefficiencies. Horizontal pricing arrangements would no doubt be subject to a very low threshold, possibly approaching zero as under current law, because it is relatively unlikely such arrangements can generate productive efficiencies (assuming they have been properly characterized). Vertical price-fixing and horizontal nonprice restraints might be subject to marginally higher thresholds, and so on, because the likelihood that they can generate productive efficiencies is somewhat greater. Of course, the antitrust agencies would face a jurisdictional restraint in assessing purely local horizontal mergers that has thus far been formally absent.

Practical Effects

In his *Summit* dissent, Justice Scalia pointed out that *McLain* had left the lower federal courts in disarray over the issue of Sherman Act jurisdiction and that the *Summit* majority missed an opportunity to clear up the resulting confusion when it found in favor of federal jurisdiction. Since then, the lower courts have continued in disarray, with an unduly large number of suits aimed at purely local activities, many of which are arguably frivolous on either jurisdictional or substantive grounds. In many of these cases, plaintiffs succeed at the jurisdictional stage only to fail on the merits as a result of their inability to prove a substantive restraint of trade *among the several states*. In our view, the geographic market power test would eliminate much of the confusion.

In *BCB Anesthesia Care, Ltd. v. Passavant Memorial Area Hosp. Ass'n* (1994), for example, the U.S. Court of Appeals for the Seventh Circuit affirmed the district court's dismissal of a Sherman Act claim brought by a physician against a local hospital. Whereas the district court dismissed the case on jurisdictional grounds, the Seventh Circuit granted summary judgment on the merits, noting the large number of Sherman Act cases in which physicians sue hospitals in federal court for revoking their staff privileges only to suffer dismissal on the merits.[27] Similarly, in *Brader v. Allegheny General Hosp.* (1995), the district court dismissed a physician's Sherman Act claim on jurisdictional grounds, but the Third Circuit reversed, ruling that it was sufficient for the plaintiff simply to allege, without any evidentiary burden, that the defendant's activities were in or substantially affected interstate commerce. On remand, the district court granted summary judgment on the merits, and the Third Circuit affirmed on appeal.[28] The entire adjudication took an additional four years and no doubt consumed considerable private and public resources. Under the geographic market power test, these cases would be dismissed at the outset on jurisdictional grounds.

Consider also *Hamilton Chapter of Alpha Delta Phi, Inc. v. Hamilton College* (1997), where a group of fraternities sued a private college that required all students to live in college housing and participate in the college meal plan. The district court dismissed the case on jurisdictional grounds. The Second Circuit reversed, finding that the college's activities had the necessary connection to interstate commerce because many of its students were nonresidents.[29] On remand, the district court dismissed on the merits for lack of market power. Here, as in *Brader*, the final decision took four years from the initial dismissal on jurisdictional grounds but was finally decided on the basis of facts that could well have been used to defeat jurisdiction under the geographic market power test.[30]

In many Sherman Act claims, the courts simply assume that jurisdiction exists. For example, in *County of Tuolumne v. Sonora Community Hosp.* (2001),[31] a family practice physician sued a local hospital, claiming that the hospital's practice of granting the privilege to perform caesarian sections only to certified obstetricians or physicians passing rigorous special training violated the Sherman Act. The district court granted the hospital's motion for summary judgment, and the Ninth Circuit affirmed. Nowhere in the decision was the issue of jurisdiction discussed, let alone adjudicated. In *Wagner v. Magellan Health Services, Inc.* (2000), a psychiatrist sued a managed care organization claiming it had blacklisted him in violation of the Sherman Act. The plaintiff alleged that the relevant geographic market was the town of Barrington, apparently in an effort to make the defendant's measured market share and likely market power appear large. The defendant in this case did not move for dismissal for lack of jurisdiction; rather, the defendant asked for summary judgment on the merits of the case, which the district court granted as the plaintiff had not properly alleged an antitrust injury.[32]

The lesson from these cases is that defendants with legitimate jurisdictional claims would rather litigate on the merits than press their jurisdictional claims and face the uncertainty and expense of an appeal on jurisdictional grounds. In the process, though, Sherman Act defendants are being deprived of a nontrivial measure of due process, with little corresponding benefit other than the opportunity for plaintiffs to extract concessions by engaging in costly discovery and then proceeding to a full trial on the merits. In the physician termination cases, it is easy to imagine that hospitals have a legitimate stake in the conduct of their staff physicians but very difficult to imagine how a uniform national rule on the subject promotes consumer welfare in any way. With even a remote threat of treble damages, many defendants no doubt settle what should be considered jurisdictionally frivolous federal claims. By establishing a clear and substantively reasoned basis for Sherman Act jurisdiction, the geographic market power test would prevent waste of judicial resources and restore defendants' due process rights. It holds out the prospect that the proper treatment of novel business practices can be more quickly and reliably discerned by allowing states to innovate their own rules where the resulting effects are completely internal to the state.

Normative Justification: Competitive Federalism

The geographic market power test applies the framework of competitive federalism to the specific context of antitrust. Just as antitrust policy is premised on the conviction that economic competition best promotes consumer welfare, competitive federalism is premised on the conviction that political competition best promotes the general welfare of the citizenry.

The sole concern for Sherman Act jurisdiction under our test is whether the defendants' conduct in one state results in a monopoly overcharge that spills across state lines. Where the monopoly overcharge is confined to the defendants' home state, that state's antitrust regulators can adequately address the problem. Political competition between states will result in optimal, although not necessarily uniform, antitrust policy with due regard for experimentation. When the monopoly overcharge spills across state lines, the citizens of neighboring states bear a portion of the losses when firms restrain trade in their home state unchallenged by home-state antitrust regulators. If the restraining firms are careful to keep their goods and their capital out of the neighboring state, there is little that a state's antitrust regulators can do to address the problem under current rules regarding personal jurisdiction. With citizens of the home state bearing less than the full monopoly overcharge while—assuming the owners of the restraining firms are citizens of the state—receiving 100 percent of the benefits, the state's antitrust regulators are unlikely to pursue antitrust policy with the same zeal as in the absence of a spillover. Only in these cases is federal antitrust regulation warranted.

An alternative view is that antitrust regulation is subject to such dramatic scale economies that unlimited federal authority is clearly efficient. But this argument applies only to legal administration, not to lawmaking per se. Lawmaking is a public (nonrivalrous) good. Under the geographic market power test, states can easily capture any scale economies attributable to federal lawmaking at no cost to the federal system simply by adopting federal rules to cover their purely internal activity if they so choose. Conversely, federal courts are free to rely on state court decisions covering novel questions of law or fact purely internal to the state. The geographic market power test in no way inhibits the interjurisdictional sharing of legal rules.

The claim that scale economies in legal *administration* warrant exclusive federal authority over antitrust administration, for its part, amounts to a rejection of any kind of federalism whatsoever. In an area of law whose primary concern is the suppression of economic market power, it is somewhat anomalous to suggest that political market power reposed exclusively in the hands of the federal government is in the long-term interest of the citizenry; a monopoly of legal administration is no less alarming than a monopoly of widget making.

The geographic market power test would in fact provide incentives for a sensible allocation and exercise of regulatory and enforcement powers under a nonmonopolistic regime. Under the current system, a state can preclude federal antitrust regulators from attacking both the internal and external activities of firms doing business within the state by integrating into the activity in question. Under the state action doctrine established in *Parker v. Brown* (1943), states are free from federal antitrust prohibitions as long as they refrain from acting in an overtly commercial capacity. To the extent the current system allows federal regulators inefficiently to expand their lawmaking power over otherwise *private* business activity that is purely internal to the states, we would expect states to extend official protection to local monopolies so as to protect them from federal antitrust authority. The geographic market power test should dilute that incentive and might lead states to divest themselves of activities better performed by private firms under the state's own choice of antitrust rules.

At the same time, the geographic market power test promises to reduce the problem of concurrent antitrust enforcement. Subjecting all U.S. firms to federal enforcement by both the Department of Justice and the Federal Trade Commission, and to private civil actions, is troublesome enough without adding concurrent state enforcement. As to purely local restraints, the geographic market power test takes a first step toward limiting concurrent enforcement.

Increasing globalization is fast reducing the relative size of the U.S. economy in world markets and subjecting U.S. firms to increasing competition from foreign firms. Increasing globalization no doubt has the effect of reducing the optimal scope of federal antitrust enforcement. In response, federal regulators are likely to direct increasing attention to local markets for "nontraded goods" that are largely insulated from the competitive effects of globalization. By reserving antitrust enforcement over such markets to the states, the geographic market power test constrains potential federal excess at this front.

Competition and Learning

By allowing political competition between states to resolve internal spillovers according to local circumstances, the geographic market power test promises to hasten the rate at which antitrust law evolves toward the optimal treatment of various alleged trade restraints. The weight of federal antitrust case law and commentary evidences considerable disagreement about the nature and effect of novel business practices. Federal courts have often failed to correctly assess many such practices, with a decidedly negative effect on consumer welfare. Examples include the Court's recent reversal of the per se rule against vertically imposed maximum prices, its earlier reversal of the per se rule against vertically imposed exclusive territories, and its distinction between horizontal restraints that are unreasonable per se and those that are subject to a full reasonableness inquiry.[33] Even now, federal courts are struggling with the proper application of the Sherman Act to horizontal aggregations in so-called "network industries," for which the optimal tradeoff between allocative and productive efficiency is far from clear. At the same time, federal courts have missed an opportunity to preserve a federal system in which competitive state lawmaking could be mobilized to provide more rapid information feedback regarding the competitive effect of novel business practices on consumer welfare.

The question antitrust regulators face in reviewing horizontal arrangements under the consumer welfare standard is whether the associated productive efficiencies, if any, are likely to offset the allocative inefficiency from the creation of market power. Because horizontal mergers are likely to enhance productive efficiency by integrating productive activity, their net effect after accounting for allocative inefficiency may be to increase consumer welfare, and federal courts therefore address them under the full rule of reason. Horizontal arrangements that involve no apparent integration of productive activity are considered unlikely to generate productive efficiency, but, following the Court's recognition of the importance of properly characterizing practices that appear on the surface to constitute garden variety price fixing or other horizontal restraints, this presumption has changed.

Commentators now recognize that even though they may generate market power, horizontal restraints may also generate offsetting productive efficiencies. Naked price fixing between rival firms with large market share is unlikely to generate productive efficiencies, but business combinations seldom come so neatly packaged. Many horizontal business arrangements designed to avert moral hazard, agency, or other incentive problems may appear at first glance to have the sole effect of generating market power for the participating firms, but on closer examination they are found to generate offsetting productive efficiencies. Syndicates formed by investment banks to market initial public offerings of corporate stock, vertically imposed resale price maintenance, vertically imposed exclusive territories between horizontally situated retailers, and copyright licensing arrangements appear to fall into this category. Although courts have yet to formally adopt a full reasonableness inquiry for horizontal restraints, they have done so where nonprice restraints are vertically imposed. But even for pure horizontal restraints, including price restraints, where the participating firms' combined market share is small and increasing over time, a compelling case can be made that, absent the use of exclusionary practices, the arrangement generates productive efficiencies that outweigh any allocative efficiency from the creation of market power.[34] (Otherwise, the participating firms' combined market shares would decline over time as rivals expand production and undercut prices.)

By promoting interjurisdictional competition over optimal antitrust policy, the geographic market power test will more quickly resolve any uncertainties regarding the proper treatment of novel business practices. One need not look very far to find evidence that state competition over antitrust policy will improve the judicial treatment of novel business practices. Recall the *Mandeville* case, for example, where the defendant and its alleged coconspirators sold their sugar into a national market in which their market share was so small that they could not possibly have influenced prices. As beet buyers, they may have enjoyed market power in northern California that allowed them to impose a monopsony underpayment when buying from beet growers. But together with substantial evidence that sugar beet processing is subject to various incentive problems—including the difficulty of measuring sugar beet quality and the attendant moral hazard—the plaintiffs' willingness to enter into the challenged contract *ex ante* raises at least a modicum of doubt that the contract constituted a naked restraint. More than likely, the agreement there was designed to internalize a moral hazard that otherwise would have resulted in resource misallocation.[35] Given that the market for sugar beets was entirely local, with no possibility that a monopsony underpayment could spill across state lines, *Mandeville* stands as a poster child for the geographic market power test. By allowing the states to perform their role as laboratories for experimentation, it would ensure that the entire body of antitrust law, both state and federal, iterates more quickly toward the optimal set of legal rules.

Constitutional Principles and Statutory Intent

The geographic market power test is consistent both with the original purpose of the Commerce Clause and with a substantial body of Commerce Clause case law. The Commerce Clause was necessary to prevent states from engaging in protracted trade wars that stifled interstate commerce and undermined national prosperity. Trade wars are one form of interstate spillover in which the state erecting the trade barrier receives the benefits while imposing the costs on the citizens of other states. By focusing on the substantive nexus between the underlying goal of the Sherman Act and the alleged restraint on interstate commerce, the geographic market power test establishes a functional blueprint for identifying the exact nature of the effects necessary to circumscribe federal jurisdiction.

At first impression, such an effort to separate "interstate commerce" from purely state-internal transactions may seem wildly anachronistic. *Wickard v. Filburn* (1942), as noted, permitted Congress to legislate under the Commerce Clause so long as local activities, in the aggregate, arguably "affect" interstate commerce. At least with respect to local *economic* activities, that holding remains good law even after the modern Supreme Court's modest rediscovery of the enumerated powers doctrine. The central question, as Justice Scalia pointed out in *Summit*, is not whether Congress *may* regulate purely local activities but whether it has in fact done so with the statute under review.

While the legislative history of the Sherman Act suggests that its principal proponents in Congress intended to reach the outer limits of federal power over interstate commerce, its sponsors considered the commerce power subject to the limitation of state police powers.[36] In the words of Senator Sherman, "[t]he purpose of this bill is to enable the courts of the United States to apply the same remedies against combinations . . . that have been applied in the several states to protect local interests. If the combination is confined to a state the State should apply the remedy; if it is interstate and controls any production in many states, Congress must apply the remedy." [37] Thus, while Congress failed to foresee the dramatic changes that would take place in the national economy and the scope of general federal commerce power, its central purpose was to resolve a political spillover between states that prevented them from unilaterally regulating the trusts.

For the purpose of identifying the proper limits of Sherman Act jurisdiction, it is just as relevant to inquire into the nature and scope of this
spillover today as it was in 1890. The most important changes that have
occurred in antitrust policy since 1890 are the level of understanding
among courts and commentators about the nature of market power as an
economic spillover and the purpose of the Act as a consumer welfare prescription. The geographic market power test is a straightforward application of the Court's repeated finding that antitrust law should evolve with
advances in economic understanding and the Court's experience with various restraints.

True, the geographic market power test appears to conflict with the
Court's repeated dictum that Sherman Act jurisdiction is concurrent with
expanding federal commerce jurisdiction. But that dictum is wholly
unwarranted. The outer limits of Commerce Clause jurisprudence have
been shaped in cases (such as *Wickard*) where "Congress itself has defined
the specific persons and activities that affect commerce and therefore
require federal regulation." In contrast, "[t]he jurisdictional inquiry under
general prohibitions like . . . §1 of the Sherman Act, turn[s] on the circumstances presented in each case and require[s] a particularized judicial
determination."[38]

Recent Supreme Court decisions suggest that a majority of the justices
are anxious to re-limit federal regulatory encroachment on traditional
state police powers. At a minimum, in construing the jurisdictional reach
of federal statutes, the Court will no longer resort to the unconstrained
aggregation of local activities to identify a substantial effect on interstate
commerce. In *Solid Waste Agency of Northern Cook County v. U.S. Army
Corps of Engineers* (2001), for example, the Court struck down the Corps's
regulation of isolated wetlands under its authority, pursuant to the Clean
Water Act, to regulate "navigable waters." In the majority's view, the federal regulation of wetlands that lack any connection to navigable waters
would stretch the commerce power to its outermost limit. Absent a clear
statement of legislative intent indicating that Congress had truly meant to
go that far, the Court refused to construe the statute so broadly.

The geographic market power test is wholly consistent with this
approach to statutory construction. The test may even provide a potentially useful template for limiting general Commerce Clause jurisdiction.

On the one hand, the geographic market power test eschews the formalistic distinctions that discredited the pre–New Deal Court's efforts to circumscribe the commerce power—in particular, the distinction between "commerce" and "manufacture." Under the facts in *E.C. Knight*, for example, the test would surely have determined that the defendants' "manufacturing" operations caused sugar prices to increase in more states than one, and Sherman Act jurisdiction was therefore appropriate. Nor does the geographic market power test rely on a mechanical distinction between "direct" and "indirect" effects on interstate commerce (although it will ordinarily give effects that are economically remote from the defendants' restraint limited weight in the jurisdictional calculus).[39] On the other hand, by focusing on the substantive nexus between the underlying evil addressed by the Sherman Act—the exercise of market power that reduces consumer welfare—and the likely geographic extent of any associated spillover, the test effectively limits antitrust plaintiffs' reliance on horizontal and vertical aggregation and the nebulous but-for approach to demonstrate a substantial effect on interstate commerce. In the framework of competitive federalism, practical antitrust economics as developed by courts, commentators, and the antitrust agencies provides the substantive nexus necessary to bound the substantial effects test for Sherman Act jurisdiction.

Over time, advances in economic understanding can be used to identify the substantive nexus, if in fact one exists, between interstate commerce and Congress's goal in enacting virtually any regulatory statute. Because the Commerce Clause is inherently concerned with economic activity, it is entirely appropriate that its application should be guided by evolving economic understanding. In our view, Congress should have the authority to regulate only those activities whose effects bear a substantive nexus to the underlying economic market failure addressed by the statute and that substantially spill across state lines such that the states, acting alone, would be unlikely to correct the problem. This approach excludes from congressional regulatory authority economic spillovers the states are able to address on their own, even though in some nebulous but-for sense, these spillovers might have a substantial effect on interstate commerce.

The charge to Congress in passing Commerce Clause regulation should be to identify what it believes to be an economic market failure common to more states than one and to make a plausible case that the states, acting independently, face a political market failure precluding them from correcting the problem. This would provide the Court with a substantive basis for assessing whether the regulation falls within Congress's constitutional authority. The Court could then review the regulation under the rational basis or strict scrutiny standards, giving due deference to Congress, and uphold it, strike it down, or enforce it to the extent necessary to achieve constitutionally legitimate congressional ends. Of course, Congress is unlikely to be able to identify the exact economic nature of the market failure in any given situation, just as it was unable to do when it passed the Sherman Act. But competitive federalism provides a sufficiently broad framework that the Court could nevertheless make an initial assessment that political competition between states is unlikely to resolve the problem as Congress has identified it. As the Court gains additional experience with the subject, it may articulate the proper limits of Congress's regulatory jurisdiction more precisely and in light of concurrent advances in economic understanding.

Notes

1. Frank H. Easterbrook, chapter 8 in this volume, p. 213.

2. U.S. 322, 334 (1991) (Justice Scalia, dissenting).

3. Robert H. Bork, *The Antitrust Paradox: A Policy at War with Itself* (New York: Basic Books, 1978), 22–25, 50–66. See, for example, *Reiter v. Sonotone Corp.*, 442 U.S. 330, 343 (1979).

4. In *Hamms v. AAMCO*, Judge Posner of the Seventh Circuit Court of Appeals noted in reviewing a post-*Summit* challenge to Sherman Act jurisdiction that if two children operating competing lemonade stands agreed to fix prices, there is no clear principle under current law preventing them from being subject to the jurisdiction of the Act, even though "the effect on the national economy would be slight." 33 F.3d 774, 780–81 (1994).

5. *United States v. E.C. Knight*, 156 U.S. 1, 12, 17 (1895).

6. *Swift & Co. v. United States*, 196 U.S. 375, 398 (1905).

7. *United States v. Frankfort Distilleries, Inc.*, 324 U.S. 293, 298 (1945) (quoting *Apex Hosiery Co. v. Leader*, 310 U.S. 469, 495 [1940]).

8. *Mandeville Island Farms v. American Crystal Sugar Co.*, 334 U.S. 219, 241 (1948).

9. Ibid., 236 (emphasis added).

10. *Goldfarb v. Virginia*, 421 U.S. 773, 785 (1975).

11. *McLain v. Real Estate Bd. of New Orleans*, 444 U.S. 232 (1980).

12. Ibid., 244.

13. Ibid., 246 (quoting *Hospital Bldg. Co. v. Rex Hospital Trustees*, 425 U.S. 738, 745 [1976]).

14. *Summit Health, Ltd. v. Pinhas*, 500 U.S. 322, 329 (1991).

15. Ibid., 331.

16. Ibid., 332 (Justice Scalia, dissenting).

17. Ibid., 335 (Justice Scalia, dissenting).

18. Ibid., 336–37 (Justice Scalia, dissenting).

19. Ibid., 338 (Justice Scalia, dissenting).

20. George J. Stigler and Robert A. Sherwin, "The Extent of the Market," *Journal of Law & Economics* 28 (1985): 555. See also William M. Landes and Richard A. Posner, "Market Power in Antitrust Cases," *Harvard Law Review* 94 (1981): 937. For an alternative method of defining markets in merger cases based on "marketing concepts," see Thomas W. Dunfee, Louis W. Stern, and Frederick D. Sturdivant, "Bounding Markets in Merger Cases: Identifying Relevant Competitors," *Northwestern University Law Review* 78 (1984): 733–73.

21. Kenneth G. Elzinga and Thomas F. Hogarty, "The Problem of Geographic Market Delineation in Antimerger Suits," *Antitrust Bulletin* 18 (1973): 45.

22. David T. Scheffman and Pablo T. Spiller, "Geographic Market Definition under the U.S. Department of Justice Merger Guidelines," *Journal of Law & Economics* 30 (1987): 123–47.

23. Other empirical tests for identifying the antitrust market can be found in Gregory J. Werden, "The History of Antitrust Market Delineation," *Marquette Law Review* 76 (1992): 123–215.

24. Another rationale for choosing the narrowest market is that it leads to a standard basis for comparison across cases.

25. Similarly, as in *Summit*, the plaintiff would be free to allege that the relevant product category includes an entire collection of vertically related activities associated with general hospital services and that the relevant geographic antitrust market is the entire Los Angeles area. A hypothetical monopoly in such a broadly defined market might well cause the price of eye surgery to increase in neighboring states, but the exclusion of a single eye surgeon from the market would be extremely unlikely to generate market power.

26. Type I errors occur when the court allows jurisdiction over defendants whose activities later prove on the merits to have no substantive interstate component. Type II errors occur when the court denies jurisdiction to plaintiffs whose claims would prove on the merits to have a substantive interstate component.

27. *BCB Anesthesia Care, Ltd. v. Passavant Memorial Area Hosp. Ass'n*, 36 F.3d 664, 667 (7th Cir. 1994) (listing cases).

28. *Brader v. Allegheny General Hosp.*, 167 F.3d 832 (3rd Cir. 1999).

29. *Hamilton Chapter of Alpha Delta Phi, Inc. v. Hamilton College*, 128 F.3d 59, 67 (2d Cir. 1997).

30. *Hamilton Chapter of Alpha Delta Phi, Inc. v. Hamilton College*, 106 F.Supp.2d 406 (N.D.N.Y. 2000). See, also, *Lifeline Ltd. No. II v. Connecticut General Life Ins. Co.*, 821 F.Supp. 1201 (E.D.Mich. 1993) (dismissing antitrust action based on merits but not on jurisdiction); *Patel v. Scotland Memorial Hosp.*, 91 F.3d 132 (4th Cir. 1995) (affirming dismissal on merits and not on jurisdiction); *Brown v. Our Lady of Lourdes Medical Center*, 767 F.Supp. 618 (D.N.J. 1991) (dismissing on the merits but not on jurisdiction); *Tropical Air Flying Services, Inc. v. Carmen Feliciano de Melecio*, 158 F.Supp.2d 177 (D. Puerto Rico 2001) (dismissing antitrust action on merits but not on jurisdiction). But see *Tice v. Hoff*, 29 F.3d 634, (9th Cir. 1994) (affirming on jurisdictional grounds dismissal of claim, because the claim was not too particular in alleging nexus with interstate commerce).

31. *County of Tuolumne v. Sonora Community Hosp.*, 236 F.3d 1148 (9th Cir. 2001).

32. *Wagner v. Magellan Health Services, Inc.*, 121 F.Supp.2d 673 (N.D. Ill. 2000). See also *Levine v. Central Florida Medical Affiliates, Inc.*, 72 F.3d 1538 (11th Cir. 1996) (affirming dismissal on merits of antitrust action by physician against Orlando area hospital); *Betkerur v. Aultman Hosp. Ass'n.*, 78 F.3d 1079 (6th Cir. 1996) (granting summary judgment with no discussion of jurisdiction).

33. See *State Oil. v. Kahn*, 552 U.S. 3 (1997); *Continental TV v. GTE Sylvania*, 433 U.S. 36 (1977); *BMI v. CBS*, 441 U.S. 1 (1979). The Court's tendency to condemn prematurely novel business practices under the per se rule is puzzling, given the recognized judicial norm that the per se rule should apply only after the Court has had sufficient experience with the practice at hand to make an informed judgment regarding the probable effect on consumer welfare.

34. The Court applied this reasoning to overturn the per se rule against vertical division of territories in *GTE Sylvania*.

35. See Jeanine Koenig Balbach, "The Effect of Ownership on Contract Structure, Costs, and Quality: The Case of the U.S. Beet Sugar Industry," *The Industrialization of Agriculture: Vertical Coordination in the U.S. Food System*, eds. Jeffrey S. Royer and Richard T. Rogers (Aldershot, UK: Ashgate Publishing, 1998), 155–84. Among other things, she reports that the American Crystal Sugar Company was ultimately bought by a cooperative of growers. This vertical integration by a horizontal combination of growers was apparently designed to reduce the transaction costs involved in measuring the quality of sugar beets.

36. Robert H. Bork, "Legislative Intent and the Policy of the Sherman Act," *Journal of Law & Economics* 9 (1966): 31–35; and Andrew I. Gavil, "Reconstructing the Jurisdictional Foundation of Antitrust Federalism," *George Washington Law Review* 61 (1993): 658, n. 114. See also Richard A. Epstein, "The Proper Scope of the Commerce Power," *Virginia Law Review* 73 (1987): 1413. Indeed, Congress viewed the Court's proscription of discrimination against interstate commerce in *Wabash, St. Louis & Pacific Ry. Co v. Illinois*, 118 U.S. 557 (1886) as a major impediment to the states' ability unilaterally to control the trusts, whose goods invariably moved in interstate commerce.

37. *Congressional Record, 51st Cong.*, 1st sess., 1890, vol. 21, 2456–57.

38. U.S. 322, 329 (1991) (Justice Scalia, dissenting) (citing *Gulf Oil Corp. v. Copp Paving Co.*, 419 U.S. 186, 197, n.12 [1974]).

39. What is more, whether the defendants' goods are in the "stream of commerce" is neither a necessary nor a sufficient condition to establish federal jurisdiction. An effective restraint by firms whose sales are entirely within their home state may cause prices to increase outside the state even though the defendants' goods never cross state lines. Alternatively, the defendants may sell their goods in a national market in which they have absolutely no hope of affecting prices, even though they have market power in their local intrastate market. The sole question relevant to Sherman Act jurisdiction is whether the alleged restraint affects prices outside any state in which the restraint operates.

10

Federalism and the Enforcement of Antitrust Laws by State Attorneys General

Richard A. Posner

I will first offer an analysis—an economic analysis, naturally—of federalism, and I will then apply it to two related questions. The first, to which I will devote the bulk of my attention, is whether state attorneys general should be permitted, as they are under existing law, to enforce federal antitrust laws in suits brought on behalf of the state's residents. The second is whether states should be permitted, as they also are under existing law, to enact and enforce their own, state antitrust laws. Although my analysis is primarily theoretical, the appendix at the end of this chapter reports the results of a limited empirical study that I have conducted.

Some Economics of Federalism

When the state itself, in its propriety capacity—for example, as a purchaser of road-building materials—is injured by a federal antitrust violation, its suing the violator for redress is relatively unproblematic and in any event inevitable: It is the injured victim. Serious problems arise,

This is the revised text of the keynote address given on April 21, 2003, at the conference, "The New Antitrust Paradox: Policy Proliferation in the Global Economy," sponsored by the American Enterprise Institute. I thank Adele Grignon and Daniel Levine for their helpful research assistance and Frank Easterbrook and John Lopatka for helpful comments on a previous draft.

however, when it sues in an essentially public capacity, as a substitute for or a competitor of the federal antitrust enforcement authorities.

But first some framing thoughts about the theory of federalism. Imagine an industry composed of a single firm, a monopolist, or, at the other extreme, of fifty separate firms; my reason for choosing the number fifty is obvious. On the one hand, a monopolist would be able to internalize certain costs and benefits that would be externalized under a competitive organization of the industry. On the benefits side are new, imitable inventions and ideas, where monopoly is a substitute for patents, copyrights, and trade secrets as methods of internalizing the benefits from innovation. On the costs side are competitive costs that do not generate net social welfare gains, such as advertising and marketing expenditures that primarily merely affect the market shares of firms selling essentially identical products; manufacturing facilities that have excess capacity; and other respects in which competition creates duplication without fully offsetting benefits.

On the other hand, the competitive organization of the industry would give consumers more choices (and at lower prices, assuming that the avoidable costs of competition previously noted are not too great). It would also promote diverse approaches to inventive activity, which is important to those who believe as I do that Darwinian theories of the inventive process, which model it as a trial-and-error process that is optimized by diversity among inventors in the same way that biological evolution is promoted by genetic diversity, are the best theories that we have of the inventive process.

Now it might seem that a monopolist could offer whatever product variety consumers wanted and achieve whatever diversity in research and development is optimal—in short, gain all the benefits that competition affords (except low prices) simply by decentralizing its marketing and research activities. But this is incorrect, especially with regard to research. The reason is that no organization can tolerate as much diversity as a competitive market can, because there must be a considerable degree of uniformity, structure, rules and reporting, and cultural conformity—a considerable degree of, in a word, bureaucracy—in any large organization. It is an imperative of management. Without considerable uniformity, an organization ceases to be an organization; centripetal forces dominate. The fact that so many mergers disappoint investors illustrates how combining different corporate cultures under the same roof, like combining different ethnic cultures in the same nation, is a trick that is extremely difficult to pull off.

This analysis transfers pretty well I think to the issue of federalism. On the one hand, there are unitary, monopolistic governments such as that of France and until recently the United Kingdom (to speak only of democracies), and on the other hand, there are federal systems such as that of the United States, Germany, Switzerland, and Canada. The monopolistic governments are "efficient" in the same sense as the monopoly supplier of some good or service; they internalize externalities and (what is actually an aspect of cost internalization) minimize duplication. But they fall down in their encouragement of variety and innovation. France is overcentralized, because the imperatives of management limit the degree to which it can achieve through bureaucratic subdivisions the benefits of decentralization. In contrast to local and regional government units in a country such as France, U.S. states exhibit considerable variety in the services they offer their residents. This variety reflects both cultural, economic, and demographic differences among the populations of the different states and the tugs of competition, because it is relatively easy for individuals and firms to relocate from one state to another. Emigration from a nation is of course more difficult and costly.

Justice Holmes long ago aptly described the states as isolated laboratories for social experiments. What he meant was that a state could experiment with some novel form of regulation, or of configuring the extent or delivery of state services, and the results of the experiment would be observed by other states. If the experiment was successful, it could be emulated by the other states or adopted by the federal government within its domain. There are innumerable examples from our history of social experiments conducted at the state level. These experiments range from early antitrust and regulatory law, "progressive" social welfare legislation, abortion reform, and novel sanctions for sex offenders to voucher systems, the privatization of prisons, and the state welfare reforms in Wisconsin and elsewhere that led up to the national welfare reform of the 1990s. The analogy to Darwinian theories of innovation is very close.

But the considerable advantages of federalism coexist with considerable disadvantages, namely negative externalities (external costs as distinct from external benefits) that tend to be greater than the negative externalities created by competitive markets. Individuals and firms cannot move from state to state with the same ease with which they can switch from buying one producer's product to buying another's. States have, to an extent, a captive market, and as a result, there is less competitive pressure on them than there is on private business firms. States also have opportunities to export costs, in much the same way that a polluting firm can in the absence of legal liability export costs. For example, a state that contains valuable mineral resources can, by imposing a severance tax on them, shift some of the costs of the state's government from the state's taxpayers to the consumers of the resources in other states or nations, assuming demand for the resources by nonresidents is not perfectly elastic. State taxes on interstate users of a state's highways could have similar effects, and so could state tort rules slanted in favor of residents, for example, a rule that exempted negligent in-state manufacturers from liability to nonresidents injured by their negligence or that imposed strict liability on nonresidents who injured state residents, however careless the residents were. State antitrust suits, which are a form of tort suit, can have the same result.

But just as there are legal rules against unwarranted cost externalization by private firms, for example, rules against pollution (or at least pollution that is not cost justifiable), Congress has the power to prevent states from trying to shift the costs of government to other states, or other costs from the shoulders of residents to those of nonresidents, by legislating under the Constitution's Commerce Clause. And the Supreme Court has long interpreted the clause to forbid of its own force, without need for congressional legislation, unreasonable state burdens on interstate commerce, which means, approximately at least, shifting costs without justification from local taxpayers to taxpayers in other states or in foreign nations, or more broadly, from residents to nonresidents. This "negative" or "dormant" interpretation of the Commerce Clause is enforced by the courts, mainly the U.S. Supreme Court. And it is (one is tempted to say, therefore) rather toothless in application because of the difficulty of determining by the methods of litigation either the costs of government services or the incidences of the taxes and other measures to which a state might resort in an effort to recoup—or shift—those costs.

It is tempting—to return to an earlier point—to suppose that a much cleaner solution to the problem of optimal decentralization of the national government than federalism would be a unitary government that, like any efficient large enterprise, organized itself into divisions, subdivisions, and so on, on functional or geographical (or both) lines, designed to strike the optimal balance between the advantages of centralization and those of decentralization.[1] But this would be unsatisfactory for the same reason that a monopolist's decentralizing its operations would not generate the same product variety and innovative progress as a competitive organization of the industry would. The unitary government would have to insist on a considerable uniformity among all its divisions and subdivisions because otherwise it would lose control. The large differences in the political cultures and institutions of the fifty states would be unthinkable if there were no states but merely regional and local offices of a unitary federal government.

Against this it can be argued that decentralization can have negative effects, for example by increasing the likelihood of corruption, because of the loss of control over subordinate officials. It can also be argued that it would be pure accident if our federal system represented the optimal amount and pattern of decentralization, because it is a historical accident that the states have the size, population, and configuration that they do.[2] The case for federalism remains somewhat conjectural.

State Antitrust Enforcement: *Parens Patriae*

I turn now to antitrust enforcement by the states, beginning with the authority, conferred in 1976 on state attorneys general by the Hart-Scott-Rodino Antitrust Improvements Act,[3] to bring suits (*parens patriae* suits) on behalf of the residents of their states under federal antitrust law. The effect, in principle at least, is to make public enforcement of federal antitrust law a competitive rather than a monopoly "market." I shall consider the pros and cons of this approach in light of the theory of federalism sketched in the first part of this chapter.

To begin, note that the state attorneys general are not the states. They are elected separately from the governor. This is significant in three related respects. First, state attorneys general are politicians, that is, elected rather than appointed officials. Second, the natural ambition of a politician who holds high state office is to be elected governor. Hence there is often a built-in tension between the attorney general and the governor of a state. In addition, the attorney general has an incentive to bring suits, regardless of their intrinsic legal merit, that confer a political benefit on him—for example, suits that benefit powerful local business or other constituencies. Third, because the attorney general is not part of the governor's administration, he lacks leverage in seeking appropriations from the state legislature. As a result, state attorneys general are chronically underfunded.[4] They cannot afford large staffs and so they cannot reap the benefits of specialization. Nor can they afford to hire top-quality lawyers. These resource-related handicaps are particularly serious in a highly technical, expert-witness-intensive, specialized field of law such as federal antitrust law.

The coalescence of these factors suggests a strategy for a state attorney general that is in fact observed. The strategy consists of bringing high-profile lawsuits that attract publicity to the attorney general and promote the interests of politically influential state residents (including corporations that have headquarters or extensive operations in the state) at the expense of nonresidents, including nonresident competitors of resident enterprises. (For some statistical evidence, see table 1 in the appendix on page 263.) The strategy is constrained however by the fact that the resources available for such litigation are likely to be very limited unless the litigation has a realistic prospect of generating a large money judgment or settlement for the state or unless several states join in the litigation (as they frequently do—see table 2 in the appendix on page 264), enabling a pooling of resources. The latter is often the more feasible method of economizing on litigation expenses even when damages are the relief sought. The reason is that judgments or settlements obtained in *parens patriae* litigation generally are distributed to the state residents on whose behalf the suit was brought and, if there is money left over, to charities designated by the state attorney general,[5] although the court may award attorney's fees to him.

It is easy to see why antitrust *parens patriae* suits might be attractive to state attorneys general. Firms headquartered or operating within the state are likely to face competition from nonresidents, and they will be grateful if the state's attorney general incurs the expense of suing those competitors; he may also have somewhat greater credibility with the courts than a competitor plaintiff would have. And major antitrust violations are likely to have effects in multiple states, facilitating joint action and therefore resource pooling by state attorneys general. What is more, as shown by the *Microsoft* case, if the U.S. Department of Justice brings an antitrust suit, the state attorneys general may be able, by bringing parallel suits that are then consolidated with the Justice Department's suit, to take a free ride on the department's investment in the litigation.[6]

The antitrust strategy of state attorneys general that I have just sketched obviously has a potential to generate socially perverse consequences. The use of the antitrust laws to harass competitors is an old story but a true one, and given the political incentives of state attorneys general, the risk is great that in deciding whether to bring an antitrust suit against a competitor of a resident enterprise a state attorney general will not be scrupulous in the exercise of his enforcement discretion and will bring and press the suit even if unconvinced of its merit. This is a form of protectionism. In addition, I worry that state attorneys general will try to channel the moneys recovered in their suits to charitable uses that advance their political agenda.

And if, as is common (as I noted earlier), there are multiple state plaintiffs, there will be coordination costs that will make it more difficult to settle the case than it would be if there were only a single plaintiff. This was a factor in the length of time that it took to settle the *Microsoft* litigation, where there were initially eighteen state plaintiffs as well as the U.S. Department of Justice. Indeed, it is not fully settled, because some of the state plaintiffs refused to settle and are appealing the district judge's rejection of their position.[7]

So there is a considerable downside to *parens patriae* antitrust suits, but we should consider whether there may be a significant upside. I think not. Because of the resource constraints that I have mentioned, it is unlikely that state attorneys general will be sources of innovative antitrust doctrines or methods of proof—and in fact, I know of no examples where they have been. (A separate question, which I'll discuss shortly, is the contribution to antitrust thinking made by the enactment or interpretation of state antitrust laws.) In principle, by offering competition in public enforcement of federal antitrust laws to the U.S. Department of Justice, the state attorneys general keep the department on its toes and offer alternatives that a monopoly would foreclose. When the 2000 presidential election resulted in a change in personnel in the Justice Department that resulted in a willingness to settle the case on terms more favorable to Microsoft than the Clinton administration had been prepared to do, several of the states, as I already mentioned, refused to accede to the settlement and thus offered the courts a competitive alternative to the Justice Department.

But there are four reasons to doubt the value of such competition. The first is its one-way character. The state attorneys general can offer only harsher antitrust enforcement than the Justice Department. They cannot, by not suing, offer the courts a gentler alternative to the department's enforcement policies, because their decision not to sue does not bind anyone. They can pile on, but they cannot remove the department from the pile. The danger is that interstate businesses will be forced to conform their business practices to the most restrictive state interpretation of federal antitrust law.[8] In fairness to the state attorneys general, their national association has issued horizontal-merger and vertical-restraint guidelines, thus providing some uniformity of enforcement policy, but, not so commendably, the guidelines are harsher than the corresponding guidelines of the Justice Department and the Federal Trade Commission.[9]

Second, even if the states could not bring *parens patriae* antitrust suits, private individuals and firms harmed by antitrust violations would be able to bring suits under federal antitrust law for redress of the injury. Competitors and customers of Microsoft are not bound by the Justice Department's settlement and can—and have—sued Microsoft on their own. The class action device enables the aggregation in a single suit of antitrust injuries too slight to warrant the expense of individual suits. The *parens patriae* suit is in effect a class action, and while class actions have plenty of problems, I know of no evidence that *parens patriae* suits solve them. Third, there is competition in antitrust enforcement at the federal level by virtue of the overlapping jurisdictions of the Justice Department and the Federal Trade Commission; increasingly, there is competition at the international level as well. Fourth, despite the potential bonanzas that *parens patriae* damages suits might seem to offer, the limited funding of state attorneys general has, perhaps in conjunction with other factors, resulted in an extraordinary paucity of antitrust *parens patriae* suits (see table 3 in the appendix on page 264).

To summarize, nothing in the theory of federalism lends support to authorizing state attorneys general to bring *parens patriae* suits under federal antitrust law. But the case against such authorization would be weakened if state attorneys general were appointed rather than elected officials, a reform that is independently desirable.

State Enforcement of State Antitrust Laws

Concerning the question of allowing states to have their own antitrust laws, the case for federalism, and so for an affirmative answer, is stronger. There is no necessary connection between a state antitrust law and enforcement by the state attorney general, because private enforcement of state antitrust law is possible and indeed common. In addition, if antitrust violations that did not affect interstate or foreign commerce were not actionable under state law, there would be a law enforcement vacuum, because the Commerce Clause of the U.S. Constitution would not authorize federal action against such violations, either. To that (rather tiny) extent, state antitrust law is secure. But Congress could preempt state antitrust law insofar as applicable to interstate or foreign commerce; such preemption, in areas as various as securities law and pensions, is commonplace and of unquestioned constitutionality. We should consider the pros and cons of it.

On the one hand, dual enforcement, as I noted earlier in reference to state enforcement of federal antitrust law, provides a competitive alternative to the U.S. Justice Department's monopolizing antitrust enforcement; but as we have also seen, the department would not have a monopoly even if there were no state antitrust laws, because of private suits under federal antitrust law and also because of the Federal Trade Commission. On the other hand, unlike the case of dual or multiple enforcement of the same laws, state antitrust law provides an opportunity for doctrinal competition—and the states have taken that opportunity, notably in the widespread rejection by the states of the *Illinois Brick* doctrine.[10] That doctrine, an interpretation of federal antitrust law by the Supreme Court, precludes antitrust suits by indirect purchasers, for example, consumers who purchase from the dealers or distributors that are the direct purchasers from the antitrust violators and that pass on much of the overcharge caused by the violation to their own purchasers, that is, the consumers. Although personally I think the *Illinois Brick* doctrine is sound, this is far from certain. Its contours, moreover, are controversial, and it is valuable to have diversity and experimentation in this area, from which a consensus may someday emerge.

But there is a downside to permitting states to reject *Illinois Brick*, and that is the danger of double recovery. In a suit by direct purchasers under federal antitrust law, there is no passing-on defense; that is the *Hanover Shoe* corollary of *Illinois Brick*.[11] Suppose the total overcharge to direct purchasers is $1 million, and of this, $500,000 is passed on to indirect purchasers. The total damages are only $1 million ($3 million after trebling), but if direct purchasers sue under federal law and indirect purchasers sue under state law, the defendant may be forced to pay total damages of $4.5 million after trebling. It is possible, despite the dual-sovereignty doctrine that allows a piling on of state and federal penalties for the same conduct, that the courts would hold that an antitrust defendant cannot be forced to pay total damages in excess of three times the total cost that has been imposed, which is to say the sum of the portion of the overcharge that the direct purchasers did not pass on and the portion that was passed on to indirect purchasers.[12] Possible, but far from assured.[13]

Given that most antitrust enforcement nowadays is private, the significance of state antitrust law that overlaps with federal law is not so much multiple suits against the same defendant as multiple theories in the same case to the extent that federal and state antitrust law differ—and this form of duplication is relatively costless. The *Illinois Brick* issue is an exception because rejection of the doctrine of that case enables additional suits. It is an exception that has both an offsetting benefit in constructive legal competition and a cost in potential overdeterrence.

I would be inclined to forbid the states to apply their antitrust laws to antitrust violations that occur in or affect interstate or foreign commerce.[14] I am even more convinced that Congress should repeal the provision of the Hart-Scott-Rodino Act that authorizes *parens patriae* antitrust suits by the states, although the small number of these suits makes repeal a low-priority item. As a second-best solution, I would like to see state attorneys general converted from elected to appointed officials. But this is not, I hasten to add, because I expect governors to be less politically motivated than other elected officials but because attorneys general would exercise some discretionary authority even if they were appointed—and it would be exercised in a more professional manner if they were not politicians—and because their antitrust enforcement activities would be better funded if they were allies rather than rivals of the governor. Better funding should increase the quality of enforcement.

Appendix: Empirical Analysis

I have tried to collect data on the actual experience of the states' exercise of their authority to bring federal antitrust *parens patriae* suits. This is not easy to do, because the state attorneys general do not report such data, but I believe that my Westlaw search has recovered virtually all the cases.

Table 1 shows that in little more than a third of the cases, all the defendants are residents of the plaintiff state(s), and in almost half, none of the defendants is a resident. These data support my conjecture that *parens patriae* litigation is a method of protecting resident companies from competition from nonresidents.

As shown in table 2, roughly a third of these suits are brought by more than one state's attorney general. I call such suits "multistate."

In table 3, notice how few antitrust *parens patriae* suits have been brought: an average of roughly one and a half per state over the *entire* twenty-seven-year period since the enactment of the Hart-Scott-Rodino Act. This paucity of suits makes it unlikely that the *parens patriae* power has much significance for the enforcement of federal antitrust law.

TABLE 1
DEFENDANTS RESIDING WITHIN PLAINTIFF STATE(S)

	Single-State Litigation	Multistate Litigation	Both Single- and Multistate Litigation
	Number (Percent)	Number (Percent)	Number (Percent)
All Defendants	24 (45.3)	5 (20.8)	29 (37.7)
Some Defendants	5 (9.4)	7 (29.2)	12 (15.6)
No Defendants	24 (45.3)	12 (50)	36 (46.8)
Total	53 (100)	24 (100)	77 (100)

SOURCE: Author's calculations.

TABLE 2

SINGLE- AND MULTISTATE FEDERAL ANTITRUST SUITS FILED UNDER
PARENS PATRIAE AUTHORITY

Type	Number of Suits	Percentage of Suits
Single-State	53	68.8
Multistate	24	31.2
Total	77	100

SOURCE: Author's calculations.

TABLE 3

FEDERAL ANTITRUST SUITS BROUGHT BY STATE ATTORNEYS
GENERAL UNDER PARENS PATRIAE AUTHORITY

Year	Number of Suits	Percentage of All Suits Filed
Before 1976	11	14.3
1976–1980	7	9.1
1981–1985	12	15.6
1986–1990	18	23.4
1991–1995	15	19.5
1996–2000	7	9.1
2001 to present	7	9.1
Total	77	100

SOURCE: Author's calculations.

Notes

1. See Frank B. Cross, "The Folly of Federalism," *Cardozo Law Review* 24 (2002): 1–59, 18–29.

2. Ibid.

3. Hart-Scott-Rodino Antitrust Improvements Act, 15 U.S.C. § 15c (2000).

4. State antitrust budgets tend to be minute. See Robert M. Hahn and Anne Layne-Farrar, "Federalism in Antitrust," *Harvard Journal of Law and Public Policy* 26 (2003): 877–921, 888–90. For example, New York's antitrust budget in fiscal 2002 was only $2.5 million, compared to $130.8 million for the U.S. Department of Justice. Ibid., 889, table 1.

5. See Susan Beth Farmer, "More Lessons from the Laboratories: Cy Pres Distributions in *Parens Patriae* Antitrust Actions Brought by State Attorneys General," *Fordham Law Review* 68 (1999): 361–406.

6. See Hahn and Layne-Farrar, "Federalism in Antitrust," 892–907.

7. In an article defending the role of state attorneys general in federal antitrust litigation, the former chief of antitrust in the New York attorney general's office makes certain representations concerning my activity in the mediation of that case. See Harry First, "Delivering Remedies: The Role of the States in Antitrust Enforcement," *George Washington Law Review* 69 (2001): 1032–34. His representations are inaccurate, except in one respect: I was indeed appalled by the unreasonable and irresponsible position taken by several of the state attorneys general in the mediation. He is incorrect, however, in stating that I "did not deal directly with the states until near the end of the mediation process." Ibid., 1032. I did not deal much with Mr. First, because he attended only one of my meetings with the plaintiffs' side of the litigation, but I dealt continuously with Tom Miller, the attorney general of Iowa, who was the lead representative of the state attorneys general in the mediation. Thus, it is also false that "the states were not actively consulted for a substantial part of the mediation process." Ibid., 1033. He says that apparently I "thought that the mediation was hopeless once it was clear that the states intended to play an active role, coming forward with views somewhat at variance with the Justice Department's." Ibid. At the last moment, the states upped the ante, making demands that it was plain that Microsoft would never accept. He accuses me of "impatience" in terminating the mediation when the states unexpectedly escalated their demands (ibid.); yet it was only after four months of almost full-time mediation that, faced with the intransigency and incompetence of the states, I decided the case would not settle, and threw in the towel.

8. Donald L. Flexner and Mark A. Racanelli, "State and Federal Antitrust Enforcement in the United States: Collision or Harmony?" *Connecticut Journal of International Law* 9 (1994): 532.

9. See National Association of Attorneys General, antitrust protocols, www.naag.org. The NAAG has been called "a modern heir to the populist tradition"

of antitrust law. Jonathan Rose, "State Antitrust Enforcement, Mergers, and Politics," *Wayne Law Review* 41 (1994): 126.

10. For an outdated list of the rejecting states, see *California v. ARC America Corp.,* 490 U.S. 93, 98 n. 3 (1989). The doctrine itself was announced in *Illinois Brick Co. v. Illinois,* 431 U.S. 720 (1977).

11. See *Hanover Shoe, Inc. v. United Shoe Machinery Corp.,* 392 U.S. 481 (1968).

12. See Kevin J. O'Connor, "Is the Illinois Brick Wall Crumbling?" *Antitrust,* Summer 2001, 37; Stephen Calkins, "An Enforcement Official's Reflections on Antitrust Class Actions," *Arizona Law Review* 39 (1997): 427, n. 79; Ivy Johnson, "Restitution on Behalf of Indirect Purchasers: Opening the Backdoor to *Illinois Brick,*" *Washington & Lee Law Review* 57 (2000): 1037.

13. See John E. Lopatka and William H. Page, "Indirect Purchaser Suits and the Consumer Interest," *Antitrust Bulletin* 48 (2003): 564–65; Johnson, "Restitution on Behalf," 1038, n. 230.

14. The case against permitting states to bring enforcement actions under either state or federal law is even greater in the case of international transactions. See Edward T. Swaine, "The Local Law of Global Antitrust," *William and Mary Law Review* 43 (2001): 627–785.

11

State Antitrust Enforcement: Empirical Evidence and a Modest Reform Proposal

Michael DeBow

The question of whether the American system of antitrust federalism makes for good antitrust law is once again on the public agenda. The proximate cause for its return to currency is the strange spectacle provided by the various government antitrust suits against Microsoft Corporation.

In November 2002, the U.S. district judge in charge of the *Microsoft* litigation approved a settlement agreement between the U.S. Department of Justice and Microsoft. Of the nineteen states that had sued the company, one (South Carolina) dropped its suit and sixteen others agreed to the November 2002 settlement. Massachusetts and West Virginia, however, objected to the settlement and have appealed the district judge's approval. In what sounds like a bad joke, West Virginia's attorney general announced he would assign his sole antitrust lawyer to work on the appeal.[1] Thus, two states—accounting for roughly 2.9 percent of the U.S. population—are delaying the close of the most significant piece of antitrust litigation in the past decade, involving the most valuable company in the U.S. economy.

Unsurprisingly, experts have questioned the wisdom of involving individual states in antitrust enforcement, at least when undeniably national matters—such as the future of Microsoft—are at stake.[2] Congress, at the initiative of Rep. Sensenbrenner (R-Wisconsin), has authorized the establishment of an Antitrust Modernization Commission with an eye to examining the role of state attorneys general in enforcing antitrust laws.[3] Most prominently, Judge Richard Posner of the U.S. Court of Appeals for the Seventh Circuit has proposed to limit the role of state antitrust enforcers.

Judge Posner served as a court-appointed mediator in the *Microsoft* litigation. His effort ended unsuccessfully in April 2000, and press accounts maintain that Judge Posner blames the plaintiff states for the failure of the mediation process.[4] In subsequent talks and publications on the role of antitrust in the "new economy," Judge Posner proposed—without mentioning the *Microsoft* litigation by name—that the states should be "stripped of their authority to bring antitrust suits, federal or state, except under circumstances in which a private firm would be able to sue."[5] Alternatively, he proposed giving the federal authorities "a right of first refusal" with respect to antitrust suits; if a federal suit were filed, private and state suits would be preempted. Judge Posner has since elaborated on these suggestions in the revised edition of his antitrust treatise and in his contribution to this volume.[6]

After a brief summary of the uniquely American system of antitrust federalism, this chapter presents empirical data on the states' antitrust enforcement record over the past decade. It shows that the *Microsoft* litigation is an exception—albeit a very significant exception—to a general record of limited state activity coupled with substantial conformity to traditional antitrust doctrine. The chapter reviews Judge Posner's theory and proposal in light of that evidence and concludes with a slightly more modest proposal for federal reform.

Antitrust Federalism

Antitrust law in the United States has been a joint federal-state pursuit from its inception. The first U.S. antitrust statute was passed by the state of Kansas in March 1889. By the time Sherman Act was adopted in July 1890, at least twelve more states had passed their own antitrust statutes.[7]

A dual system made a good deal of sense as of 1890, given the traditional understanding of the limited reach of Congress's powers under the Commerce Clause. On this view, the federal commerce power was limited to the regulation of "selling, buying, and bartering, as well as transporting for these purposes," with the word "commerce" "used in contradistinction to activities such as manufacturing and agriculture."[8] The Congress that passed the Sherman Act clearly subscribed to this interpretation,[9] and the same perspective informed the Supreme Court's early decision on the Act's reach in *United States v. E.C. Knight* (1895).

According to the original understanding, the division of labor between federal and state antitrust statutes and enforcers was straightforward: State enforcement was directed at local, intrastate violators, and federal authorities could reach business behavior that restrained interstate trade.

An initial burst of state enforcement activity lasted until World War I.[10] Afterward, though, the states played only a limited role, and the post-1937 expansion of the federal commerce power rendered state antitrust statutes largely redundant. After the Supreme Court's decisions in *United States v. Darby* (1941) and *Wickard v. Filburn* (1942), the federal commerce power was, for all practical purposes, unlimited.[11] The federal antitrust laws could be used to attack virtually any anticompetitive activity anywhere in the country, and state antitrust took a decided back seat to federal law and policy. One commentator quipped in 1961 that the state statutes "have been so dead that it may be wondered whether it would have been unethical in recent years for lawyers in most states to tell their clients to ignore them."[12]

Renewed interest in state antitrust law came in the 1970s. In 1976, Congress augmented the role of the states by passing two key statutes. The Hart-Scott-Rodino Act granted parens patriae authority to the states, and the Crime Control Act of 1976 led to the appropriation of $25 million over three years to aid state antitrust enforcement. This new funding enabled twenty-five states to establish antitrust programs in their state attorneys general offices for the first time.[13]

Reagan Revolution, National Association of Attorneys General Counterrevolution, and Reconciliation

In due course, the congressional attempt to empower state attorneys general came into conflict with the Reagan administration and its firm commitment to a set of antitrust policies based on the work of the Chicago School of antitrust analysis. This new learning in antitrust favored a limited role for the law, focused almost exclusively on horizontal price-fixing and large horizontal mergers in concentrated markets with high entry costs.[14]

The Reagan antitrust enforcers' adherence to these minimalist policies prompted a strong reaction from a group of state attorneys general.

Working through the National Association of Attorneys General (NAAG), the dissident attorneys general created their own alternative antitrust bureaucracy. In 1983, NAAG established a Multistate Antitrust Task Force to coordinate the states' efforts. The task force's Reagan-era handiwork included NAAG enforcement guidelines concerning vertical restraints (in 1985) and horizontal mergers (in 1987).[15]

NAAG's antitrust agenda differed sharply from the Reagan administration's (particularly regarding vertical restraints), and the rhetoric that suffused NAAG's efforts in this period was fiery. Lloyd Constantine, the top antitrust lawyer in the New York attorney general's office and a leading proponent of the NAAG approach to antitrust, saw the 1980s as "a 'dark age' for antitrust when favored economic theory was elevated above marketplace reality and the rule of law." Reagan antitrust enforcers, Constantine averred, were engaged in "civil disobedience" in their prosecutorial decision making.[16]

The end of the Reagan administration saw the beginnings of a thaw in NAAG's attitudes toward federal enforcers. For his part, in 1988, Mr. Constantine "called for the establishment of a regime of collective and coordinated enforcement among the federal and state antitrust agencies."[17] A substantial reconciliation between the states and the federal authorities did appear to take place during the first Bush administration. An Executive Working Group on Antitrust was established in 1989, apparently at the instigation of U.S. Assistant Attorney General James Rill.[18] Composed of the five Federal Trade Commission (FTC) commissioners, the head of the Antitrust Division, and five NAAG representatives, the working group coordinates state and federal enforcement activities in order to avoid duplication of effort. The group promotes the sharing of information and the cross-deputization of attorneys to encourage the joint prosecution of cases. Several joint federal-state investigations and prosecutions were executed during the first Bush administration.[19]

Relations between the states and federal antitrust enforcers during the Clinton administration remained cordial, with a significant number of joint federal-state prosecutions taking place.[20] Additional formal steps in federal-state cooperation included the adoption of the Protocol for Increased State Prosecution of Criminal Antitrust Offenses in 1996[21] and the Protocol for Joint Federal/State Merger Investigations in 1998.[22] To be sure, federal and state enforcers do not always agree—witness *Microsoft*.

On the whole, though, the tone of the federal-state relationship in antitrust today is quite different from the Reagan era. At this stage, it seems unlikely that the antitrust direction of the second Bush administration will differ very much from the policies of the Clinton or first Bush administrations. (Here again, the decision to settle the *Microsoft* litigation is an exception.) Barring dramatic events, federal-state relations on antitrust are likely to conform to the pattern of the recent past.

The States' Enforcement Record, 1993–2002

What precisely, though, is that pattern? In the eyes of their defenders, the states have grown into powerful players in the antitrust arena. Constantine was convinced in 1990 that "the states have secured their position of equality in the government enforcement hierarchy," with the NAAG Antitrust Task Force "as de facto a third national antitrust agency."[23] More recently, in 2002, Patricia Conners, the chair of the NAAG Multistate Antitrust Task Force, opined that "[i]t's well-settled that state attorneys general have the ability to bring multi-state matters or even single-state matters that, in effect, have an impact on national policy."[24] Such presumptions of authority and ability, however, stand in marked contrast to the empirical record. State antitrust enforcement is neither as common nor as aggressive as is suggested by the just-quoted remarks. One can state with a high degree of confidence that the states' lawsuits against Microsoft were anomalies; state antitrust on the whole has been, for the past decade, a fairly dull business.

There does not appear to be a central registry of information about state antitrust activity. (NAAG is reportedly working on such a database.) Accordingly, I compiled a list of state enforcement proceedings for the past decade (from 1993 through 2002) from the indices of legal trade publications, especially the Bureau of National Affairs's *Antitrust and Trade Regulation Reports* and the Commerce Clearing House's *Trade Cases*. In addition, I reviewed standard antitrust reference books covering the ten-year period. Given the nature of this research, the results are probably incomplete and less than comprehensive. Still, they provide at least a general overview of the nature of the states' enforcement activities during this time.

TABLE 1

ANTITRUST COMPLAINTS FILED IN COURT, 1993–2002

Case Type	Number Filed by States	Number Filed by Department of Justice
Sherman 1 cases	52 (including 7 filed cooperatively with a federal agency)	523 (including 51 civil, 472 criminal)
Sherman 2 cases	10	11
Merger cases	47 (including 12 cooperative)	115
Vertical cases	11 (including 5 cooperative)	—
Total	120	649

SOURCE: Author's case research.

My review showed that the states filed 120 antitrust actions between 1993 and 2002.[25] Twenty-one were suits brought by more than one state; I have counted each of these as a single suit. Most of the cases reported here were commenced and settled during the period shown. A few were filed during the period studied but are still pending (as with *Microsoft*). Another handful were begun before the period, but are included in my results because a significant event occurred during the period studied (that is, settlement or judicial disposition of the case). Table 1 provides a breakdown of the state cases. Data on enforcement proceedings by the U.S. Department of Justice are shown for comparison.[26] The federal data were obtained from the Antitrust Division's Workload Statistics.[27]

Two features of the data stand out.[28] First, the level of state activity is low, particularly in comparison to federal enforcement efforts. On average, the states brought twelve cases per year (five horizontal, five merger, one vertical, and one monopolization)—not exactly a tidal wave. By contrast, during fiscal years 1993–2002, the Department of Justice brought an average of forty-seven criminal price-fixing cases and twelve merger cases per year.

Second, the composition of the states' caseload was not what many feared when NAAG first declared its independence from Reagan-era antitrust. The relatively large number of bid-rigging and horizontal price-fixing cases is consistent with enforcement priorities suggested by Chicago

School economic analysis, as is the small number of vertical cases.[29] The nontrivial number of merger cases might cause some concern, but on closer inspection, the cases hardly demonstrate a desire on the part of states to move heavily into this area. Twelve of the states' forty-seven merger cases appear clearly to have been joint efforts with either the Antitrust Division or the FTC; some of the remainder may have been as well, although this is not clear from published reports.

Both in scope and direction, then, state antitrust enforcement has fallen far short of NAAG rhetoric. Enforcement levels are low because state governments tend not to appropriate much money for antitrust enforcement. Few states devote more than 2 percent of their attorney generals office budget to antitrust matters. West Virginia's lone antitrust attorney, slaving away on the *Microsoft* appeal, is more typical than Florida's antitrust division, with a staff of 23 and a $2.5 million budget.[30] The NAAG revolution has never been well funded.

The failure of state enforcement to depart sharply from federal priorities is also partially explained by the much higher level of federal-state cooperation, compared with twenty years ago. Moreover, federal antitrust law casts a large shadow over state antitrust statutes. Statutes and case law in thirty-eight states direct judges hearing antitrust actions under state statutes to consult federal antitrust law for, at the least, guidance.[31] This acts as a check on the ability of state attorneys general to press novel theories of liability in state enforcement actions. If the federal courts follow an efficiency-oriented analysis, it will be difficult for state attorneys general to buck that trend by suing under state statutes.

The Posner Critique

Judge Posner's indictment of state antitrust enforcement makes three main points. First, the states do not bring significant resources to the enforcement arena; instead, they free ride the efforts of the federal agencies. Second, the states' attorneys are not sufficiently skilled to do antitrust analysis and litigation well. Third, state enforcement officials are likely swayed by local interest group pressure in ways that make it unlikely they will use antitrust to promote consumer welfare.[32] The data strongly confirm Judge Posner's first criticism; provide no evidence one way or the other on the second criticism; and mildly support the third.

Resources. As noted, state enforcement levels are low, most likely for the reason identified by Judge Posner. Moreover, a significant portion of the states' caseload can be characterized as either joint federal-state matters or "follow-on" state suits filed in the wake of a federal investigation and suit. I count 24 such suits out of the grand total of 120 state antitrust suits I identified as originally filed during 1993–2002. This lends some support to Judge Posner's view of the states as free riding the federal enforcement effort, although a conclusive judgment would require additional information on the relative contributions of state and federal agencies to joint enforcement projects.

Bias. Judge Posner's charge that state attorneys general may be "excessively influenced by interest groups that may represent a potential antitrust defendant's competitors" is not a concern—at least, not a distinctly *federal* concern—so long as the economic consequences of an enforcement action are felt only inside the enforcer's jurisdiction. Quite a few of the cases brought by state attorneys general fit this description: They involve local businesses and fall outside a reasonable definition of "interstate commerce." Some cases have an almost quaint, Norman Rockwell–like quality: price-fixing among auto repair facilities in small-town Illinois and Minnesota; operators of Chinese-language tour buses in New York City and horse-drawn carriages at Independence Hall in Philadelphia; the overly cooperative conversations between a father and son who managed competing radio stations in Vernal and Roosevelt, Utah.[33] While one might quibble over the market significance of a particular case or the commitment of public funds to prosecuting it, it is hard to argue that state governments should not be allowed to bring antitrust suits against such obviously "local" businesses.

In addition to such purely local concerns, state and local governments have successfully brought cases against price-fixing in the markets for vitamins and milk, to name two. Such cases will seem beneficial, or at worst benign, to most antitrust skeptics. Beyond obviously local cases and hard-core antitrust offenses of price-fixing, however, state enforcement becomes much more problematic.

Each state's economy interacts with the economies of all the other states, as well as the economies of the United States's international trading partners. In that context, state officials—particularly elected officials—face strong incentives to favor in-state interests at the expense of outsiders or of broader social welfare concerns. Antitrust parochialism can generate benefits for local businesses, consumers, and officials, while its costs are exported to out-of-state investors and consumers. This type of state antitrust parochialism is Judge Posner's true concern, and the *Microsoft* litigation provides an alarming example. Robert Hahn and Anne Layne-Farrar have described the states' involvement in that litigation as a function of local special interest pressures:

> [T]he idea that it is the state government's job to serve its corporate constituents is so ingrained that elected officials do not try to conceal their complicity. Shortly after California and several other states decided to reject the settlement, a local newspaper reported that California Attorney General Bill Lockyer said "his resolve was hardened after listening over the weekend to advice from technical experts and officials from Microsoft's competitors, such as IBM, AOL Time Warner Inc., Sun Microsystems Inc. and Novell Inc." The State of California subsequently took the lead in the continuing litigation—in particular, by providing funding. As one press account confirmed, "Microsoft's competitors lobbied California lawmakers and Governor Gray Davis to approve the extra $3.7 million for antitrust enforcement."[34]

Problems of local bias and attendant externalities should be expected to loom particularly large in cases involving mergers and vertical restraints. Mergers may threaten local job loss, and vertical restraints may threaten locally owned retail outlets. (State horizontal enforcement should generally have pro-consumer effects.) But in both the merger and vertical areas, the states' record is less troublesome than the *Microsoft* litigation might lead one to suspect. While parochialism and externality concerns are theoretically well grounded, they do not find much empirical support in the states' actions to date.

Mergers. A state attorney general's overriding interest is likely to be with the local effects of any proposed merger—including the possibility of the loss of local jobs, the headquarters operations of the target firm, and the like.[35] These same concerns drove state legislatures to interfere with the market for corporate control by enacting antitakeover statutes to block hostile takeovers.[36] State antitrust actions against proposed mergers threaten to treat friendly takeovers in the same way, and for the same reasons.

The NAAG 1993 Horizontal Merger Guidelines invite state attorneys general to take "noneconomic" goals into account in making merger enforcement decisions. Section 2 of the guidelines states that, in addition to effects on consumer welfare through price increases, "mergers may also have other consequences that are relevant to the social and political goals of the Guidelines. For example, mergers may affect the opportunities for small and regional businesses to survive and compete." Such considerations, say the guidelines, "may affect the Attorney General's ultimate exercise of prosecutorial discretion."[37]

Such parochialism is on display in the consent decree negotiated by the attorney general of Maine in *Maine v. Connors Brothers Ltd.*[38] The acquiring firm, a Canadian fish processor, was permitted to acquire the assets of a Maine-based competitor only by agreeing, inter alia, to invest $12 million in the target firm's Maine facilities over a twelve-year period (with the first $7 million to be invested in the first three years); to continue to produce sardines and other products at the Maine facilities for the twelve-year period of the decree; and to use its best efforts to ensure that "the largest possible proportion of the fish processed annually at its Maine facilities consist of fresh fish landed in the U.S. by U.S. fishermen."

Another state merger case shot through with parochialism was Pennsylvania's attempt to undo Russell Stover Candies' acquisition of the Whitman Chocolates assets from Pet, Inc. The state's interest in the acquisition seems to have derived almost entirely from Russell Stover's plans to close Whitman's only manufacturing facility, which was located in Philadelphia and employed 600 people. In denying the state's request for injunctive relief, the district judge noted that "nothing in the Clayton Act or other federal antitrust laws addressed Pennsylvania's concern about the plant closing." The president of the affected union thanked the attorney general for his efforts "to protect the jobs of our members," and argued that "this case points out the need for having a state antitrust statute, which could have strengthened the state's case in this matter."[39]

Clear cases of parochialism, however, are anomalous. The run of merger cases brought by the states during the period studied—a total of forty-seven—did not obviously suffer from this defect. Instead, the vast majority of cases—twelve of which were pursued cooperatively with the FTC or the Justice Department—appear, at least on the surface, to be concerned with the effects of the challenged merger on consumer welfare, rather than on local effects on employment or competitors.

Vertical Restraints. The law on vertical restraints was a central area of disagreement between the Reagan administration and NAAG. In this context, local concerns strongly tempt state attorneys general. First, the typical case will pit local retailers and other distributors against manufacturers owned predominantly by out-of-state investors, and a state attorney general will care more about the happiness of local distributors than about the efficiency vel non of a given vertical arrangement. (A press release announcing a case against "unconscionable resale price maintenance" will scan better than a learned disquisition on the efficiency of curtailing free-rider problems in distribution networks.) Second, vertical restraints lawsuits have often resulted in substantial settlement amounts, at least a portion of which are typically paid to the state attorney general's office.[40]

Even so, the states can hardly be blamed (or credited) for the continuing viability of that area of antitrust.[41] As noted, the record for 1993–2002 shows only eleven state enforcement cases that were primarily vertical in nature. Disgruntled dealers and distributors, in contrast, file many vertical restraints suits.[42] If the states were preempted in this field, vertical restraints law would continue on unchanged, in the absence of congressional action to clear up the muddle of the current vertical case law.

The Potential for Abuse

On the whole, the states' antitrust enforcement activity fits comfortably within the mainstream of antitrust prosecutorial discretion. This does not necessarily mean, however, that state antitrust enforcement should be left undisturbed. While *Microsoft* is an exception, it is a very large and troubling exception, and one that manifestly belies cooperative pronouncements from states' attorneys general. As a matter of political economy, moreover, the Posnerian analysis of the *potential* for much more aggressive—and counterproductive—state use of the antitrust statutes is plainly right. Informal constraints that have so far prevented state attorneys general from exhausting their perceived authority—again, excepting *Microsoft*—may eventually fail.

For most of U.S. history, state attorneys general performed a routine (albeit important) function as their state's top lawyer. In the 1980s, however, some of the occupants of these offices began to stake out a much more expansive, activist role. (The NAAG antitrust revolt was an important aspect of this story, as was the opposition of some attorneys general to Reagan administration environmental and civil rights policies.) The state attorneys general slipped their constitutional traces during their crusade against the tobacco industry in 1994–98. These suits had no basis in existing law, and improperly involved the attorneys general in tax and regulatory questions that were properly within the legislatures' domains. For three reasons, the tobacco litigation raises disturbing questions about state antitrust enforcement.

First, the tobacco litigation has emboldened state attorneys general to "reform" other national industries, such as investment banks and pharmaceutical producers.[43] In the former instance, the attorney general of New York negotiated a settlement with ten major investment banks that, inter alia, insulates securities analysis from the firms' investment banking activities and provides for the payment of $1.4 billion in fines and penalties.[44] In the latter case, various state attorneys general are pursuing several legal theories directed primarily at drug firms' pricing policies, with the goal of lowering the states' expenditures on prescription medicines.[45] These aggressive attempts by state attorneys general to set national policy through litigation may make it more likely that states will pursue more aggressive antitrust enforcement in the future.[46] Second, as it happens, many of the state tobacco lawsuits contained an antitrust claim. The manifest flimsiness of those claims shows that the attorneys general are not above reading the notoriously open-ended antitrust statutes in undisciplined and improper ways.[47] Third, the tobacco litigation raises the ominous prospect of a close partnership between state attorneys general and the private bar in antitrust enforcement.[48] Such an arrangement would trump the resource constraints that have so far precluded a more aggressive and destructive pattern of state antitrust enforcement.

A Modest Reform Proposal

The somewhat perplexing pattern just sketched—general state deference to traditional antitrust doctrines, coupled with the glaring *Microsoft* "exception," aggressive rhetoric, and disturbing possibilities—suggests a federal reform agenda that goes far enough to curb the worst possible abuses—but no farther. Reform proposals should be informed by this and other pragmatic considerations.

Judge Posner's proposal to abolish state parens patriae suits and to limit states to proprietary antitrust suits would almost certainly touch off a heated political battle, with little chance of enactment. Opponents could draw strength from the behavior of the states during the 1993–2002 period—specifically, the dearth of evidence that state antitrust enforcement to date has significantly harmed consumers' interests. By the same token, of course, the fairly small number of state cases suggests that little would be lost if the states were put out of the antitrust enforcement business. The deterrent effect of the states' presence is also small. If the states were banished from the arena, the threat of federal as well as private lawsuits would remain. In most areas of the law except for those very small, very local cases that are pursued by some states today, life would go on unchanged. Even so, an acrimonious debate might well erase much of the good feeling that seems to have developed between the states and federal enforcers since 1989. Coupled with a failure to enact a reform bill, such a debate might herald another period of chilly relations between the states and the federal authorities—a chill that could well have negative implications for consumer welfare.

Furthermore, the effective congressional preemption of a field of law is always difficult. In the antitrust area, the task would be complicated by the fact that many state constitutions have provisions prohibiting monopolies, and many states also have "little FTC acts" that contain language similar to FTC Act section 5's prohibition on "unfair methods of competition." Because section 5 is read as empowering the FTC to take action against conduct that would also violate the Sherman or Clayton Acts, it could be argued that the little FTC acts should be read in the same fashion, with the result that antitrust violations would survive the preemption of the state antitrust statutes alone. Accordingly, any federal legislation designed to preempt the states from the antitrust field would have to deal with both the state constitutional provisions regarding monopolies and the little FTC acts or risk the state attorneys general resorting to one or both of these sources to resurrect state enforcement on different grounds. Preempting only the antitrust side of the little FTC acts would be difficult, and preemption of state constitutional provisions raises federalism concerns of an even higher level. Such an intrusion on state sovereignty would be highly controversial. In light of such pragmatic considerations, two reforms—slightly more modest than the Posner proposal—merit consideration.

A Market-Enhancing Role for State Attorneys General. Judge Posner would have state governments retain the right to bring antitrust suits for direct injury (for example, from bid-rigging). In addition, it makes sense to allow states to prosecute local horizontal price-fixing conspiracies, which may often be more obvious to local enforcement personnel than to federal officials. Prosecution of these cases does not involve elaborate doctrinal tests and would not allow the states to upset national antitrust policy as set by federal enforcement agencies in other areas that do involve more in the way of economic expertise—particularly merger policy. Furthermore, continued state vigilance against bid-rigging and price-fixing would raise the stakes for those business people contemplating such behavior. The possibility of jail time appears to be a more effective deterrent than increased fines (up to a point), so that a continued state presence with respect to behavior that is unambiguously harmful to consumer welfare would likely have a positive effect.

A bill under consideration by the Alabama legislature[49] stakes out just such a role for the state, following a decision by that state's supreme court that limited the reach of its antitrust statute to purely intrastate commerce.[50] This bill, developed by the Alabama state attorney general's office, offers a model for a federal reform effort that is less ambitious than a wholesale repeal of the *parens patriae* powers of state attorneys general.[51] The bill expressly adopts the federal law's definition of "horizontal competitors," "resale price maintenance," and "non-price vertical restraints," then excepts the last two from the state's antitrust jurisdiction. The bill then declares, "Any contract, combination, conspiracy, or agreement among horizontal competitors that attempts to fix prices or divide markets or allocate customers among those horizontal competitors shall be unlawful."

Such a statute would enable the states to continue to prosecute the kind of cases—horizontal price-fixing agreements—that make up the bulk of their current caseload. By expressly importing the federal law on agreements among horizontal competitors, such a statute would place a state attorney general in a supportive, rather than a potentially disruptive, role in antitrust enforcement.

Strengthened Federal Oversight. In a friend of the court brief filed in the *Microsoft* litigation, the U.S. Department of Justice argued strongly that it alone represented the interests of the "American public" in antitrust actions where injunctive relief is sought.[52] Although the district judge hearing the case declined to rule on this point, it seems likely to be heard on appeal.

Regardless of how the issue is eventually resolved in the *Microsoft* litigation, federal law should require a formal notice to the U.S. Department of Justice of any state antitrust suit that includes a request for injunctive relief.[53] To prevent state antitrust suits that are designed to promote local interests over the interests of consumers nationwide, the department should clearly be given the authority to move the court to dismiss such actions when the department thinks that the interstate aspects of the litigation outweigh the in-state interests asserted by the plaintiff state. A strong version of this legislation would direct the judge to grant the department's motion unless the court found extraordinary facts that compel denial.

Given the small number of state cases filed in any given year, such legislation would not result in an onerous new burden on the federal agencies. At the same time, more effective federal control over state antitrust cases with national implications would provide effective protection against the risks of state parochialism and abuse.

Notes

1. Ted Bridis, "West Virginia Joins Massachusetts in Microsoft Antitrust Appeal," Associated Press, December 2, 2002, available at http://biz.yahoo.com/ap/021202/na_fin_us_microsoft_2.html

2. See generally Robert H. Hahn and Anne Layne-Farrar, "Federalism in Antitrust," *AEI-Brookings Joint Center for Regulatory Studies Working Paper* 02-9 (Washington, D.C.: AEI-Brookings Joint Center for Regulatory Studies, September 2002), available at http://aei.brookings.org/admin/pdffiles/working_02_9.pdf.

3. *Antitrust Modernization Commission Act of 2001*, H.R. 2325, 107th Cong., 2d sess. (2001). "Sensenbrenner Introduces Antitrust Study Commission Legislation," June 27, 2001, available at http://www.house.gov/judiciary/news_062701.htm. Sensenbrenner's proposal was eventually approved as part of the Department of Justice's reauthorization legislation enacted in November 2002. 21st Century Department of Justice Appropriations Authorization Act, Pub. L. No. 107-273, 116 Stat. 1758 (2002).

4. Ken Auletta, "What Kept Microsoft from Settling Its Case?" *The New Yorker,* January 15, 2001, 40; Ken Auletta, *World War 3.0: Microsoft and Its Enemies* (New York: Random House, 2001), 340.

5. Richard A. Posner, "Antitrust in the New Economy," *Antitrust Law Journal* 68 (2001): 940 (footnote omitted).

6. Richard A. Posner, *Antitrust Law* (Chicago: University of Chicago Press, 2001), 281–82.

7. David Millon, "The First Antitrust Statute," *Washburn Law Journal* 29 (1990): 141; James May, "Antitrust Practice and Procedure in the Formative Era: The Constitutional and Conceptual Reach of State Antitrust Law, 1880–1918," *University of Pennsylvania Law Review* 135 (1987): 495, 499. May also notes that several state constitutions contained language at the time condemning monopolies and the like, but these provisions were apparently directed more at government grants of monopoly licenses than at private firms. Ibid., 499, nn. 9, 11.

8. *U.S. v. Lopez*, 514 U.S. 549, 585–86 (1995) (Justice Thomas, concurring) (collecting authorities). See generally Randy E. Barnett, "The Original Meaning of the Commerce Clause," *University of Chicago Law Review* 68 (2001): 101; Richard A. Epstein, "The Proper Scope of the Commerce Power," *Virginia Law Review* 73 (1987): 1432–42.

9. *Cantor v. Detroit Edison Company*, 428 U.S. 579, 632–35 (Justice Stewart, dissenting); Gregory J. Werden and Thomas A. Balmer, "Conflicts Between State Law and the Sherman Act," *University of Pittsburgh Law Review* 44 (1982): 49–56.

10. See generally May, "Antitrust Practice and Procedure in the Formative Era"; and James May, "The Role of the States in the First Century of the Sherman Act and the Larger Picture of Antitrust History," *Antitrust Law Journal* 59 (1990): 93.

11. This remains true despite the Supreme Court's recent decisions in *U.S. v. Lopez*, 514 U.S. 549 (1995), and *U.S. v. Morrison*, 529 U.S. 598 (2000), which struck down two federal statutes as beyond Congress's authority under the Commerce Clause. The statutes dealt with activity—possession of firearms in school zones and violent behavior directed at women, respectively—not easily classified as commercial. As a result, the Court was able to decide the cases without rethinking the "substantial effects" test it has applied to the regulation of commercial activity since the New Deal era. As Justice Thomas—the only justice who appears willing to rethink the "substantial effects" test—explained in his concurring opinion in *Morrison*, "By continuing to apply this rootless and malleable standard, however circumscribed, the Court has encouraged the Federal Government to persist in its view that the Commerce Clause has virtually no limits. Until this Court replaces its existing Commerce Clause jurisprudence with a standard more consistent with the original understanding, we will continue to see Congress appropriating state police powers under the guise of regulating commerce." *Morrison*, 529 U.S. at 627 (Justice Thomas, concurring).

12. James A. Rahl, "Toward a Worthwhile State Antitrust Policy," *Texas Law Review* 39 (1961): 753.

13. Alan D. Maness, "State Antitrust Enforcement: Its Evolution and Future Direction," *Antitrust Bulletin* 27 (1982): 831.

14. The canonical texts are Richard A. Posner, *Antitrust Law: An Economic Perspective* (Chicago: University of Chicago Press, 1976), and Robert H. Bork, *The Antitrust Paradox: A Policy at War with Itself* (New York: Basic Books, 1978). Another very useful treatment is Frank H. Easterbrook, "Workable Antitrust Policy," *Michigan Law Review* 84 (1986): 1696.

15. NAAG Vertical Restraints Guidelines, *Antitrust and Trade Regulation Report* 49 (BNA) No. 1234, at 996 (Dec. 5, 1985) (current guidelines, adopted in 1995, at *Trade Regulation Reports,* vol. 4 (CCH), par. 13,400, p. 21,151); NAAG Horizontal Merger Guidelines, *Trade Regulation Reports*, vol. 4 (CCH), par. 13,405 (current guidelines, adopted in 1993, at *Trade Regulation Report*, vol. 4 (CCH), par. 13,406, p. 21,193).

16. Lloyd Constantine, "The Mission and Agenda for State Antitrust Enforcement," *Antitrust Bulletin* 36 (1991): 835, 838. Another chair of the NAAG Antitrust Task Force remembered the 1980s as "dark days" when "state and federal antitrust authorities looked and talked at each other only down their noses." Laurel A. Price, "Report from Officialdom," *Antitrust Law Journal* 62 (1993): 249–50. For the administration's position regarding the scope of its prosecutorial discretion, see William F. Baxter, "Separation of Powers, Prosecutorial Discretion, and the 'Common Law' Nature of Antitrust," *Texas Law Review* 60 (1982): 661.

17. Constantine, "The Mission and Agenda for State Antitrust Enforcement," 836 (describing his remarks to the 22nd Annual New England Antitrust Conference in 1988). Constantine left the New York attorney general's office in 1991 and entered private practice. His firm, Constantine and Partners, was lead plaintiffs' counsel for "five million of the nation's merchants" in the Visa/MasterCard antitrust litigation, which

was settled in April 2003 for $3.05 billion, "the largest antitrust settlement in history." *In re: Wal-Mart Stores, Inc. et al. v. Visa U.S.A. Inc.* and *MasterCard International Inc.*, accessible at the firm's website, http://www.cpny.com/debitcase.ihtml.

18. Laurel A. Price, "Sixty Years of Federal Antitrust Enforcement: A State Perspective," *Antitrust Bulletin* 39 (1994): 854 .

19. American Bar Association Section of Antitrust Law, *Antitrust Law Developments*, 3rd ed. (Chicago: ABA, 1992), 618–19 (discussing the first Bush administration's federal-state cooperation).

20. Barry E. Hawk and Laraine L. Laudati, "Antitrust Federalism in the United States and Decentralization of Competition Law Enforcement in the European Union: A Comparison," *Fordham International Law Journal* 20 (1996): 37–39 (collecting Clinton-era cases). See also Laurel A. Price, "Roundtable Discussion with Enforcement Officials," *Antitrust Law Journal* 63 (1996): 965–66 ("We have now come to understand federal-state cooperation to mean, 'If you have a good case, let's come together and do it right.'").

21. *Antitrust and Trade Regulation Report* (BNA), no. 1755 (March 28, 1996), 362.

22. *Trade Regulation Reports*, vol. 4 (CCH), par. 13,420, p. 21,213.

23. Constantine, "The Mission and Agenda for State Antitrust Enforcement," 840.

24. "Interview with Patricia Conners, Chair, NAAG Multistate Antitrust Task Force," *The Antitrust Source* (May 2002), available at http://www.abanet.org/antitrust/source/archives.html.

25. Details on all the cases I reviewed are available on AEI's website, at http://www.aei.org/events/eventID.244,filter./event_detail.asp.

26. In addition to the Department of Justice, the Federal Trade Commission is entrusted with antitrust proceedings, most of which it handles administratively. The commission did, however, file twenty-three federal cases over this time period, the great majority (twenty-one) of which were merger cases. In addition, the FTC filed twenty-two actions for civil penalties over alleged violations of FTC orders and alleged failures to comply with premerger notification requirements.

27. See "Antitrust Division Workload Statistics, FY 1993–2002," U.S. Department of Justice website, http://www.usdoj.gov/atr/public/12848.htm.

28. My conclusions are broadly consistent with those drawn by Professor First from examining the enforcement record of the New York state attorney general's office during the period from March 1999 to February 2001. Harry First, "Delivering Remedies: The Role of the States in Antitrust Enforcement," *George Washington Law Review* 69 (2001): 1015–25.

29. The standard Chicago position is that antitrust should not concern itself with vertical restraints. See Bork, *The Antitrust Paradox*, 297 ("all vertical restraints are beneficial to consumers and should for that reason be completely lawful"); Richard A. Posner, "The Next Step in the Antitrust Treatment of Restricted Distribution: Per Se Legality," *University of Chicago Law Review* 48 (1981): 6.

30. "Oregon Attorney General Hardy Myers Appoints New Chair and Vice Chair of NAAG Multistate Antitrust Task Force," (November 29, 2001), available at National Association of Attorneys General website, http://www.naag.org/news/pr-20011129-or_antitrust.php. For data on other states' antitrust offices, see Hahn and Layne-Farrar, "Federalism in Antitrust," 11–13.

31. American Bar Association Section of Antitrust Law, *Antitrust Law Developments*, 5th ed. (Chicago: ABA, 2002), 811.

32. Posner, "Antitrust in the New Economy."

33. See, respectively, *Illinois v. Hensley*, 2000-1 Trade Cases, par. 72,772, p. 86,615 (Ill. Cir. Ct., Jan. 11, 2000); *Minnesota v. Tim Amdahl Chevrolet Co.*, 1993-1 Trade Cases, par. 70,275, p. 70,370 (Minn. Dist. Ct., June 10, 1993); "State Imposes $150,000 Penalty on Operators Fixing Tour Bus Prices," *Antitrust & Trade Regulation Report* (BNA), no. 1921 (Aug. 5, 1999), 182; "Horse Carriage Companies Settle Pennsylvania's Price Fixing Charges," *Antitrust & Trade Regulation Report* (BNA), no. 1668 (June 16, 1994), 667; *Utah v. Evans*, 1998-2 Trade Cases, par. 72,361, p. 83,412 (Utah Dist. Ct., Nov. 25, 1998).

34. Hahn and Layne-Farrar, "Federalism in Antitrust," 16 (citations omitted).

35. The incentive for elected state attorneys general to take this view has been mentioned in several articles, including David A. Zimmerman, "Why State Attorneys General Should Have a Limited Role in Enforcing the Federal Antitrust Law of Mergers," *Emory Law Journal* 48 (1999): 346–49; Jonathan Rose, "State Antitrust Enforcement, Mergers, and Politics," *Wayne Law Review* 41 (1994): 117–22; Robert H. Lande, "When Should States Challenge Mergers: A Proposed Federal/State Balance," *New York Law School Law Review* 33 (1990): 1065, 1067–69 (discounting the idea); Robert B. Bell, "States Should Stay Out of National Mergers," *Antitrust* (Spring 1989): 37, 39.

36. Roberta Romano, "The Future of Hostile Takeovers: Legislation and Public Opinion," *University of Cincinnati Law Review* 57 (1988): 457; *CTS Corp. v. Dynamics Corp. of Am.*, 481 U.S. 69, 100–1 (1987) (Justice White, dissenting).

37. NAAG 1993 Horizontal Merger Guidelines, 3–4, available at www.naag.org/issues/pdf/at-hmerger_guidelines.pdf.

38. 2000–2001 Trade Cases (CCH), par. 72,937, p. 87,973 (Me. Superior Court, March 29, 2000).

39. "Pennsylvania Fails to Win Injunction to Block Merger in Boxed Chocolates Sector," *Antitrust & Trade Regulation Report* (BNA), no. 1614 (May 13, 1993), 583.

40. Large multistate settlements of vertical cases in the 1993–2002 period include those with Keds (1994, $7.2 million); Reebok (1995, $9.5 million); American Cyanamid (1997); Zeneca, Inc. (1997, $3.9 million); Nine West (2000, $30.5 million; FTC also sued); and Toys R Us (2000, $50 million). Earlier settlements include Toyota (1984, conduct remedy); Nintendo (1991, coupon recovery; FTC charges settled as well); and Mitsubishi (1992, $7.95 million). American Bar Association Section of Antitrust Law, *Antitrust Law Developments*, 5th ed. (Chicago: ABA, 2002), 829–30.

41. Such a claim is made, from time to time, by the proponents of state antitrust. Lloyd Constantine, for example, has stated that state attorneys general are "the primary enforcer of the law" in this area. Constantine, "The Mission and Agenda for State Antitrust Enforcement," 844.

42. Steven C. Salop and Lawrence J. White, "Economic Analysis of Private Antitrust Litigation," *Georgetown Law Journal* 74 (1986): 1005, 1008 .

43. For a description of these initiatives, see Michael S. Greve, "Federalism's Frontier," *Texas Review of Law & Politics* 7 (2002): 93.

44. "SEC, NY Attorney General, NASD, NASAA, NYSE and State Regulators Announce Historic Agreement to Reform Investment Practices," press release, December 20, 2002, New York State Attorney General website, http://www.oag.state.ny.us/press/2002/ dec/dec20b_02.html.

45. For an overview, see Michael S. Greve, "States Rights on Steroids," *Federalist Outlook*, no.14 (Washington, D.C.: AEI Press, September 1, 2002), available at http://www.aei.org/publications/pubID.14296/pub_detail.asp

46. In a recent interview, NAAG Multistate Antitrust Task Force Chair Patricia Conners showed little concern for state restraint in the antitrust realm. She was asked, "To what extent do you think it matters, or should matter, to the states whether a federal antitrust agency has made a clear decision on what national policy should be in a particular enforcement scenario?" Her answer: "Setting national policy is not within the exclusive realm of the federal enforcement agencies. That is not how our system of concurrent enforcement works. Under our system, any plaintiff in any antitrust matter may affect national antitrust policy through the development of case law, whether the plaintiff is a federal enforcement agency, a private plaintiff, or a state attorney general. It's well settled that state attorneys general have the ability to bring multi-state matters or even single-state matters that, in effect, have an impact on national policy. And to the extent that private plaintiffs can do it, and have done it, the state likewise should be able to do it without causing a lot of pause out there. In the Reagan years, of course, the state attorneys general were the ones bringing cases of national impact because the federal agencies were taking a passive approach to antitrust enforcement. So, to the extent that a national policy exists, even if the policy is one of non-enforcement, I think it's obviously important for a state to take that into account in approaching its own views on antitrust issues. *To the extent that there is no policy out there, then a state or set of states should have no compunction nor be disinclined to pursue cases that establish national policies. That's in essence what happened in Microsoft, and there was absolutely nothing inappropriate about it.*" Interview with Patricia Conners (May 2002).

47. The federal district judge who presided over Texas's tobacco lawsuit ruled that the state's antitrust theory failed the *Brunswick* "antitrust injury" test. *Texas v. Amer. Tobacco Co.*, 14 F. Supp. 2d 956, 969–70 (E.D. Tex. 1997). For more on the difficulties of using antitrust theories in tobacco litigation, see Michael L. Dolan, "The Minnesota Tobacco Case—Reasoned Antitrust Analysis Goes Up in Smoke," *Hamline*

Law Review 25 (2001): 193. See also Michael DeBow, "The State Tobacco Litigation and Separation of Powers in State Governments: Repairing the Damage," *Seton Hall Law Journal* 31 (2001): 563; "Report of the Task Force on Tobacco Litigation," *Cumberland Law Review* 27 (1997): 577.

48. It is worth noting that the plaintiff states in the *Microsoft* litigation hired the Washington, D.C., firm of Williams and Connolly as outside counsel, and that Microsoft agreed, as part of its settlement with California and six other states, to cover "a total of $25 million in legal fees, plus $3.6 million for technical experts and other resources to help ensure [Microsoft] complies with the settlement's terms." Jonathan Krim, "Microsoft Offered States Deal on Legal Fees." *Washington Post*, December 14, 2002. It is not known at this point how much of this amount the states would pay to outside law firms.

49. "Alabama Antitrust Act," S.B. 331 (Ala. Legis. 2003).

50. In *Abbott Laboratories v. Durrett*, 746 So.2d 316 (Ala. 1999), the Alabama Supreme Court reasoned that "the Alabama Legislature was aware toward the end of the 19th century and at the beginning of the 20th century, when it first enacted these antitrust statutes, that its ability to regulate antitrust activity was limited in that it did not have the power to directly regulate transactions involving interstate commerce." As a result, the court concluded that "the field of operation of Alabama's antitrust statutes . . . is no greater today than it was when the laws were first enacted."

51. If Congress proves unwilling to make this adjustment to the role of the states, then state legislators and state attorneys general committed to the consumer welfare view of antitrust should take up the issue. The radicalization of the state attorneys general demonstrated by the tobacco litigation has generated a backlash, including the creation of the Republican Attorneys General Association (RAGA) and renewed interest on the part of business groups in supporting conservative candidates in state attorneys general races. Because there is comfort in numbers, RAGA would be well-advised to become an active counterweight to NAAG's influence on the antitrust activities of state attorneys general. Republican attorneys general who admire Ronald Reagan would be hard pressed to find a more appropriate way to demonstrate their allegiance to what his administration stood for than to try to replicate Reagan-era antitrust enforcement policies at the state level.

52. "Memorandum Amicus Curiae of the United States Regarding Microsoft Corporation's Motion for Dismissal of the Non-Settling States' Demand for Equitable Relief" (April 15, 2002), available at U.S. Department of Justice website, http://www.usdoj.gov/atr/cases/f10900/10980.htm.

53. For the Supreme Court's most recent discussion of the states' power to seek injunctive relief in federal antitrust cases, see *California v. American Stores Co.*, 495 U.S. 271 (1990).

12

Multijurisdictional Antitrust Enforcement: A View from the *Illinois Brick* Road

William F. Adkinson Jr.

It has been more than twenty-five years since the U.S. Supreme Court's still-controversial ruling in *Illinois Brick Co. v. Illinois* (1977), limiting the federal antitrust private treble damages remedy to direct purchasers. Much ink has been spilt over the Court's refusal to allow indirect purchasers (including, typically, consumers) to recover for injuries from antitrust violations. Some of the comments, pro and con, reflect passionate beliefs about the rights of injured parties; others, analytical judgments about the desirable level of deterrence, optimal incentives for antitrust law enforcement, and judicial economy.

More significantly, *Illinois Brick* produced a fierce political struggle. Opponents of the decision—principally, state attorneys general and consumer advocacy groups—lobbied Congress to reverse the Supreme Court's interpretation of federal antitrust law. When those efforts proved futile, many states amended or construed their laws to permit actions by indirect purchasers. In *California v. ARC America Corp.* (1989), the Supreme Court unanimously upheld these "*Illinois Brick* repealers."

The *Illinois Brick* Court feared that permitting recovery by indirect purchasers would create unacceptable complexity, reduce incentives for enforcement actions by direct purchasers, and unfairly expose defendants to the potential for multiple and inconsistent liability. But the Court's path from

---

I am grateful to Michael Greve for helpful comments and to Andrew Gavil for useful discussions and insights. Any errors are my sole responsibility.

Illinois Brick to *ARC America* presents a paradox: *Illinois Brick* provoked state indirect purchaser statutes that created even greater problems than those that the *Illinois Brick* Court sought to avoid. This resulted from the Court's repeated failure to account for the predictable political responses to its actions, especially in the states. Congress lacked the political will to revise *Illinois Brick* or to rein in the disparate state responses repudiating the doctrine. In hindsight, the Court could and should have foreseen both responses—state repudiation and congressional paralysis. When both materialized, the Court proved unwilling or unable to prevent the states from undermining the basic policies *Illinois Brick* sought to serve.

The *Illinois Brick* paradox arguably flows from a regrettable transformation in the judiciary's view of the logic of U.S. federalism and federal preemption. At a deeper level, though, *Illinois Brick* illustrates the danger, in a multijurisdictional context, of devising optimal policies without adequately considering the potential that constituent jurisdictions will reject those policies in favor of their preferred alternatives. That elementary point, in turn, has profound implications for questions of global antitrust governance. Even among the polities in our federal system—connected though they are through a web of institutional arrangements, and operating as they do under an ironclad constitutional command of federal supremacy—the states have managed to protect a perceived right to make separate antitrust policy choices *in derogation of federal policy*. By comparison, the capacity of global institutions to constrain independent antitrust policymaking by sovereign nations is less than the federal government's ability to restrain state action. Thus, proposals for supranational antitrust governance could well provide a cure worse than the disease. In that light, we should support ongoing efforts to promote global antitrust convergence and cooperation through procedural coordination and dialogue on substantive issues. Such efforts, although not panaceas, hold the promise of real progress in addressing the problems created by concurrent multinational jurisdiction while providing a foundation for broader convergence.

Federalism: Jurisdiction and Enforcement

The *Illinois Brick* paradox resulted from two fundamental tensions in U.S. antitrust enforcement. The first is dual sovereignty—the concurrent authority of the federal government and each of the states to regulate competitive conduct. The second is the division of antitrust enforcement authority among public and private agencies and, in particular, the legal authority or "standing" of private parties to bring antitrust actions under federal or state antitrust law.

Dual Sovereignty. Dual sovereignty is a basic feature of U.S. law: The federal government has jurisdiction throughout the country, and each individual state has jurisdiction within its borders. In antitrust law, as in other areas, this can lead to overlapping authority. The federal antitrust laws prohibit restraints on trade or acts of monopolization "among the several states, or with foreign nations." There are strong indications that the framers of the Sherman Act intended, consistent with general views at the time, that the federal government should have exclusive authority in interstate matters and that the states should have authority in local matters. Herbert Hovenkamp, a leading expert in the field, has observed that:

> For many members of Congress [in 1890] the value of federal legislation under then-existing conceptions of the commerce clause power was that purely intrastate restraints and monopolies would be within the exclusive jurisdiction of state courts applying state law. However, restraints that crossed state lines and operated in more than a single state should for many purposes be outside the jurisdictional reach of any individual state; at that point federal law would be empowered.[1]

This division of labor, however, has long lost its vitality. Federal authority is near-universal: No "matter how local the operation which applies the squeeze," federal antitrust jurisdiction exists so long as "it is interstate commerce that feels the pinch."[2] Conversely, state antitrust laws routinely reach restraints that are located entirely or in part in a different state. Thus, the federal antitrust laws apply to many local activities that would, in general, be subject to state control as well, leading to potentially conflicting federal-state jurisdiction.

Such conflicts could be resolved by limiting state authority over conduct subject to federal jurisdiction. Two doctrines are of relevance here.

First, the Commerce Clause in its so-called "dormant" application restricts the reach of state law, not only to directly regulate interstate commerce, but also where it would unreasonably burden or discriminate against interstate commerce. Second, the Supremacy Clause ensures that federal law preempts conflicting state laws. Preemption applies not only when the federal statute expressly supplants state laws, but also when Congress has manifested its intent to "occupy the field" or where there is an "actual conflict" between state and federal law. However, the courts have refused to significantly limit state antitrust authority under either of these doctrines.

State antitrust regulation of interstate activity is generally not held invalid due to its impact on interstate commerce. Barring the enactment of state antitrust statutes that discriminate against out-of-state companies or consumers, the courts will generally sustain state antitrust statutes even when they manifestly affect national markets. Thus the courts have generally upheld state antitrust laws affecting national markets even when those statutes prohibit practices that are legal under federal law or provide remedies that are broader than those available under federal law. Similarly, under the Supremacy Clause, the Supreme Court has construed federal preemption of state antitrust laws very narrowly, on the theory that "Congress intended the federal antitrust laws to supplement, not displace, state antitrust remedies."[3] For example, in *Exxon Corp. v. Governor of Maryland* (1978), the Supreme Court upheld a state law requiring oil companies to extend price discounts uniformly to all retailers. Although federal law permitted discriminatory discounts in some circumstances, the Court found no impermissible conflict simply because the state statute prohibited conduct permitted under federal law. The Court also sustained the Maryland statute against a dormant Commerce Clause challenge.[4]

In short, "[f]ederal antitrust law now easily reaches many restraints that are 'confined' to a state, provided that there is an effect on interstate commerce. On the other hand, state antitrust laws have been used repeatedly to reach restraints that are located entirely or in part in a different state."[5] Thus, the same activity will frequently be subject to regulation by state and federal antitrust laws. Over long stretches, a shared consensus on antitrust policy has limited conflicts among competing sovereigns. Tensions and conflicts, however, have arisen. Those events cast considerable doubt on the capacity of our legal and political system to establish clear and sensible jurisdictional boundaries. The *Illinois Brick* controversy, as we shall see, is a clear case in point.

Enforcement: Public and Private. A distinctive feature of U.S. antitrust law is the remarkable fragmentation of enforcement authority. At the federal level, the U.S. Department of Justice and the Federal Trade Commission (FTC) have authority to enforce the antitrust laws. Other federal regulatory authorities (such as the Federal Communications Commission and the Department of Transportation) also enforce competition rules within the industries under their supervision. In addition, each state attorney general's office may enforce its own state's laws.

This fragmentation of enforcement authority creates frequent opportunities for conflict between public enforcers, especially between federal enforcers and state attorneys general. To resolve such conflicts, some federal enforcers have advocated a commonsense approach to exercising prosecutorial discretion. For example, Deputy Assistant Attorney General Deborah Platt Majoras has questioned the role of state attorneys general in "cases of national significance," while recognizing that "the state attorneys general should enforce the antitrust laws in matters of local reach."[6] But the federal agencies have little power to prevent perceived intrusions by states into national matters. Federal-state conflicts, especially the increasingly aggressive posture of state attorneys general—as evidenced, for example, by some states' refusal to end the litigation against Microsoft even after the federal government had decided to settle the case—have become a source of considerable concern.[7]

Of even greater practical importance, U.S. antitrust law—in contrast to the competition regimes of virtually all other countries—permits enforcement by private plaintiffs claiming an injury as a result of anticompetitive conduct. (Almost all states likewise permit private actions, although the relief available varies.) Private enforcers operate as so-called "private attorneys general," supplementing the enforcement efforts of public agencies. Specifically, the antitrust laws authorize lawsuits by "any person . . . injured in his business or property by reason of anything forbidden in the antitrust laws," to obtain treble damages as well as attorney fees. For the purposes of antitrust law, states are considered "persons" and so may seek redress under the federal statutes if they are injured by an antitrust violation. This includes treble damages and injunctive relief. In addition, Congress has authorized state attorneys general the right to bring so-called *parens patriae* actions to recover for injuries to natural persons residing within their states.

The Supreme Court has generally interpreted the private enforcement provisions broadly, invoking "the plainly stated congressional objective that the private treble-damages action plays a paramount role in the enforcement of the fundamental economic policy of the nation."[8] Measured by the sheer number of enforcement actions, private parties are by far the most important enforcers of the federal antitrust laws. For example, a Georgetown Law Center study found that private actions comprised more than 95 percent of the antitrust actions filed in 1977 and more than 90 percent in 1984.[9] More recent data confirm the primacy of private actions. In 1998, the Justice Department filed 85 cases and the FTC filed 40 antitrust challenges, while private plaintiffs filed 548 antitrust actions in federal court (and an unknown number in state court).[10] To be sure, government enforcement actions may have special significance in deterring some forms of private anticompetitive conduct. Conversely, some nontrivial percentage of private enforcement actions consists of "follow-on" suits in the wake of government enforcement proceedings.[11] Such actions may ratchet up penalties, but they do nothing to increase the risk of detection for firms that engage (or might want to engage) in anticompetitive conduct. Despite those qualifications, there is no question about the existence of a huge differential in enforcement activity.

It is far less clear whether private enforcement contributes to a sensible and efficient antitrust enforcement regime. Despite our heavy reliance on private antitrust enforcement, it has long been recognized that private parties' enforcement efforts may be inefficient and, indeed, inconsistent with the goals of the antitrust laws. Those dangers merit some discussion, as they form the backdrop for *Illinois Brick* and its aftermath.

The Pitfalls of Private Enforcement

The federal and state antitrust statutes provide for public enforcement by the real attorneys general and other agencies. Why then is it desirable to have extensive enforcement by *private* attorneys general?

One possible justification—perhaps, the most intuitively appealing justification—is a principle of corrective justice: Private actions provide a mechanism through which injured parties can obtain compensation from wrongdoers. In antitrust and other torts, the private enforcement right is given to victims of the wrongful conduct. Their recovery is tied to the amount of damage they suffer and, thus, clearly tailored to a compensatory objective. But this justification is less attractive than it appears at first sight. In the context of redressing consumer injuries, the injury to any one consumer from an antitrust violation is typically so small that compensation serves little useful purpose (especially in comparison to the costs of a private enforcement system). Losses incurred by competitors, distributors, and other businesses allegedly harmed by anticompetitive conduct may be more severe, making the compensation rationale potentially stronger in such cases. However, such private enforcers are especially likely to use the antitrust laws to achieve unintended results. The antitrust laws protect competitive *markets*, not individual market *participants*. Individual firms that feel threatened by a competitor are unlikely to draw that distinction. They are likely to look to their own interests, not the statutory objectives, and to sue when a competing firm's conduct is altogether *too* competitive.

For these reasons, among others, economists typically view private enforcement not as a means of corrective justice, but as one of optimal enforcement.[12] From that perspective, we should seek to design a system that will induce enforcement efforts that efficiently deter violations, while minimizing the total costs of enforcement. These costs include the costs of the operating enforcement system and losses due to undeterred violations. They also include the costs imposed by the potential for errors in the legal system (for example, the deterrence of efficient transactions that would enhance consumer welfare due to the potential that liability will erroneously be imposed under the antitrust laws).

It is possible, under some circumstances, that private parties may be more efficient law enforcers than government officials, either because they face more efficient incentive structures or because they have advantages in identifying and attacking violations. For example, if public funding of enforcement efforts is set at suboptimally low levels, enforcement by private parties could be seen as a mechanism for increasing enforcement efforts.[13] Similarly, private parties may have informational advantages in certain circumstances over public enforcers. Firms have a close and continuing familiarity with the business dealings that usually are the focus of these disputes, giving them information about potential wrongdoing and its impact in the market that enforcement officials generally cannot match.

Those advantages, however, are neither unambiguous nor decisive. For example, private parties' informational advantages could be conveyed through presentations to the public enforcers. The U.S. government's prosecution of Microsoft was brought after extensive discussions with Microsoft's competitors, who complained that Microsoft's conduct was anticompetitive.[14] Presentations by private parties are also quite common in the context of the premerger clearance process. Federal enforcement officials are open to receiving such information—although they evaluate it with appropriate skepticism when it comes from competitors or others who may have interests other than promoting competition. Similarly, *public* enforcers are likely to have informational advantages in some settings (especially in pursuing cartels and other clandestine conduct). The decade-long experience with the Department of Justice's leniency program reveals government's strong comparative advantage in obtaining information to uncover and prosecute cartels.[15] The government is likely to expend considerable effort to uncover cartel activity because it is politically popular, can result in very large penalties, and lies at the heart of an antitrust agency's mission. By offering immunity from criminal enforcement to the first informant, the Justice Department has induced cartel members to become informants, not only disclosing the cartel's existence, but also helping to develop compelling evidence with which to convict the other members. Private parties have no such tool. Indeed, the threat is that private actions can reduce a potential informant's willingness to seek leniency from the Justice Department.[16]

The central problem with private enforcement, though, lies in the difficulty of devising incentives that will direct private attorneys general into enforcement actions that maximize (or at least enhance) general social objectives, as distinct from private gains. The standard model of private law enforcement usually assumes a well-defined task for the enforcement agent. This minimizes agency problems: The principal (the government) can readily ascertain whether the enforcement agent has achieved his or her goal (and make or withhold payment accordingly). The Sherman Act's broad prohibitions against restraints of trade and monopolization, in contrast, are notoriously vague and uncertain. While economic analysis has increasingly become a touchstone for assessing whether conduct is anticompetitive (and therefore appropriate for condemnation under the antitrust laws), there are large areas of uncertainty in applying the antitrust laws to particular conduct. Vagueness means over-inclusion: The laws capture a vast range of private conduct that is in fact competitive and efficient. As a result, effective monitoring of private antitrust enforcers may not be possible.

Of course, there are also reasons to question the incentives of government enforcers, and it would be quite mistaken to compare private enforcers with idealized government enforcers.[17] Still, if we were to conclude that the antitrust laws are underenforced (all things considered), it would be relatively easy to adjust the incentives and conduct of *public* enforcers. In contrast, it is fiendishly difficult to adjust the incentives facing private enforcers. To curtail the risk of private overenforcement, we should have to "rewrite the substantive law to eliminate over-inclusion."[18] Pending such an ambitious (and probably counterproductive) endeavor, private enforcers' interests in enforcing antitrust law will continue to conflict with the goals of the antitrust laws. For example, the treble-damage remedy is often defended as a means of improving the incentives for private enforcers to invest in the (costly) detection and prosecution of surreptitious anticompetitive conduct. But the availability of enhanced damages also encourages private plaintiffs to turn a routine contract dispute into an antitrust suit or to concoct new antitrust theories that actually suppress robust competition.

Unfortunately, private enforcers with interests that are potentially adverse to competitive goals appear to be the norm, not the exception. Data from the Georgetown study indicate that the potential for abuse is enormous. The study found that more than one-third (36.5 percent) of all private actions were brought by competitors, and more than one-fourth (27.3 percent) were brought by distributors or dealers of the defendant. In contrast, less than one-tenth (8.7 percent) were brought by final customers, and another 12.5 percent were brought by customer companies.[19] Examining the data set further, Kenneth Elzinga and William Wood found that about 30 percent of actions were brought by competitors and another 35 percent by dealers or terminated dealers. Actions by input purchasers and final customers accounted for only 10.1 percent and 8.5 percent, respectively. They offered a blunt assessment:

Of all the litigation surveyed in the data set, less than one-fourth (21.5 percent) involved plaintiffs whose economic relationship with the defendant was of the character where there was likely to have been a genuine welfare loss to be remedied or alleviated by the litigation. To put the matter more starkly, over three-fourths of the treble damage litigation was of an economic character where economists potentially would not expect efficiency enhancing consequences if the plaintiffs prevailed.[20]

Even actions purporting to vindicate consumer interests can raise concerns. Most important, it is not clear that treble-damages recoveries for consumers result in expanded investments in uncovering hard-to-detect anticompetitive conduct. As noted, government actions result in a small but significant number of follow-on private cases.[21] Because recent government cases are focused on cartels and other activities directed at ultimate consumers, private actions on behalf of consumers (those most likely to be procompetitive) are likely to disproportionately involve offenses that the government has already punished. Moreover, because consumers generally have very small stakes in any antitrust action, private actions to vindicate their interests are generally brought by class action lawyers, who may make very poor private attorneys general.[22] These class action attorneys may have incentives that substantially differ from the interests of the class they purport to represent. In particular they may have strong incentives to settle the case for a small total recovery as long as the attorney's fees are substantial.

Private actions increase the total penalties for antitrust violators, thus enhancing their incentives to abide by the law. But more enforcement or the piling on of additional penalties may not serve consumers well. Deputy Assistant Attorney General Deborah Platt Majoras emphasizes the potential harm:

> The greatest danger in over-enforcement of competition laws and over-remedying is that they will retard legitimate, procompetitive behavior. . . . Piling on multiple layers of enforcement or relief may also provide windfalls to other market participants, which further distorts the market away from what competition itself would create. And, of course, it places unnecessary burdens on

enforcement agencies, courts, and parties—costs that ultimately the taxpayers we serve will bear.[23]

Increased deterrence could be achieved at far lower cost by simply enhancing the penalties imposed through public enforcement. Too, public enforcers have more options with regard to the types of penalties that may be imposed and can focus them on individuals who are directly involved in the unlawful conduct. Most importantly, they can seek prison terms and also have fines imposed directly on individuals.

Precisely in recognition of the potential misalignment between private incentives to sue and the utilitarian, competitive objectives of the antitrust statutes, courts have sought to weed out claims by plaintiffs who are likely to have motives inconsistent with the purposes of the antitrust laws. The best-known mechanism for preventing competitor misuse is the requirement that plaintiffs must establish an "antitrust injury"—that is, an injury of the type the antitrust laws were intended to prevent. Conduct that injures a competitor, but not competition generally, is not actionable under the antitrust laws.[24] Similarly, courts have used the antitrust injury doctrine to prevent plaintiffs from transforming disputes best addressed as "breach of contract or business tort" claims into antitrust actions.[25]

Even where antitrust injury is clear, courts have held that it may not be sufficient to confer standing to sue. In particular, courts have denied standing to claimants whose injury is too remote, especially when the existence of other potential enforcers ensures that denying standing is "not likely to leave a significant antitrust violation undetected or unremedied."[26]

The Trip Down the *Illinois Brick* Road

The *Illinois Brick* problem arises precisely in this situation: Anticompetitive conduct has injured a variety of private parties, and the court must decide which victims have standing to sue under the antitrust laws. In a complex and specialized economy, the production and distribution of any given good will involve a long chain of transactions within and among firms. Price-fixing conspiracies or other anticompetitive acts raising prices may occur at any point in the chain. Such actions will likely have economic consequences down the rest of the chain, and perhaps up the chain as well. Consequences can even run sideways, affecting competitors or suppliers of complementary products.

The *Illinois Brick* Court ruled that only direct purchasers have standing to recover damages under the antitrust laws for monopoly or cartel overcharges, denying standing to all indirect purchasers throughout the chain of distribution. Ultimate consumers, whose welfare the antitrust laws were designed to protect, are typically indirect purchasers. In one swoop, the Supreme Court "disabled" this large class of private antitrust enforcers. That aspect of the decision explains why the seemingly dry subject matter provoked heated debate in legal and academic circles and fierce struggles in the political arena.

The right of those who purchase *directly* from a monopolist or cartel to recover damages for the resulting overcharge has of course long been recognized. In *Hanover Shoe, Inc. v. United Shoe Mach. Corporation* (1968), the Court unanimously held that a direct purchaser's recovery could not be reduced on the theory that the direct purchaser had "passed on" part of the overcharge in the price he charged to his customers. The ruling, it bears emphasis, makes no sense as a form of compensation for injured parties, because the direct purchaser may seek damages even if he recouped his losses by charging higher prices (and the indirect purchaser may bear the loss without a right of recovery).

What, then, of private parties who are the indirect victims of anticompetitive conduct further down the chain? That, in a nutshell, is the question of *Illinois Brick*. There, the state of Illinois and local jurisdictions sued cement makers who had conspired to fix the price of concrete blocks. The blocks were sold to masonry contractors, who used them on construction projects, typically working under general contractors. The final consumers—the *Illinois Brick* plaintiffs—alleged that the inflated prices builders paid for concrete blocks increased the amount they paid for the projects.

Justice White's majority opinion emphasized the need to have the rule "regarding pass-on in antitrust damages ... apply equally to plaintiffs and defendants,"[27] lest the door be open to duplicative recoveries. In other words, indirect purchasers could recover only if the Court overruled *Hanover Shoe*. In considering this choice, Justice White emphasized that "attempt[s] to trace the complex economic adjustments to a change in the cost of a particular factor of production would greatly complicate and reduce the effectiveness of already complex treble damage proceedings. . . ." He affirmed *Hanover Shoe*'s "judgment that the antitrust laws will be more effectively enforced by concentrating the full recovery for the overcharge in the direct purchasers rather than by allowing every plaintiff potentially affected by the overcharge to sue only for the amount it could show was absorbed by it."[28] Thus, pass-on theories of liability would raise unacceptable risks of inconsistent recoveries. Attempts to reduce this risk would magnify the complexity of proceedings, while dissipating private plaintiffs' incentives to bring actions. The Court's solution was to allow only a single class of private parties to bring damage actions, centralizing the right of action in direct purchasers.

The decision provoked a stinging dissent by Justice Brennan, joined by Justices Marshall and Blackmun, chastising the majority for flouting the will of the Congress. Restricting the private right to bring a treble damage action, in their view, flew in the face of the broad wording of the private treble damages provision, its expansive objectives of compensation and deterrence, and a tradition of judicial support for those legislative objectives. In a separate dissent, Justice Blackmun scolded the majority for its "wooden" insistence on consistency with *Hanover Shoe*, thereby making "still another congressional action" necessary.

The sharp division of academic opinion was reflected in acerbic exchanges between Professors Posner and Landes in support of *Illinois Brick* and Professors Harris and Sullivan against.[29] To Harris and Sullivan, a "fundamental disagreement regarding the appropriate uses of economic theory" lay at the heart of the differences. They argued that "[t]he neoclassical 'theory of the firm'" utilized by Landes and Posner did not "describe[] how firms actually behave."[30] For their part, Landes and Posner argued that they simply used the basic apparatus of economic theory. They found Harris and Sullivan's criticisms "incorrect or irrelevant," and denounced their adversaries' advocacy of indirect purchaser actions as "based on a series of economic errors."[31] Regarding the failure to compensate indirect purchasers, Landes and Posner contended that the indirect purchasers could be expected to pass through price decreases reflecting the expected damage awards. More persuasively perhaps, they emphasized the primacy of efficient enforcement over compensation and insisted that effective enforcement protects everyone from violations. Moreover, as noted, using antitrust litigation to compensate indirect purchasers makes little sense, because in virtually all cases, the harm to any individual will be small and the costs of providing compensation large.

As Justice Blackmun had predicted in his dissent, efforts at legislative repeal were launched immediately in Congress, tailored in various ways to meet some of the Court's concerns. Senator Kennedy and Congressman Rodino introduced bills five days after the decision was handed down. According to Senator Kennedy, the decision "virtually eliminated the consumers' and other indirect parties' rights." Senator Hart accused the Court of having "flouted the will and purpose of the Congress in a most crass fashion."[32] In particular, the decision was viewed as a direct rebuff to provisions of the Hart-Scott-Rodino Act passed by Congress just the previous year. That law granted state attorneys general the right to sue as *parens patriae* for treble the damages incurred by state residents from violations of federal antitrust laws. (Not surprisingly, the National Association of Attorneys General and forty-seven states filed an amicus brief in *Illinois Brick* arguing in favor of allowing indirect purchaser suits.) The *Illinois Brick* Court met this objection by observing that the *parens patriae* provision was not meant to create new rights, but merely to provide a new device for enforcing existing rights of recovery.[33] That observation was technically correct. It remained true nonetheless that *Illinois Brick* rendered the newly conferred authority much less potent.[34]

Efforts to overturn *Illinois Brick* continued for years, with repeal legislation introduced in Congress in each of the following three sessions of Congress. Members of Congress who sought to repeal *Illinois Brick* received prominent support from state attorneys general. In addition, a variety of consumer advocacy groups, including the Consumer Federation of America and Congress Watch, promoted repeal efforts. All these efforts, however, came to naught.[35] But the anti-*Illinois Brick* forces waged a far more successful campaign on a different front—the states. Beginning in California in 1978, state legislatures across the country passed "*Illinois Brick* repealers," granting indirect purchasers remedies under state antitrust and unfair competition laws. State courts construing existing state statutes achieved the same result.

Illinois Brick repealers embodied a variety of approaches to administering claims by indirect purchasers. The resulting substantial variations among state indirect purchase statutes increased complexity and resulted in duplicative proceedings in state and federal courts. The consequences were much worse than those the *Illinois Brick* Court feared would result from allowing indirect purchasers to bring actions under federal law. A 1983 American Bar Association (ABA) Antitrust Section Task Force painted a bleak picture:

> The state statutes compound the problems the Supreme Court sought to eliminate in *Illinois Brick*. Because there can be simultaneous federal direct purchaser actions and state indirect purchaser actions, defendants are exposed to risks of multiple recovery. Discovery and pretrial proceedings in state courts are not always coordinated with federal court proceedings, which can result in inefficiency and duplication of effort.[36]

Again federal legislation was proposed, now designed to deal simultaneously with the question of indirect purchaser actions under federal law and the conflicting state statutes. Like the earlier attempts to overrule *Illinois Brick*, however, those efforts proved unavailing. Lawsuits under the state statutes, meanwhile, kept proliferating.

And so, a dozen years after *Illinois Brick*, the Supreme Court was compelled to address the question of whether federal law preempted state *Illinois Brick* repealers. In *California v. ARC America Corporation* (1989), several states had filed actions in federal court for their losses resulting from a nationwide conspiracy to fix cement prices. They sought damages as direct and indirect purchasers, resting their indirect purchaser claims in part on their state *Illinois Brick* repealers. The defendants had established a settlement fund for all claims, but the district court refused to allow indirect purchasers to recover from the fund. The Ninth Circuit affirmed. Four states appealed, and thirty-five other states filed an amicus brief seeking reversal.

The Supreme Court reversed. State *Illinois Brick* repealers, the Court held, were in no way foreclosed by federal statutes or their judicial interpretation. As in *Illinois Brick*, Justice White wrote for the—now unanimous—Court. (Justice O'Connor and Justice Stevens did not participate.) His preemption analysis was unexceptional but for the inescapable irony that the state laws he upheld not only repealed *Illinois Brick*, but also imposed greater complexity and costs than he, or the Court, had been prepared to countenance in *Illinois Brick*.

The result in the *ARC America* case flowed largely from the fact that *Illinois Brick* was expressly limited to construing federal law and from the indisputable proposition that "Congress intended the federal antitrust laws to supplement, not to displace state antitrust remedies."[37] Far more problematically, however, Justice White rejected the appellees' claims that state indirect purchaser statutes were "contrary to Congressional purposes" and "interfered with accomplishing the purposes of the federal law that were identified in *Illinois Brick*."[38] In dismissing those contentions, White proffered three arguments, none of them persuasive.

First, he noted the obvious fact that the state laws did not directly affect remedies under federal law. That is true, but trivial: Of course, state laws do not themselves preempt or otherwise directly affect rights under federal law. But those state statutes established conflicting enforcement policies that led some private antitrust plaintiffs to pursue their claims in separate state court proceedings. This posed an even greater threat to coherent and efficient antitrust enforcement than the *Illinois Brick* Court sought to avert by preventing indirect purchaser actions.

Second, Justice White emphasized that "any complication of federal direct purchaser actions in federal court would be minimal," because "many indirect purchaser actions would be heard in state court." That, too, reflects an ostrich-like attempt to ignore the overall policy impact. The claim is not that indirect purchaser actions will pose no "complications"—only that they will pose no complications *in a federal proceeding*, in federal court. But of course, on any reasonable interpretation, the central concern in *Illinois Brick* was the risk to defendants and to rational law enforcement—not merely to federal courts. The "remedy" Justice White identified—stratagems by federal courts to ensure that the indirect purchaser actions are pursued in separate state court proceedings—perversely increases the complexity of the overall system of antitrust enforcement. Not surprisingly, scholars and commentators almost uniformly recommend precisely the opposite tack—consolidation of actions in federal courts.[39]

Third, Justice White discounted concerns that state indirect purchaser actions could decrease incentives for direct purchasers to sue. Those concerns, as noted, had played a prominent role in *Illinois Brick*. But of course indirect purchaser claims in state actions may reduce the ability and willingness of defendants to pay damage awards to direct purchasers, and thereby reduce direct purchasers' incentives to bring actions. This is clearly true when, as was the case in *ARC America*, there is a fixed fund for recovery.

In substance, then, the *ARC America* decision unanimously upheld the right of states to effectively overrule *Illinois Brick* by adopting contrary state policies. As a consequence, today about half the states (with half the population) permit indirect purchasers to recover.[40] A similar number permit *parens patriae* actions by their state attorneys general on behalf of indirect purchasers. These provisions are routinely utilized in antitrust litigation. Moreover, instead of being brought as part of a consolidated federal action, indirect purchaser actions are typically filed in multiple state courts, producing a "burgeoning current wave of indirect purchaser antitrust suits."[41] Follow-on suits on behalf of indirect purchasers have been brought in the wake of several recent international criminal cartel cases brought by the Department of Justice for vitamins, lysine, citric acid, and high fructose corn syrup. FTC challenges to settlements of pharmaceutical patent litigation and other enforcement activity have also resulted in indirect purchaser follow-on actions.[42] Ironically, this near-wholesale repeal of *Illinois Brick* has itself been tempered by the difficulty of certifying classes of indirect purchasers, due largely to the very complexities that caused the *Illinois Brick* court to bar indirect purchaser actions in the first place.[43]

Judicial Error or Political Economy?

Illinois Brick poses a paradox: "[A] series of individually logical decisions has led . . . to precisely the type of risk of double recovery that the Court in *Illinois Brick* sought to avoid."[44] Donald Baker puts it more bluntly:

> The reality is that the Supreme Court [in *Illinois Brick*] did not eliminate the risk that it feared. Instead the Court set in motion a series of events that have magnified this risk far beyond what anyone imagined in 1977. First, of course, *Illinois Brick* generated a strongly adverse political reaction. Congress ducked the issue, but various state legislatures responded with the "*Illinois Brick* Repealer" acts. . . . Then the Supreme Court upheld these laws in *ARC America* under perfectly normal preemption principles.[45]

At first inspection, the bizarre result suggests a Supreme Court that ignores, or is indifferent to, the actual impacts of its decisions. One can certainly tell a coherent story along those lines. In the wake of *Hanover Shoe*, the Court confronted glaring inefficiencies and unfair results if it did not decide *Illinois Brick* in a symmetrical fashion by prohibiting indirect purchaser recovery. In the face of a political uproar and widespread repudiation in state legislatures and courts, the Supreme Court in *ARC America* decided that it could tolerate not only the unfairness of indirect purchaser recovery, but also the incoherence of conflicting state and federal antitrust rules and inefficiency of separate antitrust proceedings. The *ARC America* Court's deference to the states does not really reflect a systematic respect for "federalism." After all, the Court that manufactured the *Illinois Brick* paradox also wiped out the last remaining limitations to federal authority over local transactions under the Sherman Act.[46] In other words, federal authority is unlimited. But so is the room for opportunistic state interferences with federal policy. In this morass of concurrent jurisdiction, the Court resolutely refuses to draw any line except one—the *ARC America* line, which protects the federal courts from the mess but leaves antitrust enforcement as a whole severely burdened.

One cannot tell a purely judicial story, however, without reference to the political process and the Justices' often mistaken expectations of that process. *Illinois Brick* may have reflected sound economics, but it did not reflect good political judgment. The decision was unlikely to have staying power "because the bright-line rule was so arbitrary vis-à-vis some real antitrust victims that it was always likely to generate a political counter-revolution to overturn it."[47] With respect to the contours of that response, the *Illinois Brick* Court missed two salient institutional facts: the inertia of federal political institutions and the states' powerful incentives to avoid limits on indirect purchaser claims.

By constitutional design, the federal legislative process is built to favor inertia over energy and the opponents of new legislation over its proponents. Bicameralism, the presidential veto, and numerous other obstacles effectively require a supermajority for the enactment of legislation, including legislation to override Supreme Court statutory decisions. The advocates of an *Illinois Brick* override—state attorneys general and consumer groups—never managed to assemble a sufficiently large array of forces to overcome these hurdles. Most other potent interests were found on the fence, or else on the other side. Significantly, the plaintiffs' bar generally did not join in the federal efforts to overrule *Illinois Brick*, apparently out of agreement with the majority's assessment that concentrating authority increased the likelihood that enforcement actions would be brought. The legal establishment, for its part, was undecided.[48]

So, the political forces for an *Illinois Brick* override were frustrated in Congress. But of course, the political demand for reform did not simply disappear; it migrated to the state level. That phenomenon will occur under any federal system. It is particularly likely where, as here, the disappointed constituencies include state officials—state attorneys general who had lost their opportunity to bring *parens patriae* action on behalf of consumers (and registered voters). Once the state *Illinois Brick* repealers were enacted and then upheld in *ARC America*, institutional obstacles and inertia at the federal level shifted in favor of the *advocates* of indirect purchaser actions. Despite widespread discontent with the chaotic regime that has resulted from the *Illinois Brick* paradox, would-be reformers have been unable to overcome the fierce opposition of consumer advocates and state attorneys general, and Congress has failed to act. The executive branch similarly failed to provide a strong voice for efficient antitrust enforcement.

The likely source of this near-abstention is a concern for states' rights, coupled with political sensibilities. The Justice Department's amicus brief in *Illinois Brick* plotted a middle road regarding indirect purchaser actions— perhaps politically astute in retrospect—arguing that indirect purchaser actions promoted the "principle that victims of antitrust laws should recover for their losses, and served the policy of promoting the private enforcement of the antitrust laws."[49] To guard against the obvious risk, the Justice Department argued that procedural devices designed to bring several classes of victims together in a single action should be used to reduce the burden of damage determination and the risk of multiple recovery. In *ARC America*, the Reagan Justice Department filed a brief arguing *against* preemption. While emphasizing that indirect purchaser statutes may not make for good antitrust policy, the department found principles of federalism more compelling than the policies of *Illinois Brick*. Thus, the federal executive and judicial branches of the federal government were united in recognizing the states' prerogative to set their own antitrust policies. It is hardly surprising that the legislative branch lacked the will to establish a uniform national policy.

Scholars and antitrust practitioners almost uniformly view the situation as a serious burden on the enforcement system, but have generally been unable to develop effective and politically viable solutions. To this day, indirect purchaser reform remains, if not a hot topic, at least a serious and active issue to policymakers, antitrust practitioners and scholars. In 2001, the ABA Antitrust Section prepared a report, "State of Federal Antitrust Enforcement," for the new administration, which in part lamented the potential for "duplicative, resource consuming and chaotic state-by-state adjudication of similar and related actions"[50] and advocated consolidation of actions in a single forum. Various proposals to modify rules governing complex litigation (primarily mass tort litigation) could also empower federal courts to consolidate and coordinate indirect purchaser suits. The American Law Institute's Complex Litigation Project has "extensively addressed the problems of federal-state coordination" and "proposed a new 'Complex Litigation Statute.'"[51] Most recently, in April 2003, the Antitrust Section devoted two full afternoons to panels discussing antitrust remedies. Although a five-dollar fine had been placed on the mention of *Illinois Brick*, the issue was raised repeatedly, with participants emphasizing the increasing importance of indirect purchaser claims in class action litigation. Neither massive professional discontent nor the substantial costs of the existing regime, however, seem likely to dislodge the institutional and interest group deadlock that stabilizes the *Illinois Brick* paradox.

Lessons for Global Antitrust Enforcement

The problems that arise in the federal antitrust system are magnified in the global context. Nearly one hundred jurisdictions now have antitrust laws. This multiplies the potential for jurisdictional overlaps especially since many jurisdictions impose a version of the expansive "effects" test, asserting jurisdiction over extraterritorial conduct that has a domestic impact. Business is conducted increasingly on a global basis, so that mergers or other transactions will frequently impact markets in many countries. (The burdens imposed by multiple reviews in the merger context are among the most frequently cited inefficiencies of globalized antitrust enforcement.) International coordination is rendered more difficult by the greater diversity in views regarding the importance and design of competition policy and the absence of a central authority with even nominal authority to impose uniformity. As a result, issues of fairness of multiple liability, inconsistent legal requirements, and complexity—central to the *Illinois Brick* controversy—dominate the international antitrust landscape. Against this backdrop, the *Illinois Brick* paradox holds important lessons for international antitrust enforcement and coordination.

The first lesson is the difficulty of making centrally determined antitrust policies—even sound policies—"stick" with member-states. The U.S. government is well equipped, at least as a matter of constitutional authority, to redress state interferences with interstate commerce and to ensure the coherence of its regulatory schemes. We have an unquestioned doctrine of federal supremacy and a long tradition of constitutional doctrines barring state discrimination and meddling in interstate commerce. In the antitrust context, we have a sophisticated federal regulatory apparatus. For all the disagreement about enforcement authority, remedies, and the disposition of some high-profile cases, we also have a remarkably broad professional consensus on the objectives and basic doctrines of substantive antitrust law. That consensus is fortified through agency rulings and standing practices, as well as a fairly robust body of federal judicial precedents. For what it is worth (and, with respect to indirect purchaser actions, it is not worth a lot), federal and state antitrust agencies are tied through a web of intergovernmental institutions and informal arrangements that serve to reduce friction and conflicts. Despite all those advantages, however, our political system has been unable to implement the policy choices made in *Illinois Brick*. Ultimately, the states overran the federal policy choice, with consequences that hardly anyone would care to defend. Federal agencies were unable or unwilling to force states to bend.

International institutions have none of the advantages just sketched. The legal authority of international rulemaking and adjudicatory bodies (such as the World Trade Organization) is poorly developed and, frequently, intensely controversial. There is no Congress with even nominal authority to impose uniformity. Indeed, international norms recognize broad authority of nations to apply their laws to extraterritorial conduct, and comity places only limited constraints on the exercise of that authority. Antitrust law is highly controversial even with respect to its broad objectives and contours. Thus, attempts to force international agreement on a binding substantive rule— even a sensible rule—may do more harm than good. Even if adopted (for example, by means of "side payments" to recalcitrant countries), any rule will set back the expectations of some constituencies. Those constituencies will then turn to their national governments, which will often accede to their demands. International bodies will prove incapable of policing the evasions even when the aggregate costs exceed those of having no rule at all. A series of international *Illinois Brick*–style paradoxes is hardly a far-fetched scenario.

Second, *Illinois Brick* illustrates the devilish problems posed by decentralized enforcement. National enforcers are bound to be driven by parochial considerations, and formal international constraints (such as a nondiscrimination or "national treatment" rule) are unlikely to prove sufficient to constrain such conduct—just as the rather more robust body of U.S. antitrust law does not preclude its strategic deployment by state attorneys general. For this reason, Andrew Guzman has urged the extension of enforcement rights to private parties, on the theory that such parties are less likely than governments to be biased by national or other constituency-oriented considerations.[52] Practical experience with private antitrust enforcement in this country, however, including especially the *Illinois Brick* saga, counsels great caution about use of private actions as a possible corrective to governmental biases. One person's corrective is another person's distortion. If private enforcers are unlikely to be guided by parochial biases, they are equally unlikely to be guided by considerations of global efficiency.

Steering them in that direction would prove inordinately difficult, and perhaps impossible. The most likely but also most suspect complainants, producers harmed by "excessive" competition, can always play to government parochialism through the simple device of complaining to, or leaning on, government enforcers. (Those governments need not be their own: Having been rebuffed in the United States, Microsoft's *American* competitors are now imploring *European* authorities to rein in their mighty competitor.)[53] Thus, the principal effect of private enforcement may be to reinforce a parochial bias even where political authorities, in the interest of comity and reciprocity, might be inclined to resist the temptation. One well-known set of situations arises when U.S. citizens sue foreign nationals for conduct largely occurring overseas. In the leading case of *Hartford Fire Insurance Co. v.*

California, the Supreme Court confirmed that the Sherman Act extends to wholly foreign conduct "that was meant to produce and did in fact produce some substantial effect in the U.S."[54] There, British reinsurers were held to be subject to suit under the Sherman Act for allegations that they had conspired to require U.S. insurers to make changes to standard policy terms that the latter issued in the United States. The Court held that although the conduct was *permitted* by U.K. law, considerations of comity should not prevent the exercise of jurisdiction, since a conflict would arise only if the antitrust laws were applied to conduct *required* by U.K. law. The decision has proved extremely controversial; British officials have described U.S. extraterritorial jurisdiction as "exorbitant."[55] More recently, foreign nationals have brought antitrust suits in U.S. courts, alleging antitrust violations for activities undertaken outside the United States and seeking to recover for injuries incurred outside the United States. (The plaintiffs claim that the Sherman Act applies because the conduct also had an anticompetitive impact within the United States that injured other people, citing the language of the Foreign Trade Antitrust Improvements Act of 1982.) Such actions may override the policy decisions of foreign governments to permit certain conduct and to limit enforcement authority to agencies.[56] In short, private enforcers may exacerbate as well as counteract domestic biases, increase conflict, and reinforce neutral, centrally determined rules.

The sought-after goal of harmonization confronts disagreements on the proper role and implementation of competition policy, as well as the tendency of individual nations to abuse antitrust policies for parochial and protectionist purposes. Either way, coordination problems will be far more common and pronounced under an international regime than in the federal context, and institutional capacities for remedying them are far less developed. We should therefore be modest and circumspect about international antitrust harmonization and, before establishing binding regimes, emphasize informal means of developing a broader consensus on the goals and objectives of competition policies. The International Competition Network (ICN), the most recent initiative to improve global antitrust enforcement, appears well-designed to accommodate these realities.

The ICN serves as "a forum for antitrust agencies from developed and developing countries to formulate and develop consensus on proposals for procedural and substantive convergence in antitrust enforcement."[57]

Founded in 2001, it has quickly grown to more than seventy members who cumulatively account for a large majority of global gross domestic product. The ICN does not exercise any rulemaking function but, rather, develops guiding principles and recommendations for voluntary implementation by member agencies. The ICN rests on the recognition that the United States (or European Union) cannot establish antitrust enforcement policy for the rest of the world. Sound antitrust enforcement requires a deep and shared "culture of competition." The first step is to build an understanding of one another's laws and institutions and of the economic principles that give antitrust laws their reason for being.[58]

The focus on building consensus and voluntary implementation recognizes limitations inherent in imposing views on other sovereign powers and reflects the intractability of coordinating international antitrust without such measures. The United States has considerable bargaining leverage in treaty negotiations and trade talks, but these tools of diplomacy offer only limited opportunity to prod foreign governments on antitrust policy, and especially on how such policies are implemented. Success will depend on the difficult task of convincing other jurisdictions of the soundness of antitrust analysis as it has evolved in the United States. Our own approach has changed significantly over the past forty years, and is still evolving. We must expect that relatively new antitrust enforcement regimes will require considerable time to develop clear views of what antitrust should be, and longer still to reassess them in light of experience. The ICN has the twin virtues of allowing concrete progress on specific matters while laying the groundwork for broader convergence.

Illinois Brick illustrates the danger of devising "optimal" policies without adequately considering the potential for constituent jurisdictions to reject those policies in favor of their preferred alternatives. It underscores the potential advantages, in the global antitrust context, of cooperative processes that seek to improve antitrust coordination in particular areas and, perhaps, to lay the groundwork for more extensive harmonization. If the *Illinois Brick* paradox comes to serve as a warning sign on the road toward ambitious international coordination efforts, it will have done some good after all.

Notes

1. See Herbert Hovenkamp, *Antitrust Law: An Analysis of Antitrust Principles and Their Application*, vol. 14 (New York: Aspen Law and Business, 2003): 290.

2. *Hospital Building Co. v. Trustees of Rex Hospital*, 425 U.S. 738, 743 (1976).

3. *California v. ARC America Corp.*, 490 U.S. 93, 102 (1989). Indeed, under the so-called state action doctrine, states may immunize certain conduct of private actors that would otherwise violate the federal antitrust laws, where the state is pursuing a policy that it has "clearly articulated and affirmatively expressed" and that is "actively supervised by the state itself." *California Retail Liquor Dealers Ass'n v. Midcal Aluminum, Inc.*, 445 U.S. 97, 105 (1980).

4. *Exxon Corp. v. Governor of Maryland*, 437 U.S. 117 (1978).

5. Herbert Hovenkamp, "State Antitrust in the Federal Scheme," *Indiana Law Journal* 58 (1983): 379 (footnotes omitted).

6. Deborah Platt Majoras, "Antitrust and Federalism," Address before the New York State Bar Association (January 23, 2003), 18–19, http://www.usdoj.gov/atr/public/speeches/200683.htm.

7. Editors' note: See chapter 10 by Richard Posner and chapter 11 by Michael DeBow in this volume.

8. *Illinois Brick Co. v. Illinois*, 431 U.S. 720, 755 (1977) (Justice Brennan, dissenting).

9. See Steven C. Salop and Lawrence J. White, "Private Antitrust Litigation: An Introduction and Framework," in *Private Antitrust Litigation: New Evidence, New Learning*, ed. Lawrence J. White (Cambridge, Mass.: MIT Press, 1988), 4.

10. Kevin J. O'Connor, "Federalist Lessons for International Antitrust Convergence," *Antitrust Law Journal* 70 (2002): 425–26.

11. Thomas Kauper and Edward Snyder found that, from 1973 to 1983, follow-on cases accounted for less than 10 percent of private actions. Thomas E. Kauper and Edward A. Snyder, "Private Antitrust Cases that Follow on Government Cases," in White, *Private Antitrust Litigation*, 333. This percentage may have increased in recent years due to the Justice Department's increased success in ferreting out cartels through its leniency program.

12. The debate dates back to the seminal contributions by Gary S. Becker and George J. Stigler, "Law Enforcement, Malfeasance, and Compensation of Enforcers," *Journal of Legal Studies* 3 (1973): 1–18; William M. Landes and Richard A. Posner, "The Private Enforcement of Law," *Journal of Legal Studies* 4 (1974): 1–46.

13. An alternative to private enforcement could be to simply increase the funding for public enforcement. But political considerations surrounding budget allocations may limit the feasibility of increasing enforcement budgets.

14. See, for example, Ken Auletta, *World War 3.0: Microsoft and Its Enemies* (New York: Random House, 2001), 4–7.

15. Scott D. Hammond, Director of Criminal Enforcement, Antitrust Division, "A Summary Overview of the Antitrust Division's Criminal Enforcement Program," Address before New York State Bar Association (January 23, 2003), http://www.usdoj.gov/atr/public/speeches/200686.htm.

16. Acting Assistant Attorney General R. Hewitt Pate, "Anti-Cartel Enforcement: The Core Antitrust Mission," Remarks before the British Institute of International and Comparative Law Third Annual Conference on International and Comparative Competition Law (May 16, 2003), 12, http://www.usdoj.gov/atr/public/speeches/201199.htm The same logic applies to private actions by U.S. citizens.

17. See generally William Shughart and Fred McChesney, *Causes and Consequences of Antitrust: The Public Choice Perspective* (Chicago: University of Chicago Press, 1995); Thomas J. DiLorenzo, "The Origins of Antitrust: An Interest-Group Perspective," *International Review of Law and Economics* 5 (1985): 73–90.

18. Landes and Posner, "The Private Enforcement of Law," 40.

19. Salop and White, "Introduction and Framework," in White, *Private Antitrust Litigation,* 4.

20. Kenneth Elzinga and William Wood, "Costs of the Legal System in Private Antitrust Enforcement," in White, *Private Antitrust Litigation,* 131.

21. Kauper and Snyder, "Private Antitrust Cases that Follow on Government Cases," in White, *Private Antitrust Litigation,* 333.

22. John C. Coffee, Jr., "Rescuing the Private Attorney General: Why the Model of the Lawyer as Bounty Hunter Is Not Working," *Maryland Law Review* 42 (1983): 215–88.

23. Deborah Platt Majoras, "Antitrust Remedies in the United States: Adhering to Sound Principles in a Multi-Faceted Scheme," Address before Canadian Bar Association National Law Section (October 4, 2002), 2, http://www.usdoj.gov/atr/public/speeches/200354.pdf.

24. *Cargill, Inc. v. Monfort of Colorado, Inc.,* 479 U.S. 104, 116 (1986); *Atlantic Richfield Co. v. USA Petroleum Co.,* 495 U.S. 328 (1990); *Brunswick Corp. v. Pueblo Bowl-O-Mat, Inc.,* 429 U.S. 477 (1977).

25. See American Bar Association Section of Antitrust Law, *Antitrust Law Developments,* 5th ed. (Chicago: ABA, 2002), 849.

26. *Associated General Contractors of California v. California State Council of Carpenters,* 459 U.S. 519, 541, 542 (1983).

27. *Illinois Brick Co. v. Illinois,* 431 U.S. 720, 728 (1977).

28. Ibid., 735.

29. See William M. Landes and Richard A. Posner, "Should Indirect Purchasers Have Standing to Sue under the Antitrust Laws? An Economic Analysis of the Rule of *Illinois Brick,*" *University of Chicago Law Review* 46 (1979): 602–35; Robert Harris and Lawrence Sullivan, "Passing on the Monopoly Overcharge: A Comprehensive Policy Analysis," *University of Pennsylvania Law Review* 128 (1979): 269–360; Landes and Posner, "The Economics of Passing On: A Reply to Harris and Sullivan," *University of*

Pennsylvania Law Review 128 (1980): 1274–79; Harris and Sullivan, "Passing On the Monopoly Overcharge: A Response to Landes and Posner," *University of Pennsylvania Law Review* 128 (1980): 1280–90 (defending indirect purchaser suits).

30. Harris and Sullivan, "A Response to Landes and Posner," 1289.

31. Landes and Posner, "A Reply to Harris and Sullivan," 1279.

32. Subcommittee on Antitrust and Monopoly of the Senate Committee on the Judiciary, *Fair and Effective Enforcement of the Antitrust Laws: Hearings on S. 1874* (95th Cong., 1st sess., 1977), 17 (statement of Senator Hugh Scott).

33. *Illinois Brick*, 734 n.14.

34. Courts have "generally denied *parens patriae* recovery with respect to indirect purchasers" in federal actions. American Bar Association Task Force, "Report of the American Bar Association Section of Antitrust Law Task Force to Review Proposed Legislation to Repeal or Modify *Illinois Brick*," *Antitrust Law Journal* 52 (1984): 848 (hereinafter "1983 Task Force Report").

35. Well into the 1990s, the National Association of Attorneys General remained active in petitioning Congress to overturn *Illinois Brick*. See Donald L. Flexner and Mark A. Racanelli, "State and Federal Antitrust Enforcement in the United States: Collision or Harmony?" *Connecticut Journal of International Law* 9 (1994): 519. These activities waned, however, after state *Illinois Brick* repealers were passed. Jonathan Rose, "State Antitrust Enforcement, Mergers, and Politics," *Wayne Law Review* 41 (1994): 76 n.15.

36. 1983 Task Force Report, 849.

37. *California v. ARC America Corp.*, 490 U.S. 93, 102 (1989).

38. Ibid.

39. See, for example, Andrew I. Gavil, "Federal Judicial Power and the Challenges of Multijurisdictional Direct and Indirect Purchaser Antitrust Litigation," *George Washington Law Review* 69 (2001): 860–901; ABA Section of Antitrust Law, "The State of Federal Antitrust Enforcement," *Report of the Task Force on the Federal Antitrust Agencies* (2001), 22–24, http://www.abanet.org/antitrust/antitrustenforcement.pdf; American Bar Association Section of Antitrust Law, "Report of the Indirect Purchaser Task Force," *Antitrust Law Journal* 63 (1995): 993.

40. Donald I. Baker, "Federalism and Futility: Hitting the Potholes on the *Illinois Brick* Road," *Antitrust* 17 (Fall 2002): 16.

41. Andrew I. Gavil, "An Equally Divided Supreme Court Fails to Clarify the Role of Federal Supplemental Jurisdiction in Indirect Purchaser Actions," *FTC Watch*, no. 544 (May 8, 2000), http://www.antitrustinstitute.org/recent/67.cfm.

42. See, for example, Ronald W. Davis, "Indirect Purchaser Litigation: ARC America's Chickens Come Home to Roost on the *Illinois Brick* Wall," *Antitrust Law Journal* 65 (1997): 376; William H. Page, "The Limits of State Indirect Purchaser Suits: Class Certification in the Shadow of *Illinois Brick*," *Antitrust Law Journal* 67 (1999): 3–4; Gavil, "Federal Judicial Power," 876–78; Joel M. Cohen, "Navigating Multistate Indirect Purchaser Lawsuits," *Antitrust* 15 (Summer 2001): 31.

43. See Page, "The Limits of State Indirect Purchaser Suits," 1–39.

44. Cohen, "Navigating Multistate Indirect Purchaser Lawsuits," 30.

45. Baker, "Federalism and Futility," 17–18.

46. See chapter 9 (pages 223, 229–32) by Johnsen and Yahya in this volume.

47. Baker, "Federalism and Futility," 18.

48. A year after the decision, the ABA Section of Antitrust Law took no position on whether recovery should be limited to direct purchasers. It "emphasize[d] that any legislation should . . . correspondingly modify or overrule *Hanover Shoe* to permit" defensive use of the passing-on theory. ABA Task Force, "Report of the American Bar Association Section of Antitrust Law Task Force on Legislative Alternatives Concerning *Illinois Brick Co. v. Illinois,*" *Antitrust Law Journal* 46 (1978): 1141. The majority report proposed consolidating indirect purchaser claims in a single forum as "the only practical alternative available for adjudicating claims asserted by indirect purchasers and sellers at different points in the chain of production and distribution."

49. Brief for the United States as Amicus Curiae in *Illinois Brick Co. v. Illinois*, no. 76-404 (Jan. 1977), 4.

50. American Bar Association Section of Antitrust Law, "The State of Federal Antitrust Enforcement," 23.

51. Andrew Gavil has described how this proposal and other legislative and judicial modifications to the current rules governing complex litigation could substantially reduce the problems raised by state indirect purchaser actions. Gavil, "Federal Judicial Power," 885.

52. Andrew Guzman, "Choice of Law: New Foundations," *Georgetown Law Journal* 90 (2002): 883–940.

53. John R. Wilke and Brandon Mitchener, "Microsoft Rivals Allege Antitrust in New EU Case," *Wall Street Journal*, February 17, 2003, A1.

54. 509 U.S. 764, 796 (1993).

55. American Bar Association Section of Antitrust Law, Antitrust Law Developments, 1117, n.12.

56. *Kruman v. Christie's International PLC*, 284 F.3d 384, 399–401 (2002) (finding U.S. antitrust jurisdiction but reserving standing question); *Empagran S.A. v. F. Hoffman-LaRoche, Ltd.*, 315 F.3d 338, 357 (D.C. Cir. 2003) (finding U.S. antitrust jurisdiction); *Den Norske Stats Oljeselskap AS v. HeereMac Vof*, 241 F.3d 420, 427–28 (2001) (upholding dismissal for lack of jurisdiction).

57. Assistant Attorney General Charles A. James, "International Antitrust in the Bush Administration," Address before the Canadian Bar Association Annual Fall Conference on Competition Law (September 21, 2001), 8–9, http://www.usdoj.gov/atr/public/speeches/9100.htm.

58. Deputy Assistant Attorney General William J. Kolasky, "International Convergence Efforts: A U.S. Perspective," Address before the International Dimensions of Competition Law Conference (March 22, 2002), 3, http://www.usdoj.gov/atr/public/speeches/10885.htm.

13

Toward a Domestic Competition Network

William E. Kovacic

Modern discussions about pursuing convergence among dissimilar competition policy systems focus mainly on differences among national or multinational jurisdictions. Efforts to address the divergence acrossnations in antitrust procedures, substantive standards, and implementation capabilities typically assume that individual jurisdictions have achieved harmony within their own borders. For example, when we speak of attaining convergence of competition policy between the United States and the European Union, we tend to overlook the question of whether those jurisdictions have developed internally consistent analytical principles and coherent mechanisms for making competition policy within their own borders. The energy devoted to addressing cross-border phenomena tends to deflect attention away from considering the consequences of decentralized authority and institutional multiplicity within individual jurisdictions.

In many countries, though, national competition agencies share power to enforce antitrust commands and shape competition policy with other government bodies and private actors.[1] In the United States, authority to prosecute antitrust claims is vested in two federal antitrust agencies, the governments of the individual states, and private parties. For mergers in some industries, sectoral regulators such as the Federal

The views presented here are the author's alone. The author is grateful to Richard Epstein and Michael Greve for many useful comments and suggestions.

Communications Commission and state public utility commissions also exercise power to perform competition policy reviews. The decentralization of authority can generate the same tensions and divergent policy outcomes within any single jurisdiction that we observe internationally.

This chapter makes the case for using convergence techniques from the international policy field to improve the development and implementation of competition policy within the United States. In particular, the establishment of a Domestic Competition Network (DCN)—modeled roughly on the International Competition Network (ICN), in which the U.S. antitrust agencies participate actively[2]—would help the United States exploit the benefits of decentralized decision making while reducing the costs associated with distributing enforcement and other policy-making responsibilities across many actors.

The U.S. Competition Policy System

Institutional Fragmentation. "Competition policy" is the sum of various means by which government bodies influence the amount and type of business rivalry in the economy.[3] In the United States, a complex collection of policy instruments and institutions shapes the rules of the competitive process, and law enforcement is highly decentralized.[4] By statute and judicial decision, many public institutions and private entities enjoy power to enforce antitrust commands governing such behavior as abuse of dominance, horizontal price fixing, mergers, and vertical contractual restraints. No other legal system in the world distributes the decision to prosecute antitrust rules so widely.

Merger enforcement provides an example. In the typical merger case, several entities have power to challenge a transaction. Two federal agencies, the Department of Justice (DOJ) and the Federal Trade Commission (FTC), share authority to review mergers and establish policy guidelines. Since the late 1940s, the federal competition authorities have coordinated merger enforcement through a liaison arrangement that determines which agency will review a specific transaction.[5]

Since the mid-1980s, the state attorneys general have emerged as a second significant public institution for antitrust merger control. Acting under the federal antitrust laws or, in rare cases, under state antimerger laws, the states have conducted antitrust reviews of mergers and have sued to challenge several transactions. The states and the federal antitrust agencies have developed agreements that promote cooperation in reviewing transactions of common interest.

In addition to public enforcement, the U.S. competition policy system authorizes private parties to challenge antitrust violations, including anticompetitive mergers. Eligible private candidates include competitors, customers, and suppliers of the merging parties. Although Supreme Court decisions since the late 1970s have placed formidable standing hurdles in the path of competitors, private actions brought by rivals of the merging parties remain possible.[6]

The possibility of enforcement by entities other than the federal antitrust agencies points to an important anomaly in U.S. antitrust doctrine. The merger guidelines issued by the DOJ and the FTC are less restrictive than Supreme Court decisions that, in the 1960s and early 1970s, imposed stringent limits on horizontal and vertical transactions.[7] The Supreme Court has not issued an antitrust merger decision dealing with liability standards since 1975, and the Court has not repudiated the pillars of its merger jurisprudence of the 1960s. Nonfederal government plaintiffs can invoke (and occasionally have relied upon) the more restrictive Supreme Court precedents. This underscores a vital feature of the U.S. antitrust system: Intervention by nonfederal government entities diminishes the capacity of federal antitrust authorities unilaterally to use prosecutorial discretion to adjust the boundaries of merger control or other elements of antitrust policy.[8]

Antitrust Enforcement by Sectoral Agencies. In several sectors, antitrust agencies share responsibility for formulating and implementing competition rules, including merger standards, with other government agencies. Shared authority is common in industries that are or have been the subject of regulation that governs entry, exit, and rate-making. Prominent illustrations include the following:

- *Airlines.* The Department of Transportation has exclusive authority to approve certain agreements between U.S. airlines and foreign carriers and to grant antitrust immunity for such agreements. In these matters, the DOJ plays an advisory role exclusively.

- *Electric Power.* Transactions involving energy companies are subject to competition policy review or challenge by the DOJ or the FTC, the Federal Energy Regulatory Commission, the public service commission of each state in which the parties do business, and, for some transactions, the Securities and Exchange Commission (exercising powers granted by the Public Utility Holding Company Act).

- *Financial Services.* The DOJ shares competition policy jurisdiction over mergers involving banks with three federal banking regulators: The Office of the Comptroller General, which reviews transactions involving national banks; the Federal Deposit Insurance Corporation, which reviews transactions involving federally insured, state-chartered banks that are not members of the Federal Reserve System; and the Board of Governors of the Federal Reserve System, which reviews transactions involving banks that create a state-chartered bank that is a member of the Federal Reserve System.[9] In general, banking regulators apply standards similar to those established under § 7 of the Clayton Act and must consider a report filed by the DOJ before completing their own assessment of a transaction.

- *Railroads.* Jurisdiction over mergers involving railroads resides solely in the Surface Transportation Board. The DOJ provides nonbinding advice to the board, which must consider, but need not heed, the DOJ's recommendations.

- *Telecommunications.* Mergers involving telecommunications service providers usually are subject to competition policy review or challenge by the federal antitrust agencies (the DOJ ordinarily reviews mergers involving telephone companies, and the FTC has reviewed mergers involving cable television firms), the Federal Communications Commission,[10] and the public service commission of each state in which the parties do business.

In most instances, review by any one authority is concurrent and nonexclusive. In other words, acquiescence in a transaction by any one government agency usually does not preclude a separate challenge by any other entity. Approval of a transaction, subject to certain concessions, by one agency does not preclude another regulatory gatekeeper from insisting upon further concessions.

Collateral Institutions. All of the institutions just described have explicit authority to enforce competition rules. In addition, various other government agencies devise regulations or enforce statutes that have an important impact on the competitive process by, for example, determining the ability of firms to enter specific markets or expand production in existing lines of business. Notable examples include the regulation of advertising and entry by producers of food and pharmaceuticals; the administration of processes that grant intellectual property rights, such as patents; and rules and policies that govern public procurement.

Academics, policymakers, and practitioners are becoming increasingly aware that the decisions of bodies such as the Food and Drug Administration, the Patent and Trademark Office, and the Department of Defense deeply influence business rivalry—perhaps as much as the enforcement of traditional antitrust rules.[11] A significant part of the work of public antitrust agencies today takes place at the intersection with regulatory regimes involving intellectual property and procurement. It is impossible to discuss the major determinants of U.S. competition policy without expanding the focus beyond antitrust enforcement to account for institutions that implement these and other systems of regulation.

Rationales for Decentralization and Institutional Multiplicity

Three basic rationales can be offered to support duplicating federal government functions, including antitrust enforcement: competition, diversification, and institutional comparative advantage.[12]

Competition. A monopolist supplier of a government service might behave in ways that resemble the performance of a monopolist supplier of goods or services in a private market—produce quantities below optimal levels, exert too little effort to reduce costs, or fail to innovate in carrying out its functions.[13] Thus, one reason to have two or more agencies perform the same government function is to foster interagency competition, with the objective of increasing the output and improving the quality of the product that the agencies are intended to supply.

Congress can create interagency competition in several ways: by giving the two agencies identical enforcement duties; by establishing overlapping but nonidentical enforcement mandates; or by assigning two entities dissimilar responsibilities in the same general field of policy. In the last two cases (creating overlapping or dissimilar mandates), Congress can make the enforcement terrain of either agency contestable by indicating that future allocations of enforcement powers and resources will depend on how each agency executes its existing duties.

Recent experience with bid protests in the federal procurement system shows how new entry can change the behavior of a government agency monopolist. In the 1980s, Congress viewed the General Accounting Office (GAO), then the sole government administrative forum for resolving contract award disputes, as being excessively hostile to complaints by disappointed offerors. In 1984, Congress gave overlapping protest jurisdiction to the General Services Board of Contract Appeals (GSBCA), which proceeded to treat protesters more favorably. Rivalry between the GAO and the GSBCA increased protester success rates and spurred procedural innovations by both bodies that bolstered the ability of protesters to collect information useful in overturning purchasing agency decisions.[14]

It is important to underscore one aspect of the relationship between the GAO and the GSBCA that forced each entity to account for, and respond to, the behavior of its counterpart. The GAO and the GSBCA had concurrent jurisdiction over protests involving computers and telecommunications equipment and services. A disappointed offeror could file a protest with either body. Forum self-selection by protesters was a crucial motivating tool for the GAO and the GSBCA. Each protest forum knew that the demand for its services was elastic and that users chose a forum based on a mix of "price" and quality factors.[15] The forum that provided the superior price-quality package took adjudication business away from its rival.

Diversification. The diversification rationale has several elements. The first deals with the difficulty of identifying an optimal approach for accomplishing an objective amid conditions of limited information and uncertainty. When the United States embarked on a new scheme of economic regulation (antitrust) in the late nineteenth and early twentieth centuries, there were uncertainty and disagreement about the best way to implement new competition policy commands. Congress decided to endorse three implementation options: enforcement by private parties in the courts, enforcement by the DOJ in the courts, and enforcement by an administrative tribunal (the FTC) akin to the then recently established Interstate Commerce Commission.[16]

One way to test the merits of different implementation options is to conduct a natural experiment with more than one technique. Experimentation generates an empirical basis for determining what the long-term enforcement system should be. Actual experience provides insights for adjusting the mix of enforcement institutions by revealing which techniques are successful and which are not.

A second diversification rationale is to ensure against the possibility that any single enforcement entity may fail to execute its responsibilities (for example, through sloth, corruption, or flawed institutional design), leaving an important public policy goal unfulfilled. Redundancy creates alternative paths for implementation if any single approach fails. The more vital the government function, the stronger the case for diversifying sources for supplying it.[17]

Institutional Comparative Advantage. The solution to competitive concerns arising from mergers in network industries sometimes involves orders that mandate access to essential facilities or impose nondiscrimination requirements on the owner of such facilities. The design and implementation of mandatory access and nondiscrimination requirements can confront antitrust agencies with oversight tasks, such as the review of tariffs and the monitoring of other access terms, that are better suited for traditional regulatory agencies. Collaboration between the antitrust agency and the sectoral regulator might be necessary to produce the best result. For example, one might assign primary responsibility for reviewing a merger's competitive effects and conceiving a remedy to an antitrust authority and give a sectoral regulator responsibility for routine monitoring of the remedy.

Potential Costs of Decentralization and Multiplicity

The application of the rationales just discussed—especially the competition rationale—to antitrust policymaking is hardly unproblematic. It may be difficult, without a substantial expenditure of resources to evaluate the results of each agency's activities, for Congress or any other monitoring body to determine which agency is worthy of receiving a larger budget or greater authority.[18] More importantly, the U.S. antitrust system contains major limits on how strongly interagency competition can shape enforcement agency behavior. Unlike the bid protest process, firms cannot self-select the antitrust agency that will review conduct for which jurisdiction is shared. For example, at the federal level, parties to a proposed merger cannot determine which agency will investigate the transaction by filing a premerger notice with a favored agency. Because the DOJ and the FTC allocate merger enforcement matters between them, the volume of merger "business" flowing to each agency is largely insensitive to the substantive quality of each agency's analysis or the cost of information demands that each agency imposes.

The lack of self-selection in merger control means that the equilibrium of enforcement policy and transaction planning might be set by the enforcement agency with the strongest preferences for intervention. An agency unilaterally can impose a more interventionist policy, because parties to a merger must assume that the more interventionist agency could receive their transaction in the clearance process. A loosening of government enforcement standards, however, requires the consent of all potential government prosecutors. One agency can defeat the other agency's move toward greater permissiveness simply by adhering to the status quo. Put differently, the multiplicity of competition policy agents complicates efforts by any single agent to establish consistent enforcement policies. Unless Congress or the courts establish binding rules that apply to all prosecutorial agents, policy adjustments under-taken by any one agent can be undermined by the decisions of other agents. Parties planning transactions must take seriously the preferences of the most intervention-minded enforcement agent.

Achieving competition and diversification in the supply of services by government bodies entails additional coordination and administrative costs. The first is greater expenditures for institutional overhead associated with duplicating central administrative and management functions. If the consolidation of antitrust enforcement authority would occur by having one entity absorb all or most of other entities' antitrust professionals and support staff, the main financial savings from consolidation would be to eliminate some overhead resources consumed by the disappearing entities. Such savings, though, would be modest. A unification of competition policymaking authority that only eliminated duplicative overhead would generate relatively small cuts in public expenditures.

A second cost consists of resources that the agencies spend to coordinate conduct where purely independent decision making could be harmful. One form of coordination involves the allocation of potential cases and investigations. As mentioned previously, the DOJ and the FTC have devised an interagency clearance mechanism to ensure that both entities do not simultaneously review the same antitrust matter or sue the same defendant for identical conduct. The clearance process sometimes involves active, intense participation by high-level DOJ and FTC officials. Its operation consumes relatively few out-of-pocket agency resources, but can create serious interagency friction and cause costly delays.

Interagency coordination also involves preparing enforcement guidelines. For areas in which different competition agencies have active enforcement programs, it is not unusual for each agency to adopt a somewhat distinctive analytical approach. Devising joint guidelines involves extensive negotiations to harmonize analytical methods and resolve disagreements. Consolidating enforcement authority in a single institution would reduce the cost and therefore might increase the output, of such guidance.

A third cost consists of additional resources that companies spend to inform themselves about the decision-making tendencies of multiple institutions rather than one. Regulatory outcomes can depend heavily on how individual regulators exercise their discretion. The importance of discretion in policymaking causes regulated firms to spend substantial sums to identify the tastes and idiosyncrasies of incumbent regulatory decision makers. The cost of learning about and monitoring the habits and preferences of multiple bureaus exceeds the cost of mastering the traits of a single institution.

When two or more agencies enforce the same laws, differences in law enforcement approaches may emerge. If agencies apply dissimilar analytical techniques or standards, a fourth cost of competition and redundancy is the expense that businesses incur to evaluate commercial plans and strategies under different enforcement approaches. Accounting for what they learn in studying formal acts and informal signals of policymakers, firms must evaluate contemplated moves in light of how different regulators with similar enforcement portfolios might evaluate their behavior.

National Multiplicity and International Convergence

In addition to the costs just described, policymaking fragmentation at the national level exacerbates the difficulty of establishing international cooperation and consensus. Complex, overlapping competition policy regimes exist in countries other than the United States. Foreign competition policy systems feature conflicts that arise between the following:

- Multinational regional competition policy regimes and the antitrust laws of individual member-states. This is a continuing issue of concern in the relationship between the competition policy apparatus of the European Commission and the competition agencies of the member-states of the European Union.

- The operation of national competition regimes and sectoral regulatory frameworks. For example, in recent years, Germany has liberalized its postal services and telecommunications sectors and has created a new institution to perform residual regulatory tasks (such as setting access prices for bottleneck facilities). The legislation creating the new independent regulatory body does not clearly define the respective competition policy roles of the German Cartel Office and the independent regulator. This ambiguity has led to disputes between the Cartel Office and the regulator concerning a variety of competition policy issues.

- Decisions by national competition authorities and regional competition policy bodies within the same country.[19]

- Agencies of the national government that share power to review the competitive effects of mergers.[20]

In each instance, intrajurisdictional rivalries inhibit the ability of national governments to establish common policies and procedures with their foreign counterparts.

From the perspective of the United States, the existing design of domestic institutions for making competition policy could inhibit progress toward international convergence on competition policy processes and substantive standards. Decentralization and multiplicity in U.S. competition policymaking complicate the attainment of a nationwide consensus about the appropriate content of procedures and substantive requirements. This is evident where two or more independent institutions exercise overlapping authority and there is no hierarchy of authority to make binding decisions. The DOJ and the FTC may be seen as lacking the ability to speak authoritatively to foreign governments about U.S. competition policy because their pronouncements do not bind other institutions, such as sectoral regulators and state attorneys general, which independently exercise policymaking power over a wide range of business activity.

Coordination of competition policymaking for individual transactions among foreign competition authorities becomes more costly where the preferences of several domestic agencies, rather than one institution, are relevant to the policy outcome. For example, a foreign competition authority can negotiate common terms with its competition policy counterparts, but it must also await the outcome of sectoral regulator proceedings in the same matter. Competition authorities may lack mechanisms for sharing information and views with the sectoral regulators in the same way that they share information and views with their antitrust counterparts.

Ensuring the Selection of Superior Policies: Toward a Domestic Competition Initiative

The rationales favoring a multiplicity of enforcement bodies run into difficulty if the jurisdiction in question lacks mechanisms for ensuring that the most efficient enforcement instrumentalities or policies ultimately prevail.

To some extent, the litigation of cases before the federal courts provides a vehicle for establishing doctrinal principles that constrain all potential enforcement agents. Analytically flawed efforts to continually expand the zone of antitrust enforcement concerning any single form of behavior eventually would be subject to control by judicial interpretations that delineate substantive standards and procedural requirements. One presumes that liability theories that are truly perverse in their efficiency consequences ultimately would be subject to litigation and rejection in the courts.

Yet, not all poorly conceived enforcement measures, public or private, result in full litigation on the merits and the publication of judicial opinions. Nor is litigation necessarily an available or effective means to correct errors in policymaking—for example, the issuance of guidelines—that take forms other than litigation. It may be necessary to consider other devices by which superior norms are identified and by which various enforcement agents are persuaded to accept the superior norms.

It is possible that Congress and other policymakers will reassess the rationality of the U.S. antitrust enforcement system and undertake significant adjustments, including the withdrawal of prosecutorial power from selected public authorities or private entities that currently exercise important competition policy functions. Such a change, however, seems unlikely. The institutions or entities that now enjoy prosecutorial power will not volunteer to surrender it or acquiesce in measures to curb their authority. Legislative committees that have vested enforcement power in institutions subject to their oversight will not choose to curtail the responsibilities of such bodies. The existing decentralization of competition policy authority seems largely impervious to significant change.

Recent experience with international efforts to promote competition policy convergence suggests other paths that the United States might take to realize the benefits of decentralization while reducing its costs. The development of competition law internationally indicates that progress toward widely accepted norms regarding substantive standards, procedures, and institutional capacity might occur in three steps:[21] decentralized experimentation at the national or regional level, the identification of best practices or techniques, and opting in to superior norms by individual jurisdictions.

The World Trade Organization and the Organisation for Economic Co-operation and Development, among other global and regional networks, are devoting significant effort to competition policy convergence issues. But among the international institutions that are facilitating the process of convergence, the most intriguing institution for U.S. domestic purposes is the ICN. Created in the fall of 2001, the ICN is a virtual network of competition agencies representing nearly eighty jurisdictions. The ICN operates through working groups consisting of government officials and representatives from academia, consumer groups, legal societies, and trade associations. One group has focused on merger control and has prepared a widely praised body of guiding principles and best practices for notification practices and procedures. Other working groups have addressed competition advocacy and capacity building in emerging markets. ICN has considerable promise to promote the development of an intellectual consensus about competition policy norms.

A domestic equivalent to ICN could serve similar ends in identifying best practices that have emerged through experience with decentralized policy-making and in promoting the adoption of superior analytical techniques and procedures. A DCN could pursue a variety of "soft" convergence strategies to achieve greater consistency and simplicity in competition policy. Possibilities for a DCN include the following:

- Creating working groups of representatives of public institutions that share competition policy authority for various matters, such as reviewing mergers.

- Holding conferences to address policy questions of common interest.

- Engaging government bodies that lack a formal antitrust portfolio (for example, the Food and Drug Administration and government procurement authorities) in discussions about how their choice of policies and implementation techniques affects the competitive process.

- Promoting the allocation of competition agency resources to conduct retrospective assessments of the effects of past policies.

- Encouraging public bodies to issue guidelines that delineate their enforcement intentions.

- Developing interagency protocols that clarify substantive standards and procedures.

These measures would serve to make enforcement processes and substantive standards more transparent. Where significant differences across agencies become apparent, the identification of the differences can provoke discussion and criticism and may stimulate adjustments. A DCN could become a platform for a continuing assessment of U.S. competition policymaking institutions.

The development of a DCN also would highlight an important condition of leadership in a world of multiple decision makers. Success in guiding the refinement and acceptance of competition policy norms is likely to come to agencies that generate the best ideas. Achieving intellectual leadership requires competition agencies to spend resources on what FTC Chairman Timothy Muris has called "competition policy research and development."[22] A strong research agenda and commitment to policy analysis are necessary to identify superior norms and persuade other authorities to opt in. Progress toward widely accepted norms is likely to be gradual, and a patient investment in long-run engagement promises to yield the greatest rewards. In today's environment, the continuing reevaluation of the intellectual foundations and institutions of competition policy becomes an increasingly important component of a sensible antitrust agenda.

Notes

1. The decentralization of authority in the United States is described in William E. Kovacic, "Lessons of Competition Policy Reform in Transition Economies for U.S. Antitrust Policy," *St. John's Law Review* 74 (2000): 375–83. The increasing role of private enforcement in Argentina, Canada, the European Union, and the United Kingdom is examined in Symposium, "Private Enforcement of Competition Laws," *International Business Lawyer* 31 (August 2003): 149–201.

2. The origins of and rationale for the International Competition Network are reviewed in William E. Kovacic, "Extraterritoriality, Institutions, and Convergence in International Competition Policy," *American Society of International Law Proceedings* 97 (2003): 309–12.

3. See William E. Kovacic, "Institutional Foundations for Economic Legal Reform in Transition Economies: The Case of Competition Policy and Antitrust Enforcement," *Chicago-Kent Law Review* 77 (2001): 281–86 (discussing concept of "competition policy"); Timothy J. Muris, Chairman, Federal Trade Commission, "State Intervention/State Action—A U.S. Perspective," remarks before the Fordham Annual Conference on International Antitrust Law and Policy (New York, October 24, 2003), available at http://www.ftc.gov/speeches/muris/fordham031024.pdf.

4. See Andrew I. Gavil et al., *Antitrust Law in Perspective: Cases, Concepts and Problems in Competition Policy* (St. Paul: Thomson West, 2002), 923–30; William E. Kovacic, "The Influence of Economics on Antitrust Law," *Economic Inquiry* 30 (1992): 295.

5. The "clearance" mechanism by which the Department of Justice and the Federal Trade Commission decide which agency will treat matters over which both share jurisdiction is described in ABA Section of Antitrust Law, *The Merger Review Process,* 2nd ed., ed. Eileen K. Gotts (Chicago: ABA, 2001), 133–34.

6. See ABA Section of Antitrust Law, *Antitrust Law Developments*, 5th ed. (Chicago: ABA, 2002), 838–69.

7. The disparities between existing Supreme Court merger jurisprudence and the current federal merger guidelines are noted in William Blumenthal, "Clear Agency Guidelines: Lessons from 1982," *Antitrust Law Journal* 68 (2000): 5–27.

8. For a discussion of how the decentralization of prosecutorial power eliminates the ability of any single enforcer to adjust the impact of a statutory command through the exercise of discretion, see William E. Kovacic, "Private Monitoring and Antitrust Enforcement: Paying Informants to Reveal Cartels," *George Washington Law Review* 69 (2001): 781.

9. See ABA Antitrust Section, *Antitrust Law Developments*, 1317–22.

10. See ABA Antitrust Section, *Antitrust Law Developments*, 1271–73.

11. See, for example, Federal Trade Commission, "To Promote Innovation: The Proper Balance of Competition and Patent Law and Policy" (October 2003), available at http://www.ftc.gov/os/2003/10/innovationrpt.pdf (discussing how

institutions responsible for granting intellectual property rights can affect competitive process); and William E. Kovacic, "Competition Policy in the Postconsolidation Defense Industry," *Antitrust Bulletin* 45 (1999): 421–87 (examining how policy choices made by the U.S. Department of Defense affect competition among suppliers of weapon systems).

12. Segments of this section are adapted from William E. Kovacic, "Downsizing Antitrust: Is It Time to End Dual Federal Enforcement?" *Antitrust Bulletin* 41 (1996): 505–40.

13. See William A. Niskanen, "Nonmarket Decision Making: The Peculiar Economics of Bureaucracy," *American Economic Review* 58 (1968): 300–301 ("the passion of reformers to consolidate bureaus with similar output . . . seems diabolically designed to . . . increase the inefficiency (and, not incidentally, the budget) of the bureaucracy").

14. See William E. Kovacic, "Procurement Reform and the Choice of Forum in Bid Protest Disputes," *Administrative Law Journal of American University* 9 (1995): 461–513. Concluding that the protest reforms of the 1980s elicited excessive scrutiny of purchasing agency decisions, Congress ended this experiment in 1996 by eliminating the GSBCA's protest authority.

15. The "price" of pursuing a protest is chiefly a function of the cost of adjudicating a claim before the forum. GSBCA protests generally were more expensive than GAO protests because GSBCA used discovery processes (such as depositions) whose use often gave the protester valuable information but raised the cost of challenging the purchasing agency's decisions. Successful protesters were permitted to recover reasonable attorneys fees. For a protester, the "quality" of a protest forum is a function of the likelihood of obtaining a favorable ruling and the form of remedy that the protest forum is likely to provide. The GSBCA generally offered protesters a higher quality "product" because it ruled against the government more often than the GAO and often ordered more expansive relief.

16. For an important recent interpretation of the origins of the U.S. antitrust system at the turn of the twentieth century, including the decision to diversify the enforcement system by creating the Federal Trade Commission, see Marc Winerman, "The Origins of the FTC: Concentration, Cooperation, Control, and Competition," *Antitrust Law Journal* 71 (2003): 1–97.

17. One reason to maintain the Air Force, the Army, and the Navy as distinct bodies (rather than establish a single armed service) is to provide multiple independent centers for developing new tactics and weapon systems. An integrated armed service might suppress or ignore meritorious ideas about tactics or weapons that threaten established ways of doing things. See Thomas L. McNaugher, *New Weapons, Old Politics: America's Military Procurement Muddle* (Washington, D.C: The Brookings Institution, 1989), 38–48.

18. The importance of and difficulties associated with assessing the consequences of public antitrust enforcement are addressed in William E. Kovacic, "Evaluating

Antitrust Experiments: Using Ex Post Assessments of Government Enforcement Decisions to Inform Competition Policy," *George Mason Law Review* 9 (2001): 843–61.

19. See Roger Alan Boner and William E. Kovacic, "Antitrust Policy in Ukraine," *George Washington Journal of International Law* 31 (1997): 8–10 (describing broad distribution of decision-making power among national and regional competition officials in Ukraine).

20. See Michael G. Cowie and Cesar Costa Alves de Mattos, "Antitrust Review of Mergers, Acquisitions, and Joint Ventures in Brazil," *Antitrust Law Journal* 67 (1999): 113–57 (describing difficulties that arise from the distribution of antitrust merger oversight authority across three institutions of the national government in Brazil).

21. This discussion uses the model of convergence presented in Timothy J. Muris, "Competition Agencies in a Market-Based Global Economy," prepared remarks at the Annual Lecture of the European Foreign Affairs Review (Brussels, Belgium, July 23, 2002), available at http://www.ftc.gov/speeches/muris/020723/brussels.

22. See Timothy J. Muris, "Looking Forward: The Federal Trade Commission and the Future Development of U.S. Competition Policy," remarks for the Milton Handler Annual Antitrust Review (New York, December 10, 2002), available at http://www.ftc. gov/speeches/muris/handler.

14

Postscript: In Defense of Small Steps

Richard A. Epstein and Michael S. Greve

The "domestic" and "international" parts of this book reflect a striking contrast: In the United States context, there is broad agreement among all authors both with respect to the general analysis and the direction of institutional reform; at the international front, there is sharp disagreement on both scores, but especially with respect to institutional questions. We did not invite the contributors with the intention of producing this (or any other) particular conclusion. Nor, however, do we believe that the result obtained—domestic unanimity, international disagreement—is fortuitous. Rather, the contrast reflects, in our judgment, an important lesson about the difficulties of institutional design in multijurisdictional settings. (The lesson applies beyond the antitrust context, but we shall stick to our present knitting.)

As an empirical observation, jurisdictions compete—and firms and individuals choose their jurisdictions—on any number of margins, including antitrust policy. Wolfgang Kerber and Oliver Budzinski disentangle the various meanings of "competition" in this context with admirable analytical clarity. Their first type of competition is "yardstick competition," whereby autarkic states (without any other exchange or relation) compete, in a metaphorical sense, by learning from the innovations, wise or foolish, that other autarkic states make in formulating and implementing antitrust policy. Because this form of competition does not pose enforcement conflicts with respect to general antitrust policy or individual cases, Kerber and Budzinski argue that yardstick competition will generally yield beneficial (or at least, not systematically deleterious) results. Thereafter, we can follow the logic of Kerber and Budzinski as they gradually relax the stringent assumptions of the autarky model and first permit goods and services, then firms and individuals, to cross borders. Under the most relaxed assumptions, firms are permitted a free choice of competition law, much as U.S. corporations may choose an exclusive state charter.

We agree with much of Kerber and Budzinski's fair-minded analysis. Sketching a theme developed at greater length by Andrew Guzman, they rightly suggest that cross-border trade may induce jurisdictions to utilize antitrust policy for strategic ends. The collective pursuit of such objectives by many nations will almost invariably reduce global welfare. The ability of firms to choose applicable antitrust laws by relocating to this or that juris-diction will tend to exacerbate the incentives for strategic behavior (although the force of that effect will depend on a variety of factors, such as the extent to which other jurisdictions apply their own laws extraterritorially). Finally, Kerber and Budzinski conclude that the corporate choice-of-law model is generally inapplicable to the antitrust context. Just so: Contractual choice of law works in contractual settings and fails in cases of monopoly so long as the negative effects of any decision fall on outsiders to the firm. Competition is, as it were, a limited tool for deciding the proper competition policy.

Still, we take issue with Kerber and Budzinski on a central point. They invoke the Hayekian model of decentralized learning in a marketplace to explain why such competition should lead to favorable results, but we are as yet unpersuaded by their sunny conclusions. The Hayekian insights work well to explain the origin of incremental improvements in contracting prac-tices among law merchants *who already work in competitive markets*. The con-straints of competition force them to develop their positions in constructive ways because the options of cartelization and combination are independ-ently blocked. Once those structural constraints are removed, however, we are much less sanguine that local practices will be governed by a disinter-ested search for better practices. Nothing, alas, prevents those who seek to cartelize local markets from learning about how best to do this by watching and imitating successful cartelization efforts elsewhere. So long as internal constitutions are imperfect, the Japanese champions of quotas for rice importation can learn from the Americans, who have perfected the art in sugar. Yardstick competition may work with respect to administrative improvements that are worth having under any set of substantive norms, such as improved enforcement techniques or merger registration proce-dures.[1] On substantive questions, however, the lessons only bite if there is an antecedent commitment to open markets, which yardstick competition can neither advance nor retard.

Kerber and Budzinski mention two instances of institutional yardstick learning: the international diffusion of American antitrust law over the twentieth century, and the transmission of German antitrust doctrines to the European Union (EU) (and, subsequently, from the EU to member-states). We are in no position to assess the social welfare effects of those events, but Judge Diane Wood's illuminating remarks on the international proliferation of antitrust law put us in a rather skeptical frame of mind. We can, moreover, think of one striking counterexample—a dramatic improvement in substantive antitrust policy that had nothing to do with institutional learning in a Hayekian sense.

We have in mind, of course, the transformation of American antitrust law circa 1980. That unambiguous improvement resulted from pathbreaking scholarship, not local politics, and it was implemented in a highly centralized fashion by federal agencies and federal judges. In putting antitrust law on a solid foundation, William Baxter, Robert Bork, and Richard Posner took their bearings from economics, not successful state experiments. There were none: States were the places that ran cartels of the *Parker v. Brown*–style cartels described by Frank Easterbrook.

As both Michael DeBow and William Adkinson show, the states' response to the antitrust revolution was principally resistance, not adaptation and further marginal improvement. Undoubtedly, substantive antitrust law remains much in need of such overhauling. For example, the application of standard antitrust doctrines—which rest on an assumption of increasing marginal costs—to network industries poses difficult questions, especially at the intersection with intellectual property law. No one, however, would seriously hold out the states' contribution to the *Microsoft* litigation or the sprawl of state "indirect purchaser" actions as a success. (See DeBow and Adkinson, respectively.) And surely, Richard Posner is right that state attorneys general offices are not the places to look for constructive innovation at antitrust law's uncertain frontier. Theoretical and practical improvements are far more likely to come, as they have in the past, from the University of Chicago and the Federal Trade Commission.

In fairness, Kerber and Budzinski recognize that effective yardstick competition depends on institutional preconditions that are unlikely to be generated by strategically acting states. They conclude their chapter with a broad proposal for an international multilevel system that would permit institutionalized learning and, at the same time, resolve the jurisdictional conflicts, limit the transaction costs, and reduce the opportunities for strategic behavior that bedevil the existing, near-anarchic regime. They are hopeful that political institutions can find the appropriate mix of centralization and decentralization in light of economies of scale, the scope of competition problems, the heterogeneity of policy preferences among member-jurisdictions, and other salient considerations.

While Kerber and Budzinski are anything but starry-eyed about the basis and the prospects of their proposal, it is still fair to note its distinctly European flavor. It depends in the end on a high degree of confidence in stable bureaucratic organization and cooperation, the application of impartial expertise in designing institutions and executing policies, and the ability of political institutions to operate in a public-interested fashion. If Americans generally find such confidence hard to come by, that may be because we live in a more contentious society whose political institutions seem too fragmented to permit their ready integration into the sort of overarching design that Kerber and Budzinski envision. Put more directly, our own ongoing experiment in multilevel antitrust governance has proven largely incapable of sustaining sensible and efficient jurisdictional boundaries.

Hence, the striking contrast mentioned at the outset: Our "international" contributors argue over whether it is possible to establish an order to define, protect, and preserve efficient jurisdictional boundaries, and about what that would take. Among the "domestic" contributors, that theoretical dispute is displaced by the uniform conviction that all defensible federalist boundaries have crumbled. Their self-imposed task is to find out how to reestablish those boundaries in one form or another.

International Antitrust

The "international" contributors forcefully advocate a wide range of views. At one end of the spectrum, Andrew Guzman calls for harmonization—that is, the articulation and enforcement of a uniform body of antitrust laws by an international body, most likely the World Trade Organization (WTO). At the other extreme, Paul Stephan favors international autarky in which each state pursues whatever antitrust law it chooses, restrained only by its treaty obligations with individual nations. An intermediate position, urged here first by John McGinnis and then by Michael Trebilcock and Edward Iacobucci, defends an extension of the current WTO legal regime, which embraces a "national treatment" principle that prohibits discrimination against foreign producers without specifying the content of national antitrust law.

The inherent difficulties presented by these choices all stem from the simple Coasean point that positive transaction costs can ruin a good day. As Andrew Guzman observes, if transaction costs were low enough, nations could negotiate with each other until they adopted those solutions that maximized total output between them, making whatever side payments are needed to ensure that no side loses in the exchange. Any two-party agreement might, in principle, impose costs on third persons, but in a zero transaction cost world, these would instantly disappear. The excluded party would costlessly negotiate with the other players for their mutual gain, making or receiving any side payments if necessary. The process would not be subject to any practical upper bound, but would continue immediately and inexorably until all parties came within the grand alliance. The need to choose between the three alternatives would vanish like the wind. Alas, transaction cost barriers preclude this happy outcome. The number of nations involved is very great, and their level of sophistication on antitrust issues varies enormously, so it is hard to predict in the abstract what path will lead toward a principled and coordinated resolution of international trade policies.

Guzman's plea for harmonization rests on the conviction that local trade policies are unnecessarily duplicative, arguably inconsistent, and suffer from an incurable home court advantage that is quick to register the local gains from certain policies while ignoring their external costs. He hopes that all divergent interests will be brought to the table at a single point in time so that consistency and simplicity will be joined with coherence that is not possible to achieve by ad hoc interventions and agreements. One implicit premise of his argument is that the international process could operate at a level that works better than the domestic ones because the incentives are more sensibly aligned. One immediate response, strongly suggested by Diane Wood's sobering observations, is that Guzman may hold naïve expectations as to how well international bodies are able to work. The honest differences of opinion over an ideal competition policy are very great. National governments are often willing to make concessions in favor of small businesses and infant industries, and the hard question is why they should be denied that (dubious) right for autonomous choice in some international regime in which one size is made to fit all.

Both Trebilcock and Iacobucci as well as McGinnis pursue different versions of this theme. They argue that the nondiscrimination rule embodied in the national treatment standard of the WTO offers the best solution: Each nation holds to its own policy of choice on competition issues so long as it does not impose additional burdens on foreign nations. The principle is easier to operate than one that tries to undertake substantive harmonization at the international level, but it also ensures that whatever gains are generated internally are shared by firms from outside the country who operate within it. The authors defend different versions of the national treatment principle. Trebilcock and Iacobucci would restrict its extraterritorial operation to inbound commerce and treat antitrust rules that affect outbound commerce as a trade rather than an antitrust question. McGinnis fears that the regime suggested by Trebilcock and Iacobucci would dilute exporters' incentives to lobby for open borders. He would welcome WTO jurisdiction only (and precisely) with respect to national antitrust rules that operate as a protectionist trade barrier. Despite that important difference, the authors are united in their desire to constrain the authority and discretion of international institutions. If one lacks confidence in the abilities or motivations of international bureaucrats, limits on their substantive discretion are likely to cut out disastrous, not welcome, interventions.

As the authors acknowledge, though, even a formal antidiscrimination rule (in either version) proves somewhat problematic. Its success or failure may well depend on a variety of circumstances. The ratio of imports to exports clearly makes a difference: For example, a nation that has little production in a given industry pays a far lower price when it imposes restrictions on external producers than one that sports robust domestic production. Yet, even these calculations are incomplete, because domestic consumers in the affected industry may press for liberalization of trade restraint in order to reduce the costs of production for their own goods, including those bound for sale in export markets. In addition, much depends on whether the nondiscrimination policy extends to de facto as well as de jure distinctions. Nondiscrimination is hard to achieve when neutral laws have concealed purposes and effects that hurt foreign firms. The level of international cooperation in enjoining de facto as well as de jure discrimination, though, is likely to be limited. Solving the problem at the level of rules, moreover, is only part of the battle. The interpretation and application of the rules in distinctive situations may make it hard to apply an antidiscrimination norm even after it is on the books. McGinnis is willing to go very far in entrusting international bodies with the authority to police evasions, but his resolve carries the price of permitting such bodies to burrow deep into domestic policy arrangements.

Doubts of this sort have led Paul Stephan to take a far more skeptical stance against all forms of international cooperation. His preferred regime allows each nation to set its own policy and to enforce it as it sees fit. That rule would allow any individual nation to give extraterritorial effect to its own substantive laws, so that a given practice by one firm could in principle be subject to review in many different countries where its economic effects are manifest. (Presumably, the impact of this go-it-alone policy could be reduced by bilateral treaties between nations or by cooperation on a spot basis where the gains are evident to both.) Intriguingly, Stephan also argues that at least in knowledge-intensive economic sectors, overly protective policies may create short-term strategic gains only at the price of long-term losses in innovation and competitiveness. If that is right, (some) countries may have a powerful incentive to adopt global welfare-enhancing policies on their own accord. But at root, Stephan believes that the incentives that govern international bodies, not to mention their own substantive preferences, should lead people away from any dewy-eyed expectations of any substantial gains from cooperation.

We are duly impressed by the closeness of the argument. In principle, we would gladly support harmonization if *we* could write the rules of the game to ensure that export cartels and antidumping proceedings were a thing of the past. But we are not likely to be accorded this great power soon—which makes us once again apprehend the danger of runaway "harmonization." However, we think that the go-it-alone strategy might be too pessimistic in light of some of the modest advances that have been made in trade policy in recent years. We incline therefore to the nondiscrimination rule or national treatment principle, with all its ambiguities and limitations. Even that modest endorsement, however, will require modification in light of the domestic experience.

The United States: Antitrust Crisis?

The disagreement between Guzman and Stephan, with Trebilcock and Iacobucci and McGinnis in between, is not primarily one of substantive policy. In the end, all authors (including, we suspect, Paul Stephan) could live with some version of a national treatment or nondiscrimination rule as one element of an international antitrust order. The disagreement, rather, is rooted in questions of political economy and, in particular, differences of opinion about the extent to which international institutions, given the political forces that operate on them, are likely to get the rules "right." In light of our limited experience with such institutions, the authors are compelled to operate with presumptions and burden-of-proof arguments. Start with the undeniable costs of decentralized decision making by parochial nations, and the presumption (Guzman avers) runs toward harmonization. Start with the public choice dynamics that afflict central political institutions (in the fashion of McGinnis and Stephan), and the harmonizers bear an enormous burden. Because the costs and benefits on both sides are highly conjectural, there is no way to bring the debate to closure. It may be informed, however, by our experience with the actually existing multijurisdictional antitrust regime of the United States. With respect to international harmonization efforts, the "domestic" essays in this volume counsel great caution.

While the U.S. Constitution is much more than a mere free trade pact among states, it is also and at least that. In addition to specific prohibitions against the sorts of protectionist state practices that are the basic stuff of international trade agreements (such as duties), the Constitution contains explicit nondiscrimination norms, such as the Full Faith and Credit Clause and the Privileges and Immunities Clause. The dormant Commerce Clause, in its modern incarnation as a nondiscrimination rule, may be a judicial invention (as its critics charge), but it surely tracks the original constitutional logic.[2] One may quarrel about the precise extent to which the vision of a "common market" animated the Founders, but the Constitution plainly embodies powerful background presumptions for free trade and competitive federalism. Quite obviously, though, the constitutional story has not played out that way. Post–New Deal jurisprudence is a mere shadow of a competitive constitutional order. It has proven inordinately difficult to sustain efficient jurisdictional rules and distinctions.

In some settings, those rules are tolerably straightforward. Recall the theme of our Introduction: In contractual settings with zero third-party costs, the parties to the transaction should be allowed to choose their legal rules. A close second-best default rule is the "Delaware principle" of American corporate law, which unambiguously designates the corporation's charter state law as the applicable set of rules. Notably, however, we honor that principle mostly in the breach. The principle governs corporate law—but not securities law.[3] It governs, thanks to some splendid judicial footwork, credit card and mortgage markets—but not insurance markets: Here, federal law (the McCarran-Ferguson Act) explicitly exempts state protectionism of the rankest kind from dormant Commerce Clause review.[4] Look over the range of U.S. economic regulation, and it turns out that the corporate law regime is anything but a paradigm. It is a huge outlier, which appears to owe its survival largely to an exogenous event (World War II).[5]

Because political institutions fail to adopt sensible jurisdictional rules when the choice is tolerably straightforward, it is hardly surprising that they should fail at that task when the rules are tricky. In noncontractual settings, or in contractual settings with massive third-party costs (such as antitrust), it is devilishly difficult to figure out the correct jurisdictional and choice-of-law rules.[6] For that reason, it makes sense to operate with nondiscrimination rules as default principles rather than ironclad constitutional norms: When conceptual distinctions cut too wide a swath, let the legislature tailor the rules to any given context.

The monstrous fly in this ointment is that Congress almost never clarifies or specifies jurisdictional rules; instead, it mows them down. The most encompassing congressional power, the authority to "regulate" interstate commerce, was originally envisioned not as a vehicle for the affirmative federal regulation of private conduct but primarily—according to Madison's later recollection, exclusively—as a means of breaking down state interferences with interstate commerce.[7] Congress was supposed to undertake the job that the courts have picked up under the dormant commerce doctrine. Far from sticking to its primary task, however, Congress has almost never utilized its commerce power to that end. In its best moments, it has refrained from eviscerating efficient jurisdictional regimes—and even such instances of beneficial abstention (for example, the federal "failure" to accede to Ralph Nader's demands for a national corporation law in the 1970s) seem largely fortuitous. In short, Congress typically rejects the option of solving jurisdictional conflicts through rules against aggression and discrimination. Instead, central intervention almost always takes the form of affirmative regulation of private conduct.[8] That move may often be sensible: In contexts where one cannot specify optimal jurisdictional rules with any kind of confidence, uniform regulation of private transactions may be the better part of wisdom. But the shift in strategy implies a change in perspective. Now, the vertical problem dominates: How much authority should be left to the states in formulating policy and in enforcing their own and federal antitrust rules?

The authors of the Sherman Act legislated against a background understanding of "dual federalism"—that is, the notion that regulatory affairs belonged either to the states or to the national government, but not to both at the same time. As several of our authors note, though, the constitutional doctrines that enshrined dual federalism were dismantled by the New Deal. State and federal antitrust authority now extend concurrently over the entire range of private transactions, from the local lemonade stand to multinational mergers.[9] At the same time, the massive extraterritorial effects of many "local" cartels, coupled with the minimum contacts rule, guarantee enormous overlap among state jurisdictions, with all the attendant risks of duplication and conflict.

All of our "domestic" authors urge some form of sorting along the vertical dimension. Bruce Johnsen and Moin Yahya demonstrate, to our satisfaction, that the extension of American antitrust law to local events at the outer limits of congressional power is unwarranted. Relying on modern economic scholarship, they formulate an intelligible "geographic market power" test that would put purely local anticompetitive conduct beyond the scope of federal enforcement. Their judicially manageable test tracks the intuitive distinction between "national" and "local" economic affairs that informed the authors of the Sherman Act back in 1890. One might quarrel with the policy prescription ("leave local monopolies to the states") on casual empirical grounds—for instance, the contention that the prosecution of local monopolies may help to distract federal antitrust agencies from more questionable, or perhaps affirmatively harmful, enforcement activities on a national scale. Such ad hoc arguments, however, strike us as misdirected. Johnsen and Yahya argue quite plausibly that antitrust nationalism does after all entail costs. Surely, there are better ways of remedying the enforcement biases of federal agencies.

Much tougher problems arise over state interference in national antitrust matters—or, to put it more neutrally, the state enforcement of federal rules in a multijurisdictional setting. To be sure, the enforcement of central rules requires some level of decentralization. That is not a problem when the rules are tolerably clear; when the local enforcers' incentives are reasonably well aligned with the central authority's; and when that authority has at its command reasonably efficient means of monitoring and disciplining the locals. In antitrust law, however, none of those conditions holds. The rules are anything but hard and fast. States have every incentive to shirk and free ride and to manipulate enforcement to their own advantage. The federal government appears to lack, at least under current law, an authoritative means to shut down ill-conceived or parochial state enforcement proceedings.

William Adkinson's essay on the strange fate of "indirect purchaser" suits under federal antitrust statutes provides a powerful illustration of the crucial difference between mere administrative decentralization and divided authority. The Supreme Court's *Illinois Brick* decision barred such lawsuits under federal law in the interest of coherent antitrust enforcement (among other reasons). Powerful interests, however, insisted on broad-based private antitrust enforcement. That demand proved insufficient to produce a congressional override of *Illinois Brick*—but it was more than adequate to produce multiple defections at the state level, which the Supreme Court duly blessed. State "*Illinois Brick* repealers" present the very problems of inconsistent law enforcement that the original decision meant to curtail— except, as Adkinson shows, on a much greater scale.

Richard Posner's and Michael DeBow's chapters on the problems of state (rather than strictly private) antitrust enforcement highlight a slightly different facet of the problem. The states' conduct in the course of the *Microsoft* antitrust proceeding and, in particular, the decision of some states to hold out for additional concessions even after the federal government had decided to settle the matter have prompted Judge Posner, no stranger to these matters, to advocate a wholesale repeal of state attorneys' general *parens patriae* authority to litigate antitrust cases on their citizens' behalf. Michael DeBow's useful compilation of state antitrust actions over the past two decades suggests that *Microsoft*-style interferences with interstate commerce are rare exceptions to a pattern of generally modest and harmless, if somewhat parochial, state antitrust enforcement. On the basis of that evidence, DeBow urges a more limited proposal than Posner's to curb the potential for state overreach. More specifically, he would permit state *parens patriae* actions involving purely in-state horizontal restraints, while strengthening federal oversight over all antitrust lawsuits seeking injunctive relief. DeBow volunteers, however, the grim thought that *Microsoft* may be a harbinger rather than an outlier. Most distressingly, and quite credibly, he suggests that the relatively low level of state antitrust enforcement may have something to do with the ready availability of alternative means of exploiting out-of-state actors, such as general-purpose prohibitions against deceptive trade practices. As state attorneys general gain experience in antitrust litigation, their costs of bringing the next case decrease at the margin, thus increasing the potential for exploitative antitrust prosecutions.

A funny thing, it appears, happens on the way from export cartels and other forms of interstate exploitation to central harmonization: The horizontal dimension of the problem—which, at the outset, *was* the problem—drops from sight, and institutional actors (and for that matter academics) turn their eyes to the question of preserving some vertical equilibrium. One possible "solution" is our existing arrangement of divided and concurrent state and federal authority over the entire range of private conduct. As noted in the Introduction, though, that is not an equilibrium but a jurisdictional state of nature. The existing, informal intergovernmental arrangements described by DeBow have undoubtedly helped to reduce friction and conflict. But their efficacy appears to depend on highly contingent factors, such as a general agreement among state and federal enforcers on substantive antitrust policy. Even the more muscular intergovernmental cooperation proposed by William Kovacic would provide only partial relief: When the states decide not to play, the result is *Microsoft*.

The search for a firmer, more stable federal-state balance typically rests on casual empirical averments. States justify their aggressive posture by complaining about the federal government's alleged "abdication" at the antitrust front, while corporations and federal officials lament the states' "interference with national affairs" and observers ruminate about "the role of the states" in a federal system. (DeBow's essay provides examples of such rhetorical maneuvers.) To our minds, that debate will remain fruitless without some explicit recognition that the vertical dimension is derivative on the horizontal question. One cannot determine what the central government should be able to do to rein in the states, antitrust-wise or otherwise, without some prior understanding of what states may do to one another—just as one cannot delineate the proper scope of government without some prior comprehension of what individuals may do to one another. Try to run the argument the other way around, and there's no end of trouble.

The essays in this volume buttress the point. Frank Easterbrook has proposed to turn the notorious "state action" doctrine of *Parker v. Brown* on its head so that it would bar state export cartels and exploitation. His position gathers its devastating force precisely because it focuses on horizontal, state-to-state effects, as distinct from abstract considerations of a "federalism balance." Johnsen and Yahya's proposal to bar federal antitrust jurisdiction over purely in-state antitrust infractions presents the flipside of the Easterbrook theory. It isolates antitrust matters that *have no* horizontal extraterritorial effects; for precisely that reason, the vertical question has a clean solution.

Posner, DeBow, and Adkinson rest their analysis and policy prescriptions concerning antitrust enforcement by state and private attorneys general and private attorneys general on a variety of arguments, from the inadequate expertise and resources of state enforcers (Posner) to the efficient enforcement theories pioneered by Posner and adopted here by Adkinson. While we do not necessarily disagree with those claims, we do think that a more explicit identification of horizontal concerns would strengthen the authors' case. When West Virginia or Massachusetts decides to bar or penalize some private transactions that originated in

Washington state but had adverse effects within their territories, it seems difficult to deny them that right. Yet, their choice may vitiate Washington's equally respectable right to tolerate the conduct and to reap its benefits. We may choose to handle that difficulty, in a manner of speaking, by granting Washington an equal right to retaliate in some other forum. But this approach runs the inherent risk of escalation because no one can identify what tit works for which tat. Therefore, while a universal rule of mutual aggression is neither incoherent nor inherently contradictory, its capacity to metastasize makes it a highly unlikely legal regime to maximize joint gains. And so one migrates, in the context of states' rights as in the context of private rights, to the opposite pole—a universal rule of nonaggression, coupled with monopolistic federal enforcement. Against this backdrop, Posner's and DeBow's seemingly drastic policy prescriptions look not only plausible but well-nigh inescapable.

If that conclusion seems startling, that may be so because American antitrust law, as well the public and political and academic debate about it, has to all intents ceased to address the state-to-state antitrust dimension. Internationally, that dimension drives the debate and the search for solutions; here at home, we have largely suppressed it. Concerning the causes of that distortion, we venture two guesses, neither of them inspiring.

First, governments acting in concert may move from nondiscrimination rules to full-scale harmonization for good or bad reasons. Among the possibilities are genuine difficulties in specifying workable nonaggression rules; a universal desire to play in a better-than-second-best world; and a desire to entrench unilateral advantages. In all events, however, governments will resist a wholesale transfer of sovereign authority and instead insist on retaining some independent interpretive and enforcement authority. In part, that demand reflects a desire to preserve options to commit *ex post* opportunism, and in part, it may reflect an earnest desire to monitor the terms of the original bargain. Either way, though, the subordinate governments typically preserve some power to protect or, as the case may be, to revise the original bargain. Invariably, central "harmonization" in fact translates into joint production (both in rulemaking and in enforcement), with all its attendant problems. The brief discussion by Kerber and Budzinski suggests that the EU's antitrust apparatus is lumbering toward that same outcome.

The second, perhaps more potent factor is a predilection for collusion and monopoly by government actors. *Ex ante*, that preference translates into an insistence on rules that entrench unilateral advantages; *ex post*, it translates into an unwillingness to challenge sister-state aggression even when the rules forbid it. A few examples, loosely derived from the contributions to this volume, illustrate the point.

Richard Posner's collection of state antitrust actions, contained in the Appendix to his chapter, shows that roughly half of those cases involved exclusively out-of-state defendants. That evidence, Posner writes, supports his claim that state antitrust enforcement often serves parochial ends and, specifically, the protection of in-state producers. That conclusion, which is mildly supported by DeBow's study, is probably right, but one cannot justify it from Posner's data without knowing more about the individual cases. Suppose a single state (say, California) is a near-monopolistic supplier of a particular product (say, raisins), and suppose the state organizes the producers into a hard-core cartel: A consuming state's antitrust challenge would (by stipulation) involve only out-of-state defendants. But it would be anything but parochial or protectionist. Quite the contrary: It would only replicate on the domestic level the ability of the federal government to use a similar effects tests to chase after foreign cartels that sell on American soil.

Where, then, were the consumer-states in *Parker v. Brown*? If Frank Easterbrook is right, as surely he is, about the extraterritorial effects of California's raisin cartel, one would expect the affected states to have pressed the point (if not as litigants, then at least in an amicus capacity). Somewhat puzzling, however, *no* state (except of course California itself) participated in the case, even though it is hard to believe that all states had export cartels of their own to defend. Similarly (or perhaps in contrast), numerous states participated in *Summit Health* (1991), the case that established the boundless extension of the Sherman Act criticized by Johnsen and Yahya—*in support of that extension*. In the *Microsoft* litigation, the district judge heard elaborate arguments from the eighteen states that insisted on prosecuting Microsoft even after the federal government had decided to settle the case—but not a word from the states that declined to participate, including Microsoft's home state of Washington.

The harsh fact, and the point of our excursion into the states' antitrust litigation positions, is that states are highly likely to mobilize antitrust rules and enforcement for protectionist and exploitative purposes—and highly *un*likely to contest aggression by sister-states. That asymmetry may help explain the political robustness of our unconscionable "state action" doctrine even in the face of withering criticism (such as Easterbrook's). California's raisin cartel collected its rents from all over the country, thus diluting the incentive of any individual state to contest the imposition. Every state, moreover, has interest groups that desire to exploit and discriminate on some margin; so long as these interest groups can influence local policy, no state has a strong incentive to publicly insist on firm, across-the-board antidiscrimination rules. Those incentives, mind you, operate even when states faithfully register local preferences. Introduce a whiff of agency problems between the governors and the governed, and the situation deteriorates: For the governing class, mutual state exploitation ("I shall let you rob my citizens if you let me do likewise to yours") becomes the preferred solution. "Harmonization," it turns out, may institutionalize mutual exploitation as well as nonaggression. Political dynamics may make the former more likely than the latter.

What Is To Be Done?

Our brief survey of the impressive contributions to this volume suggests—to us at least—three lessons about the management of jurisdictional problems in antitrust policy.

The first lesson, here as in most other settings, is this: Keep it simple, stupid. Instead of aiming at a comprehensive—but usually elusive—solution, it is usually best to tackle, first and energetically, incontrovertible institutional errors. The domestic policy proposals presented by Easterbrook, Johnsen and Yahya, DeBow, Posner, and Adkinson all fall squarely into this category of "fixes" for glaring inefficiencies. (If anything, the proposals strike us as too modest; for example, we would cheerfully defend a wholesale bar, in all but purely local cases, against indirect purchaser suits in federal or state court, under either federal or state law.) The problems here are political, not intellectual. The intellectual temptation is to run from politically difficult questions toward more complicated schemes that seem more acceptable—precisely because they skirt or obscure the core problems. That way, we think, leads to disaster.

For analogous reasons, we are impressed by Diane Wood's observation that the international arena offers opportunities for a low-cost elimination of inefficiencies and exploitation, and we wholeheartedly subscribe to her urgent advice to put those opportunities at the top of the international agenda. The United States invented export cartel exemptions. We do not need the WTO or the EU to un-invent them; we can and, in our judgment, should revoke them unilaterally, just as we can unilaterally promote free trade.[10]

In addition to export cartels, Judge Wood lists antidumping laws, agricultural policy, and certain sectoral arrangements (such as telecommunications) as prime candidates for a piecemeal but impressive international antitrust agenda. Diplomats, trade lawyers, and international bureaucrats, of course, classify those issues as "trade" issues. Antitrust, in contrast, is one of the "Singapore issues" on which the WTO was to move after the trade agenda had supposedly been settled. The de facto collapse of the WTO's Doha Round has thrown into disarray an international agenda that would have the WTO move methodically from trade to more complex and robust forms of harmonization.[11] That development provides added support for Judge Wood's advice to advance an international antitrust agenda in trade areas with massive antitrust implications—because the intellectual case here is straightforward; because the territory is more familiar than the mystifying field of corporate organization; and because measurable progress and tangible benefits at these fronts would build transnational confidence and possibly understanding.

Second, as already mentioned, we would support an international nondiscrimination or national treatment principle in antitrust. Consistent with our first point, we agree entirely with Trebilcock and Iacobucci's implicit warning against constructing an international antitrust regime from the vantage of the hardest possible case, the international mega-merger. A jurisdictional rule that settles half the problems with a tolerable rate of error is vastly preferable to a system of rules that produces monstrous errors over the entire range.

We incline to qualify even this cautious endorsement. Our skepticism extends not so much to the difficulty of procuring agreement on such a principle. On that score, Andrew Guzman's proposal of national "side payments" seems sensible, especially given the likely nature of such payments: If industrialized countries wish to obtain developing countries' assent to an international antitrust order, they will likely have to surrender their agricultural subsidies and import restrictions. We would welcome the liberalization of agricultural markets, both at home and abroad, with or without an antitrust "swap." Our reservations, therefore, only extend to the difficulty of stabilizing a nondiscrimination principle and of arresting a future slide into the kind of harmonized joint production and vertical-horizontal government collusion that afflict U.S. antitrust law. Supporters of the nondiscrimination principle have acknowledged this point but, to our minds, given insufficient thought to the problem. John McGinnis, for example, defends an antitrust nondiscrimination norm on the grounds that free trade agreements increase countries' incentives to achieve protectionist objectives by means of antitrust policy.[12] That is so. But an antitrust nondiscrimination norm will have the same effect in some other dimension—or perhaps in its own dimension: Countries will migrate from discriminatory rules to discriminatory enforcement. In resisting the ensuing clamor for additional, far more intrusive interventions and more muscular international authorities, it is extremely difficult to define a compelling stopping point, let alone one that is politically tenable.[13]

Third, and finally, we return to our starting point: For us, as for several contributors to this volume and especially those with administrative antitrust experience (Diane Wood and William Kovacic), the key issue is in one sense trying to build a consensus on what practices should be legal and which ones should not. "Soft" harmonization may well help to reduce friction and, perhaps, the range of substantive disagreement. It is hard to see the downside to this form of institutional learning, and we think that there is room for an incremental migration toward free trade and competitive markets up and down the line. If the right attitudes are adopted, the regime choice becomes less pressing because more voices will be heard in favor of a political agenda that has a long and illustrious intellectual history—even if it has been honored as much in the breach as in the observance.

Notes

1. For more on international harmonization of these matters as a means of reducing transaction costs, see Douglas H. Ginsberg and Scott H. Angstreich, "Multinational Merger Review: Lessons from Our Federalism," *Antitrust Law Journal* 68 (2000): 219–37.

2. Justice Thomas and Justice Scalia, the two harshest critics on the Supreme Court of the dormant Commerce Clause, would both enforce the antidiscrimination purposes of the doctrine under textual constitutional provisions, such as the Privileges and Immunities Clause and the Import-Export Clause. See, for example, *Camps Newfound/Owatonna v. Town of Harrison*, 520 U.S. 564, 609 (1997) (Justice Thomas, dissenting).

3. See Roberta Romano, *The Advantages of Competitive Federalism for Securities Regulation* (Washington, D.C.: AEI Press, 2002).

4. For financial regulation, see *Marquette National Bank of Minneapolis v. First Omaha Service Corp.*, 439 U.S. 299 (1978) and *Smiley v. Citibank (South Dakota)*, 517 U.S. 735 (1996). For insurance regulation, see *Prudential Ins. Co. v. Benjamin*, 328 U.S. 408 (1946). State insurance regulation does remain subject to some residual scrutiny under the Due Process Clause and Equal Protection Clause. See *Metropolitan Life Ins. Co. v. Ward*, 470 U.S. 869 (1985).

5. Congress had every intention to order corporate law along the lines of the 1934 Securities Act and in fact managed to wipe out choice of law for investment advisers (1940). Then the war intervened. See Donald E. Schwartz, "Federalism and Corporate Governance," *Ohio State Law Journal* 45 (1984): 547.

6. Andrew Guzman, "Choice of Law: New Foundations," *Georgetown Law Journal* 90 (2002): 883–940.

7. Letter from James Madison to J. C. Cabell (February 13, 1829), reprinted in *The Records of the Federal Convention of 1787*, vol. 3 (New Haven: Yale University Press, 1966), 478.

8. This is true with respect to both regulation and taxation. See, respectively, Jonathan Macey, "Federal Deference to Local Regulators and the Economic Theory of Regulation: Toward a Public Choice Theory of Federalism," *Virginia Law Review* 76 (1990): 265–91; and Kathryn L. Moore, "State and Local Taxation: When Will Congress Intervene?" *Journal of Legislation* 23 (1997): 171–212.

9. Richard Posner suggests that purely local activities are beyond the scope of congressional authority. In our view, *U.S. v. Lopez*, 514 U.S. 549 (1995) and *U.S. v. Morrison*, 529 U.S. 598 (2000) explicitly *reaffirm* the "aggregation" principle of *Wickard* with respect to all economic activities—including, we presume, the sorts of activities that might prompt antitrust complaints.

10. See Jagdish Bhagwati, "Introduction: The Unilateral Freeing of Trade Versus Reciprocity," in *Going Alone: The Case for Relaxed Reciprocity in Freeing Trade*, ed. Jagdish Bhagwati (Cambridge, Mass.: MIT Press, 2002).

11. The disastrous Cancun meeting took place in September 2003, after the AEI conference on which the contributions to this volume are based but before the completion of this postscript.

12. We have singled out John McGinnis—whose contribution appears in this very volume—to reduce our own and our readers' search costs. The criticism would more fairly be directed against more romantic WTO supporters than McGinnis.

13. As noted earlier, McGinnis's resolve in having international authorities police evasions suggests this danger.

Index

transparency of, 71, 74–75
Technological innovation and success of
  virtuous competition model, 92
Telecommunications and sector agency
  antitrust enforcement, 319
Territoriality
  inefficiencies of, 82–83
  and jurisdictional diversity, 81–82,
    157–64
  and national regulatory power, 85, 86
  and state jurisdiction issue (U.S.),
    13, 16–17, 25, 191
  See also Extraterritorial antitrust
    enforcement
Third party effects and antitrust, 3, 5, 24
  See also Consumer welfare
Thomas, Clarence, 283n11
Tobacco litigation and abuse of state
  attorney generals' role, 278–79,
    287n50
Tompkins, Erie Railroad v. (1938), 25
Trade policy
  agreements vs. competition policy, 86
  benefits of open trade for U.S., 92
  and competition policies, 68, 152–72
  jurisdiction as central to, 7–15
  and labor productivity, 87
  liberalization as goal of competition
    laws, 180–81
  public choice effects, 109, 111–12,
    135
  strategic trade theory, 70–71
  and traditional barriers, 74–75, 186
  See also Closed vs. trade economy
    competition behavior; Discrim-
    ination in trade; International
    trade; Market access; Nondis-
    crimination trade rule
Transaction costs
  of diversity in competition laws,
    99–100, 127, 147n2, 152,
    153–54

and drive for harmonization, 109,
  110, 114, 117–18, 182–83
and lead jurisdiction approach, 166
in multi-agency U.S. antitrust
  enforcement, 323–24
and unworkability of harmonization,
  337
Transfer payments for inequities in
  cooperation, 110, 118
Transitory jurisdiction, viability of,
  29n15
Transparency
  and dispute resolution, 185–86, 187
  international disagreements on, 170
  lack of, 74–75, 78–79, 86
  and nondiscrimination trade rule,
    141
  See also Information availability
Transportation Department, U.S., 319
Treaty of Rome (1958), European,
  72–73, 178
Trebilcock, Michael J., 118, 143, 337,
  338–39
Treble damages remedy, 288, 296–97,
  300
TRIPS (Agreement on Trade-Related
  Aspects of Intellectual Property
  Rights), 76, 145–46, 179
Tyson, Swift v. (1842), 24–25

Underregulation and jurisdictional
  issues, 105–8, 117
Unfair trade practices regulation,
  180–81
Unitary vs. federal governments and
  innovation, 254–56
United Brands Co. v. Commission, 94n12
United Shoe Machinery Corp., Hanover
  Shoe, Inc. v. (1968), 261, 299, 300
United States
  antitrust innovation in, 132
  benefits of trade openness for, 92

About the Authors

William F. Adkinson Jr. is senior policy counsel at The Progress & Freedom Foundation, where he has written on competition, intellectual property, and regulatory issues. Before joining PFF, Mr. Adkinson was an associate at Wilmer, Cutler & Pickering in Washington, D.C., and he has also served as an attorney with the Office of Policy and Planning at the Federal Trade Commission. Mr. Adkinson currently serves as vice president for programs of the National Economists Club. His articles have appeared in *Antitrust* and the *Washington Times*.

Oliver Budzinski is a senior research fellow with the Department of Economics Economic Policy Unit at the University of Marburg. Mr. Budzinski specializes in the fields of international economics, economic and competition policy, ecological economics, monetary economics, and the theory and management of complex systems. His work has been published in *Constitutional Political Economy* (2003), *Current Issues in Competition Theory and Policy* (2002), and *International Institutions and Multinational Enterprises: Global Players, Global Markets* (2004).

Michael DeBow is professor of law at Samford University's Cumberland School of Law and an adjunct professor of health care organization and policy for the School of Public Health at the University of Alabama at Birmingham. From 2000 to 2004, Professor DeBow also served in the Office of the Attorney General of the state of Alabama. His previous positions include special assistant to Assistant Attorney General Douglas Ginsburg in the Antitrust Division of the Department of Justice and law clerk for Judge Kenneth W. Starr at the U.S. Court of Appeals for the District of Columbia.

The Honorable Frank H. Easterbrook was appointed to the U.S. Court of Appeals for the Seventh Circuit in 1985. Prior to his appointment, he served as a law clerk to Levin H. Campbell of the U.S. Court of Appeals for the First Circuit, and as deputy solicitor general of the United States. In 1979, Judge Easterbrook joined the faculty at the University of Chicago Law School, where he served as the Lee and Brena Freeman Professor of Law, and where he currently holds the position of senior lecturer. He is a former editor of the *Journal of Law and Economics*, coauthor (with Daniel R. Fischel) of *The Economic Structure of Corporate Law*, and author of numerous articles, several of them scholarly.

Richard A. Epstein is the James Parker Hall Distinguished Service Professor of Law at the University of Chicago Law School, where he has taught since 1972. Since 2000, he has been the Peter and Kirstin Bedford Senior Fellow at the Hoover Institution. Professor Epstein has been a member of the American Academy of Arts and Sciences since 1985, and a senior fellow at the Center for Clinical Medical Ethics at the University of Chicago Medical School since 1983. He has edited the *Journal of Legal Studies* and the *Journal of Law and Economics*, and at present, he is a director of the John M. Olin Program in Law and Economics. Professor Epstein's books include *Torts* (1999), *Free Society: Reconciling Individual Liberty with the Common Good* (1998), and *Takings: Private Property and the Power of Eminent Domain* (1985).

Michael S. Greve is the John G. Searle Scholar at the American Enterprise Institute in Washington, D.C., where he serves as the director of the Federalism Project. Mr. Greve cofounded and, from 1989 to 2000, directed the Center for Individual Rights, a public interest law firm which served as counsel in many precedent-setting constitutional cases, including *United States v. Morrison* (2000) and *Rosenberger v. University of Virginia* (1995). He currently serves on the Board of Directors of the Competitive Enterprise Institute. Mr. Greve has written widely on constitutional and administrative law, environmental policy, civil rights, and federalism. His books include *The Demise of Environmentalism in American Law* (AEI Press, 1996) and *Real Federalism* (AEI Press, 1999).

Andrew T. Guzman is professor of law and the director of the International Legal Studies Program at the University of California at Berkeley's Boalt Hall School of Law. Prior to joining the faculty at Boalt, Professor Guzman was a visiting assistant professor of law at the University of Chicago Law School and a law clerk for Chief Judge Juan R. Torruella of the U.S. Court of Appeals for the First Circuit. Professor Guzman is on the board of editors of the *International Review of Law and Economics*, and the board of advisors for the *Berkeley Journal of International Law* and the *Berkeley Business Law Quarterly*. He has written extensively on international regulatory cooperation, international law, and international trade.

Edward M. Iacobucci is associate professor of law at the University of Toronto Faculty of Law. Professor Iacobucci was a visiting professor of law, University of Chicago Law School in 2003, and a John M. Olin Visiting Fellow at Columbia University Law School in 2002. Prior to joining the Faculty of Law, he was the John M. Olin Visiting Lecturer at the University of Virginia in 1997–98 and served as law clerk at the Supreme Court of Canada for Mr. Justice John Sopinka in 1996–97. Professor Iacobucci's areas of interest include corporate law, competition law, and law and economics more generally.

D. Bruce Johnsen is professor of law at George Mason University, a leading center for law and economics scholarship. Professor Johnsen's work focuses on the law and economics of property rights. He has held positions in the Department of Management at Texas A&M University, the Office of Economic Analysis at the U.S. Securities & Exchange Commission, and the Department of Legal Studies at the Wharton School of the University of Pennsylvania.

Wolfgang Kerber is professor of economics at the University of Marburg, where he has been a member of the faculty since 1997. Professor Kerber's research focuses on evolutionary market theory, competition policy, evolutionary economics, institutional economics (especially law and economics), competitive federalism, and European integration. He is coeditor of *Party Autonomy and the Role of Information in the Internal Market* (2001), and his recent articles have been published in *Fordham International Law Journal* (2000), *European Journal of Law and Economics* (2002), and *The Future of Transnational Antitrust—From Comparative to Common Competition Law* (2003).

William E. Kovacic is the general counsel of the Federal Trade Commission, which he joined in June 2001. He is on leave from The George Washington University Law School in Washington, D.C., where he has served as a professor since 1999 and has taught antitrust, contracts, government contracts, and comparative government procurement law. He previously served as an attorney-advisor to Commissioner George W. Douglas of the Federal Trade Commission. Professor Kovacic's recent articles have appeared in the *Connecticut Law Review* and the *Supreme Court Economic Review*.

John O. McGinnis is professor of law at Northwestern Law School, where he teaches constitutional and international trade law. Professor McGinnis clerked for Judge Kenneth Starr of the District of Columbia Circuit, and served as a deputy assistant attorney general in the Office of Legal Counsel at the Department of Justice in the Reagan and George H. W. Bush administrations. Professor McGinnis was recently named to the advisory committee on labor standards and NAFTA, and was selected to be on the register of panelists to settle WTO disputes.

The Honorable Richard A. Posner was appointed to the U.S. Court of Appeals for the Seventh Circuit in 1981, and served as the chief judge from 1993 to 2000. Prior to his appointment, Judge Posner taught at the University of Chicago Law School for twelve years; earlier he had held several positions in Washington, including law clerk for U.S. Supreme Court Justice William J. Brennan Jr., assistant to the Solicitor General Thurgood Marshall, and general counsel of President Johnson's Task Force on Communications Policy. Judge Posner's contributions to the field of law and economics, like the many honors he has received, are too numerous to be listed. He is the author of the landmark *Antitrust Law* (2d ed. 2001), as well as *Economic Analysis of Law* (6th ed. 2003), and the founder of the *Journal of Legal Studies*.

Paul B. Stephan joined the University of Virginia School of Law faculty in 1979. He is the Lewis F. Powell Jr. Professor, teaching courses on international relations theory, comparative law, emerging markets, and international business transactions. Before joining the faculty, Professor Stephan clerked for U.S. Supreme Court Justice Lewis F. Powell Jr. He has written extensively on international law, international economics, corruption, and the history of the Cold War.

Michael J. Trebilcock is university professor and professor of law and economics at the University of Toronto, where he has taught since 1972. During his tenure, Professor Trebilcock has held the positions of fellow in law and economics at the University of Chicago Law School, visiting professor of law at Yale Law School, and global law professor at New York University Law School. He received the Canada Council Molson Prize in the Humanities and Social Sciences in 1999 and was elected president of the American Law and Economics Association in 2002.

The Honorable Diane P. Wood was appointed to the U.S. Court of Appeals for the Seventh Circuit in 1995. From 1993 to 1995, Judge Wood was a deputy assistant attorney general for the Antitrust Division of the Department of Justice, and from 1981 to 1993, she taught at the University of Chicago Law School. Judge Wood is known for her expertise in the field of antitrust law, both in the United States and around the world, and her long list of publications includes articles in the *Chicago Journal of International Law* and the *Harvard Journal of Law and Public Policy*.

Moin A. Yahya is a visiting assistant professor of law at the University of Alberta, Edmonton, Canada. He teaches contracts and business associations. Mr. Yahya previously served as an antitrust economist with the Competition Bureau in Ottawa, where he provided economic analyses of merger and civil nonmerger cases, and worked on antitrust enforcement guidelines. Mr. Yahya's previous papers and presentations include "A Positive Theory of Regulator Finance" and "The Law and Economics of Torts and Bankruptcy."